GREED AND INJUSTICE IN CLASSICAL ATHENS

GREED AND INJUSTICE IN CLASSICAL ATHENS

Ryan K. Balot

PRINCETON UNIVERSITY PRESS PRINCETON AND OXFORD

Published by Princeton University Press, 41 William Street,
Princeton, New Jersey 08540
In the United Kingdom: Princeton University Press, 3 Market Place,
Woodstock, Oxfordshire OX20 1SY

Library of Congress Cataloging-in-Publication Data

Balot, Ryan K. (Ryan Krieger), 1969–
Greed and injustice in classical Athens / Ryan K. Balot.
p. cm.
Includes bibliographical references (p.) and index.
ISBN 0-691-04855-X (acid-free paper)
1. Avarice—Greece—Athens—History. 2. Distributive justice—History. 3. Athens (Greece)—Politics and government. 4. Philosophy, Ancient. I. Title.

B187.A85 B35 2001
178′.0938′5—dc21 2001021483

British Library Cataloging-in-Publication Data is available

This book has been composed in Janson

Printed on acid-free paper. ∞

www.pup.princeton.edu

Printed in the United States of America

10 9 8 7 6 5 4 3 2 1

MATRI MATERTERAE VXORI OPTIMIS

Contents

Preface and Acknowledgments

I HAVE written this book for scholars in ancient history and political theory, in the belief that each discipline has much to offer the other. My inquiry into Athenian political thought is primarily historical and contextual, but I have tried to broaden its focus by asking questions inspired by modern ethics and political thought. My goal has thus been to create an interdisciplinary work, in more than one way. Within the ancient context, first, I argue for marked continuities between the Athenian poetic and historiographic traditions, on the one hand, and the discourse of fourth-century Athenian political philosophy, on the other. These generically distinct ways of approaching ethics and politics, however apparently self-contained, enrich and inform one another in recognizable ways. Second, in uncovering the ethical assumptions of Athenian poetry and historiography, and in approaching the systematic reflections of Plato and Aristotle, I utilize contemporary political theory. I hope thereby to have clarified the distinctiveness of Greek political ideas, and to have created the potential for dialogue between ancient and modern notions of distributive justice and individual virtue. Finally, I regard the "history of ideas" not as a history of self-contained debates or as a reflection of social forces but rather as an integral part of social and political process. I envision a genuine dialectic between ideas and the role they played in forming the self-conceptions, and thus the behavioral dispositions, of people in antiquity. The topic of greed is well suited to bringing together these diverse discourses in a systematic and coherent way.

This book first took shape as my doctoral dissertation at Princeton University. There I received generous fellowships from the Classics Department, the University Center for Human Values, and the Charlotte Elizabeth Procter fund. Josiah Ober, my thesis supervisor, first encouraged me to pursue this topic and provided help, encouragement, and inspiration until its completion. Through his example and through many conversations, he opened my eyes to the possibility of studying ancient history in a theoretically compelling way. Brent Shaw gave characteristically insightful and balanced advice throughout. He was a sure guide through many difficult historical pathways. Robin Osborne read the entire manuscript, forcing me to think and rethink; after first getting me interested in Greek history, he has generously offered guidance for a decade. For their suggestions on individual chapters, I thank Ewen Bowie, George Kateb, and the participants in the graduate seminar at Princeton's University Center for Human Values. Sandy Robertson kindly made available to me materials from his forthcoming book *Greed* in advance of publication and helped me clarify my thinking at a variety of levels. For many invaluable conversations about ethics, I thank three friends from graduate school—Mark Erwin, Kyle Hudson, and Jeremy Goldman. Among others who provided timely advice and encouragement, I thank Ian Morris, Andrew Ford, Gregory Nagy, Joshua Katz, Ruel Tyson, Philip Stadter, Mark Toher, Tara Silvestri, Randy Ganiban, and Sara Forsdyke. Brigitta van Rheinberg and Chuck Myers at Princeton University Press have offered generous support as I transformed my dissertation into a book, and Brian MacDonald's learned and careful copyediting helped make it better and more readable.

In the course of writing this book, I joined the faculty at Washington University in St. Louis. Here I received a generous research grant, which helped me complete the project. I am grateful to my colleagues in the Department of Classics, especially George Pepe, Bob Lamberton, and Susan Rotroff, all of whom offered important suggestions and guidance. My colleagues in the Department of History, Hillel Kieval and Derek Hirst, helped me understand the potential significance of the project for historians of later periods. One of my students, Brad Atwell, provided editorial assistance and saved me from many errors and inconsistencies.

My greatest debts are to three family members. My oldest readers are my mother, Elizabeth Miranne, and my Aunt (whom I call "Nanny"), Mary Joe Krieger. My wife, Carroll, has had the deepest impact on this book—she provided support and clarity at the most important moments. I dedicate the book to the three of them.

In order to make the work more accessible to students of both classics and politics, I have translated all Greek passages and included transliterations of key Greek terms and passages. I have defined Greek words at first use and often thereafter, particularly if there is a long gap between a word's appearances. I have generally used the familiar anglicized forms in transliterating Greek names—for example, Socrates instead of Sokrates and Achilles instead of Akhilleus.

For Greek and Latin texts, I have usually referred to the standard Oxford Classical Texts. In translating from Greek and Latin, I have generally consulted both older and more recent Loeb Classical Library translations and adapted them in order to emphasize key terms and points in particular contexts. Exceptions are listed in the first section of the bibliography.

Abbreviations

AP	Aristotle *Athēnaiōn Politeia* (*Constitution of the Athenians*)
DK	Hermann Diels and Walther Kranz, eds., *Die Fragmente der Vorsokratiker*. 6th ed. Berlin: Weidmann, 1966–67.
Fornara	Charles W. Fornara, *Archaic Times to the End of the Peloponnesian War*. Translated Documents of Greece and Rome, 1. 2d ed. Cambridge: Cambridge University Press, 1983.
HCT	A. W. Gomme, with Antony Andrewes and Kenneth J. Dover, *A Historical Commentary on Thucydides*. 5 vols. Oxford: Clarendon Press, 1945–81.
HGP	W.K.C. Guthrie, *A History of Greek Philosophy*, 6 vols. Cambridge: Cambridge University Press, 1962–81.
IG	*Inscriptiones Graecae*. (Berlin: G. Reimer, 1873–.
LSJ	*A Greek-English Lexicon*. Compiled by Henry George Liddell and Robert Scott. Revised and augmented throughout by Sir Henry Stuart Jones. 9th ed., with supplement. Oxford: Oxford University Press, 1968.
ML	R. Meiggs and D. M. Lewis, eds., *A Selection of Greek Historical Inscriptions to the End of the Fifth Century BC*. Oxford: Clarendon Press, 1969.

1

Introduction

GREED is central to ancient Athenian history, ideology, and political thought. It motivated political action and occupied the attention of contemporary analysts of civic conflict and imperialism. I want to explore various facets of greed in Athenian society and political discourse from roughly 600 to 300 B.C. I use the term *greed* to refer to acquisitiveness or an excessive desire to get more. Greed is a primarily materialistic type of desire, which is characteristically expressed by the attempt to satisfy bodily urges through the acquisition of money, material goods, and power. Occasionally, materialistic acquisitiveness shades off into an excessive desire to get power for its own sake. But, for reasons that will become clear, I do not focus in the first instance on ambition, that is, the excessive desire for honor or status.[1]

The most important observation we can make is that greed is rarely something an agent predicates of himself. Rather, members of a moral community use the concept to criticize others, and classical Athenians developed a wide array of terms for precisely this purpose. In archaic and classical Athens, this critique tended to take one of two basic forms. The first is more important from the perspective of society and hence more important for the present book: the idea that greedy agents violated canons of fair distribution among equal individuals or groups. As a violation of equality and fairness, greed was inevitably linked to injustice and therefore identified as a leading cause of civic strife. Perceptions of greed thereby became a primary stimulus to political action, and greed itself became a dominant feature of political thought. The second form of critique focused on the greedy individual himself, rather than his violation of the just claims of others. Here the critique is that greedy desires reveal an impoverished conception of what it means to live as a human being. They diminish the person as such and detract from his genuine happiness and well-being. This is the ethical perspective on greed and it tends to

[1] Robertson 2000 offers an excellent and highly stimulating account of the materialism involved in greed in contemporary America. As Plato (*Rep.* 558c–559d) saw, there are, of course, natural and necessary desires to get more, but greed by definition is an *excessive* form of desire. By contrast with materialistic greed, seeking honor was seen as being the proper aim of political life; see Aristotle *Nicomachean Ethics* 1095b22–23.

focus on individuals apart from their social setting. Because the second critique tends to occupy philosophers rather than practical political agents, it is less important than the first for understanding the relationship between ideas and history.

Greed not only featured in the contemporary *perceptions* of politics but also motivated individuals and groups—and even Athens itself—throughout Athenian history in the archaic and classical periods. Greed does not respect the scholar's distinction between social history and literary representation. As Greenblatt has said, "Language, like other sign systems, is a collective construction; our interpretive task must be to grasp more sensitively the consequences of this fact by investigating both the social presence to the world of the literary text and the social presence of the world in the literary text."[2] My working hypothesis is that as political events influenced literary and philosophical condemnations of greed, so too did key texts help stimulate certain types of political action.[3] Accusations of greed inspired radical attempts at self-justification; they unified the self-proclaimed "oppressed" and motivated them to seek justice; they led to philosophical defenses of self-aggrandizement and critiques of conventional morality. Finally, as I argue in the epilogue, traditional critiques of greed stimulated Plato to conceive of justice in a distinctive way and to develop a hierarchical opposition between material appetites and other, "higher," forms of desire.

To substantiate and complicate this account of greed, I first analyze Aristotle's treatment of greed in *Nicomachean Ethics* book 5 and in his analysis of human nature, commercial trade, and civic strife in the *Politics*. This chapter, by far the most technical discussion in the book, deals with questions of the psychology of action and the difficult Aristotelian schema of the virtues and vices. Having elicited from Aristotle a working concept of greed and its place in Greek moral evaluation, I then turn to the heart of the book—the evolving role of greed in Athenian history and political thought.

The complexity of Aristotle's account, I argue, results from the long Athenian discourse on greed, which began in the sixth century, when Solon adapted traditional ethical models in order to censure the greed and injustice he witnessed among both the upper and lower classes. Solon articulated a civic definition of the individual according to which self-restraint and distributive fairness are the core features of proper political participation. In the fifth century, Herodotus and Thucydides realigned the terms of Solon's discourse. They proposed that Athenian democracy

[2] Greenblatt 1980, 5.

[3] In interpreting the relationship between text and context, I have been most influenced by LaCapra 1983; 1985; Chartier 1990; Baker 1990; Kramer 1989.

created ideological harmony between the elite and the demos, which enabled Athenians to solve the problem of greed within the polis by channeling their acquisitive impulses outward against other Greeks. The greed that had once characterized competing groups within Athens now became the prevailing attribute of the city as a unified whole. But this ideological consensus was destroyed in the late fifth century, when members of the elite, resentful over the demos's greed in managing the empire, initiated two oligarchic revolutions. Their conduct justified the contemporary interpretation of the oligarchic coups of 411 and 404 as exemplifying elite greed in action. In the post-revolutionary period, Lysias used the Athenian experience of elite greed as a democratic rhetorical weapon, while Xenophon rehabilitated the aristocratic ideal by showing that civic worth was the exclusive prerogative of the traditional aristocracy. In the *Republic*, Plato confronted the legacy of aristocratic greed by designing a polis that was specifically free from greed and injustice and ruled by self-controlled, fair-minded aristocrats.

Although I trace the history of and discourse on greed from Homer through Plato, my analysis is selective rather than comprehensive. I focus on turning points in the archaic and classical periods—the Solonian crisis, the advent of imperialism, the oligarchic revolutions in the late fifth century, and the early fourth-century recollection of those revolutions. I have excluded material that would naturally figure in an encyclopedic study. In particular, I do not offer an account of the Peisistratid tyranny, because our sources on the contemporary discourse in that period are basically non-existent. I also forgo treatment of the Attic orators, because my specific focus is on how the discourse on greed was made practically effective in the oligarchic revolutions of the late fifth century, and on how Plato's philosophical account of justice constituted a response to those revolutions.[4]

My focus on greed, I am aware, runs the risk of anachronistically inventing a category of investigation that the Greeks themselves would not have recognized. A more familiar approach, no doubt, would be to conduct a semantic study of the Greek term *pleonexia* (greediness), and to footnote passages where other words seem to mean the same thing; Weber did exactly this in a Bonn dissertation of 1967.[5] The past decade, in fact, has witnessed the publication of two wide-ranging semantic studies, Fisher's *Hybris* and Cairns's *Aidōs*. Both aim to identify the precise meaning and semantic range of their key words. Both employ a rigorous philological method that scrutinizes the usage of these important

[4] In future work, however, I plan to approach Isocrates' treatment of the Athenians' imperialistic greed.

[5] Weber 1967.

terms in an extraordinary range of texts in the archaic and classical periods. Both are fundamentally similar to North's excellent study *Sophrosyne* in 1966. The result, in each case, is a comprehensive account that illuminates the meaning of the targeted words and, secondarily, the meaning of passages in which they are found. In their scope and discipline these works are the worthy fruits of classical philology and demonstrate its formidable powers to clarify meaning.[6]

Still, I have chosen to call this a book about greed, rather than *pleonexia*, for several reasons. First, although greed provoked criticism in the works of Homer, Hesiod, and Solon, none of them used the term *pleonexia*. Barring one exception, this term is found only in extant prose literature.[7] Hence, focusing on the term *pleonexia* runs the risk, in its own right, of artificially hiving off entire domains of culture that are relevant to the concept of greed. The enabling assumption of this project is the possibility of expressing the concept of greed in other words. Thus, even though *pleonexia* is the most important single term for my history,[8] I also discuss passages where the concept of greed is being discussed in other words. Among the more significant of these synonyms are *koros* (greed or satiety), *philochrēmatia* (love of money), *aischrokerdeia* (base covetousness), and *epithumia chrēmatōn* (desire for money), along with a variety of periphrastic expressions suggesting the idea of grasping for more in excess of what is needed, useful, or just.

Second, a more straightforwardly lexical method would itself construct arbitrary categories of analysis. The semantic range of key cultural abstractions—such as *hubris*, *aidōs*, and *sōphrosunē*—is wide enough that tracing instances of a particular term and its associated forms sometimes involves discussing passages that have little in common with each other, apart from the presence of the term in question. The lexical method usually makes no attempt to clarify the connections between apparently disparate passages, or to show what intervening events and thoughts brought about a transformation.[9] The method depends on the desired

[6] Fisher 1992, Cairns 1993, North 1966. The English translations of their titles are, roughly, "Arrogance," "Sense of Shame, Modesty," and "Temperance."

[7] The term *pleonexia* occurs only once in extant classical poetry, in Euripides *Iphigeneia at Aulis* 509, while its associated noun (*pleonektēs*) and verb (*pleonektein*) do not appear at all; see Weber 1967, 77. See Weber 1967, 16–25, for an account of roughly equivalent terms in the era before Herodotus.

[8] Of *pleonexia* the philosopher Gregory Vlastos once said, "I despair of an adequate English translation," though he fell back on "greed" or "covetousness" as the best rough equivalents (Vlastos 1973, 116n16).

[9] Cairns 1993 does engage with other terms, such as *aischros* (shameful, ugly) and *sebas* (reverence), but generally focuses on *aidōs* (shame, modesty) and grammatically related forms of *aidōs*. As Adkins 1994 points out, however, major social changes, such as the Athenian Empire, "come and go without leaving a ripple" (182) on the surface of the study

goal, and my goal here is to explain how the social practices of greed gave rise to a sophisticated discourse and how, in turn, that discourse shaped and stimulated cultural practices, self-representations, and political behavior in a particularly important period of Athenian history.

Before I turn to Aristotle, a variety of specifically Greek concepts about ethics and politics must be set in relation to one another. The most straightforward way to erect a framework is to examine a paradigmatic figure, who reappears throughout this book—the Callicles of Plato's *Gorgias*.[10] Callicles, I stress, is a useful paradigm, but, like all paradigms, he fails to capture the specificity of many cases that must be understood on their own terms. Callicles is best known for his attack on conventional justice, and his assertion of another, in his view more genuine, conception of justice based on what he calls the "law of nature." Callicles disparages conventional morality as a self-interested tool of power. The craven masses, he argues, "frighten the stronger and those able to have more [*pleon echein*], so that they do not have more [*pleon echōsin*] than themselves, and they say that the desire to get more [*to pleonektein*] is shameful and unjust, and that injustice [*to adikein*] consists in seeking to have more than others [*to pleon tōn allōn zētein echein*]" (483c1–5). The ordinary mass of humanity, in other words, has set up a self-regarding system of law and morality in order to prevent the powerful from taking whatever they happen to desire.

Callicles' representation of conventional justice already invokes the key terms of the first critique of greed—that it is unjust. Even before describing his own desires, he begins by contesting the notions of justice and injustice promoted by the masses of ordinary citizens. His formulation must be understood against the background of the Greek conception of citizenship as a form of sharing in the political, economic, and religious life of the community.[11] The usual Greek expression for this "sharing" is *metechein tēs politeias* (to share in the political community).[12] Citizens perceive themselves as possessing in common all the divisible goods of the community, in particular power (*kratos*), political office or honor (*timē*), and material goods (*chrēmata*). The simplest formulation we can offer is that citizens view justice as having an "equal share" (*to ison*), or a "just share" (*to dikaion*)—notions that are given content by an agreed-

---

of *aidōs*, which poses problems for the book's attempt to place *aidōs* at the center of Greek ethics.

[10] Following Dodds 1959, 12–15 (cf. Kerferd 1981, 52), I believe that Callicles was a real person in the late fifth century who held views similar to those attributed to him in the *Gorgias*.

[11] Ostwald 1996; Schofield 1999, 141–49.

[12] See, e.g., Aristotle *Politics* 1268a24, 1268a27–28, 1302b26–27, 1306b10–11.

upon principle of distribution.[13] Consequently, citizens are opposed to those who want to have "more," or to have a "greater share" (*to pleon*), and they therefore construe "injustice" as meaning "having more than a fair share."[14] Callicles' argument, then, is that through defining appropriate "shares" in collective goods and through convincing others of the justice of their definitions, the weak masses keep the intelligent and powerful from seeking to have more than their share.

To conventional justice, Callicles opposes his own conception of "natural justice," according to which powerful individuals follow their innate instincts to get more and more. He thus embraces greed and injustice, as they are conventionally understood: as the excessive desire to get more—more than one has, more than others have, and especially more than one deserves as a matter of *distributive* fairness. In his words, "Nature itself, I think, shows that it is just [*dikaion*] that the better man should have more [*pleon echein*] than the worse and the stronger more than the weaker. Nature shows that this is so in many areas—among other animals, and in whole cities and races of men, that the just share [*to dikaion*] is decided in this way: the stronger rules over [*archein*] the weaker and has more [*pleon echein*]" (483c9–d6).[15] He considers the attempts by the powerful to gratify their desires to be a law of nature. Following the law of nature is Callicles' recommendation for how it is best to live a human life—with disregard for conventional strictures, and in pursuit of power and the satisfactions of one's natural desire to get more.[16] Thus he contests the notion of distributive fairness to which he is subjected in conventional society, on the grounds that the powerful and intelligent deserve more than a conventionally determined "equal share"; they deserve, he imagines, as much as they can get.

[13] The notion of having "equal shares" can derive from a principle of simple equality (often called "arithmetic equality") or from a principle of "proportional equality" (or "geometric equality"). The first of these, characteristic of democracy, means simply that everyone is equal and therefore deserves an equal share; the second, characteristic of democracy's critics, that in some morally relevant respect, such as the respective contributions they make to group projects, individuals are unequal and therefore deserve a correspondingly unequal (or proportional) share in collective distributions. On the idea of "two equalities," see Harvey 1965, 1966; Vlastos 1973, 183–96.

[14] Gutglueck 1988, 25–26, offers a brief consideration of some of these issues.

[15] If understood generously, Callicles is offering a conception not simply of self-interest but of justice, which ultimately appeals to impartial notions that are independent of the aims of any given individual: see Cooper 1999d, 52–53; Irwin 1995, 102–4; Dodds 1959, 15. The principle of charity is crucial here, since Callicles' initial claims point only to the self-interest of those able to employ brute force. Furthermore, even if Callicles sometimes suggests that he could fulfill his ideals as a democratic orator, his impulse is the tyrannical one, and he is an absolute elitist; see Dodds 1959, 13; Kahn 1983, 100.

[16] Callicles' notion of happiness is discussed by Irwin 1995, 104–6; Kahn 1983, 97–102; Cooper 1999d, 51–57; North 1966, 161–62.

This contest over what counts as *fair* distribution is a central part of the history I trace. Because all citizens "share in" the collective goods of their respective communities, a question of distributive justice immediately arises: according to what principle are such "shares" to be distributed to members of the community? In the *Politics*, Aristotle says that every polis lays claim to a sort of justice (1280a9–10), but the particular principle of distributive fairness in any given polis depends on the prevailing notion of proportional equality (*to kat' analogian ison*), according to which citizens receive differential shares in collective goods depending on their relative worth and merit in promoting the common good.[17] If distributive fairness is based on a concept of "the equal share" (*to ison*), then injustice in distribution means taking "the greater share" (*to pleon*), that is, taking more than one's fair share of a community's divisible goods. Through constructing unorthodox arguments about what counts as fair, Callicles attempts to justify his bitter rejection of equality and his repeated emphasis on getting "the greater share." The ways in which such arguments were made is itself a crucial feature of Athenian history in our period.

Arguments must be made in the first place because the distributing community does not enforce its values by means of an "invisible hand," nor does the power to enforce values emanate from any single or particular source, such as a tyrant, or the elite, or those in political power at a given moment. Rather, the members of a community enforce and maintain collective sentiments through their private and public relations with one another and, in particular, through their use of shared evaluative language.[18] Hence, in the chapters that follow, I consider greed within a constellation of other values by which the members of a community enforce their shared notions of distributive fairness and of appropriate individual desires and deserts. Greed itself should be considered one of the most powerful evaluative tools in the arsenal of Athenian rhetoric. Those who invoked greed were by implication placing themselves on the side of the community and its interests, against those who were, through their excessive acquisitiveness, allegedly violating shared communal standards of fair distribution. But when is "enough" enough? And, conversely, when is "too much" too much?

As Aristotle recognized in his discussions of justice in the polis, in *Politics* 3 and 5, these questions cannot be answered on any abstract, a priori basis.[19] But that does not mean they can be treated idiosyn-

[17] *Politics* 1280a25–34, 1281a4–8, 1282b14–24, 1301a25–28.

[18] On the capacity of language to enforce values, see the suggestive account of punishment found in Foucault 1979; within classical history, see Cohen 1992.

[19] Of course, such questions *can* be answered aprioristically, as they were by Plato and Aristotle himself. But theorists' answers hold relatively little weight in practical political

cratically. Instead, they are answered by arguments explicitly made within the prevailing conventions and ethos of particular political cultures in force at a given time. These conventions define the ethical framework within which particular answers are made possible.[20] Given the undoubted fact of social conflict, however, is it legitimate to say that Athenian standards of distribution, for example, were prevalent or shared? The archaic and classical discourse on greed offers prima facie evidence to the contrary: it is the reality of social conflict that lies behind the use of greed as a pejorative ideological label. Put simply, what one person calls just and fair distribution may look, to someone from a different socioeconomic group or evaluative perspective, like outrageous exploitation. How are such disputes to be adjudicated? Should we be saying that one group of people is *really* greedy according to prevailing standards, while another is *really* acting justly, however its ideological rivals describe it? Or does the devil lie not in the details but rather in the description?

To pose the issue differently, the problem lies not in discovering the meanings of words—everyone essentially knew the *meaning* of the vocabulary used to express the idea of greed—but rather in understanding or arguing about the criteria of applying the terms correctly in specific contexts.[21] This problem is at least as old as Thucydides (cf. 3.83): especially in times of crisis, evaluative terms are peculiarly susceptible to reinvention and revaluation in the light of changing sensibilities and the breakdown of traditional order. Even so, reevaluated moral expressions or ideas must be presented in terms of familiar and widely acceptable notions of morality, social relations, and collective commitments. Otherwise, they look like bizarre neologisms or the ravings of heterodox fringe groups and, as such, they have no purchase in the community to which they are meant to appeal. In other words, they lack evaluative or ideological force because they cannot tap into the community's deepest, preexisting beliefs about politics, economics, and society. Writing the history of greed as an ideological and theoretical concept means coming to terms with the different ancient attempts to use greed in political argument by

---

situations, where everything depends on rational arguments made within the framework of preexisting conventions and beliefs.

[20] That only certain sets of arguments and moral claims are possible in given social circumstances underlies Foucault's helpful formulation of the "problematic": "But the work of a history of thought would be to rediscover at the root of these diverse solutions the general form of problematization that has made them possible—even in their very opposition; or what has made possible the transformations of the difficulties and obstacles of a practice into a general problem for which one proposes diverse practical solutions. . . . [Problematization] develops the conditions in which possible responses can be given; it defines the elements that will constitute what the different solutions attempt to respond to" (Foucault 1984, 389).

[21] Skinner (1988b, 121–23) offers a neat formulation of this distinction.

fitting it into the prevailing framework of other generally accepted moral sentiments.

Having attained some clarity about the context of Callicles' critique, we can now ask what Callicles wants for himself in the first place.[22] His conception of human flourishing depends on a close connection between power and desire. In his view, natural justice entails "that the man who is going to live as a man ought, must allow his appetites [*epithumias*] to be as great as possible instead of repressing [*kolazein*] them, and be able by means of his courage and intelligence to satisfy them in all their intensity by providing them with whatever they happen to desire" (491e8–492a4). To Callicles, power is the coefficient force that connects desire and possession, whereas desire is the meaningful directing spirit behind power. In practice this means that strong men will rule states and use their power to "have more" than their subjects; Callicles always connects ruling (*archein*) and having more (*pleon echein*) as the twin facets of justice according to nature (cf. 488b4–5, 490a1–5, 491c6–d2). He has difficulty conceiving of someone with power who chooses not to exploit that power for his own material advantage, unless that someone has been so benighted by conventional morality as to lose touch with his natural instincts. Callicles' desire, then, is twofold: he desires power as an instrumental good, and he desires other unspecified material pleasures that his power will enable him to enjoy.

As for these other pleasures, Callicles emphasizes satisfying his "appetites" (*epithumias*, e.g., 491e9, 492a2–3),[23] and he shows a strong tendency to idealize "intemperance" (*akolasia*)—both of which suggest a materialistic, bodily focus.[24] As Aristotle later pointed out, temperance (*sōphrosunē*) and intemperance (*akolasia*) have to do with pleasures of the body, particularly those pleasures, such as touch and taste, that human beings share with other animals and which, therefore, appear "slavish" (*andrapodōdeis*)

[22] On Callicles' notion of happiness, see n.16.

[23] In his note on 491a4, Dodds (1959, 292) rightly points out that there are two questions involved here: Socrates asks Callicles to explain who is he talking about and what they desire; Dodds rightly says that the answer to the second question "is never formally given but is implicit in the tirade which begins at 491c5" (292).

[24] Callicles himself, under pressure from Socrates' interrogation, comes to identify his conception of happiness, the gratification of appetites, with indiscriminate hedonism. Kahn (1983, 102–5) rightly points out that "Plato makes Callicles an indiscriminate hedonist rather than a more selective pursuer of preferred passions, like the timocratic or plutocratic man of *Republic* VIII" (104). But then he more plausibly withdraws that admission (499b6–8), so that in the end the status and objects of his own appetites are left unclear. Cooper (1999d, 69–75) offers a compelling analysis of Callicles' withdrawal and the ways it can improve his position. As Kahn (1983, 104–5) points out, if Callicles had focused on "the pursuit of power and wealth," then his position would be more defensible.

and "bestial" (*thēriōdeis*) (*EN* 1118a1–3, 1118a23–26).[25] Concluding his account of temperance and intemperance, Aristotle says that the temperate individual must harmonize his "appetitive part" (*to epithumētikon*) with reason (*EN* 1119b15–16). Hence, Callicles desires power for the sake of materialistic, probably bodily, pleasures, which will satisfy the enlarged appetites that he considers a part of any good human life.

In Plato's *Republic*, the "appetitive part" (*to epithumētikon*) of the soul is one of three constitutive parts, the others being reason and aspiration. Plato describes the appetitive part as follows: "We have called it the appetitive [*epithumētikon*] part, because of the intensity of its appetites [*epithumiōn*] for food, drink, sex, and all the things associated with them, but we have also called it the money-loving [*philochrēmaton*] part, because such appetites [*epithumiai*] are most easily satisfied by means of money" (580e2–581a1). Immediately thereafter, Plato reiterates that this part is money-loving (*philochrēmaton*) and profit-loving (*philokerdes*) (581a6–7).[26] Money, as the paramount instrumental good, is the means to gratify physical urges, and thus is grouped together with such gratification in a single part of the soul. Earlier Plato had said that the appetitive part was "by nature most insatiable for money" (*chrēmatōn phusei aplēstotaton*) (442a6–7) and most apt to attempt "to enslave and rule over the classes it is not fitted to rule" (442b1–2). It attempts, in other words, to rule over reason and aspiration, even though, according to Plato, it is harmful to the individual if it does so. The appetitive part of the soul is in many ways analogous to Callicles, the individual who is dominated by his appetites. Like Callicles, the appetitive part of the soul desires power over the other parts, along with materialistic satisfactions and pleasures.[27]

Central to Callicles' own self-understanding is his greed to get more—more bodily pleasures and more of the means, such as power and wealth, to satisfy them. We have seen that it is nearly impossible to mention such uninhibited desires without also arguing with the conventional belief that they are unjust. Society criticizes individuals like Callicles for their violation of fairness. In the *Gorgias*, though, Socrates opens up another line of

[25] With Aristotle's connection between the intemperate pleasures and bestiality, one may compare Callicles' invocation of the animal world to explain the truth of his view of natural right (483d3); cf. Kahn 1983, 99.

[26] On the apparent complexity of this part of the soul, see Annas 1981, 128–30; Cooper (1999b, 126–30) demonstrates the essential unity of the appetitive part, which is rooted in its relation to the body and bodily pleasure.

[27] At the end of the *Republic* (588b–590b), Plato finally represents this appetitive part as a many-headed beast—like the Chimera, Scylla, or Cerberus—that wants to enslave the other parts. This image anticipates Aristotle's claim that the appetites are what we share with animals. Our reason, by contrast, which is represented by the human being, is what makes us distinctively human. This is a powerful and, as we shall see, persistent type of attack on those who share Callicles' ideals.

critique by subjecting Callicles' notion of happiness to scrutiny. He poses an apparently simple question: will Callicles' "strong man" be self-controlled (*sōphrona*)? Will he be master of himself (*enkratē*) (491d7–e1)? Callicles thinks the very idea conventional and dim-witted; self-control and moderation are for him the virtues of the weak.[28] In order to limit the appeal of Callicles' enlarged appetites, Socrates compares Callicles' ideal to the repellent life-style of a bird called the *charadrios*, which, an ancient commentator says, eats while it excretes.[29] Needless to say, this is a filthy and disgusting conception of happiness.[30] Socrates' argument is typical of an entire tradition of discourse about greed, ranging from Solon to Herodotus to the Anonymus Iamblichi, all of whom question the conception of happiness that drives those who pursue the ideals of greed. Their arguments are all designed to show that excessive desires are unworthy of the greedy agent's humanity, and that they do not ring true to his genuine aspirations—if only he could see what those aspirations are.[31] After further arguments, Socrates seems to win the debate, though Callicles remains unconvinced. Callicles' response, too, is typical of an entire tradition of stubbornly greedy agents: they simply do not care to hear, and certainly do not believe, that they are impoverished by their greed.[32] Quite the opposite.

At this point it is necessary to complicate my picture in two ways. First, I have focused on the excessive materialism that is a central object of criticism, but the desire to get more material goods is usually linked to the desire for other types of socially constructed goods. Herein lies another contest over the moral significance of desires to get more. Wealth

[28] North (1966, 96–97, 159–65) discusses the opposition between *sōphrosunē* (self-control) and *pleonexia* in the *Gorgias*.

[29] On the nature of this bird, see Dodds 1959, 306; it has been identified with the stone curlew.

[30] As Cooper (1999d, 69n60) shows, this argument does not deter Callicles from maintaining his viewpoint, although he is annoyed at having to talk about such things. Socrates must make further arguments in order to exploit the weaknesses of Callicles' position; on the quality of these arguments, see Cooper 1999d, 69–75.

[31] The attack on impoverished conceptions of happiness and humanity does not, of course, necessarily undermine all possible attacks on justice as a social virtue; it merely illustrates the difficulty of conjuring up a feasible conception of happiness while also rejecting justice. I return to these issues in the epilogue, where I discuss Plato's *Republic*. Often attacks on the impoverished conceptions of happiness of individual agents use the image of gluttony, which is closely allied to greed; cf. *Gorgias* 518e–519b and chapter 4.

[32] This explains the emphasis on Callicles' lack of shame compared with Socrates' other interlocutors (e.g., 482e6–483a2; 487b1–2; 494c5): he must be able to say what he really thinks despite conventional disapproval. On shame in the *Gorgias*, see Irwin 1995, 122–24. Another way of putting this is to say that Callicles pays little attention to the "spirited part" of his soul (*thumos* or *to thumoeides*), as Plato defines it in the *Republic*, which is honor-loving (*philotimon*); on the "spirited" part, see Cooper 1999b, 130–36.

has a socially constituted meaning in specific cultures: it creates power for the rich, and it makes them prestigious. As the sociologist Viviana Zelizer has demonstrated, money is not an absolutely fungible, uniquely rationalizing, and universally abstract medium. Instead, people employ material "goods simultaneously as markers of their social rank, as indicators of other shared collective identities, and as signals of their individuality."[33] As a result, their desires for such goods are defined not only with reference to the goods themselves, but also with reference to the symbolic and cultural associations of those goods in specific contexts. By extension, the possession of certain culturally situated goods helps to define an individual's identity and his relationship to the wider society.

In the *Iliad*, for example, Agamemnon robbed Achilles of his captive girlfriend Briseis because he wanted a material sign of his own status. In response, Achilles accused him of base greed and condemned him as a leader who "feeds fat" on his people (2.231). Such disputes involving accusations of greed could also be contests over the social and moral significance of the desire to get more. Critics who exploited the rhetoric of greed, such as Achilles, tended to emphasize the base corporeality of desires in order to deflate the opponents' pretensions to honor. Those, on the other hand, who tried to satisfy their desires, such as Agamemnon, might well view themselves as noble and their desires as honorably motivated. Furthermore, they might, like Agamemnon, view their eventual possession of the desired goods as a mark of status and honor—rather than something to be ashamed of. The historical interest lies in the conflict and in the kinds of arguments that could be made on either side. It is necessary to try to understand the psychology of the desiring agent himself as much as the arguments of those who labeled him, critically, "greedy."

The second complication concerns the individual's role within society. Because of its location at the intersection of the discourses on injustice and excessive desire, the classical discourse on greed illuminates one of the deepest conflicts of Greek civilization generally. As many have seen, Greek culture highly valued the agonistic "virtues" of competition, the individual striving for more, and the promotion of the self as opposed to, and even at the expense of, the common good.[34] At the same time, the Greeks, like other ancient Mediterranean peoples, lived in a culture defined by scarcity of resources and the continual threat of famine, shortage, and economic breakdown. Consequently, Greek culture had to devise sophisticated mechanisms of social control whereby the communally sanctioned striving for more would also be sufficiently limited to permit

[33] Zelizer 1994, 212; Parry and Bloch 1989.

[34] See Adkins 1960; 1972, with references to older discussions; Irwin 1995, 102–4.

the community as such to flourish. A key feature of Greek moral thinking was precisely the attempt to place limits on excessive behavior; language and morality, the mechanisms of communal censure, operated with laws and other strictures to limit individual self-aggrandizement. Still, there is an obvious tension between the individualistic virtues of competition and the communal framework within which those virtues became meaningful—between what Adkins has called the "competitive" and the "cooperative" virtues of Greek culture.[35]

The key issue in resolving that conflict is the collective education of the individual. MacIntyre has shown that the greedy agent, driven to acquire more unjustly, subjectively experiences competition differently from those who abide by the prevailing ethics of their communities:

> For those possessed by *pleonexia* the *agōn*, the contest, becomes something quite other than it was in the games or for Pindar. It becomes an instrument of the individual will in grasping after success in satisfying its desires. Of course in any society where contests are central to activity, the victor will achieve the prizes of success and will at least appear to be and will probably in fact be nearer than others to satisfying his desires. But the achievement and the excellence recognized by himself, by the community and by such people as the poet whose task it is to praise that achievement and that excellence are what is valued primarily; it is because they are valued that prizes and satisfactions attach to them; *not* vice versa.[36]

Prizes, pleasure, and satisfaction are, in other words, the second effects of outstanding achievement and the exemplification of excellence. They should be an afterthought, not what is valued in the first instance. Greedy agents like Callicles have it the wrong way round; they subordinate their intelligence and courage, their proper virtues, to getting more for themselves. They can be taught to do this by their culture. Thus, the tempering of desire remains an individual problem, but must also be viewed within the framework of a society called upon to educate individual desires as it participates in the formation of moral consciousness. As it must appropriately limit individual acquisitiveness, so too must society, in urging individuals to compete, promote a proper understanding of the values that underlie competition from the start. Plato saw this clearly in his critique of contemporary society's education of its citizens:

> Or do you agree with the general opinion that certain young men are corrupted by sophists—that there are certain sophists with significant influence on the young who corrupt them through private teaching? Isn't it rather the very people who say this who are the greatest sophists of all, since they educate

[35] The classic treatment is Adkins 1960; Adkins 1972, 8–9.
[36] MacIntyre 1984, 137.

> them most completely and make young and old, men and women, into precisely the kind of people they want them to be?
>
> When do they do that? he asked.
>
> When many of them are sitting together in assemblies, courts, theaters, army camps, or in some other public gathering of the crowd, they object very loudly and excessively to some of the things that are said or done and approve others in the same way, shouting and clapping, so that the very rocks and surroundings echo the din of their praise or blame and double it. (Plato *Rep.* 492a5–c2)

It is right and proper that a community should criticize individuals for excessively desiring more, on the grounds that their greed leads to injustice, and perhaps that it diminishes the individuals themselves. In making such critiques, though, the community as such—here, with Plato, I am thinking of classical Athens—opens itself to the criticism that, through its own excessive desires (e.g., its imperialism), it has taught its individual citizens to be greedy from the start. If individual greed leads to civic conflict, then the greed of a polis like Athens leads to strife within the international community of Greek states. My hope is to show that greed was a nodal point in the arguments and behaviors of classical Athenians, who considered themselves, simultaneously, to be individuals, members of a polis, and members of an international community.

To clarify the historical distinctiveness of ancient Greek greed as well as its similarities to later conceptions, one can examine the role of greed in theoretical and cultural analysis in later texts and systems of thought. A vice of individual psychology and social relations, greed figures in a variety of modern cultural representations. The richness of the discourse derives in part from greed's role as a central dialectic in political thought since the time of the ancient Greeks. Space permits only the most schematic representation of greed's role in Rome, the Middle Ages, and modernity, but even a sketch of the long, complex history of greed illustrates its potential as a force of moral destabilization and its elasticity as a category of social disapproval. Highlighting key changes in the conception and theoretical use of greed provides a provocative background against which to understand the ancient Athenian discourse on greed.

Roman authors censured greed because it leads to an inappropriately luxurious life-style (*luxuria*), moral turpitude, and forgetfulness of Rome's ancestral customs (*mos maiorum*).[37] The Roman discourse on greed (*avaritia*) suggested that the individual lust for riches gradually eroded the social and personal values that had made the Republic great in the first place: values like simplicity, frugality, and moderation. Describing the

[37] See, e.g., Livy 34.4.3, 36.17.4–5, 37.54.18–23, with Luce 1977, 230–97.

early Romans, Sallust invokes a key opposition between glory and greed: "They desired glory, but were liberal with their money; they wanted unbounded glory, but riches won honorably [*gloriam ingentem, divitias honestas volebant*]" (*Bell. Cat.* 7.6). Like his Greek predecessors, Sallust positioned greed in a clear hierarchy of value according to which greed represented base, materialistic desires, the converse of the praiseworthy pursuit of honor and glory. Sallust argues that ambition is not very different from virtue (11.2), but that "Avarice [*avaritia*] implies a desire for money [*pecuniae*], which no wise man covets. It is a kind of deadly poison, which renders the most manly body and soul effeminate. It knows no bounds and can never be satisfied: nor can either abundance or want make it less" (11.3).[38] Avarice, the paramount materialistic desire, poisons and weakens the body; Greek authors, too, linked the discourse on greed with that on masculinity and expressed anxiety over the destructive insatiability of acquisitive desires.

Sallust's notion of avarice takes money as its object, but his description of the influx of wealth into Rome shows that greed to get more quickly assumed a wider focus: "As soon as wealth [*divitiae*] came to be a mark of distinction and an easy way to win renown, military commands, and political power, virtue began to decline. . . . Riches [*divitiis*] made the younger generation a prey to luxury [*luxuria*], avarice [*avaritia*], and pride [*superbia*]" (*Bell. Cat.* 12.1–2). In other words, wealth had come to be desirable not only in itself, but also because it was the means to status in the form of conspicuous display, as well as to political power. This is a common triad in theoretical discussions of greed at Rome: wealth, status, and power are clustered together in the diverse understandings of greed's role in causing Rome's decline.

Starting in the middle Republic, the discussion of avarice was conditioned by Rome's acquisition of a Mediterranean empire, which made enormous reserves of wealth available to any Roman leaders willing to fight for it, and thereby catalyzed the elite's preexisting ethic of competition in disastrous ways. Elite competition for money and prestige ultimately destroyed the institutional framework that had made that competition meaningful in the first place. In his famous preface, Livy wrote, "The less wealth there was, the less greed [*cupiditatis*]; recently riches have brought in avarice [*avaritiam*], and self-indulgence has brought us, through every form of sensual excess, to be in love with death both individual and collective" (*Preface* 12). Livy regards greed as the product, rather than the cause, of Rome's initial acquisition of wealth. The swarm of desires created by the influx of wealth harmed the state by destroying Rome's collective ideals in favor of a newly individualistic ethic. As Feld-

[38] On Sallust's concept of *avaritia*, see Earl 1961, 13–14, 34–39.

herr explains, "*Luxuria*, the force that has corroded the Roman state, shuts off the individual from the collective life of the state."[39] Roman political thinkers and historians embedded greed deeply within their analyses of social unrest, individual competition, and the wide framework of characteristically Roman desires to get more prestige and power. As we shall see, the Greek discourse also embeds greed within wider frames of reference that included honor and social esteem, but greed was always a term of contamination, a way of destroying the "purity" of a desire to win honor or prestige.

The Roman discourse was appropriated by the late antique and medieval discussions of avarice, which concentrated on the destructive moral consequences of avarice when it operated in the soul of a single individual. The "goods" that people get by successfully satisfying their greed stop being good for the individual after a certain limit; avarice is a disordered desire that makes the individual less than he should be. Avarice also drives people to violate proper social relations among members of their own communities or, in the Christian conception, among all human beings.[40] The hierarchy of value, codified late in the classical period by Plato, was Christianized; the two basic Athenian critiques of greed continued to exert influence but now with more emphasis on the welfare of the individual.

As one of the seven deadly sins, avarice occupied a place of particular prominence in medieval reflections upon sin and humanity. Much of the discussion of greed in late antiquity and the early Middle Ages was concerned to reconcile two biblical statements about the priority of pride and avarice in the classification of vices. According to Ecclesiasticus 10:13, "Pride is the beginning of all sin," whereas Saint Paul held that "Cupidity is the root of all evil things" (1 Tim. 6:10). Little has argued that pride held primacy of place among the vices in the early medieval period, usually through the explicit subordination or subsuming of avarice within it; later, however, avarice rose in importance in tandem with the rise of a mercantile, as opposed to an agrarian, economy.[41] Throughout the medieval period, different authors tried to reconcile the apparent biblical contradiction by offering a broader interpretation of avarice. Saint Augustine, for example, "juxtaposed the two texts and urged the

[39] Feldherr 1998, 115. Rome's tendency to fall prey to greed can of course be documented in much earlier periods, as when the people's greed caused internal strife because of their dissatisfaction over the distribution of booty from Veii in ca. 390 B.C. For discussion of this episode in Livy, see Miles 1995, 82–87, and esp. Livy 5.20.1–4, 5.24.4–8.

[40] Sacks (1998, 267–311) traces how medieval and early modern thinkers played out the predominantly Aristotelian themes of *pleonexia* and injustice in their own distinctive social and political contexts.

[41] See Little 1971; 1978.

reader to adopt a broad understanding of avarice, that is, as an inordinate desire for anything and not simply for money. . . . The devil had been made to fall by avarice, and everyone knows that this avarice consisted not in a love of money but in a love of power."[42] My reconstruction of the Greek discourse on greed makes Augustine's interpretation more comprehensible, because power, like money, is often the instrumental means to satisfy shameful, even fundamentally destructive, appetites. Similarly, Hugh of Saint-Victor, the twelfth-century theologian, defined avarice as an immoderate desire for "having," without clarifying the objects of that desire. In the fourteenth century, John Wyclif has his allegorical character Phronesis remark that "the true opposite of avarice is *ordinatus amor temporalia* [well-ordered love of temporal things], because that vice is really *inordinatus amor temporalia* [disordered love of temporal things]," again a wide-ranging and excessive desire for a variety of earthly goods.[43] Avarice thus proved suitably elastic for thinkers who wanted to illustrate the underlying relationship between excessive acquisitiveness and pride. Under the pressure of biblical interpretation, Augustine and others devised a notion of greed that linked its materiality with desires for other goods such as power.

Greed's elasticity also set it up as the habitual bedfellow of other vices in diverse theories about the root causes of social instability. As Hirschman has remarked, "The major passions had long been solidly linked to one another in literature and thought, often in some unholy trinity, from Dante's 'Superbia, invidia e avarizia sono / le tre faville ch'anno i cuori accesi (Pride, envy, and greed are / the three sparks which have inflamed hearts)' to 'Ehrsucht, Herrschsucht, und Habsucht (ambition, thirst for power, and greed)' in Kant's *Idea for a General History*."[44] In a wide-ranging study of the Aristotelian and medieval roots of the sixteenth-century condemnation of monopoly, Sacks has shown that greed for material goods usually leads outward to the harsh exploitation of and control over others.[45] Much of the discourse against monopolistic greed is directed against upper-class lords who allegedly want to get possession of power, wealth, and everything else in exorbitant degree. Of a variety of rebellious tracts written from the fourteenth to the sixteenth century, Sacks notes, "Recurring is the image of 'these gorgious Gentlemen' acting with 'crueltie and covetousnesse,' as well as injustice, against their tenants, treating them 'slavishly,' enclosing pastures, ditching and hedging, taking 'by violence all away,' not content 'except that they may also sucke . . .

[42] Little 1971, 20.

[43] Bloomfield 1952, 189; this remains the classic work on the seven deadly sins in medieval literature.

[44] Hirschman 1977, 20–21.

[45] Sacks 1998.

our bloud and marrow, out of our veines and bones'."[46] Both in the Greek context and in these later discourses, such all-encompassing greed is particularly associated with aristocrats, especially those with tyrannical ambitions. Such ambitions often involve enslaving others, gluttonously consuming their livelihoods, and using violence liberally to achieve unjust aims.

In late medieval Europe, as a profit economy became more prominent, reactions to money were ambivalent: on the one hand, money facilitated the development of urbanism, commerce, and manufacture, but it also inspired graphic denunciations because of its morally corrosive effects. In particular, it was envisioned as a form of filthy refuse: speaking of gothic manuscripts, Little writes, "In one of these drawings a worried looking ape, with his right paw under his chin and his left paw under his knee, defecates three coins into a golden bowl. Another shows a hybrid man defecating coins into a bowl held by an ape."[47] Avarice was thus explicitly and unambiguously tied to a disgusting form of materiality. Money was gross because it changed hands constantly, touched everyone, and thereby became filthy. Gross materiality, as we saw in Socrates' critique of Callicles, was also an integral element of the Greek rhetoric of condemning greed.

In an altogether different way, the connection between money and feces survives even today: a recent television commercial advertising the online investment firm E-trade begins with doctors surveying the anus of a patient and concluding, "This man has money coming out of the 'wazoo'!"[48] By investing with E-trade, the idea must be, we can all manufacture wealth in an act of literal intestinal fortitude. This is disgusting but obviously meant to be funny and strangely appealing—and that appeal in itself points to the transformation that has occurred in the modern period. Historians have long held that a central transformation in views of avarice came about especially in the Scottish Enlightenment. By contrast with the radical denunciations of avarice in the Middle Ages, Scottish Enlightenment thinkers rechristened greed as "rational self-interest," and gave it the job, as Hirschman has shown, of countervailing other, even more destructive passions, such as the lust for glory and power.[49] Different thinkers conjured up different ways in which that countervailing was possible, but one of the best known, Mandeville, proposed in his *Fable of the Bees* that the "Skilful Management of the Dex-

[46] Sacks 1998, 287.

[47] Little 1978, 34.

[48] This television commercial aired during the National Football League's Super Bowl 2000 (January 30, 2000).

[49] Hirschman 1977, esp. part 2; Parry and Bloch 1989, 17–19.

trous Politician" could turn "private vices" into "publick benefits."[50] If greed as "avarice" was considered responsible for *countervailing* ambition and hunger for power, then, by definition, greed—that is, cupidity for money—must be differentiated from ambitious self-aggrandizement. As greed became a morally agreeable feature of society, it was also more narrowly focused on money, rather than explicitly connected to other social vices like the hunger for power. The conception of one's narrow self-interests as "private vice, public benefit" gradually became a central tenet of Anglo-American philosophical liberalism and an ideological mainstay of market capitalism. By pursuing our own narrowly defined self-interests, the theory goes, we create economic surplus, reduce prices, and learn to deal peacefully with others in the rationally driven marketplace.

In contemporary society, it stands to reason, "greed" is a massively overdetermined concept. The ethical critique of the greedy individual prevails: he demeans himself as a human being by taking more than he needs or could use; he has a narrow, impoverished conception of himself and his life. At the level of social evaluation, however, we have inherited sharply conflicting traditions. On the one hand, greed is considered a politically destructive and socially divisive desire, which must be restrained within strict limits if society is to flourish. In Wimbledon's view, for example, "covetousness prompted men not only to oppress widows and motherless children, to bear false witness, and to turn free men into bondmen, but even to deny their own kin and to break faith with their friends."[51] We will see many of the same themes—enslavement, oath breaking, and deceit—in the classical Greek discourse on greed.

On the other hand, as many now suppose, the "invisible hand" of the marketplace so arranges individual activity, however self-interested and vicious, that society as a whole capitalizes on individual greed, winning advantages for itself that are otherwise unattainable. Thus greed, in the guise of rational self-interest, contributes to social and economic flourishing through the production of ever expanding surplus.[52] Despite powerful, especially Marxist, critiques of market capitalism, the system and its underlying ideology have shown remarkable staying power in the contemporary Western world.[53] Even as late as 1936, Keynes wrote that

[50] See Hirschman 1977, 18.

[51] Sacks 1998, 283.

[52] A recent popular sociology of greed, that of Shames 1989, emphasizes that excessive acquisitiveness has had negative consequences for greedy individuals and their families, but it is striking that the term "justice" does not appear in the index and has not entered into the author's thinking about greed in contemporary American society. Greed today is a matter of excess; much less, however, a matter of justice.

[53] Indeed, despite formidable critiques from a Marxist perspective and elsewhere, the no-

> Dangerous human proclivities can be canalized into comparatively harmless channels by the existence of opportunities for money-making and private wealth, which, if they cannot be satisfied in this way, may find their outlet in cruelty, the reckless pursuit of personal power and authority, and other forms of self-aggrandizement. It is better that a man should tyrannise over his bank balance than over his fellow-citizens.[54]

The following chapters show that Keynes's fundamental distinction between power and wealth as objects of the acquisitive appetite is impossible in classical and archaic Athens. They also suggest that Keynes provides a deeply inaccurate picture of desiring agents in any period.

The activities of corporate America in recent decades show that the lust for money is deeply entrenched in the culture, and recent cultural discourse illustrates clearly the enduring legacy left by the Scottish Enlightenment. To quote Gordon Gecko, the classic corporate raider in the 1987 movie *Wall Street*: "Greed—for lack of a better word—is good. Greed is right. Greed works. Greed clarifies, cuts through, it captures the essence of the evolutionary spirit. Greed in all its forms: greed for life, for money, for love, knowledge, has marked the upward surge of mankind, and greed—you mark my words—will not only save Teldar Paper, but that other malfunctioning corporation called the USA."[55] Gecko himself is a highly unappealing character, but he captures the underlying materialism of even the most wide-ranging form of greed he can imagine.

Over the course of two millennia, greed underwent contextual variations in scope, standard objects, and ethical evaluation. The same is true in the ancient Greek world: Callicles exhibits the widest possible range of immoral desires to get more, but the scope and standard objects of ancient Greek greed are subject to change depending on the specific context under examination. To take one example among many, the Athenian elite in Solon's day differed from Thucydides' imperialists in wanting land, not empire, and in wanting an exclusive hold on power within the city, rather than dominance over other Greeks. In the chapters that follow, I chart and explain the transformations in greed—in how it was understood as such, in what political contexts it assumed importance, and in

tion that individual greed is good for society at large has had remarkable staying-power in our culture. A recent television documentary (*Greed—with John Stossel*, a one-hour ABC-TV program aired Tuesday, February 3, 1998), set out to show that, despite what people think at first glance, even outrageous examples of individual accumulation actually serve our financial interests and well-being at all levels of society.

[54] Keynes 1973, 7:374; cf. Hirschman 1977, 134.

[55] *Wall Street*, Twentieth Century Fox, 1987, directed by Oliver Stone, screenplay by Stanley Weiser and Oliver Stone.

how it became socially meaningful to individual agents.[56] Tracing that history will, I hope, have implications for our current evaluation of greed, both through illustrating that greed has a fundamental relationship to power as well as money, and through offering a historical perspective on the potential for greed to undermine social cohesion.

[56] Cf. Parry and Bloch 1989, 23: "What money means is not only situationally defined but also constantly re-negotiated." This applies, as I argue, not only to money but also to other forms of wealth, and to the desires that drive agents to seek wealth.

2

Greed in Aristotle's Political Thought

> At the root of wealth one therefore discovers a corrupted disposition, a perverse will, a pleonexia—the desire to have more than others, more than one's share, to have everything.
> *J.-P. Vernant*[1]

THE notions of greed and respect for fair distribution did not arise in tandem with theoretical reflection about politics. These were very old concepts in Greek thought: in book 1 of the *Iliad*, for example, Achilles wrangles with Agamemnon over the appropriate distribution of shares in honor and material wealth, a quarrel that drives the action of the later narrative. Along with the idea of appropriate distribution came a nascent conception of justice and a dispute over its content. Achilles argued that he was entitled to a certain "share" (conceived in such terms as *moira*, *dais eïsē*, *geras*, *timē*) in the distribution of spoils as a function of his worth to the community, which he estimated in primarily military terms. At least in the poem's first scene, however, Agamemnon argued that status was a more important determinant of distribution than military valor by itself (see chapter 3). This dispute, the first recorded in the Greek world over precisely which principle of justice was to apply to collective distributions within a community, offers a clear perspective on the justifications that typically lie behind such arguments. Inaugurated in the *Iliad*, the tradition of thinking about communities in terms of "shares" in divisible goods animates Aristotle's own discussion of justice in book 5 of the *Nicomachean Ethics*. Aristotle's systematic account of justice, in turn, clarifies his ethical evaluation of excess acquisitiveness and constitutes a useful starting point for the history of greed in classical Athens.[2]

Aristotle's analysis provides a powerful theoretical model that can then be tested and played off against earlier discussions of and cultural prac-

[1] Vernant 1982, 84.

[2] Aristotle was not an Athenian citizen, but because he was deeply engaged with Athenian politics and those who reflected upon it, such as Plato, his work is a useful starting point. Aristotle spent much of his life in Athens, probably more than thirty years. On Aristotle's complex relationship with Athens, see Strauss 1991; on the biographical details, see Ross [1923] 1995, 1–6.

tices deriving from greed. As a result, his discussion constitutes a valuable template against which to view earlier treatments. To be more precise, the meanings and roles assigned to greed (usually expressed by the Greek term *pleonexia*) in Aristotle's *Ethics* and *Politics* do not define a "focal meaning" that is present in every usage and in every author who treats it.[3] Instead, Aristotle writes at the end of a long tradition of reflecting on and experiencing greed as an integral part of political life. His predecessors continually adapted the notion to their own historical circumstances and for their own intellectual purposes. After using Aristotle's conception in order to understand the psychological roots of greed, along with the ways in which it was censured, I then trace the intellectual and social history that led, through various reinterpretations, to the account given by Aristotle.

Aristotle's several discussions of greed define three issues. First, in his treatment of particular injustice in *Nicomachean Ethics* 5, he tries to define the relationship between excessive desire for more and injustice in distribution. Second, in the *Politics*, he notes the general tendency of human beings to yield to acquisitive desires by nature and the limited purchase that education has on restricting that tendency. He elaborates the point, which had already become clear in Plato's portrait of Callicles, that greed is rooted in human physicality—in the bodily urges that make us anxious to get more. Third, he observes certain distinctions in the quality and practice of greed in different social classes. He notes, in particular, that the desire for more becomes more wide-ranging as it moves up the social scale, until it becomes, in its manifestation among tyrants, the tyrannical desire to possess the entire state, along with its material goods and all the people who inhabit it.

Greed and Unfairness in Distribution in *Nicomachean Ethics* 5

> If Aristotle is to be our guide, the unjust person is no victim of any kind. He is dominated by only one vice, greed. That is why he breaks the rules of law and fairness. He just wants more of

[3] Owen (1986, 217), relying ultimately on Wittgenstein, says, "For the idea that an expression has *focal meaning*, that is to say that it has a primary sense by reference to which its other senses can be explained, seems to have been first clearly set out and exploited in an argument for Plato's Forms." For the concept of a "focal meaning" as used by, e.g., Fisher 1992 in studying *hubris*, see Adkins 1995, 452–53, who rightly notes the difficulties in arguing that complex concepts have a single or core meaning to which every particular usage is somehow connected.

everything, material goods, prestige, and power.
And the impact of his greed falls entirely upon
others, who receive less than they deserve thanks
to his grasping conduct.
Judith Shklar[4]

In *Nicomachean Ethics* 5, Aristotle offers an account of the virtue of justice. In accordance with his usual practice, he tries to show that this virtue is an intermediate state between a vice of excess and a vice of deficiency. In practice he focuses on the vice of excess, greed (*pleonexia*), which to him accounts for the drive to get more in violation of communal canons of distributive fairness. Justice and injustice, however, are notoriously difficult to fit within Aristotle's well-organized typology of virtues and vices, because they refer both to determinate psychological structures and to external facts about fairness in contexts of collective distribution. This two-pronged conception of justice and injustice is inherited from the tradition, but it poses certain problems for Aristotle's scheme. My contention is that the problematic status of injustice within Aristotle's moral system is highly illuminating for the psychology and moral evaluation of the greedy agent throughout the tradition.

According to Aristotle, there is an ambiguity in the use of the term "justice" (*dikaiosunē*).[5] On the one hand, "general justice" is "complete virtue" (*aretē . . . teleia*, 1129b26), or the whole of virtue (*holē aretē*, 1130a9), at least insofar as it is displayed toward others (1129b27). All the other virtues are therefore considered to be parts of general justice. General justice is concerned above all with what is lawful. Its characteristic goal is to promote the common good (1129a31–35, 1129b11–26).[6] It is to be distinguished, Aristotle claims, from "particular justice," which is a part of virtue (*tēn en merei aretēs dikaiosunēn*, 1130a14) and is divided into two subspecies, distributive and corrective (1130b30–1131a1). Distributive justice, with which we are concerned, is "found in the distribution of honor [*timēs*] or wealth [*chrēmatōn*] or the other things which can be divided up [*merista*] among those who share in a political community [*tois koinōnousi tēs politeias*], for among these it is possible for one person to have a share that is either unequal [*anison*] or equal [*ison*] to that of another" (1130b31–33).[7]

[4] Shklar 1990, 28.

[5] On the distinction between "general" (or "universal") justice and "particular" justice, see O'Connor 1991, 137–39; Curzer 1995, 208–11.

[6] For discussion of the meaning of "the common good" and of certain ambiguities involved in the conception, Morrison n.d. has been helpful.

[7] On Aristotle's discussion of distributive justice, see Keyt 1991a; Miller 1995, 68–74; MacIntyre 1988, 103–13.

The vices opposed to general and particular justice are general and particular injustice. Aristotle argues for a distinction between these vices as follows:

> The proof that it [particular justice] exists is this: when a person's actions display the other vices, for example throwing away a shield through cowardice or speaking harshly out of anger or not assisting another with money because of illiberality, he acts unjustly, but not greedily [*pleonektei d' ouden*]; but when he acts greedily [*pleonektē*], he usually displays none of these vices, and certainly not all of them, but his action does display some vice (since we blame him)—in particular, injustice. (1130a16–22)

In interpreting this complicated sentence, we must recall that, in Aristotle's view, virtues and vices occupy distinct spheres of application and have distinct psychological structures. Strictly speaking, for example, the same action cannot be both cowardly and illiberal; it must exhibit one or the other vice, because an individual "action" designates not only a certain type of physical motion, but also a particular psychological structure that has given rise to the action, or that typically gives rise to it.[8] In characterizing a virtue or vice, then, Aristotle must account not only for its particular object or area of activity, but also for the disposition that characteristically gives rise to it. The quoted passage, then, is intended to show (1) that greed is a "first-order," non-overlapping vice, distinct from and on a par with all the other "first-order" vices such as cowardice or illiberality and, therefore, (2) that it is different from general injustice.[9]

In order to support this argument, Aristotle identifies seeking profit (*to kerdainein* or *kerdos*, 1130a24, 28, 31; 1130b4) as the distinctive motivation of greed (*pleonexia*) as opposed to other vices. At this point, it is crucial to see that profit seeking causes moral agents to violate distributive fairness; how the motive of greed or acquisitiveness and the context of fairness are related will have to be elicited carefully from Aristotle's cryptic remarks. Some men commit adultery, he says, because they are intemperate, but the greedy individual commits adultery for the sake of gain (*tou kerdainein heneka, dia to kerdainein*, 1130a24–28). This "profit seeking" is presented at first as greed for money (1130a24–33), and then as a wider-ranging grasping for different goods, including honor, money, and safety; or, more precisely, for the pleasure derived from gain in these areas (1130b4).

This characterization, however, poses several immediate problems for

[8] Here I am following Curzer 1995, 213. My formulation also implies the further Aristotelian view that every action is, to borrow Curzer's term, a behavior-under-a-description. For further discussion, see also 1115a17–24, 1130a24–33 with Curzer 1995, 208–9.

[9] With Curzer (1995, 209), I use the term "first order" to distinguish these vices from the "second order" vice of general injustice, in which all the first-order vices participate, but without being its equivalent.

Aristotle's system: if greed is, in one of its guises, an excessive desire for money, then how can it be distinguished from the vice of illiberality (*aneleutheria*, 1121b12–1122a17), which Aristotle says consists both in deficiency in giving and excess in getting (1121b18–19)?[10] At first glance anyway, this overlap seems to violate Aristotle's general principle that the different virtues and vices should occupy different spheres of application and have different motivational structures. The overlap also makes it unclear whether illiberality should be seen as a violation of general justice or particular justice. Similarly, the ambitious (*philotimos*) man is blamed for pursuing honor excessively or from the wrong sources (1125b8–10); this characterization also overlaps with that of Aristotle's "greedy" individual. The great-souled (*megalopsuchos*) man, by contrast, is moderate not only with regard to honor, but also with regard to wealth, power, and all sorts of good and bad fortune (1124a13–19). In other words, he respects the canons of distributive fairness with regard to the goods of fortune.[11] But this is precisely what defines the individual who embodies particular justice (cf. 1129b2–4). These overlaps with the other virtues and vices make it difficult to differentiate particular justice and injustice from other first-order vices that Aristotle has already treated.

Despite the efforts of modern commentators, the problematic status of greed, considered as the opposite of distributive fairness, persists throughout the argument. Aristotle himself signals that justice is an unusual virtue near the end of his account of particular justice: "Justice is a certain mean [*mesotēs tis*], not in the same way as the other virtues, but since it is related to an intermediate state [*mesou*], while injustice is related to the extremes [*tōn akrōn*]" (1133b32–1134a1). As most commentators have seen, justice and injustice fit awkwardly within Aristotle's schematization of virtues and vices for several reasons.[12] Apart from being only a "kind of" intermediate state, justice is also, very unusually, unrelated to any specific emotion (*pathos*), and it is not a mean relative to the individual, but rather a mean in the distribution of shares in collectively

[10] At first glance *aneleutheria*, with its alpha-privative, seems to mean "illiberality," or the lack of willingness to give what one already has rather than the disposition to take more than one should. This intuition seems confirmed by a passage in the *Eudemian Ethics* (1221a33–34), where Aristotle says, "The one who exceeds in every expenditure is prodigal, whereas the one who falls short in every expenditure is illiberal." But Aristotle says explicitly that *aneleutheria* consists both in deficiency in giving (*tēi t' elleipsei tēs doseōs*) and in excess in getting (*tēi huperbolēi tēs lēpseōs*) (1121b18–19). See further 1121b12–1122a17 with O'Connor 1991, 148–54.

[11] On the goods of fortune, see Cooper 1985.

[12] The most helpful treatments are O'Connor 1991, Curzer 1995, Williams 1980, and Irwin 1988, 424–31. For persuasive criticisms of Aristotle's account, see Williams 1980, 198–99.

held goods.[13] This key difference between justice and the other virtues comes across clearly in the table of virtues and vices found in the *Eudemian Ethics* (1220b38–1221a12), where "the just" (*dikaion*) is listed as being the mean, not between two vices or conditions of the soul, but between gain (*kerdos*) and loss (*zēmia*).[14] Although Aristotle later describes the "profiteer" (*kerdaleos*) as excessively acquisitive (*pleonektikos*, 1221a23), nonetheless gain and loss in themselves, as listed in the table, transgress an external standard of distributive fairness (*to dikaion*), but they do not define a specific motivational structure or disposition to act. Moreover, Aristotle does not mention a vice of deficiency, "trying to get or taking less than one's share," which corresponds to greed, the vice of excess that denotes "trying to get or taking more than one's share."[15]

All these problems arise because Aristotle tried to unite an external perspective on justice, which is concerned with appropriate shares in a distributive context (1129a34, 1129b8–10, 1130b31–33), with a description of justice as an internal attribute of a particular agent—that disposition, he argues, that motivates the individual to choose or distribute a just share (1129a7–9). Although Aristotle begins his treatment with a psychological account, his discussion of distributive justice as such (1131a9–1131b24) is concerned only with describing the proper ratios that figure into a mathematical determination of what is just or equal. As a result, Aristotle's greed is both an internal attribute of an individual and, paradoxically, an external feature of a distributive situation: it is at once a disposition to get more and the condition of unfairness in the distribution of goods. The latter, external perspective on justice is drawn out further by Aristotle's claim in the *Politics* that (translating literally) "justice is something [*ti*] in relation to some people [*tisi*]" (1282b20)—that is, not a characteristic of an individual but rather of a good divided up by individuals who stand in a certain relationship to one another. Hobbes tried to unite the two perspectives by considering greed (*pleonexia*) to be a "desire of more than their share" (*Leviathan* 15), but Aristotle's psychological account strongly suggests that greed is simply a dis-

[13] Sparshott (1994, 158–159) lays out these two issues very clearly. For the requirement that a virtue be a mean relative to the individual, rather than relative to the external goods with which he is concerned, see 1106b7, 1106b36–1107a1; for the standard picture of a virtue as a disposition of the soul (*hexis*) in relation to a feeling (*pathos*) that motivates an action, see 1106b16–18, 1107a2–6, *Eudemian Ethics* 1222a6–12. Justice, as characterized from the external standpoint, is a mean "relative to us" in a different sense: the individual figures into the mathematical equation that determines what the just or the equal amount is in a given distributive context (1131a15–24). But this does not imply that justice is a psychic mean within the individual's interior makeup.

[14] Hardie 1968, 202–3; O'Connor 1991, 152n57.

[15] Hardie 1968, 183–87.

position to act acquisitively, without regard for the claims of others.[16] Both possibilities seem to be indicated at different times by Aristotle's highly complex account. Beyond its combination of an external and an internal focus, greed is moreover supposed to be distinct from illiberality (*aneleutheria*) and excessive ambition (*philotimia*) on the one hand and from general injustice on the other.[17] It is difficult to imagine that, within Aristotle's tidy universe, any single concept could fully sustain such a multifaceted characterization.

Precisely for this reason, however, Aristotle's account is valuable for studying the history of greed. Aristotle may have been attracted to the notion because its elasticity, which is derived from a long tradition, suggests that it can refer both to an identifiable motivational principle and to having an excessively large amount—a larger amount than an individual is entitled to in a given context of distribution. The philosophical work that Aristotle imposes on the notion of excessive acquisitiveness illustrates certain ambiguities, and even difficulties, which are inherited from a long historical tradition.

Previous treatments have attempted to smooth out Aristotle's account by reconceiving his presentation of greed and injustice in accordance with widely acknowledged Aristotelian principles.[18] Examining one

[16] There is a tradition in political philosophy of translating *pleonexia* as "the desire for more than one's share." As MacIntyre (1984, 137; 1988, 111–12) points out, this is how J. S. Mill and Hobbes understood the term; they are followed by Irwin 1999 and Curzer 1995. MacIntyre (1984, 137) is right to criticize Mill for translating *pleonexia* (greed) as wanting more than one's share, but he goes wrong in arguing that *pleonexia* is "the wish to have more *simpliciter*, acquisitiveness as such." *Pleonexia* is an *excessive* desire to get more, not simply acquisitiveness as such, which, depending on how "acquisitiveness" is understood, might refer merely to natural or necessary desires to get more. Reeve (1988, 47, 279) comes nearer the truth when he says that it is the desire to have more and more without limit. This is certainly true of Callicles, but it is possible that a greedy agent can find himself satiated—that is, not desiring still more—once he has gone beyond ordinary limits and satisfied his inordinate desires. His desires would not then be without limit, strictly speaking; they simply would not respect *ordinary* limits.

[17] *Philotimia*, as a vice, designates an inappropriate ambition that strives to win more honor than is right: see *Nicomachean Ethics* 1125b1–25 for Aristotle's own discussion of the ambiguities associated with *philotimia*, which was often considered a virtue and a proper attribute of a male citizen. As later chapters will demonstrate, *philotimia* and associated terms were often paired with *pleonexia* as a related mode of communally destructive excess. For further discussion of *philotimia* the virtue, see Whitehead 1983.

[18] For the view that Aristotle's project of treating justice as a virtue is itself fundamentally flawed, see Williams 1980, 198; Shklar 1990, 28–32; contra Yack 1993, 159–61. As Shklar (1990) says, "The best fictional characterizations, history, biography, and our own experience tell us that the unjust person has a tangle of many motives, not merely *pleonexia*. Even if he or she begins with *pleonexia* and ambition, other dispositions soon come into play. In unjust politics *pleonexia* is joined by ideology, fanaticism, prejudice, xenophobia, and sexism" (30). For an attempt to rehabilitate the possibility that justice can be conceived as a virtue, see O'Connor 1988.

thoughtful recent treatment in some detail underlines the ambiguities and tensions in Aristotle's account. Attempting to distinguish *pleonexia* from the other vices, Curzer argues that the greedy agent wants to violate standards of distribution, rather than to get more of certain types of good. Following Hobbes to the letter, Curzer argues, "*Pleonexia* is a desire for certain goods not *qua* good, but rather *qua* more than one's share."[19] In other words, the greedy agent desires the illicit pleasures of getting more than he deserves, rather than desiring to possess an actual good, such as land or money, for its own sake. He desires to cheat others out of what they deserve. If this view is to make sense, then when Aristotle says (1130b4) that the motive of greed (*pleonexia*) is the pleasure derived from gain (*kerdos*), this use of "gain" (*kerdos*) must mean "more than one's share," and not "more of a particular good."[20]

This view purports to distinguish greed (*pleonexia*) from other vices like illiberality (*aneleutheria*), which are focused on acquiring goods because goods are desirable in themselves. It relies, however, on a highly counterintuitive interpretation both of "gain" (*kerdos*) and of Aristotle's presentation of greed in general. In his first formulations, Aristotle conceives the unjust agent as desiring to have more of some good, be it money, honor, or safety (1129b1–10, 1130a24–32, 1130b3–5). He specifically says, in fact, that greed (*pleonexia*) is motivated by the pleasure of gain (*di' hēdonēn tēn apo tou kerdous*, 1130b4). In normal fourth-century usage, "gain" (*kerdos*) refers to ordinary material profit or advantage. Only very special pleading will make it otherwise.[21] Moreover, earlier in the *Ethics*, Aristotle had defined illiberality (*aneleutheria*) with reference to "gain," saying that it consists in a deficiency in giving and excess in getting:

> But illiberality . . . is far-reaching and takes various forms. For there seem to be many kinds of illiberality. It consists in two things, deficiency in giving and excess in getting. It is not always found in its complete form, but sometimes it is divided: some men are excessive in taking, while others are deficient in giving. (1121b12–20)

[19] Curzer 1995, 215; cf. Engberg-Pederson 1988, 59.

[20] Curzer 1995, 214; Irwin (1988, 624) suggests that "When Aristotle speaks of 'gain', *kerdos*, as characteristic of *pleonexia*, he needs to restrict it to gain at the expense of another—the sort of gain that is another's loss." This approach tries to have it both ways: the greedy agent does want something for himself, but only if he gets it by violating fairness, by taking it from another who deserves it. Aristotle does not himself characterize *pleonexia* this way. Moreover, the context is insufficient to establish a different sphere for the vice. It would be hard to show that the vicious individual characterized by illiberality will, unlike the greedy, show proper respect for fair standards of distribution. Certainly Aristotle's thieves and pickpockets, who exemplify illiberality (*aneleutheria*), do not care much for distributive justice. For the purpose of distinguishing *pleonexia* and *aneleutheria* in Aristotelian terms, a different motivation, psychological structure, and object would be required.

[21] LSJ, s.v. *kerdos* I, 1–2.

The specific motive that underlies illiberality is wrongful desire for "gain" (*kerdos*, 1122a1–13).[22] Hence *kerdos* cannot be the basis of a distinction between greed and illiberality. Moreover, and more importantly, Aristotle later points out that *kerdos* means simply "gain" in the sense of having more than one had previously. In his discussion of corrective justice, Aristotle says, "These names, loss [*zēmia*] and gain [*kerdos*], come from voluntary exchange. For to have more [*pleon echein*] than one's own is called gaining [*kerdainein*], while to have less [*elatton*] than one had at the beginning is called suffering a loss [*zēmiousthai*]" (1132b11–14). Therefore, "gaining" means to have an unequal—that is, greater—amount after a transaction. The greedy agent takes pleasure in having more of a good than he had previously.[23]

Beyond such philological difficulties, this view encounters another, more serious problem. In essence, this attempted solution attributes to the greedy individual what Bernard Williams has called "counterjustice," the disposition or desire to act in ways that run specifically contrary to justice, simply for the pleasure of doing so.[24] That this is problematic is illustrated by the way Aristotle characterizes vice in general in his discussion of incontinence (*akrasia*). In his discussion of incontinence, Aristotle distinguishes the incontinent (*ho akratēs*) from the self-indulgent agent (*ho akolastos*) on the grounds that the vicious individual is not aware of his vice, while the incontinent man is aware of his incontinence (1150b36).[25] He also says that both the self-indulgent agent and the incontinent pursue bodily pleasures, but the self-indulgent man thinks it is right to do so (*oiomenos dein*), whereas the incontinent does not (1152a5–6). Like other vicious agents, therefore, the greedy person is not aware that what he is doing is wrong. Because of a perversity in his character or upbringing, he overvalues certain goods like money and wrongly believes that his acquisitiveness will lead to flourishing (*eudaimonia*) for him. This rules out the

[22] Aristotle does say that grand-scale thievery, such as that of tyrants, is not considered mean, but rather impious and unjust (1122a3–7). But this move is not legitimate; vices are defined by their objects and their motives, not by the scale of their operation. As Curzer (1995, 212) recognizes, "[I]f Aristotle applied this move consistently not only to money, but also to honor, safety, etc., he would impoverish the rest of the virtues in order to create a sphere of application for particular justice."

[23] Another problem with this view is its premise that "The sphere of particular justice is gain" (Curzer 1995, 215). The sphere of particular justice—that which justice is concerned about (*peri ho*)—is rather "honor or money or safety or whatever single term we have to encompass all these things" (1130b2–3).

[24] Williams (1985, 13–14) describes "counterjustice" as a "whimsical delight in unfairness."

[25] This problem is rightly noted by Curzer 1995, 215–16, but his solution to it, which appeals to the notion of "doublethink," is ingenious but inadequate because it finds no basis in Aristotle's thinking.

view that greed drives him to desire more than his share as such, because desiring more than his share requires that he seek to get more specifically with a view to contravening standards of distributive fairness that he himself acknowledges.[26] If the vicious agent is not aware of his vice in general, then the greedy agent cannot conceive of himself as "taking more than his share," because that description would require him to know what an appropriate share is and to desire to take more than that amount, in which case he would be not only aware of his vice but also self-conscious in his pursuit and enjoyment of it.

Now we are in a position to describe the psychology that underlies Aristotle's idea of greed. Aristotle's greedy agent must think of himself as someone who wants to get more because that is a fulfilling thing to do (he imagines), and he must believe that the share he eventually gets is a fair share.[27] On any straightforward reading of *Ethics* 5, Aristotle views greed as an excessive acquisitiveness of various divisible goods, which is driven by the pleasures of actually getting the good in question.[28] Looking ahead briefly, we will find that in his discussion of acquisitiveness in *Politics* 1, Aristotle similarly presents acquisitive agents as desiring more (i.e., more than they need or more than they already have) because they have a perverse conception of their lives or of what constitutes the good life. Aristotle's presentation in the two works tells against the idea that acquisitive agents never want goods in order to possess them per se, but rather only in order to experience the pleasures of having "more than their share." According to Aristotle's presentation in the *Ethics*, the psychological drive that underlies greed is simply that of getting more, without regard to the claims of others.[29]

There are, however, two qualifications. First, it is important to empha-

[26] Equally it rules out other versions of this attempted solution: cf. Irwin 1988, 426, 429, 624nn4–6, 635n24; Yack 1993, 159–61. Young (1988, 238) similarly believes that the distinctive motivation of particular injustice is "the desire for gain in greedy circumstances," by which he means "circumstances in which gaining requires taking what belongs to others."

[27] That this characterization does not distinguish *pleonexia* very carefully from several other vices is perhaps predictable if we recall that in the *Eudemian Ethics* Aristotle considers the "profiteer" (*ho kerdaleos*)—who apparently exemplifies the vice of injustice, according to Aristotle's table—to be a person who seeks gain from every source (*ho pantachothen pleonektikos*), while he considers the "rascal" (*ho panourgos*), who opposed the virtue of practical wisdom (*phronēsis*), to be gain-seeking by every means and from everywhere (*pantōs kai pantothen pleonektikos*) (*EE* 1221a23–24, 1221a37). Although he seems to intend to do so, Aristotle does not offer a distinct motivational structure for the vice of *pleonexia* in either work.

[28] Apparently recalling *pleonexia* (*Will to Power*, 47), Nietzsche defined the will to power as *Haben- und Mehrhaben-Wollen* (wanting to have and to have more), without referring to the agent's own reflections on justice and injustice; cf. Dodds 1959, 390.

[29] Cf. Williams 1980, 198–99.

size that he offers a characterization of greed in order to identify the characteristic motive of particular injustice. Aristotle conceives of greed as driving individuals to violate distributive fairness. He calls the greedy agent "unequal" or "unfair" (*anisos*, 1129a33, 1129b10). He lays stress on the unfairness of the greedy by making greed the specific vice that opposes particular justice. The question arises how unfairness is related to the desire to get more. In the *Ethics*, as we have seen, Aristotle rules out the self-conscious enjoyment of unfairness because vice is unconscious of itself. Therefore, the greedy individual strives to get more and, as a matter of fact, happens to violate justice along the way. As we will see in the following discussion, however, the greedy agents of the *Politics*—tyrants and oligarchs especially—are often characterized as enjoying an unimpeded ability to cheat others out of what is normally considered a fair share. The characterization offered in the *Politics*, while psychologically plausible and probably true to reality, does not fit coherently with Aristotle's characterization of such individuals in the *Ethics*, because their violation of justice is simply an external fact of their behavior, not part of their motivation. In the *Politics*, by contrast, those driven by greed sometimes enjoy their ability to outdo rivals, at least in the sense of violating with impunity their rivals' conception of fair distribution. Apart from this conflict, we find in the *Politics* that the greedy are certainly seen by others as both violating distributive fairness and as being excessively acquisitive. This is what their political rivals mean when they apply the label "greedy" to their behavior. Aristotle's presentation of greed in the *Ethics* and *Politics* includes both a psychological treatment and consideration of the distributive context within which an agent is judged. It also provides insight into the differences between how the agent views himself and how others view him. These complexities in Aristotle's different accounts derive from the difficulties of fitting the highly subtle, multiperspectival ethical and political tradition into the rigid framework of virtue and vice adopted in the *Ethics*.

Second, the question arises whether the greedy individual is unfair according to absolute principles of justice, or unfair according to the distributive principles of the political system in which he happens to live—whether or not that system is itself constructed justly. Aristotle does not settle that issue in any clear way (cf. 1131a24–32). Moreover, he believes that most people are habitually bad at judging their own merits and hence tend to make mistakes about their proper status in the distributive order, whether or not that order is itself just (1280a15–16). The real world of distribution is, to put it mildly, chaotic. Aristotle's shrewd understanding of the chaos of practical distribution informs his explanation of revolution in the *Politics*.

In light of the foregoing discussion, it is useful to view greed as operative within two moral "fields" that overlap but do not entail one another: that of fairness and unfairness, the field of distribution, and that of moderation and excess, the field of acquisition. Although the two "fields" in which greed participates can be theoretically distinguished, they are often brought together in the psychology and behavior of practical political agents.[30] We are left with a picture of greed that points in two directions—toward the excessive desires of the individual and toward the ethical context of distributive fairness within which the greedy individual is characteristically evaluated.

What are the objects of greed? For Aristotle greed is directed toward all the goods of fortune; it is a certain disposition to grab at all the divisible goods that a community (at least theoretically or imaginatively) distributes, rather than simply material goods.[31] This widening of the notion was not common in the prior tradition of Greek political thought, but is rather one consequence of Aristotle's failed attempt to bridge the gap between external facts of distribution and internal motivations. The following chapters show that, throughout the discourse on greed, greed is an excessive acquisitiveness directed primarily at two objects, wealth and power. Aristotle could have restricted his vice to these two objects, but he recognized that collectivities also distribute many other types of good, such as honor and even safety. As a result, Aristotle widened the notion in order to oppose it to the proper distribution of all divisible goods, even safety, although no previous author had attempted to construct it that way. Examining the history of Greek political thought enables us to make sense of the tensions and ambiguities of Aristotle's complex account of greed in the *Ethics*.

In keeping with Aristotle's own belief that ethics should be studied with a view to politics (1094a27–b11), let us now turn to the discussion of excessive acquisitiveness and violations of fairness in the *Politics*. We find there a telling commentary on the role of injustice in the polis and, in particular, on the complicated ways in which greed to get more enters into the history, ideology, and theory of the city-state. Aristotle's *Politics* maps out the character and political meaning of this vice in several highly illuminating theoretical discussions. If we grasp the contours of Aris-

[30] O'Connor (1991) argues that Aristotle views *pleonexia* from an "aetiological" and a "symptomological" perspective, and that these two perspectives help reconcile the problems I have mentioned. Aristotle probably should have viewed *pleonexia* in that way, but he does not, and hence I believe that O'Connor's insightful argument does not solve Aristotle's problem.

[31] MacIntyre (1988, 112) rightly points out that while *pleonexia* is a disposition, "greed" is the name of a desire; but this distinction loses importance outside Aristotle's own description of the three constituents of the soul: emotions, faculties, and dispositions (1105b19–1106a13).

totle's conception, then it will be possible to provide a detailed history of the changing events and conceptions that constitute the political and intellectual ancestry of one of Aristotle's fundamental concerns.

What Makes Human Beings Greedy?

In *Politics* 1, Aristotle inquires into possession and the art of acquiring property (*chrēmatistikēs*) (1256a1), and particularly into this art's relationship with household management (*hē oikonomikē*, 1256a4).[32] Although he begins with household management, however, his concern with acquisition leads him outward to issues of class, greed, and political stability. At first glance, Aristotle's focus is on commercial trade, but he mixes into his discussion a variety of other concerns such as bodily appetites and ignorance of the good life. As a result, this apparently self-contained discussion is closely connected with Aristotle's other interests in the *Politics* and *Ethics*. In particular, the discussion clarifies the psychological sources of greed for material goods. This materialistic greed figures prominently in Aristotle's later discussions of civic injustice and strife (*stasis*). In this section, however, Aristotle concentrates primarily on immoderation in acquisition and its causes, rather than on unfair distribution within a community—though the latter makes its presence felt throughout. In other words, he now elaborates the internal psychology of the greedy agent without emphasizing the tendency of unjust and contentious grasping to cause civic strife through its violation of fairness.

Aristotle holds that there are two types of acquisitive art, only one of which is a proper part of household management: that one is concerned to provide the household with necessary and useful items (*anankaiōn kai chrēsimōn*, 1256b29); the other, to acquire wealth in its own right, without regard for what is necessary and useful, and often without limit (1256b41–1257a1, 1257b28–30). To Aristotle, the first is a natural and necessary part of the good polis, whereas the second is not natural and is potentially destructive, but it happens also to be a necessary evil in the polis (1258a14–16).[33] On the basis of this celebrated discussion, critics have attributed to Aristotle abstract conceptions of value, price, and exchange.[34] But his fundamental aim is rather to illuminate the character

[32] Finley (1977, 150–51) lays out an important ambiguity concerning *chrēmatistikē* in this passage: first, it has a general sense of "the art of acquisition"; second, it has a more specific sense, which arises later in the argument, of "the art of moneymaking" (cf. 1256b41, 1257b2).

[33] On these distinctions, see Booth 1981, 220–26.

[34] Meikle 1979; 1991; 1995; Swanson 1992, 74–75. For the opposing view, that Aristotle never developed a fully differentiated concept of the economy, see Finley 1977; Polanyi

and psychology of human beings in their capacity as acquisitive agents and to connect these features of human nature with the household and the polis.

According to Aristotle, there is a state of nature in which heads of household satisfy their household needs by natural occupations such as hunting, fishing, and agriculture (1256a19–1256b26). Aristotle emphasizes that the items acquired by natural acquisition are useful and necessary to the household (1256b29). Nothing is accumulated beyond what the household (*oikos*) needs; desires are strictly limited to what is natural and necessary. This limitation is the result not of an inability to accumulate goods (1256b27–30), but rather of the apparently intuitive, or natural, realization that true riches are a collection of instruments (*organōn plēthos*, 1256b36) to be used by the householder for the purpose of leading the good life, and that there is no need of more tools than the master can actually use. This is the ideal picture of natural acquisition against which Aristotle judges all other forms of acquisitive behavior.

Aristotle realizes, to be sure, that nature does not always spontaneously provide all that human beings need. Rather, households are often forced to exchange commodities with other households, according to their needs (1257a22–24). In Aristotle's view, "Exchange of this sort [*hē . . . toiautē metablētikē*] is not contrary to nature . . . for it existed in order to support natural self-sufficiency" (1257a28–30)—even if this type of barter comes to involve, as it ultimately does in Aristotle's account, the use of money and then of coinage (1257a33–41).[35] In its most "natural" capacity, money has the function of merely facilitating the logistics of trade.[36]

If Aristotle's account of natural acquisition is straightforward, then complications begin to arise when he turns to unnatural acquisition, which seems on the face of it to originate in the mechanisms of commercial trade. Aristotle's evaluation of unnatural acquisition needs to be carefully elicited from the text. The central question is whether unlimited desire for gain is necessarily associated with merchants and the art of commercial trade; or can it also characterize other people, and other arts, as well? Common sense certainly suggests that insatiable greed is dissociable from commerce, but Aristotle's account of the evolution of unnat-

1968; Schumpeter 1954; Barker 1959, 359–400; Havelock 1957, 343–55; Castoriadis 1978, 691. Morris 1994 offers a good overview of current thinking about the ancient economy.

[35] For the evolution sketched by Aristotle, see Meikle 1979, 61–62; Ambler 1984, 494–96; Nichols 1983, 178.

[36] To Aristotle, money is a paramount example of that which exists only by convention and is by nature nothing; this point is proved, he says, by the case of Midas (1257b10–17). As a result, it can never be said to have a truly natural capacity, but it can be used as a medium in the process of natural acquisition.

ural acquisition seems to argue that they are virtually inseparable. To pose the problem in another way, Aristotle seems at first to disapprove of the *mode* of acquisition being discussed—that is, commercial trade based on money. Later, however, his disapproval is directed rather at the failure of unnatural acquisition of any sort to respect natural limits.[37] Herein lies a set of issues that, however tangled, reveal something important both about Aristotle's ideological presuppositions and about his understanding of the psychological roots of avarice.

After the account of natural acquisition, Aristotle suggests that, at an unspecified time, a completely different and non-natural art of acquisition arose, which he calls either *chrēmatistikē* or *to kapēlikon* (1256b41, 1257b2). Owing to this art, people began to think that there is no limit to wealth (1256b40–1257a1). Aristotle does not yet explain why the art arose in the first place, but says only that when money was invented in order to facilitate trade, people somehow, almost automatically or spontaneously, began to use it in ways different from those originally intended (1257b1–5). Specifically, the art does not view material goods as objects to be used productively by human agents but rather as objects of exchange by which profits can be made (1257a2–17). The point of the art is not to acquire and then to use wealth as a collection of instruments for the household but rather to discover the sources and methods of maximizing monetary profit (1257b4–5). Profit is thus considered an end of its own. Like medicine and other arts, Aristotle says, the art of moneymaking in this sense cannot but be unlimited in respect of its end (*telos*), which is riches and the possession of goods (1257b28–30).

The passage illustrates Aristotle's prejudice against commercial traders, whom he snidely designates "hucksters" (*kapēloi*).[38] In Aristotle's view, petty traders care nothing for the natural needs of a household, or for the proper use of goods, but rather only for profit achieved through exchanging goods. Hence their occupation is filthy and materialistic, and even stunts the growth of their characters.[39] But Aristotle is also concerned with something beyond the hucksters' mere mode of acquisition, namely their lack of respect for natural limits (1256b41–1257a1, 1257b26–29).

The greed of Aristotle's hucksters apparently stands in some relation to their occupation and status, and to their habitual use of money in the

[37] Shulsky 1991, 86–87.

[38] Wood and Wood 1978, 227–37; Saunders 1995, 95; Finley 1977, 151–52.

[39] Wood and Wood (1978, 209–57) make the clearest case for an "ideological" approach based on this passage; they suggest that in Aristotle's view "Democracy and unnatural acquisition are the political and economic dimensions of a single malady afflicting all of Greece, and particularly Athens: the replacement of the agrarian, aristocratic way of life by the base conduct and values of urban *hoi polloi* (the many)" (237).

marketplace: but what is the precise relationship here? Does the hucksters' mode of acquisition itself lead, as if inevitably, to a lack of respect for natural limits? That is, does their habitual use of money in the marketplace condition their characters to be greedy for more than they need? If so, then is this conditioning necessarily dependent on their use of money in particular, or could any type of acquisition condition the soul to become acquisitive? Does the sight of money—or handling money, or familiarity with it—in itself create desires that had never before existed, or unleash latent desires that simply needed to be catalyzed? Or, on the other hand, is the hucksters' greed merely facilitated by the existence of money, but actually caused by something else? In short, are money and commerce as such really the essence of Aristotle's account, or is there something else that remains to be analyzed?

To answer these questions, we must distinguish between the acquisitive desire that is Aristotle's focus, and the material preconditions that allow that desire to be most readily satisfied.[40] Aristotle says that money has an essential logistical function, but even the goods provided by and used in accordance with nature can be accumulated (1256b28–29). It is not the logistical conveniences of money that drive Aristotle's account; these conveniences turn out to be a necessary, but not sufficient, factor in the process Aristotle sketches. Aristotle has two overlapping, but not identical, aims in this passage. The first is to clarify the opposition between natural and unnatural acquisition in terms of the opposition between agrarian and commercial modes of acquisition.[41] The second is to elucidate the psychology of greed as a facet of unnatural acquisition, along with the mechanisms by which greed for money comes to exist in the world; but it turns out that these two aims cannot be mapped precisely onto one another. On the contrary, Aristotle's arguments indicate that greed can affect people of all sorts, not just traders. As we will see, greed originates independent of commercial trade.[42]

To Aristotle, the huckster is a paradigm of unnatural acquisitiveness. His trade does not find its limit in providing necessary goods for his own household; rather, the huckster is concerned only with acquiring more money. When Aristotle introduces the huckster's art, however, he gives no indication of why this particular perversion in the use of money arose: "At first, perhaps, it was simple, but then through experience it became more skilled in figuring out what and how to exchange in order to make the greatest profit" (1257b2–5). This hypothesis about the evolution of

[40] Most scholarly accounts reflect Aristotle's own failure to make this distinction clear: Ambler 1984, Springborg 1984, Booth 1981.

[41] See Wood and Wood 1978; my account, by contrast, finds evidence for this position in the internally conflicting logic of Aristotle's own presentation.

[42] Cf. Shulsky 1991, 87.

trading with money does little to show why such trading was originally separated from concern for the household's needs. Aristotle says merely that, in contravention of the principles of need and household usefulness, traders began to search out methods of exchange according to which monetary profit could be maximized, and, with experience, eventually discovered them. He does not, however, say that money creates or awakens desire. The most that can be inferred is that, in the marketplace, people tend to try to maximize profit, without regard for what is natural and useful, and that this is facilitated by money. Perhaps coined money intensifies preexisting desires, but greed as such may originate independent of money.

What unnatural human desires, then, is this perverse art meant to satisfy? Aristotle proposes that the greed inherent in such an art typically originates in an irrational desire to experience bodily pleasure. Such an irrational attachment to the body betrays ignorance of the nature of a truly good life (1257b40–1258a6).[43] In one scenario, practitioners of this art set their sights on life as a mere biological function rather than on the good life (1257b41–1258a1). As their desire for life *qua* biological existence is without limit, so also do they desire without limit whatever contributes to that biological function (1258a1–2). They irrationally believe that they can prolong their lives, or make the quality of their lives better, by storing up material possessions.[44] Others, however, misunderstand the good life as being a life devoted to bodily enjoyment, rather than to virtuous activity or theoretical contemplation. Such misunderstandings of the good life are at the root of greed. They explain why the greedy agent overvalues material goods in his conception of human flourishing (*eudaimonia*). In Aristotle's words:

> The cause of this state of mind is that they are serious about life [*to zēn*] but not about the good life [*to eu zēn*]; since therefore the desire for life is unlimited, they also desire without limit the means productive of life [*tōn poiētikōn apeirōn epithumousin*]. Even those who aim at the good life seek the good life as measured by bodily enjoyments [*hosoi de kai tou eu zēn epiballontai, to pros tas apolauseis tas sōmatikas zētousin*], so that, since this also appears to consist in the possession of property, all their time is spent in getting wealth; and because of this the second [i.e., unnatural] form of the moneymaking expertise has arisen. (1257b40–1258a6)[45]

[43] Very few commentators have paid attention to this short but significant passage: Lewis 1978 must be considered fundamental but has a very different focus from the one presented here; cf. Polanyi 1968, 98–99; Springborg 1984, 407–9.

[44] Polanyi (1968, 98–99) believes that Aristotle is trying to show that the "lure of wealth" (99) is subordinate to the household and society. Nichols (1983, 179) holds that "unlimited moneymaking is premised on the denial of mortality"; through melodramatic, this view tends in the right direction.

[45] There is a further relevant question, which Aristotle seems not to answer in this pas-

Attempting to understand the psychology of greed, then, Aristotle pointed, like Plato before him, to the body's viselike grip on human desire and to its tendency to pervert the individual's conception of well-being. In this section, as I mentioned, he focuses on the psychology of individual greed, rather than on its social effects or ethical evaluation. Because the polis is a partnership [*koinōnia*, 1252b28] for the sake of living well, however, it is likely that the polis as a whole will be adversely affected by members with an inadequate and potentially destructive conception of human flourishing. Moreover, depending on the external objects of their acquisitiveness, greedy individuals will likely hinder the polis from achieving its goal of self-sufficiency (1252b27–1253a1). This problem is especially acute because Aristotle reveals an uneasy awareness that his psychology of greed applies to ordinary citizen householders as well as traders. This awareness provides a lead-in to his discussion of revolution in book 5, where, he argues, greedy citizen factions create strife and civic turmoil when they struggle with one another over the city's distribution of goods.

Despite his general denigration of traders, therefore, Aristotle laments that as a matter of fact *all* wealth getters, even householders, try to increase their holdings without limit (1257b33–34). Aristotle hypothesizes that, because of their bodily urges to seek pleasure, householders tend to confuse the respective ends (*telē*) of the two types of acquisitive art. Although both arts use the same property (1257b36–37), he says, one of them has the goal (*telos*) of acquiring strictly necessary household goods, whereas the other aims at increase (*auxēsis*, 1257b38) pure and simple. By conflating these two ideas of the ultimate goal, some heads of household come to think that the function (*ergon*) of household management is to encourage householders to safeguard their property continually or to increase their holdings of money without limit (1257b40). Hence unnatural acquisition results from an improper extension of a natural motive (to supply the household), by analogy, or confusion, with the commercial motive of maximizing profit. In the process, perceived needs transgress the limits of true, natural need, and motivate men to strive for unlimited gain.[46]

Aristotle's meaning is not very clearly expressed in this passage, but his point is that the all-too-human drive to seek physical gratification tends to make human beings, including householders, pervert the natural arts

sage, namely, where does such ignorance and irrationality come from in the first place? In one sense this question replays a classic issue for Aristotle's account of nature: why do anomalies occur only rarely in the animal and plant kingdoms, whereas in human society and politics the "naturally" good life and the best polis by nature are rarely, if ever, realized in practice? For discussion of the issue, see Keyt 1991b.

[46] Springborg 1984 offers a perceptive discussion of the complicated notion of "need."

and turn them into the means of acquiring wealth.[47] His "explanation" is more plausibly read as a redescription of what is actually happening around him, rather than as an explanation of the origin of householders' greed. As a matter of observable fact, householders simply *do* violate the "natural limits" of acquisition (1257b33–34), and do in fact apply the underlying assumptions of commercial trade to acquisition of goods for the household. They thereby exceed the needs of the household, and try to acquire goods to an unlimited degree. Aristotle says that the *cause* of the householders' greed is their mistaken conception of well-being. Hence greed as such does not originate in trading activity and may be entirely unrelated to it. The advent of coinage may facilitate preexisting desires, and may even excite them; but it does not create them. Because the pleasures of the ignorant consist in excess (1258a6–7), they seek out the art that best produces excessive joy. Money may not even be involved. If, in fact, they find that the art of acquisition itself fails to procure the requisite excesses, then they pervert all their other virtues and abilities, such as courage, or the military and medical arts, in order to acquire possessions (1258a8–14). To Aristotle, this is an unpleasant comment on the very real possibility that human beings will pervert their capacities for genuine virtue because of their irrational and unnatural outlook on life, which, again, he regards as originating in their drive to experience bodily pleasure.

Aristotle's express belief in the possibility of perverting courage and the military and medical arts disrupts the self-containment of his treatment of the art of acquisition. Although the various arts have intrinsically appropriate functions, they may be perverted for the sake of other, unnatural ends. This turn is surprising, because earlier Aristotle had strictly limited his treatment of unnatural acquisition to commercial trade conducted by means of money. Now, however, Aristotle suggests that a variety of arts can be wrongly converted into moneymaking arts, which have the ultimate end (*telos*) of unlimited acquisition. This turn in the discussion is accompanied by a change in the social sectors on which Aristotle focuses his attention.

Throughout the section, Aristotle concentrates on the *kapēlos*, the petty huckster, or commercial trader, as the paradigm of unnatural ac-

[47] See Saunders 1995, 93: "By its pursuit of unlimited gain, trade breaks free of the controlling and limiting functions of political knowledge . . . not only does it become an independent sphere of activity 'disembedded' from the social and political structure . . . but it infects the attitudes of household-managers with commercial assumptions." By invoking "infection," Saunders implies that, upon seeing commercial traders in the marketplace, householders begin to overvalue non-necessary personal profit. This seems to me to neglect the importance of the householders' impoverished conception of the good life and their undue attention to bodily gratification.

quisitiveness.[48] In principle, however, Aristotle's account of unnatural acquisitiveness might apply to people of every class and status. The underlying principle of wrongful acquisition is ignorance of the good life, which involves an improper attachment to pleasures of the body. Even respectable heads of traditional households, not only hucksters, can succumb to such attachments. Even though Aristotle's original description applies to a non-citizen or lower-class group, his train of thought leads him outward in an attempt to explain how all sorts of other arts—some of which, like generalship, are presumably the exclusive province of a wealthy citizen elite—are perversely directed to satisfying greed (1258a10–14).[49] This has important implications for Aristotle's later discussions of greed as a fundamental problem of the polis.

The impression that this passage concerns a wider group of people than merely hucksters is confirmed by Aristotle's later discussion of monopoly (1259a5–1259a36).[50] Aristotle opens this account by telling the story of Thales' monopoly, which resembles the activity of traders in using cash in order to trade up for a profit. According to Aristotle, Thales was taunted with the uselessness of philosophy because of his poverty. Recognizing from his knowledge of astronomy that the olive crop would be large one season, Thales rented all the olive presses in Miletus and Chios. Finally, when the season came and the massive crop of olives appeared, Thales was able to lease his olive presses on whatever terms he wanted, thus realizing the profits of his monopoly. In light of the anecdote, Aristotle suggests that "it is easy for philosophers to become wealthy if they want, but this is not the thing they pay serious attention to" (1259a17–18).[51] According to Aristotle, philosophers have been correctly trained to view wealth for what it is, namely one of fortune's goods, but nothing to compare in importance with the development of character and intellect.[52] Genuine philosophers do not care about

[48] Finley 1977, 151.

[49] As Finley (1977, 156–58) points out, most commercial traders in fourth-century Athens were metics. But Aristotle is concerned not strictly with non-citizen groups, but rather with the implications of greed within the individual psyche and within the political community.

[50] On monopoly, see Sacks 1998.

[51] One may compare Plato *Republic* 485d10–e5 for the sentiment that it is inappropriate for a genuine philosopher (as opposed to the counterfeit kind one normally finds) to take money and the things it can purchase seriously.

[52] For a useful discussion of Aristotle's views on the goods of fortune, see Cooper 1985. Swanson (1992, 91n68) suggests that "By way of a story about Thales of Miletus, Aristotle conveys the power of intellectual activity to supplant the desire to accumulate and consume." This is true in a sense, but the accent is wrong; the proper education of desire, which should accompany an intellectual education, is decisive in turning philosophers away from moneymaking (cf. 1266b34–38). Intellectual training in itself does not make a man self-restrained and, indeed, as Thales' case shows, it could simply provide

material goods for their own sake, or for their ability to produce pleasure. Thales exemplifies the individual whose power to acquire more, which is embodied in his intelligence and "wisdom" (*sophia*), is properly restricted by his knowledge of what constitutes the human good.[53] What if Thales were not (presumptively) in control of his desires and appetites, and persistently mistook mere life and its bodily pleasures as sufficient to create the good life? The result would be that Thales would use his superior intelligence in order to satisfy his greedy desires for more. In short, he would become similar to Callicles. The internal logic of Aristotle's argument therefore suggests that, without proper training, those with power—whether that power derives from superior intelligence or from political position—are preeminently situated to pursue wealth inordinately and to take more than their share of the community's resources: by legal means, through their superior intelligence, but also by illegal means, if they pervert arts like that of the generalship for the sake of personal profit.

In light of Aristotle's discussion, it stands to reason that those of intelligence and high station who are not properly educated in regard to wealth and virtue will—like their lower-class counterparts, the hucksters—pursue wealth in ignorance of what is good for them and possibly for society at large. This idea was intimated earlier when Aristotle suggested that some heads of household might misuse their courage and their possession of the generalship art (*stratēgikēs*), in order to acquire more wealth. Up till then, the discussion had focused on legal forms of profit making, whether natural or unnatural, but the suggestion that the ignorant will pervert even their fundamental virtues for the sake of unnatural acquisition, introduces a new element of doubt about the legality of certain forms of unnatural acquisition.

It is easy to see how a doctor could come to look upon his occupation as primarily a way to gain wealth, rather than to heal. But the case of the generalship is perhaps less clear. Aristotle is referring to the improper use of political office for personal profit; or, if this profit motive is directed at other city-states rather than one's fellow citizens, then Aristotle is implying the gratification of an imperialistic urge to get more with the help of one's fellow citizens.[54] If this is true of the generalship, then why not also

---

the instrumental means to get more if it is not combined with virtues of character such as temperance.

[53] For the seven sages (including Thales) as "performers of wisdom"—an often non-Aristotelian form of wisdom that included knowledge of engineering, laws, and agriculture—see Martin 1993.

[54] For the profits attainable through holding office, see 1321a40–42, *Eudemian Ethics* 1216a24–27; for the unjust profits of empire, see 1324b3–22. The idea that the general will pursue foreign conquest for his own profit should be read carefully against Thucydides' presentation of similar subjects in his portrayal of Athenian democratic politics: see chapter 5.

of political office in general? Aristotle is suggesting, perhaps radically, that human beings' irrational attachment to the body has the potential to turn every occupation in the state—even the state itself—into a vast moneymaking enterprise.

The section on monopoly concludes with a brief analysis of state, rather than individual, monopolies (1259a21–36). Its explicit purpose is to say something useful to statesmen about replenishing the state's coffers when the treasury is empty. As Aristotle says, "For statesmen too it is useful to be familiar with these things, since many cities need business and revenues of this sort, just as a household does, but more so. Therefore some statesmen even devote their political energies solely to this" (1259a33–36). At least with respect to acquiring material goods, a polis is like a household, only bigger; a statesman is like a householder, only more important.[55] If householders pervert their proper art for the sake of unlimited gain, however, then so do statesmen.

In this connection it is striking that Aristotle offers the tyrant Dionysius of Syracuse as an example of a statesman interested in making money. Dionysius, Aristotle says, once banished a Sicilian man for making a great profit from a monopoly on iron. His reason for doing so? That the man had "discovered revenues that were unprofitable [*asumphorous*] to the tyrant's own affairs" (1259a30–31). Whichever Dionysius is meant here, his appearance in this passage cannot but call to mind all the wrongful excesses in acquisition associated with such tyrannical figures throughout the Athenian discourse on greed. The story calls to mind the long-standing question of whether rulers rule in their own interests or in those of their subjects.[56] Later in the *Politics*, Aristotle says that Dionysius levied such a burdensome taxation that within five years everyone had contributed his entire substance to the tyrant (1313b26–28). Dionysius's activities, though legal in a strict sense, are clearly unjust in both general and distributive terms (to use the language of the *Ethics*). Is Dionysius as a ruler any different from those heads of household who pervert their proper arts for the sake of satisfying greed? To anticipate the next section, both Dionyius's behavior and that of the unnaturally acquisitive householders exemplify the sort of wrongful depredation that typically causes civil strife.

Aristotle's fundamental interest in discussing acquisition, then, is not with the economy in its own right, but with desire, greed, and self-control—all of them seen against the background of Aristotle's account of human flourishing and well-being (*eudaimonia*) in the *Ethics*. By ex-

[55] Of course, Aristotle denies the equation of household and polis in the introduction to the *Politics* (1252a7–16), but in this passage he explicitly points a limited comparison between household and polis.

[56] This classic question of Greek political thought is expressed most forcibly perhaps in Thrasymachus's arguments in *Republic* 1 but is also discussed in *Politics* 3.

plaining greed in terms of human beings' misdirected desires and ignorance of appropriate goals, Aristotle's discussion illuminates his later treatment of the role of greed in causing civic breakdown. Having set the stage with a teleological vision of politics, Aristotle eventually turns to the problem of excess acquisitiveness in the polis, which was impressed on him through his knowledge of Greek history and his awareness of his philosophical predecessors. A primary concern is the question of what happens when political leaders, ignorant of the true goal (*telos*) of human life and the political community, mistake the community's well-being with its economic interests? Worse yet, what if political decision makers allow their desire for wealth to run amuck, out of a fixed indifference to the interests of their own community? Finally, and more broadly, how do partisan judgments about appropriate distribution, along with the presence of greed in human psychology and in political ideology, undermine the stability of political units? The stage is now set for Aristotle's attempt to read his economic, social, and psychological theories back onto the history of the Greek polis and, in particular, back onto the struggle between rich and poor over the polis's divisible goods.[57]

Analyzing Greed in the Polis: Revolution, Civic Strife, and Distributive Justice

> But many of those in politics are not properly called "politicians," since they are not truly political. For the political man chooses noble actions for their own sake, whereas most people choose that way of living for the sake of money [*chrēmatōn*] and unfair gain [*pleonexias*].
> (Eudemian Ethics *1216a23–27*)

Aristotle's discussion of revolution and civic strife (*stasis*) in the *Politics* follows from his discussion of distributive justice in the *Ethics*, because civic conflict often results, at least according to Aristotle, from the violation, or the perceived violation, of appropriate distributive principles.[58]

[57] In Balot (forthcoming b), I argue that Aristotle makes a transition from human psychology to civic strife in his critique of Phaleas of Chalcedon (1266a39–1267b21). The critique shows in particular Aristotle's subtlety in analyzing the interconnections between wealth, power, and honor in the psychology and civic relations of lower and upper classes, and particularly the ways in which these three eminent goods of social life are interrelated in the desires of revolutionaries.

[58] Contra Young 1988, 245, it is wrong to equate political justice and distributive justice; see the criticisms of Keyt 1988, 251–53. In Aristotle's conception, political justice is more

Equally, appropriate distributive principles are themselves usually violated, in Aristotle's account, by greed for more. For the purposes of practical politics, however, "justice," "injustice," and "excessive acquisitiveness" remain largely empty concepts as long as nothing is said about how the appropriate distribution of shares in communal goods is to be determined. Collective distribution, Aristotle explains, is effected through a system of proportional equality, according to which distributions are based on worth or desert.[59] Briefly put, this means that the ratio between the value of two "goods" (say, tracts of land) must equal the ratio between the value of two individuals (1131a14–32). Everyone agrees on the principle of proportional equality in the abstract (1131a25–26; cf. 1301b35–36), and even on the value of the goods in question (1280a18–19); but different groups disagree about the differential "worth" (*axia*) of members of the community or, differently, about the underlying principle or principles that determine their places in the proportional hierarchy.[60] Is it to be wealth, or noble birth, or freedom, or virtue—or some combination of these (1280a7–25, 1282b21–1283a23)? This question, Aristotle says, "is difficult and requires political philosophy" (1282b22–23).

If we are to discover absolute, extralegal standards of justice by looking to nature, as Aristotle ultimately hopes to do, then it becomes clearer how to determine principles by which to differentiate the worth of individual members of the community. This is part of the enterprise that Aristotle undertakes in *Politics* 7 and 8, which describe what is for Aristotle the best political system built on the foundations of philosophical insight into nature and the human good. But Aristotle is also concerned with another, altogether different project, namely the analysis and amelioration of "deviant" constitutions.[61] To this end, he recommends ways

closely linked to general justice and is concerned either with the common good or, in deviant constitutions, with the advantage of the rulers; cf. Morrison n.d., Keyt 1988.

[59] The best discussion of Aristotle's theory of distributive justice is Keyt 1991a, which concludes that by grounding his conception of absolute distributive justice in human nature, Aristotle avoids "Protagorean relativism without embracing Platonic absolutism" (1991a, 277). Yack (1993, 166–74) reads Aristotle as offering an indeterminate, political account of justice, which appeals to no extralegal standards; but this rings false in the context of Aristotle's underlying belief in natural teleology. Cf. also Barker 1959, 345; Mulgan 1977, 80–81; MacIntyre 1988, 104–5. For a general account of arithmetic and geometric notions of equality in Greek political thought, see Harvey 1965; 1966.

[60] These are, again, extremely old problems in Greek political thought and are present long before politics became an explicit focus of theoretical discussion; see Donlan 1980, esp. 32–75.

[61] This is the classic twofold division that scholars have traditionally seen in the *Politics*. It has been influentially approached as a problem of composition and explained as a change of mind on Aristotle's part: see Jaeger 1948 for the division into "utopian" and "empirical" books; for skeptical views, see Barker 1959, xliii–xliv. Rowe (1991) explains the division by suggesting that "[W]e should assume the existence of a fundamental ambivalence in Aris-

in which deviant constitutions can be made more stable, such as finding a basis for cooperation among the strongest groups in the state and ensuring that those in power show due respect to others.[62]

In practical politics, Aristotle recognizes, the moral basis of a constitution, the underlying principle that determines social worth, is an ideological rather than philosophical issue. The final form of the constitution is the outcome of competition among differing, and often conflicting, sets of beliefs about what the goals of the polis are, and about what social arrangements are just, both absolutely and in light of those goals.[63] This ideological view of morality and political order lies behind Aristotle's analysis of revolution and *stasis* in book 5, and helps explain why greed and injustice became central topics of ideological debate in the Greek polis.[64] Whatever Aristotle's recommendations for amelioration, and whatever his own views about the best polis, he recognizes that in practical politics, political arrangements and social distributions are determined by ideological "truths," which are to him only philosophical half-truths (1282b14–1284a3).[65] His appreciation of the role of free-playing ideology allows Aristotle to give a penetrating, and historically useful, account of revolution and *stasis*.

There are three causes, Aristotle says, for *stasis* and revolution (*metabolē*).[66] Most generally, internal strife is caused by a person's feeling that he, or the group with which he identifies, is suffering injustice at the hands of others, either as a matter of unjust institutional practice or as a

totle's attitude. . . . He is firmly committed to the Platonic ideal of the virtuous city; but he is also committed to the idea that political science must have something *useful* to say" (73, his emphasis).

[62] Miller (1995, 285–304) formulates two Aristotelian principles of stability: first, what he calls the "maxim of superiority," that is, "that the multitude wishing that the constitution continue to exist ought to be superior (*kreitton*) to the multitude that does not (IV 12 1296b 15–16; V 9 1309b16–18)"; and, second, that those constitutions which most closely approximate justice are most secure; cf. Yack 1993, 231–39. On Miller's use of "rights" as an analytic category in discussing Aristotle, see Cooper 1996.

[63] See MacIntyre 1988, 106–7, for further elaboration of this point.

[64] For a useful concept of "ideology" as applied to ancient history, see Finley 1983, 122–41.

[65] In this sense it might be said that, with regard to practical politics and political judgment, the existence of "objective" standards of morality is simply irrelevant; all that matters, instead, is the process of collective determination of ideological "truths" that the community will, in fact, maintain: see Waldron 1992. Contra Yack 1993, 128–74.

[66] Jowett (1885, 188) points out that these correspond to the material, final, and efficient causes that Aristotle discusses in the *Physics*; for a brief but helpful treatment of the "four causes", see Barnes 1982, 51–57; for an attempt to apply this theory to politics, see Johnson 1990, 91–114; Graham 1986. For discussion of the terms *metabolē* and stasis, see Polansky 1991, 324–27; Wheeler 1977; Newman 1887–1902, 4:282. For a very basic general account of Aristotle's discussion of revolution, see Ryffel 1956, 136–79.

matter of abuse of power within institutions that are themselves just in principle (1302a22–31). (Usually this distinction is not important in Aristotle's discussion.) In Aristotle's view this feeling can arise whether or not the agent who perceives injustice is right to do so; from the perspective of absolute justice, that is, the attitude may be either defensible or not (cf. 1302a40–b2). This perceived injustice is very vaguely conceived: it is distributive injustice but does not refer specifically to any particular imbalance—for example, of political power, of honor, or of wealth.[67] This cause is advanced as merely the most general cause of *stasis*; it is not intended to apply necessarily to every specific case.

Second, *stasis* arises from the pursuit, either separately or in combination, of gain (*kerdos*) and honor (*timē*), the latter of which refers both to political office and to general social esteem, or from the attempt to avoid their opposites, dishonor (*atimian*) and loss (*zēmian*, 1302a31–34).[68] These aims are effectively set in motion, third, by a variety of different "efficient causes," including gain, honor, *hubris*, fear, and so on.[69] It may seem surprising that gain and honor are included in both the second and third categories of causes, but Aristotle's point is that, in the second case, men desire gain and honor for themselves when they feel they are not getting enough, but in the third case they rebel against a system that supports the depredations of others, whether or not their revolution results in further gain or honor for themselves specifically (1302a34–1302b5).

At first glance, Aristotle's most general claim seems to suggest that greed as such does not motivate *stasis* and revolution. Instead, revolution is rooted in a sense of injustice, rather than the desire for more; the gain that is desired, that is, is desired under the description "just deserts," which are the distributive rewards that revolutionaries think they deserve but do not currently get. Accordingly, revolution is essentially reactive against injustice, and against suffering and depredation.[70] Those in power may declare for ideological purposes that greed is the motive of revolutionaries, but, on Aristotle's analysis, they are (strictly speaking) wrong.

Nonetheless, Aristotle points out that the greed of those in power might inspire the oppressed to rise up against their rulers, if they see

[67] Contra Mulgan 1977, 120–21; my view shares elements with that of Polansky 1991, 335. It seems clear that the *pleonexia* referred to at 1302a26 and 1302a28 is very vaguely conceived, because Aristotle says subsequently that "the things about which men engage in stasis are gain and honor and their opposites" (1302a31–32).

[68] Earlier Aristotle had explained that most voluntary wrongdoing comes about through ambition (*philotimian*) and love of money (*philochrēmatian*, 1271a18).

[69] Newman 1887–1902, 4:295 correctly observes that "now we study the causes of revolution more in detail, and the detailed study of them discloses that a sense of injustice is not always present in the minds of those who aim at constitutional change."

[70] Davis 1986.

them profiting unjustly. Like *hubris* and "preeminence" (*huperochē*, 1302b2), greed constitutes an affront to individuals or the community and often acts as a catalyst to revolution (1302b5–10). At this point, Aristotle's analysis might be accused of falling into an infinite regress: is the "greed" against which revolutionaries react—that is, the "greed" of the rulers—really unfair acquisitiveness, or is it merely a justified reaction against perceived injustice in its own right? One piece of evidence that bears on this question is that, in his account of the "efficient causes" of revolution (1302a34–1303b17), Aristotle assumes that greed and unfairness as such are actually exhibited by some power holders. But is it fair for him to attribute unfair acquisitiveness to those in power, or is their behavior also motivated by judgments about fairness? In fact, four separate issues are involved in this question, and it is helpful to distinguish them carefully from one another.

First, and perhaps most superficial, Aristotle himself has an absolute standard of correct distribution in mind, and people either adhere to it or they do not. If they do not, then they are greedy according to Aristotle's standards. In practical politics, though, the standards of distribution are determined by ideological competition and not by Aristotelian philosophy. Second, there is a difference between greedy actions and behavior that is motivated by a settled disposition to pursue one's acquisitiveness unfairly (1135b19–25). What is normally more important in politics is actual behavior, rather than underlying dispositions, because we are rarely in such a privileged position as to know men's motivations fully, but their actions are readily observable and constitute the "raw material" of ideological debate. As Aristotle points out in the *Eudemian Ethics*, "Because it is difficult to know the nature of a person's purpose, we are forced to judge what sort of person he is from his actions" (1228a15–17). This type of judgment is characteristic of political debate. The problem is that a particular action may not be genuinely indicative of a person's character or overall disposition; moreover, the motivations that lie behind even a particular action may themselves be unclear, and the action may be, so to speak, misleading. Hence a particular action may give rise to a pejorative label ("he's greedy") that is unfair to a person or misrepresents him or his motives in a single instance or in general. In discussing Aristotle's political theory, however, it is crucial to make a distinction between a person's character and his behavior, because Aristotle himself draws attention to that distinction in interpreting political behavior generally. What looks greedy to observers may in fact represent a self-conscious attempt to assert a particular principle of justice or to right certain distributive wrongs.[71]

[71] It may also be motivated by something entirely different, such as *hubris* or excessive predominance, but Aristotle does not himself engage with such complications.

Third, however, human beings, in Aristotle's view, tend to be self-aggrandizing and to make interpretations, either of others or of situations in which they find themselves, on the basis of self-interest. In his refutation of Phaleas, Aristotle says that few are amenable to education; of those who are, fewer still have actually received an appropriate education (cf. 1267b5–9).[72] Hence, when Aristotle says that perceived injustice is the cause of revolution, he means injustice perceived by self-interested, unjust human agents, who tend to interpret others' behavior, along with the rules that govern behavior, with a view to narrow self-interest. Aristotle explains that bad judgments can easily arise in these matters, because people "are making a judgment about themselves, and most men are bad judges about their own affairs" (1280a14–16; cf. 1280a20–22). As a result, it is likely that, under the pressure of their own desires to get more, human beings will never be satisfied with what they have. They will tend to feel that their particular distributive circumstances are unjust and will be driven to seek more. Perceived injustice may well be a self-interested psychological mask for those who are actually driven by greed but cannot consciously admit this, either to themselves or to others.

Finally, individuals with enough power may institute a particular set of political arrangements that tend to gratify their own desires for power, money, and honor. To them, setting up such a system may seem just in one sense: they are the powerful and hence get what they deserve. But it is open to Aristotle (and to their political rivals) to claim that rather than fighting for a principle, these people are using principles as propaganda, while actually instituting a particular system for their own advantage. If human beings in the real world are as greedy as Aristotle says, then the self-serving manipulation of political principles should be the prevalent mode of political life. "Principles" will be made to serve the baser instincts that Aristotle uncovers in *Politics* 1. Aristotle's own examples, drawn from the history of the Greek city-states, show that in his mind unjust greed as such exists and often leads to revolution. This point of view is especially clear in the *Constitution of the Athenians*.[73] In Aristotle's conception, individuals and groups strive to get more, not only when they feel unfairly treated, but also simply because they want more—more than others, and even more than they deserve. To put it in terms of *Politics* 1, this urge originates in the regrettably common tendency to desire life *qua* biological function and its attendant bodily pleasure, rather than natural human well-being.

Nonetheless, the question of whether unfairness can ever exist "as such" *should* perhaps concern Aristotle in the practical sections of his

[72] See Balot forthcoming b, for an extended discussion of the role of education in calming or inciting civic strife, with specific reference to Aristotle's critique of Phaleas.

[73] For discussion of this work and the problems of its authorship, see chapter 3.

work. Even if political agents are expressly motivated by desire for gain, who can say whether their desires for more are unjust, especially if they offer substantial arguments that they deserve what they want as a matter of distributive fairness? Practically speaking, this question can be answered only with reference to arguments made within the prevailing conventions of particular political communities. In particular, such arguments must have reference to the overarching goal for which the community exists in the first place—be it wealth, imperialism, noble actions, or the good life (1280a25–1280b10, 1281a2–4, 1324b3–5). For example, "If men formed the community and came together for the sake of wealth, then they would share in the state to the extent that they shared in the property, so that the argument of the oligarchs might seem to be powerful" (1280a25–28). Hence, unjust greed as such might be said to exist when individuals violate the distributive principles derived from the community's overarching end (*telos*). Aristotle is acutely aware, however, that even that overarching aim itself is the subject of political debate and even, when it comes down to it, armed conflict. As a result, the existence of unjust acquisitiveness in practical politics must be subject to examination within a framework of shared political values. When such values are no longer shared, the stage is set for revolution. As Aristotle says, "This is peculiar to human beings compared with other animals: that human beings alone have perception of good and bad and the just [*dikaiou*] and the unjust [*adikou*] and the other things, and partnership [*koinōnia*] in these things makes a household and a polis" (1253a15–18). In other words, when groups within a community have lost the capacity to understand justice and injustice in common, then the foundations on which their polis is built have been destroyed.

These questions of greed and distributive justice lead directly to the age-old question of Greek political thought: who or which group should be the sovereign power (*to kurion*, 1281a11) in the state—the mass of ordinary citizens, the rich, the noble, the virtuous, or a tyrant? Each asserts part of a just principle (*meros ti tou dikaiou*, 1281a9)—for example, the rich might claim power because they possess the most land (1283a31–32)—without acknowledging the just claims of others. The inability to recognize others' legitimate claims leads to the abuse of power:

> If the poor divide up the property of the rich through being greater in number, is this not unjust? No, it may be said, for it was justly resolved by the supreme authority. Then what must we call the extreme of injustice? And again, when everybody is taken into account, if the majority divides up among themselves the property of the minority, it is clear that they are destroying the state. . . . But is it just that the minority and the rich should rule? If they also do these things and plunder and take away the property of the multitude, is this just? If it is, so also is the plunder of the rich by the multitude. (1281a14–1281a27)

Hence those with power tend to destroy the state through a failure of moral vision. Unable to see that the state's welfare depends on respecting the legitimate claims of others, the faction in power tends to pursue its own acquisitiveness, arguing that it is just to do so. Its behavior may be just procedurally but not substantively.[74] Without agreement on matters of substantive justice, then, groups that receive unfair treatment will revolt. In Aristotle's picture, the "deviant constitutions" are subject to an ingrained instability because they fail to achieve a moral consensus. It is precisely the structures of political power in deviant constitutions that make power holders greedy, as a way to strengthen their positions in the state. Perhaps ironically, their attempts to create a lasting regime that will satisfy their excessive appetites are typically frustrated because they violate principles of distributive fairness. The process operates differently for the demagogue, the oligarch, and the tyrant; but, in each case, greed is deeply embedded in social relations of power.

In democracy, to say it as directly as Aristotle does, revolution is caused by the "outrage" (*aselgeian*, 1304b21) of demagogues. In a general way, this means that demagogues wrong the notables (*tous gnōrimous*) in order to curry favor with the demos, either by dividing up their estates, or imposing heavy liturgies, or by slandering them in order to confiscate their property (*dēmeuein ta ktēmata*, 1305a3–7). At Megara, for example, the demos's leaders expelled many members of the upper classes in order to have money to distribute (1304b34–38); demagogues of Aristotle's own day, by contrast, rob the rich through the courts (1320a4–6). The connotations of *dēmeuein* (to confiscate), a verb derived from the noun *dēmos*, make their intentions clear: they want money in order to distribute it to the people (cf. 1304b36–37), because that is the best way for them to retain their own positions of power. In order to court the demos's favor, ambitious men need money, not so much in order to satisfy their own acquisitiveness, as that of the poor citizens (1320a5–6), who are always greedy for material goods (1308a9–10, 1318b16–17). The greed of the demos underwrites the demagogues' depredations.

The relationship thereby established enables Aristotle to assert further that it is the structure of political power in democracies that causes the powerful—that is, the demagogues—to rob the rich of what is rightfully theirs. A destructive cycle is established, according to which demagogues want money only as a seductive instrument that helps secure their own positions of leadership, although in reality the demos is materialistic be-

[74] Miller (1995, 280–85) offers a perceptive discussion of this passage; cf. also Robinson [1962] 1995, 34–35. Yack (1993, 224–31) usefully brings up the concept of *philia* (friendship) in this connection, suggesting that one reason why distributive injustice is so offensive is that members of a political community, like friends, expect their fellow citizens to show a special solicitude in regard to their own interests and feel betrayed when this is not shown.

cause of its concern with its own enrichment as an end in itself. On the other hand, if Aristotle here presents democratic leaders as concerned primarily with power, then elsewhere he presents democracy as the paradigmatic example of a system in which citizens become magistrates principally in order to receive the emoluments of office (1321a41–1321b1).[75] In either case, however, the behavior of demagogues is always predicated on the greed of the demos. The destructive cycle explains why democracy can ultimately deteriorate into a form of tyranny (1292a17–19).

According to Aristotle, oligarchies undergo revolution for a variety of reasons, including unjust treatment of the demos, excessive expenditure, and extreme exclusivity. But greed plays a special role here. Oligarchs, Aristotle says, have a particular tendency to abuse their power for the sake of wealth (1308b31–34), because oligarchies conceive of wealth as their ultimate object and final goal (*telos*, 1311a9–10). Such a conception of the final goal shapes the framework of values within which arguments about distribution must be made. Oligarchs typically use their magistracies for personal profit (e.g., at Apollonia, 1306a6–9), rather than making magisterial expenditure for the sake of honor (1321a39–b1)—which is what Aristotle expects from the properly educated rich.[76] The reason for this is that the "dominant good" in an oligarchy, to use Michael Walzer's language, is wealth; as Aristotle declares, "Aristocracy turns into oligarchy because of the rulers' wickedness; since they distribute the city's goods contrary to worth, and they give everything or most good things to themselves, and always give the offices to the same people, since they esteem wealth above all" (1160b12–15).[77] Oligarchy is by definition the political system set up by a society whose paramount value

[75] Compare *Eudemian Ethics* 1216a24–27 and Wood and Wood 1978, 215–16.

[76] In this passage Aristotle strikingly suggests that seeking gain from office is in fact characteristic of democracy, even while he is making the point that greed among officeholders plagues oligarchies: "But as it is oligarchs do not do this [spend for the public good], but the opposite: for they seek the profits no less than the honor; therefore it is right to say that they are miniature democracies" (1321a40–b1). As Donlan (1980) has shown, the ideological claim that the wealthy use their money for the sake of the collective good goes back to the archaic period. It is this type of claim, however, that the historical experience of elite greed belies. At least in this regard, Aristotle's evidence does not suit his ideological presuppositions.

[77] For the concept of a "dominant good," see Walzer 1983, 3–30, esp. 10–13. Aristotle's claims about "dominant goods" enable us to challenge Morris's recent argument (Morris 1996, esp. 35–38) that "the one good thing" in Greece was citizen birth. In one sense, it is true that citizen birth was an important line to draw; but there is another point, more relevant to Greek political thought—that *within* the group of male citizens dominant goods varied over time and created the possibility for constitutional change of all sorts, in the direction of oligarchy or democracy. Aristotle makes this point in his comments on the variability of communal standards of worth (*axia*), which determines the hierarchy of distribution of goods.

is wealth; as a result, the behavior that is rewarded above all by that society is that which most increases the individual's own wealth. As wealth is the means to power under an oligarchy, so too is political power the means to further wealth: in discussing a revolution at Thurii, Aristotle says in an unfinished sentence, "but since the nobles had illegally acquired the entire region (for the constitution was too oligarchic, so that they were able [*edunanto*] to get more and more [*pleonektein*]) . . ." (1307a29–31, cf. 1308b31–34). Rulers who are able to satisfy their greed with impunity care little for justice and equality (1318b1–5).[78] Ironically, though, Aristotle still insists on the ideologically informed view that the upper classes in general want honor, whereas the masses want money (1308a9–10; cf. 1315a16–20, 1318b16–17), despite his diagnosis of the oligarchs' unbounded acquisitiveness.

Tyranny, in turn, copies oligarchy in making wealth (*ploutos*) its end (*telos*), because wealth provides a tyrant both with a bodyguard to secure his power and with luxury (*truphē*, 1311a11). As a result, money is both the source of a tyrant's power and the origin of his downfall; if money defends the despot, then dissolute living makes him contemptible and easy to overthrow (1312b23–25). Even when he is difficult to overthrow, the tyrant's subjects attack him because of his tendency to seize their property (1311a25–28) or because they themselves simply desire the wealth he has acquired (1312a15–16, 1312a22–24). Aristotle's tyrants desire wealth as both an instrumental means to consolidate power, and as a final goal in the form of a luxurious life-style.[79] Herein lies a peculiar conflict: the tyrant must at once restrain his impulses if he wants to continue to live extravagantly, but, in order to enjoy the typical tyrannical satisfactions, he must also fully pursue his excessive desires to acquire more—more money and, ultimately, more and more of the state as a whole.[80] Aristotle's tyrants, therefore, are scripted differently from Callicles' tyrannical ideal: rather than continually expanding their desires, they must negate their baser human urges for the sake of maintaining power. Maintaining power, of course, will then lead to further satisfaction of materialistic desires and make that satisfaction more lasting; but a

[78] In yet different formulations, oligarchs may desire the gains (*lēmmata*) of office rather than the honor (1321a41), while oligarchies sometimes become more narrow because of greed (*aischrokerdeia*), which in turn leads to democracy (1286b18–26).

[79] The latter goal is emphasized as the central focus of tyranny: "The tyrant's aim is pleasure, the king's is what is noble; therefore, tyrants are greedy for money, while kings desire honor" (1311a4–7). Note again the opposition between an ignoble desire for money and the noble desire for honor.

[80] Aristotle had already criticized oligarchs for extravagance: "Oligarchic revolutions also come about when they spend their private goods through dissolute living; for men like this seek to start a revolution and desire tyranny themselves or prepare someone else for it" (1305b39–1306a1).

balance must be struck.[81] The main point, in any event, is that the tyrant cannot *seem* to be robbing the state for his personal benefit if he wants to preserve the tyranny. In order to preserve a tyranny, the main thing is to avoid excessive appropriation of public funds for obviously private use; to appear as the state's trustee rather than its grand-scale thief; in short, to become a monarch rather than a tyrant (1314a40–1314b7, 1314b37–38, 1315a41–1315b2).[82]

Aristotle believes that the tyrant conceives of the entire state, and all its citizens, as his very own possession.[83] Unlike a genuine monarch, the tyrant takes possession of the state with a foreign bodyguard, as if he were literally attacking it from without (1311a7–8). Tyrants typically strip the multitude of citizens of their arms and treat them hubristically, while destroying the notables, who resist being enslaved (*douleuein*, 1311a12–20). In his discussion of illiberality in the *Ethics*, Aristotle mentions that "As for those who wrongly take great things from the wrong sources, such as tyrants who sack cities and plunder temples, we do not call them illiberal [*aneleutherous*], but rather wicked and unholy and unjust" (1122a3–7). Aristotle's presentation of tyrants in the *Politics* makes it clear that tyrants are not only interested in attacking other cities as a form of grand-scale greed, but also, and prior to this, they are concerned to plunder and enslave their own cities. At the level of tyranny, in fact, it becomes hard to distinguish simple greed for gain, ambition, and hunger for power. All the normal categories are blurred in the extreme situation. Does the tyrant want control over his fellow citizens in order to satisfy his lust for power; or in order to treat citizens as his slaves, and to use them as his possessions; or because he thinks that poets and history writers will call him most blessed and most honored because of his tyrannical accomplishments; or because he is most pleased with himself when he takes more than his share, and treats his fellows unfairly, and gets off scot-free? Interview a tyrant, at least an Aristotelian tyrant, and we find out that these distinctions are not part of his psychological furniture. When greed characterizes the psychology and behavior of the upper

[81] In this sense, Aristotle's tyrant must achieve the psychic balance of Plato's oligarchic man, who masters the drive for immediate pleasure in order to secure long-term material gain (Plato *Rep.* 553a1–555a8).

[82] Mulgan (1977, 133–34) has argued that Aristotle's advice that moderation is the key to preserving all sorts of constitutions "causes a problem in relation to his stated intention of preserving all types of constitution. If an extreme oligarchy or democracy is to become more moderate, will this not amount to a change in the constitution rather than a means of preserving it?" This goes too far: a polis can remain generically a democracy and still go a long way toward "moderation." Aristotle does not intend to preserve each subtype of democracy and oligarchy, but he does hope to preserve each major type.

[83] In Balot (forthcoming b), I treat the tyrant's enslavement of his own city from a different perspective.

classes, then simple materialism may be at the origin of their urges, but they quickly conceive a tyrannically greedy urge to have it all.

Aristotle's initial, abstract analysis of revolution might, if we are not careful, lead us to say that greed was often incorrectly imputed to those who tried to get more as a matter of fairness. But that is not what his later analysis and his historical evidence show. Aristotle held a more complex view of political injustice and revolution than his initial formulation indicates. Ultimately, only in the thinnest of senses can the historically greedy be said to act from feelings of being unjustly wronged rather than from the competitive desire to get more for themselves, often at the expense of others' just claims.

Conclusion

Of Aristotle's discussion of revolution, one scholar has recently written:

> The problem, then, is that the freedom which is the goal of political life is essentially negative in character. It is rooted in a reactive passion, a desire not to be ruled. For that reason it generates an anger, a righteous indignation, which has as its object the overcoming of whatever opposes it. But that is only to say that this anger has ruling as its object. However, wherever there are rulers, there will be some who are ruled. And wherever some are ruled, regardless of the justice of the rule, there will be a perception of injustice. This, in turn, will generate a righteous indignation, and potentially a new revolution with new rulers and so on. All of this is what Aristotle has in mind by suggesting that the nature of the *polis* is revolution, and by connecting revolution with frustrated eros. The very passion which is at the heart of political life insures imperfect satisfaction with political life.[84]

This unusual presentation of Aristotle contains a kernel of truth. Almost every practical regime—which is to say, the "deviant" regimes, oligarchy, democracy, and tyranny—is unstable at its very core, but not because of a desire for freedom from constraint, much less from eros. These regimes are inherently unstable because they promote and reward greed and they encourage destructive, competitive ambition (*philotimia*). Greed and ambition are at the center of every known constitution, although they are present in different forms and for different reasons depending on the constitution. People want money, not freedom from the constraints of money; they want the pleasures of rule, not freedom from rule. In this they show ignorance of the good life and yield to the urges of their base human nature. The societies they construct, consequently, encourage them to value, all the more, material goods, honor, and power. The frailty of ordinary constitutions is enhanced further by individuals'

[84] Davis 1986, 58.

profound ignorance of others' motives. People may want more because they want what is just, not simply because they are aggressive or self-aggrandizing; but their behavior is labeled "greedy" by those who have an interest in doing so, for the sake of satisfying their own greed. All too often, one imagines, the label is in any case accurate. Practical political players can only observe and interpret social behavior; they have no access to other men's minds. Hence greed becomes not just a practical problem of behavior but a virus within the community's ideological exchanges.

Aristotle's own evidence and analysis suggest that the perception of injustice is not at the core of political instability. Although we have charted certain complications with this view, Aristotle believes that the real root of political instability is self-aggrandizing behavior of every sort, and in the *Ethics* and *Politics* he offers a penetrating analysis of the psychology and causes of such behavior. Hence I do not find his approach so different from that recommended by Judith Shklar, although Shklar herself explicitly opposes her method to that of Aristotle:

> Why should we not think of those experiences that we call unjust directly, as independent phenomena in their own right? Common sense and history surely tell us that these are common experiences and have an immediate claim on our attention. Indeed, in all likelihood most of us have said, "this is unfair" or "this is unjust" more often than "this is just." Is there nothing much more to be said about the sense of injustice that we know so well when we feel it? Why then do most philosophers refuse to think about injustice as deeply or as subtly as they do about justice? I do not know why a curious division of labor prevails, why philosophy ignores iniquity, while history and fiction deal with little else, but it does leave a gap in our thinking.[85]

At least with regard to Aristotle, whose ethical model Shklar specifically means to oppose in this passage, these claims stand in need of some qualification. Aristotle provides searching accounts of the psychology and political importance of greed. Most important for the history of Athenian greed is Aristotle's connection between acquisitiveness and the violation of distributive fairness within political communities. As much as Aristotle has clarified the nature of these concepts, though, he has also opened up a cluster of questions about greed, all of which deserve historical analysis. Toward what objects did greedy individuals, groups, or city-states typically direct their acquisitiveness? Within which evaluative communities was their greed considered to be unfair? What competing arguments about greed and unfairness were in play at different historical moments? How was greed for material goods related to the desire for honor and power? How did political agents manipulate the language of greed to

[85] Shklar 1990, 16.

serve their own ideological purposes? The foregoing investigation of Aristotle has set the stage for a study of the historical events and conceptual changes that made greed a central issue to a historically minded political thinker at the end of the classical period.[86]

[86] By saying that Aristotle is "historically minded," I mean only to suggest that he used archaic and classical Greek history as the primary empirical basis for his theoretical study of politics, and that he was, as a result, influenced by the major trends that defined that history; cf. Polansky 1991, 329; Weil 1977, 202–3.

3

Solonian Athens and the Archaic Roots of Greed

THE Athenian discourse on greed was bounded on one end by Aristotle's systematic reflections on acquisitiveness and injustice. That discourse had its roots, however, in the world of archaic Athenian politics and in Solon's poetry, which thoughtfully responded to that world and defined parameters for later classical discussions. Because of his concern to limit excess acquisitiveness and to enforce distributive justice, Solon is a logical starting point. In this chapter, I want to examine Solon's distinctive way of adapting archaic poetic traditions in order to promote solidarity and patriotism among the citizens of Athens.

Aristotle found in Solon a useful interlocutor in his effort to understand greed. He engages with Solon as both an ethical thinker and a political leader—for example, in contesting Solon's view that no limit of wealth has been clearly revealed to men (*Pol.* 1256b32–34, Solon fr. 13.71),[1] and in citing Solon's recognition of the importance of having a level standard of property (*Pol.* 1266b16–18). In fact, in his account of the Solonian reform, he quotes poetry that he interprets as Solon's exhortation to the rich not "to be greedy" (*parainōn tois plousiois mē pleonektein*; *AP* 5.3):[2] "Calm the strong heart in your breast, you who had more than your fill [*koron*] of many good things, and lay down your ambitious thoughts in moderation [*en metrioisi*]; for we will not obey, nor will these things be fitting for you" (fr. 4c). In these lines, Solon is urging the rich to observe self-restraint for the sake of Athens as a whole. Elsewhere in his poetry, Solon envisioned his goal to be that of creating and enforcing fairness in distribution: "It gives me no pleasure to act by force of tyranny [*turannidos . . . biēi*], nor that the base and noble should have an equal share of their rich fatherland [*oude pieirēs chthonos / patridos kakoisin esthlous isomoiriēn echein*]" (fr. 34.7–9). Although he used different termi-

[1] As I shall argue, Aristotle's interpretation of this verse is ungenerous, but his disagreement clarifies Solon's meaning.

[2] The authorship of the *Athenian Constitution* is contested, although all are agreed that the work comes from Aristotle's school, if not Aristotle himself. Rhodes (1981, 61–63) states the case for skepticism about Aristotle's authorship; Keaney (1992, 3–19) argues for Aristotelian authorship on stylistic grounds; cf. Ostwald 1986, xx–xxi n1. For convenience' sake I refer to the author as Aristotle, but the issue of authorship does not affect my arguments here or later in the book. In citing fragments of Solon's poetry, I have used the numeration provided by West 1992.

nology and responded to different historical circumstances, Solon was participating in—even originating—the discourse on greed that Aristotle engaged with so deeply.

The surviving fragments of Solon's poetry embody a social critique in which the acquisitiveness and disruptive behavior of both rich and poor are exposed, scrutinized, and condemned. Solon's critical stance aims to shape individual dispositions with a view to self-restraint and distributive justice. His critique of greed and injustice grew out of both the archaic poetic tradition and the historical circumstances of the early sixth century. Upon examining Solon's poetry in these two contexts, we find a progression in notions of justice from Homer to Solon, organized around the central idea of acquisitiveness and its regulation by an increasingly assertive community. Ultimately Solon encouraged Athenians to view themselves, above all, as citizens of Athens rather than as assertive individualists or as members of specific groups motivated by narrow self-interest. In their capacity as citizens, they must refrain from excess acquisitiveness and observe justice for the good of their polis.[3] Solon's stature and authority in the Athenian democracy contributed to the later importance of his own formulations of Athenian social problems, but conversely the persuasive force of his formulations accounts in part for his preeminent position within the tradition.[4]

Homer and Hesiod

Recent discussions of the Homeric epics have concentrated on refining our understanding of the relationship between "Homeric society" and the historical society of Dark Age Greece. Whatever society the epics depict—one of the late eighth century, one of 800 B.C., or one created solely from the poet's imagination—they do not present a "closed" ideological picture that excludes the possibility of further debate.[5] On the

[3] Holmes (1979), developing Benjamin Constant's arguments, elucidates the essentially civic construction of the individual in classical Athens in the course of arguing that this construction is anachronistic, and potentially dangerous, if applied to modern liberal states. The civic definition of the individual begins, I believe, with Solon's formulation of individual identity within the civic context.

[4] For the importance of Solon as a "founding father" figure in the fourth-century democracy, see Hansen 1989, Thomas 1994, 119–34. Although Herodotus presents him only as a "wise adviser," Solon becomes a key political figure especially during the constitutional struggles of the late fifth century in Athens. Nonetheless, as I argue in chapter 4, Solon's moral ideas also play an important role in Thucydides' presentation of Athens, even though Solon is not named in Thucydides' text; cf. Szegedy-Maszak 1993.

[5] There has been an outpouring of recent work on the relationship between Homeric society and history: see especially Raaflaub 1997; 1998; Morris 1986; Thalmann 1998; Os-

contrary, they draw attention to the ethical disputes that tend to arise in conflicts between individuals or groups within self-consciously structured political communities. If we view politics as "a process in which questions of community organization are raised, determined, and implemented," then the Homeric epics are political texts that provide a detailed framework within which later political and ethical debates can take place.[6] Among the ethical issues they raise, the most significant is their presentation of individual acquisitiveness as a problem of collective distribution. Although the epics push the reader in certain interpretative directions, their importance for understanding Solon's poetry lies in their presentation of multiple ethical possibilities rather than in any specific conclusions they draw.[7]

The epics describe endlessly various modes of acquisition, including plundering expeditions, raids, piracy, receiving gifts of hospitality, and full-scale warfare.[8] Because, broadly speaking, material wealth had symbolic value for its possessor, the heroic code encouraged as much accumulation as possible. But aggressive modes of acquisition, such as plundering and raiding, were subject to ethical criticism. Here the *Iliad* makes a key distinction between forcible acquisition from strangers on the one hand and, on the other, improper acquisition within an already constituted group, such as the Achaean army. In these two spheres of acquisition, respectively, questions of general, retributive justice and of specifically *distributive* justice tend to arise. The role of prior compacts is of primary importance in distinguishing between the two.

In the first sphere, all communities, even those with no prior relationship, are protected by the watchfulness of Zeus, who is supposed to guar-

---

borne 1996, 137–60; Rose 1992; 1997; Qviller 1981; van Wees 1992; Hammer 1997; 1998.

[6] The quotation is from Hammer 1998, 2; Hammer (1997; 1998) and Osborne (1996, esp. 147–56) argue persuasively that the Homeric epics are explicitly political and invite the audience to entertain questions about rhetoric, leadership, and political authority. Earlier scholars (e.g., Snell 1953) once argued that Homer lacks a concept of the self or of the will and therefore cannot address serious moral issues in comprehensible ways; for criticisms of this view, see Lloyd-Jones 1971; Williams 1993, 21–49. Homer's presentation of moral psychology is different from that of later authors but the idea itself is by no means absent.

[7] Although the poems present a generally aristocratic viewpoint, they are sufficiently open-ended to provide a fertile ground for further political and ethical reflection. For a similar view that concentrates on Homer's audience rather than his later readers, see Taplin 1992, 50–53, contra Finley (1978b, 113–14), who emphasizes the lack of ambiguity in the Homeric code; for other arguments in favor of the open-ended reading of the poems' ideological stances, see Osborne 1996, 147–56, Balot forthcoming a. Thalmann (1998, esp. 272–305), argues that "the *Odyssey* tries to shut down questioning in favor of affirming hierarchy" (296); for other "aristocratic" interpretations, see Morris 1986; Tandy 1987.

[8] Finley 1978b, 51–73; van Wees 1992, 207–58.

antee justice and to secure punishment for the wicked.[9] In particular, the injustice of Paris's theft of Helen is a postulate within the poem that motivates the Trojan War and its outcome.[10] Even so, Homeric ethics actively encourages, and even requires, booty raids as a method of winning wealth and prestige.[11] Accumulating wealth brought honor, especially when the heroes acquired possessions through plundering, a prestigious mode of acquisition. As van Wees says, "Homeric princes turn to predatory warfare because those who forcibly seize the wealth of foreigners kill two birds with one stone. They get rich *and* establish themselves as warriors and men of power."[12] On the other hand, this ethic did not prevent victims of theft from regarding raiding and stealing as acts of *hubris* and violations of justice that had to be rectified by retributive violence.[13] Heroes incurred dishonor if they allowed others to take away their possessions; Neleus, for example, was extremely angry (*kecholōmenos*) over the insults he had suffered from his arrogant (*huperēphaneontes*) neighbors, and Nestor still remembers with pride how he took revenge for the outrages suffered by his father and his people (*Il.* 11.670–762).[14] There is thus a great deal of ambiguity in the first, more general sphere of acquisition. In light of the ethical conflict I have noted, it is fair to say that a key ingredient of modern notions of morality, namely impartiality, is lacking from Homeric moral conceptions.[15] The Homeric heroes operate with a double standard that they make no attempt to

[9] See Irwin 1989, 17; Lloyd-Jones (1971, 1–27) argues that Zeus is concerned with the protection of justice from the earliest times, and that, because of Zeus's will, the Trojans, like both Agamemnon and Achilles, receive "rough [reciprocal] justice" in the end (27). See, e.g., *Iliad* 16.384–93. For opposing views, which suggest that Zeus is concerned with his own honor (*timē*) but not with justice in general, see Adkins 1960, 62; Dodds 1963, 52; Finley 1978b, 140–41.

[10] A further complication is that Paris's crime against Menelaus violates the code of guest friendship (*xenia*), which they both implicitly agree to, but this does not affect my argument.

[11] See *Iliad* 6.476–81; *Odyssey* 9.39–42; 14.230–33; van Wees 1992, 207–27. For justice as retribution: see *Iliad* 11.655–803. For Hesiod the situation is less ambiguous: striving after wealth is a positive activity, but becomes negative when it involves injustice and corruption, the two primary forms of taking what rightly belongs to another. For the positive evaluation, see especially *Works and Days* 23–24; negative: *Works and Days* 37–41, 212–24, 238–47, 263–65, 320–26.

[12] Van Wees 1992, 248.

[13] See, e.g., Menelaus's speech over the dead Peisandrus at *Iliad* 13.620–39 with the comments of Fisher 1992, 154–60. See also Nestor's condemnation of the raiding Epeians at *Iliad* 11.670–762.

[14] On the dishonor incurred by heroes who cannot defend themselves, see van Wees 1992, 107.

[15] For impartiality as a fundamental requirement of moral thinking, at least in the liberal tradition, see Griffiths 1967, 177–82; Rawls 1971, 11–17; Nagel 1991; Williams 1985, 65–70.

justify. The ambivalence expressed by the Homeric poems about the morality of forcible acquisition becomes even more powerful when classical Greeks begin to consider the massively complicated moral questions associated with international, and especially imperial, relations.

The second sphere of acquisition, by contrast, concerns the distribution of goods within well-defined communities. It thus provides a model for the classical authors who focused on the problems of acquisitiveness within distributive communities.[16] The importance of fairness, in this sphere, derives from the logically prior belief that the group has claims on the individual, as a matter of distributive justice, which non-members, such as foreigners or slaves, do not have. After a hunt or a battle, for example, the community's leader was obligated to ensure a fair distribution (*isē moira* or *isos dasmos*) of meat and of spoils, and individual recipients were obligated to accept their portions or to explain to the group why their portions were unacceptable.[17] The defining scene is Achilles' dispute with Agamemnon in *Iliad* 1. By examining Achilles' arguments, we gain an important perspective on the ethical arguments and rhetorical strategies of the discourse on greed—arguments and strategies that we will meet over and over again.

Achilles makes two charges against Agamemnon, who intends to seize one of his fellow kings' prizes in order to replace Chryseis. First, he scolds Agamemnon's excessive acquisitiveness (*philokteanōtate*, 1.122), claiming that all the spoils from previous campaigns have already been distributed, and that it is wrong (*ouk epeoike*) to recall them now: "Glorious son of Atreus, greediest for gain of all men [*philokteanōtate pantōn*], how will the great-hearted Achaeans give you a prize [*geras*] now? We do

[16] The characteristics of acquisition within a collective body, as distinguished from acquisition from those with whom one has no prior commitments, are clearly brought out by John Rawls's opening remarks in an essay entitled "Distributive Justice" (1993): "We may think of a human society as a more or less self-sufficient association regulated by a common conception of justice and aimed at advancing the good of its members. As a co-operative venture for mutual advantage, it is characterized by a conflict as well as an identity of interests. There is an identity of interests since social co-operation makes possible a better life for all than any would have if everyone were to try to live by his own efforts; yet at the same time men are not indifferent as to how the greater benefits produced by their joint labours are distributed, for in order to further their own aims each prefers a larger to a lesser share. A conception of justice is a set of principles for choosing between social arrangements which determine this division and for underwriting a consensus as to the proper distributive shares" (73). It is possible to criticize this conception of justice if we think, for example, of what justice could mean in an international, as opposed to a societal, context. Do similar rules of distribution and mutual advantage apply *between* societies as well as within them? This is the difficult question confronted by a variety of fifth-century political thinkers who figure in the next three chapters.

[17] On the carefully regulated process by which the Homeric army distributes its booty, see van Wees 1992, 299–310.

not know of many things stored up in common anywhere. But the things we sacked from cities, these have been distributed [*dedastai*] already, and it is not right [*ouk epeoike*] that the army gather them all back again" (*Il.* 1.122–26). Achilles castigates Agamemnon's arbitrary, self-interested rejection of customary procedure for the sake of greed. For Achilles, the settled habits of the group should not be subject to immediate revision by the group's aggressively greedy leader. Agamemnon's disregard for the process of collective distribution shows that he values his own interests over those of the community.

Second, Achilles claims that he deserves a larger prize of honor (*geras*) than he usually receives, perhaps even a larger one than Agamemnon, because of his military prowess (*Il.* 1.163–67): "I never have a prize equal [*ison*] to yours, whenever the Achaeans sack a well-founded citadel of the Trojans; but my hands bear the greater part of the furious fighting; but whenever a division [*dasmos*] of spoils comes, your prize [*geras*] is by far greater." Achilles argues that his greater contribution to communal projects merits a proportionally greater share in the advantages derived from those projects.[18] Although the Homeric epics do not represent politics as taking place within the elaborate institutional framework of the developed polis, the standard of heroic behavior is not defined simply by harsh self-interest, or by physical force, but also by the legitimacy of one's claims as expressed in public debate. Thus the *Iliad* inaugurates a tradition of ethical reflection upon acquisition in a collective context, where communal notions of fair and unfair distribution are typically questioned and contested through rational argument. Invoking merit as a justification for receiving prizes, Achilles anticipates the Trojan Sarpedon, who also proposes that it is his front-line martial prowess that legitimates his receiving material wealth from the Lycians (*Il.* 12.310–21). Placed in a broader perspective, both passages roughly foreshadow Aristotle's later arguments to the effect that merit or worth (*axia*) ought to correlate to the possession of political power and material wealth.

Beyond making these ethical arguments, Achilles also tries to win the upper hand through scoring rhetorical points against Agamemnon. Most important, he uses the rhetoric of greed in order to deflate Agamemnon's pretense of being concerned about honor. Achilles interprets Agamemnon's attempt to take away his girlfriend Briseis as characteristic of his tendency to rob his troops of their just deserts. Achilles calls him "a king who feeds fat [*dēmoboros*] on his people, with nonentities [*outidanoisin*] for

[18] Contra Rose (1992, 43–91; 1997), Achilles' argument is not a nostalgic presentation of merit-based values that are in the process of being superseded by claims of status and inherited excellence. As I demonstrate in this and successive chapters, the idea that one's position in a collective hierarchy is based on claims to merit in areas that the community values (e.g., warfare, rhetoric) shows remarkable staying power in the Greek tradition.

subjects" (*Il.* 1.231). Achilles attacks Agamemnon in the language of gluttony, accusing him of literally consuming his own community in order to satisfy his appetite for more.[19] His attack thus participates in a wide-ranging system of archaic imagery, which linked greed to gluttony.[20] Later in the assembly, similarly, Thersites recommends leaving Agamemnon in Troy in order to "digest his prizes" (*gera pessemen*), so that Agamemnon will come to appreciate the value of his followers (*Il.* 2.236–38). He thus advances the image of the gluttonous king who devours his community in disregard of just distribution. Agamemnon's gluttonous habits of consumption show that his materialistic desires are inextricably linked with his abusive control over others, a link that Aristotle makes explicit in his representation of the tyrant. In Achilles' powerful presentation, Agamemnon was not driven by the socially approved motive of winning honor, but rather by his belly—a grossly material, vulgar motivation. By grounding greed in the materiality of the body, he anticipates Aristotle's explanation of greed as deriving from a wrongheaded conception of the good life, which overvalues bodily pleasure as a human good (see chapter 2).

Generally speaking, Achilles and Agamemnon view their quarrel in terms of outrage (*hubris*) and honor (*timē*), which are concretely signified by the seizure and possession of material goods. As Finley pointed out, however, it is difficult to untangle the social and economic significance of goods in the Homeric world, but social honor (*timē*) seems to take precedence over a narrowly economic perspective on material goods.[21] In the public assembly, however, Achilles attributes to Agamemnon precisely this sort of dishonorable materialistic greed. Even if Agamemnon views himself as pursuing honor nobly, the well-deployed rhetoric of greed enables Achilles to suggest that he has abandoned the heroic desire for honor in favor of a vulgar desire to feed fat on his people.

[19] Graver (1995) shows that Achilles' abuse of Agamemnon as a "dog-face" (*kunōpa*, 1.159) refers specifically to his materialistic greed, which recalls the dog's voracity; for parallels, cf. *Iliad* 1.225, 10.502–6; *Odyssey* 20.18–20.

[20] Nagy 1979, 312–13; cf. 225–27. For the semantics of *dēmos* as "people, community" and as "fat," see Nagler 1974, 5–9. The image of gluttony symbolically links the *Iliad*'s initial quarrel (*neikos*) with the heroic feast, where the (proportionally) equal apportionment of meat is crucial to fairness and cohesion.

[21] Finley 1978b, 117–23. As we have seen, these tight connections between honor and material goods have loosened by the time of Aristotle, whose conception of greed (especially in the *Politics*) is focused on power and material goods, rather than on honor. Cairns (1996) in fact argues that *hubris* is a kind of *pleonexia* as Aristotle conceives *pleonexia* in the *Nicomachean Ethics*, but also suggests (rightly, I believe) that *pleonexia* in the *Politics* is distinguished from *hubris*: see, e.g., Cairns 1996, 5n28, where he notes that in the *Ethics*, "Aristotle is aware that he is using *pleonexia* in an extended sense (cf. 1132a7–14, b11–18), and so it is no objection to the interpretation of *hybris* as a kind of particular injustice/*pleonexia* that elsewhere *hybris* and *pleonexia* are distinguished (e.g., *Pol.* 1302b5–9; Fisher 22–24)."

In order to exclude Agamemnon from the Greek ethical community even further, Achilles represents his own dispute with Agamemnon as an issue of general concern among the troops. He assumes the role of community spokesman when he accuses Agamemnon of feeding fat on his troops; he recognizes that it is nearly impossible to argue against the welfare of the community at large. Achilles' presentation of Agamemnon is facilitated by the Greeks' conception of distribution as occurring "in the middle" (*es to meson*). As Detienne has shown, Homer's Greeks imagined divisible goods, in particular the spoils of war, as owned in common, or "in the middle," until the moment of distribution to individuals by the group.[22] Such a conception of division enables Achilles to suggest that, by robbing even a single chief, Agamemnon is in fact robbing the entire army, even though he specifically limits his aggression to one of the other leaders (*Il.* 1.137–39). Achilles thus wins a rhetorical advantage by identifying his own interests with those of the larger group, when in reality the dispute is a manifestation of conflict between Agamemnon and the group of other, lesser kings.[23] Achilles encourages the army to restrict Agamemnon's greed for the sake of its own self-interest, but the real beneficiary of the army's involvement would be Achilles—at least in the present case.[24]

Hence this paradigmatic scene illustrates several points about the discourse on greed and fair distribution. First, the discourse on greed began as a reaction against perceived oppression within the context of collective distribution.[25] Second, the discourse originates in intra-elite competition over resources, in which interested parties try to maintain their own material privileges by restricting the self-aggrandizement of other elites and by representing their own self-interests as the interest of the wider community. But the community's interests, at least by this point, have nothing to do with the struggle, although this will change by Solon's time. Nevertheless, this intra-elite struggle took place before an assembled au-

[22] Detienne 1996, 89–106.

[23] Intraelite conflict illustrates a significant tension within Homeric ethics: leaders are encouraged to value their own honor (*timē*) over the group's welfare, but the best—even the only—way to secure one's honor (*timē*) over the long term is to show due respect to the group. For discussion of this and similar tensions relating to "competitive" and "co-operative" virtues, see Adkins 1960; 1971; Long 1970; Irwin 1989, 6–19. Rose (1997) offers a perceptive analysis of intra-elite conflict and its ideological implications within the Homeric epics.

[24] Thus where I see Achilles' defense of the community as a rhetorical strategy meant to serve his own advantage, Rose (1992, 78–80) interprets his stance more literally.

[25] Hence my analysis of elite greed and the reaction against it helps to particularize and make more concrete Raaflaub's argument (1988, 22) that "dissatisfaction with the shortcomings of aristocratic leadership" was "the immediate cause that provoked the earliest manifestations of political thought and remained one of its most cogent stimuli."

dience, which can "vote with its feet" by standing behind the arguments of one leader or another. In the *Iliad*, however, the audience does no such thing; it rather justifies Achilles' belief that the common people of this poem are a group of ciphers. But the poem suggests the possibility that, as the demos became more aware of its own authority to evaluate, it could engage more fully in the political process. As Raaflaub has argued, "[S]cenes such as those described in *Iliad* I and II attest an awareness that the masses fighting in the war and sitting in the assembly represent at least a potential power factor. Otherwise it would be futile for Achilles, Hector, and Thersites to decry the people's passiveness and lack of courage."[26] The verbal interaction within the heroic elite, as well as between that elite and the assembled people, provides a key insight into the importance of both types of struggle within early Greek political communities.

Not surprisingly, Achilles himself verbalizes a central tenet of what later became the self-consciously egalitarian effort to hold greedy aristocrats accountable to the community: the belief that members of a community deserve a share in divisible goods in virtue of their contribution to common goals, and the further recognition that shares can be distributed appropriately only when self-restraint is observed, especially by members of the elite. The difference here, of course, is that Achilles is concerned at bottom with keeping his own possessions, not with equitably distributing limited resources among all members of the community. His version of resistance to oppression can become "egalitarian" only when all members of the community, including the poor and the non-elite, assert their claims to a fair share of divisible goods; or at least when a member of the elite, such as Solon, himself makes demands that actually serve the interests of the non-elite.

A remote glimmer of proper egalitarianism is found in the remarks of the buffoon Thersites, who also accuses Agamemnon of unfairness, selfishness, and excessive desire for more: "Or is it yet more gold you want, that some son of the horse-taming Trojans brings as ransom out of Ilion, one that I or some other Achaean capture and bring in? Or some young woman, so you can . . . keep her all for yourself?" (*Il.* 2.229–33).[27] Thersites too wants his own efforts to be equitably rewarded in the distribution of goods, and he abuses his fellow soldiers for their effeminacy in allowing Agamemnon to take more than he deserves (*Il.* 2.235). He thus forges a connection between masculinity and the ability either to enact or

[26] Raaflaub 1988, 11.

[27] I suggest that this is proper egalitarianism not because Thersites is an ordinary member of the army but because his ideas about distribution, in contrast to those of Achilles, would actually benefit the mass of Achaeans, rather than simply maintaining equitable distribution among the elite.

successfully to resist greed.[28] Greed is already being constructed here as part of a "politics of masculinity," in which the excessive desire to get more, along with the ability to satisfy that desire, is recognized as a sign of manhood. This is a feature of the tradition that Thucydides and Plato's character Callicles later develop in their own respective methods of theorizing greed. The army's laughter at Odysseus's humiliation of Thersites demonstrates a general complicity in valuing the interests of leaders, especially those of Agamemnon, over their own legitimate claims. The mass of fighters is not yet ready to hear its own claims articulated before the leaders. Egalitarian interests have not yet become mainstream, but instead can be expressed only in the voice of the explicitly marginal Thersites, whose freedom of speech is similar to that of the "metanastic" figure of Hesiod and the blame poets of the iambic tradition.[29] Odysseus reinforces the aristocratic status quo, which serves his own and especially Agamemnon's vested interests. Accordingly, the scene conveys the general impression that the rulers are always right, and their authority unquestionable.

From the outset, the *Iliad* formulates the problems of greed and fair distribution within an emerging political community.[30] By focusing on the resentment that results from their unfairness, it levels an important critique against corrupt leaders who behave as if the community exists for their own sake. By contrast, the *Odyssey* provides a more thoroughgoing treatment of greed's capacity to disrupt the emerging polis. The generic expectations of both Homeric epics encouraged their composers to focus on the heroic elite, but, like the *Iliad*, the *Odyssey* represents the behavior of aristocrats in the context of increasingly self-conscious communities. Although the *Odyssey* is usually regarded as biased in favor of the aristocracy, it is equally plausible to read it as, among other things, a detailed examination of how the greed of aristocrats gone wrong creates problems for their communities. But the suitors do not represent "counterfeit" aristocrats; instead, their reprehensible behavior conflicts with aristocratic ideals and throws into question the standard aristocratic claim to

[28] See Kateb (1998, 86) for the view that the Athenian Empire later represented the "excesses of politics-as-masculinity," and Halperin (1990, esp. 99–103), who rightly emphasizes the connections between masculinity and citizen status in fifth-century Athens.

[29] See Martin 1992, 20–21; Nagy 1979, 253–64. For other treatments that view the Thersites episode as critical of the aristocrats, see Rose 1988; Thalmann 1988.

[30] Raaflaub 1997, 629–45; Morris 1986, 100–104. Manville (1990, 54–92), however, argues that "It was not until the age of Solon that any kind of public and broadly accepted definition of membership and community existed—one that would embody a formal concept of citizenship for all Athenians" (69). I believe that the Homeric epics do portray emergent political communities, but I also argue later in the chapter, with Manville, that in Athens the notions of citizenship and community came about only in Solon's era because of the unique prepolitical conditions of seventh-century Attica.

natural and inherited moral excellence.[31] They cast serious doubt on the likelihood that Ithaka will find an appropriately self-restrained leader once Odysseus is gone.

There is considerable overlap between the suitors' dishonoring of Odysseus and his household (*oikos*) and their excessive greed for both material wealth and power: while their behavior is typically criticized as hubristic (1.227, 1.368, 3.207, 4.321, etc.), they hope to acquire as much wealth and power as possible through violating Telemachus's just claims to his inheritance. By pressing the issue of Penelope's marriage, by devouring Odysseus's substance, and by attacking Telemachus, they show that their acquisitiveness is directed at once toward material goods and the power and prestige that accompany rule over Ithaka.[32] The suitors themselves believe their behavior is justified as a way of putting pressure on Penelope and Telemachus to agree to have Penelope marry one of them (*Od.* 2.85–129). For everyone else, however, the suitors are excessive and hubristic (e.g., 1.368), and Odysseus's own condemnation of them centers on their unjust plundering of his household during his absence (22.35–41, cf. 20.213–18, 24.454–62). Their behavior provides a classic example of the wide-ranging acquisitiveness of members of the elite, who want not only to satisfy their material desires but also to acquire political power and control over others.

Like the *Iliad*, the *Odyssey* explores the dialectic between leaders and their communities within the framework of the community's collective understanding of rightful ownership and its censure of illegitimate desires for more. Here, however, the community's evaluation of individuals is mediated by the elite household (*oikos*), which is the focus of the suitors' transgressions and acquisitiveness. The *Odyssey* is ambivalent about the community's power to resist the suitors' habits of consumption. Inspired by Athena, who appears as Mentes, Telemachus calls an assembly—the first since Odysseus left (2.26–27)—in order to demand publicly that the suitors stop eating up his livelihood. Even Telemachus is uncertain whether he can appropriately present his private troubles in

[31] Donlan 1980 provides the classic treatment of the aristocratic ideal of excellence; Rose (1992, 43–140) shows how this ideal is enmeshed in the ideological conditions of the production of archaic poetry, and also how the ideal is thrown into question by the Homeric epics; Thalmann (1998, 84) calls the suitors "counterfeit" aristocrats.

[32] The issue of succession in the *Odyssey* is notoriously vague and ambiguous, in part because it is wrapped up in the question of whether the Homeric *basileus* is a genuine king and monarch, as opposed to a "big man" or chieftain. For an excellent summary of the positions taken in these debates, see van Wees (1992, 281–98), who argues, against Finley (1978b, 82–91) and Halverson 1986, that Homeric *basileis* are kings whose monarchic rule is heritable. I am inclined to agree that the *Odyssey* contains many hints pointing toward Telemachus's possession of a monarchic entitlement, but he must assert his claim before it will be taken seriously.

the public assembly (2.44–45), but he clearly expects his community to help both from concern for its reputation (2.64–66) and from religious fear (2.66–67, 2.141–45). Mentor elaborates the message of collective responsibility: "Now I hold it against you other people (*allōi dēmōi*), how you all sit silently, and never with an assault of words check the suitors, though they are few and you are many" (2.239–41). The poem emphasizes the fictional Ithakan community's responsibilities to individuals but also its utter inability to behave decisively against a united group of greedy aristocrats. As those aristocrats see it, the real threat to their positions comes rather from Telemachus's supporters abroad (2.325–30).[33] For Telemachus and other Ithakans in his camp, any other hope of justice rests with the gods, not with the community itself. The religious framework, within which justice will be realized through the agency of the gods, is more pronounced in Hesiod, but here too the gods are invoked as champions of a social order in which the greed and exploitation of the mighty are restricted in accordance with standards of divinely ordained social justice.[34]

Like Achilles in the *Iliad*, Telemachus presents the suitors' greed through the image of extravagant ingestion: speaking to Athena, who has adopted the guise of Mentes, he says, "Dear stranger, would you be scandalized at what I say? This is all they care about, the lyre and the singing. Easy for them, since without penalty they eat up [*edousin*] the substance of a man whose white bones lie out in the rain and fester somewhere on the mainland, or roll in the wash of the breakers. If they should see him returning to Ithaka, all of them would pray to be lighter on their feet instead of richer men in gold and clothing [*aphneioteroi chrusoio te esthētos te*]" (1.158–65; cf. 1.250–51, 1.377–78). Similarly, Nestor counsels Telemachus, "Do not wander for a long time away from home, leaving your possessions, and in your house men so overbearing [*huperphialous*], for fear they divide up all your property and devour it [*phagōsi ktēmata dassamenoi*], so all your journey will have no profit" (3.313–16). In their hunger for more, the suitors have abandoned aristocratic excellence and the desire for honor, choosing instead a path of objectionable materialism. The *Odyssey* draws special attention to gluttony as a symptom of the perverse banqueting on Ithaka. The suitors' greed for more perverts and destroys proper feasting, which marks off human civilization as opposed to both the barbarity of the uncivilized and the divinity of the gods, who receive honor from proper sacrifices. If, as some scholars maintain, the

[33] West 1988, 128.

[34] Hence Raaflaub (1988, 18) overemphasizes the idea that "the problems tackled by political thought fit into an entirely human framework of cause and effect"; cf. Morris 2000, 174, who also underemphasizes the religious framework of Telemachus's appeal.

suitors represent an emerging class of oligarchs,[35] then they are subject to precisely the criticism that Aristotle later levels against oligarchs—namely, that they exploit their power for the sake of profit, rather than spending their money on public works in order to win honor from the community (cf. *Politics* 1306a6–9, 1321a39–b1).

As Solon was later to express it, these aristocrats cannot "order the merriment of their present banquet in peace" (*parousas / euphrosunas kosmein daitos en hēsuchiēi*; fr. 4.9–10)—a sentiment that evokes the *Odyssey*'s condemnation of the Ithakan leaders in order to cast the leaders [*hēgemones*] of sixth-century Athens in an appalling light. Such is the suitors' *hubris* that they "fear no one" (2.199), not even Odysseus himself (2.246–51); they haughtily reject the prudent warnings of Halitherses (2.161–76) and Mentor (2.229–41), and begin to abandon even their pretenses at justification. At times they justify themselves by pointing to their courtship of Penelope, but at other times they simply warn that they are unstoppable, even by Odysseus himself (2.246–51). Like Achilles and Agamemnon, they have the power to disregard the community's evaluation, but unlike those heroes they come to abandon the project of self-justification in their raw rhetoric of power and self-interest. As the fictional Ithakan community begins to acknowledge its own responsibility to its individual members, and as Telemachus summons help from that community, the suitors reject a communal identification altogether, banding together with their own group like pirates or predators, and occupying an oppositional stance in relation to that community. The *Odyssey*'s ethical critique of the suitors' greed illustrates their deep perversions of the aristocratic ideal—an ideal best represented by Odysseus, who was "as gentle as a father" to his dependents (e.g., 2.234). While its critique provides resources for later egalitarian criticisms of elite greed, and while the assembly represents a potential power factor, the epic itself does not positively promote an ideal of egalitarianism.

For the positive articulation of an egalitarian ideal, we must turn to Hesiod. Hesiod (as I call the persona of the author in the *Works and Days*) used a critique of both elite and nonelite greed as an instrument of self-definition and self-justification. Hesiod embodies the values of the "middling" farmer who opposes himself both to the injustice and rapacity of the elite, and to the laziness of the needy poor, who, as he imagines, are in a shameful condition of dependence on others.[36] In his famous distinction between two types of Eris (Strife)—one that fosters war and

[35] Rose 1992, 99–102; Whitman 1958, 306–8.

[36] For Hesiod as a "middling" agriculturalist, see Morris 1996 and Hanson 1995, 91–126; Hanson argues vigorously against Millett's view (1984) that Hesiod is a "peasant." I have also found useful Osborne 1996, 143–47, and Lamberton 1988, 105–33, in reading Hesiod's poetics in context.

destruction, the other that rouses the sluggish to work (*WD* 11–26)—Hesiod implies that his own agrarian competitiveness is not destructive but rather productive. He thereby constructs a space of appropriate acquisition for himself and his fellow farmers, who grow eager to increase their wealth when they see the prosperity of their neighbors: "Neighbor rivals neighbor as he hastens after wealth [*aphenos*]" (23–24). "This Strife is good [*agathē*] for men" (24) because it encourages them to seek wealth justly through ideals of self-reliance and hard work. In a concise formulation, Hesiod recommends, "Work with work upon work," (382), or, in other words, build up a modest estate over time through persistence, knowledge, and self-reliance (311, 349–51, 361–62).

As Hesiod articulated the ideals of "middling" agriculturalists, he also graphically charted the destructive failings of those above and below his "middling" position. There is a close correspondence, ensured by the gods, between work and success; "both gods and men are angry with [*nemesōsi*] an idle man," and "hunger is wholly suitable for a lazy man" (302–4). As a result, agricultural failure and the poverty that accompanies it cause shame for the needy: "Vile shame [*aidōs*] accompanies the needy man, shame, which both greatly harms and benefits men. Shame is attached to poverty [*anolbiēi*], confidence to prosperity [*olbōi*]" (317–19). The ethos of hard work, by contrast, leads to god-given wealth over time, because the gods ordained that human beings should work their land (397–98). The wealth of the successful farmer is just and lasting because it is the gods' gift (225–37, 300–301, 308–9, 320; cf. the *ploutodotai* [givers of wealth] at 126). By carving out a space of just acquisition, Hesiod defines himself in opposition to the needy poor.

More importantly, however, Hesiod aligns himself with the natural agricultural cycle, justice, and the providence of Zeus, who takes care to limit the self-aggrandizement of the powerful.[37] The primary thrust of Hesiod's social criticism is directed against the unjust and greedy upper class, which exploits its position of power in order to acquire more. Hesiod condemns the injustice and *hubris* of "bribe-devouring" (*dōrophagous*) kings (38–39), who pervert their judicial authority in order to satisfy their greed.[38] He thus elaborates the egalitarian rhetoric of greed by developing a social critique of the rich and powerful, and he does so, again, through the image of gluttonously ingesting food.[39]

[37] For associations between the poet, the justice of Zeus, and the natural agricultural cycle, see Lamberton 1988, 109, 122–23; on Hesiod's concern for justice and fairness as the new virtues of his society, see Donlan 1980, 26–34. For Hesiod's positive evaluation of acquisition, see *Works and Days* 11–26; Weber 1967, 19.

[38] On *dikē* and *hubris* in Hesiod, see Fisher 1992, 185–200; Nagy 1985, 39–40, 57–59, 62–63.

[39] For this element in Hesiod's critique, see also Morris 1996, 28–30. Martin (1992, 20–

Hesiod envisions two paths to unjust enrichment by the elite: "Wealth [*chrēmata*] should not be plundered [*harpakta*]; that which is given by the gods is far better. For if someone takes great riches [*olbon*] violently, or steals it with his tongue, which often happens when profit [*kerdos*] deceives the mind of men, and shamelessness tramples down their shame, then the gods quickly make him powerless, and make his house small, and wealth [*olbos*] attends him only for a brief time" (320–26). As Howe has shown, Hesiod's mention of "seizing" wealth refers to the practices of raiding and plundering typical of Homeric heroes.[40] Hesiod's agrarian ideology finds a potentially prestigious heroic practice unacceptable because of its injustice. Homeric heroes typically fail to consider the perspective of those they plunder, because they do not have prior obligations to them within a self-conscious community. For Hesiod, by contrast, Zeus himself, along with the other gods, guarantees the integrity of all property, at least insofar as he punishes raiders (238–39) and even brings down their cities along with them (238–47). He thus evokes a sense of Zeus's watchfulness and the possibility of retributive justice—both of which fit squarely into what we called the first sphere of acquisition in the *Iliad*.[41] Hence, no special social compact is needed to make raiding and looting morally unacceptable.

The second path involves both a greedy rhetorician and crooked judges. "Stealing with the tongue" refers to exploiting false rhetoric in the lawcourts, or to using deception or bribery in dealing with judges, in order to win advantages. It is characteristic not necessarily of the elite but rather of men like Hesiod's brother Perses, who, Hesiod says, cheated him out of his proper inheritance: "For we had already divided up [*edassameth'*] our share [*klēron*], but you seized the greater share [*polla harpazōn*] and carried it off, giving great glory to our bribe-swallowing lords [*basilēas dōrophagous*], who love to judge this kind of case. Fools! They do not know how much greater the half is than the whole [*oude isasin hosōi pleon hēmisu pantos*], nor what great advantage there is in mallow and asphodel" (37–41). This quotation became a trademark of those railing against an acquisitive and exploitative elite. In Plato's *Republic*, for example, Socrates mentions the line in order to rule out greed among his upper-class Guardians. As Socrates says, "If . . . a thoughtless, adolescent

---

21) shows that Hesiod is related to Thersites in traditional archaic poetics in that both are marginalized, though verbally adept, figures who blame and criticize their social superiors: Hesiod is entitled to *parrhēsia* because of what Martin calls his "metanastic" status—that is, his status as an "exterior insider" (14).

[40] Howe 1958.

[41] In our later discussion of the hawk and nightingale fable, it will emerge that Hesiod views justice as a distinctively human characteristic, which separates human beings off from the animal kingdom. On the interpretation of this fable, see, also Lamberton 1988, 121–24.

idea of happiness [*eudaimonias*] seizes [a Guardian] and drives him to use his power to take everything in the city for himself, he will understand that Hesiod was truly wise when he said that somehow 'the half is greater than the whole' [*pleon einai pōs hēmisu pantos*]" (466b7–c3).

Both Perses and the "bribe-devouring kings" are at fault because of their respective ways of exploiting the courts to satisfy their greed, which embodies a wrongheaded conception of glory and of true human happiness. Hesiod's original dispute with his brother is, like the dispute between Agamemnon and Achilles, a compelling case of excessive acquisitiveness that violates canons of fair division, where each party clearly has prior claims on and obligations to the other. Perses' excessive desire to get more has led him to take more than his share of the divisible good of their inheritance. Thus, beyond diminishing Perses and the judges as human beings, their greed also creates resentment among people like Hesiod himself and, therefore, the potential for unrest. The "half" is worth more than the "whole" in the same way that the "equal share" contributes more to the health of a polis than desire for the "greater share."

Already in the early archaic period, then, Hesiod laid out clearly the terminology of distributive "shares," which Aristotle adapted to his own conceptions of just distribution in the polis. His proverbial statement "the half is greater than the whole" is perfectly suited to his accusation that the dispensers of justice are too foolish to see that their greed violates the fairness upon which the community's stability and welfare are based. The traditional, simple fare of the farmer, mallow and asphodel, represents a rejection of elite excess and self-aggrandizement in favor of the collective advantage. For Hesiod, of course, this collective advantage is a matter of divine ordinance, rather than practical politics: Zeus prospers the cities of fair-minded men (225–37). For Aristotle, by contrast, distributive fairness itself created communal stability through the workings of individual psychology. Between these two theoretical visions of the just city, Solon acts as an important transitional figure.

Solon's Reform

In both the recent and more distant past, historians have tended to view Solon either as a forward-looking democrat or as a conservative elitist intent on preserving aristocratic privileges.[42] I believe he was neither.

[42] The startling spectrum of opinions on this question can be revealed by the following two quotations: "According to our hypothesis, it was the purpose of archaic codifications to secure the political and economic status quo for a ruling class that was especially concerned

Rather, he was a reformer who aimed to stabilize Athens by defining the political community and by defusing the materialistic elite competition that threatened to destroy it. Although his reform gave benefits to both the elite and the demos, Solon's sights were set on the good of Athens as a whole, rather than that of any narrow group.

If we examine the content of the reforms, we find that Solon was not a partisan of the elite or the demos but granted qualitatively different privileges to each group depending on what he believed it deserved (cf. fr. 5). Both aristocrats and the demos won obvious legal and social rewards from the reform. On the one hand, aristocrats maintained their positions of wealth and power: Solon did not engage in a wholesale redistribution of agricultural land, nor did he increase the opportunities for the nonwealthy to hold the highest political offices (*AP* 7.3). Considering the demos's desire to have more, the aristocrats got off easily and had most of their privileges preserved. Moreover, by regulating office holding through a new system of wealth-based classes (known as *telē*), Solon stabilized the elite by eliminating any exclusiveness based on birth (*AP* 7.3–4). At many levels, therefore, Solon was concerned with regulating the elite and with preserving elite unity.[43]

On the other hand, the demos received unambiguous benefits of its own: Solon reenlisted men who had been enslaved; he banned debt bondage (*AP* 6.1; Plut. *Sol.* 15.3); he provided for legal appeals to a court of ordinary Athenian citizens (*AP* 9.1; Plut. *Sol.* 18.2); and, above all, he "freed the black Earth" of its marker stones (*AP* 12.4, fr. 36.3–7), which arguably means that he abolished the premonetary obligations owed to the elite by sharecroppers of some sort, who were known as "sixth-parters" (*hektēmoroi*). Not all of this can be attributed to a concern with elite self-regulation.[44] Moreover, Solon provided for a probouleutic council that included ordinary citizens (*AP* 8.4; Plut. *Sol.* 19.1), and for the demos's own scrutiny of magistrates after their term of office (Arist. *Pol.*

with its own group interests" (Eder 1986, 292, speaking especially of the Solonian reform and the Twelve Tables at Rome). Contrast Wallace 1997, 11: "Solon himself established Athens's first democratic constitution, from amid a popular revolutionary movement that was by no means unique in Greece and under intense political pressure from ordinary people, many of whose perspectives he shared." For a judicious overview of the controversy, and its interpretation in a vast range of modern scholarship, see Rhodes 1981.

[43] The view that Solon's reform primarily benefited the elite has gained ground recently; see Eder 1986, Osborne 1996, Foxhall 1997, Mitchell 1997; cf. Aristotle *Politics* 1274a15–21.

[44] For the traditional picture of a more democratically inclined Solon, see Linforth 1919; Hignett 1952, 102–9; Ehrenberg 1973, 56–73; Forrest 1966, 160–74; Murray 1993, 181–200; and now Wallace 1997.

1274a15–17, 1281b32–34; cf. Isoc. 7.26, 12.147).[45] The picture that emerges is thus neither of a solely aristocratic Solon nor of an altogether democratic Solon, but rather that of a reformer who geared his provisions precisely in order to benefit different groups in Athens who had qualitatively different interests at the time of the reform.

Perhaps Solon's most important law was his outlawing of debt bondage. By enacting this measure, Solon rigorously defined the Athenian citizen body and created the Attica of small landholders found in the classical period. In other words, Solon aimed to preserve Athens specifically through the creation of solidarity based on citizenship.[46] Thus, his reform amounted to nothing less than the creation of a genuinely political sphere in Athens, where, during the seventh century, the elite had successfully rejected the newly collective polis ethic that was then developing throughout central Greece.[47] Ian Morris has argued persuasively that Athens embarked on the path to becoming a polis in ca. 750 but then reversed this trend ca. 700, when the elite reinstituted a social and political organization resembling that of ninth-century Attica, with a "distinct elite and a dependent peasantry."[48] Solon's reform helped undo this elitist, prepolitical social structure by legally defining the Athenian citizen body and ensuring that Athenians entered into relationships with one another specifically as citizens. By formally defining the citizen body, Solon ruled out the possibility that the rich could acquire their social inferiors as slaves. He thus also defined proper and improper realms of acquisition within Attica. Accordingly, it might be said, Solon refounded the Athenian polis after the polis ideal was in abeyance for over a century.

What pressures culminated in the need for such wide-ranging measures both to regulate elite competition, to create elite unity, and to guarantee privileges, especially citizenship, for the demos? First, in early sixth-century Athens, the demos was much more assertive than the weak assembly of Homer's poems; instead of remaining a potential power factor, it had become an actual source of power, possibly capable of supporting a tyrant. That the demos could exert pressure is indicated by a reform from which it benefited; considering the range of Solon's reforms, it is difficult to see why any benefits would have been given to the lower classes unless they demanded them, and unless they had the power to insist. Their power may have consisted in their ability to support a tyrant. After all, Peisistratus rose to power, some thirty years later, on the

[45] See Wallace 1989, 53–54; 1997, 18.

[46] Manville 1990, 124–56; Morris 1987, 205–10.

[47] For an overview of seventh-century Attic archaeology, see Morris 1987, 57–217; 1998, 1–91; Osborne 1989.

[48] Morris 2000, 302; cf. Morris 1987.

strength of his leadership of the demotic "men of the hill" (Hdt. 1.59.3; *AP* 13.4). Because the aristocracy wanted to maintain its power for as long as possible, it had a strong interest in limiting social unrest, even if that meant making certain concessions to the demos.

Second, the archaeological record indicates that Solon legislated during a donnybrook of materialistic elite competition, which had lasted since at least 700. The context for Athens's elite competition was its political and administrative conservatism during the seventh century: unlike other political units of central Greece, the Athenians did not adopt hoplite warfare, or participate in colonization, or build monumental temples. In Attica, the focus of conspicuous elite display was still at tombs, rather than at major sanctuaries.[49] While the rest of central Greece saw a shift in dedications away from graves to public sanctuaries, which marked the rise of a newly collective ethic, Attica did not develop monumental religious architecture until around 600 or shortly thereafter. Seventh-century Athenian burials, moreover, point to the existence of an elite burying group that used primary cremation in imposing shaft graves as a means to assert status. This method of disposal is a self-consciously archaizing reference to both the Attic past and to Homeric burial, and it linked the Attic elite with heroes and outstandingly wealthy foreign men, who also began to dispose of their dead in ostentatious ways at precisely this period.[50] Tomb display could take a variety of forms, including mounds, the construction of mudbrick tombs with painted plaques, funerary markers surmounted by sphinxes, and, by 600, stone sculptures.[51] These monuments got more elaborate and ostentatious over the course of the seventh century, as Attica saw a trend toward monumentality outside the grave.[52]

Most importantly, members of the Attic elite began to destroy elaborate banquet services in nearby offering trenches outside the grave; the pottery, with its protomes and figurines, was designed to call to mind precious metals and ivory, while the banquet setting itself recalled the banquets characteristic of the *Odyssey*. As Houby-Nielsen has written, "the deliberate destruction of the banquet service can then be said to have denoted an extraordinary, heroic male *mnema* [memorial], involving

[49] Morris 1987, 191; Whitley 1994, 58; Osborne 1989. De Polignac (1995, 81–88) also shows that Athens, in another unusual move, maintained the "traditional monocentric concept of the city" (88), as opposed to the bipolar religious organization arising throughout much of Greece in the archaic period.

[50] Houby-Nielsen 1992, 352–54; Morris 2000, 292–305. Houby-Nielsen (1992, 353) points to similarly ostentatious graves in Gordion in Phrygia and Salamis in Cyprus, as well as the "princely tombs" of Italy in the seventh century B.C.

[51] Morris 1998, 19, 31–32; Houby-Nielsen 1992; 1995; Morris 1987, 128–39.

[52] Whitley 1994, 54.

the destruction of property of precious metals and ivory, and to have expressed the status of the dead man as head of a household with the right and power to give a banquet."[53] These elaborate deposits put a fine point on Solon's complaint that the leaders of the community "do not know how to order the merriment of their present banquet in peace" (*parousas / euphrosunas kosmein daitos en hēsuchiēi*; fr. 4.9–10)—a verse that brings the Panhellenic vocabulary of civic disruption home to conservative Attica in a particularly incisive way.[54] The archaeological record displays the fruits of aristocratic greed, which drove members of the elite to desire more and more in order to win points over their rivals.[55] In particular, the use of Homeric forms of self-expression is an ideological move purporting to show that Attic aristocrats had the same foreign ties, lifestyle, and importance within their societies that Homeric heroes had within the Homeric poems. Through their conspicuous display, elite Athenians tried to claim for themselves the status of Homeric heroes.

Their claim had more than symbolic overtones. Cultivating the look of Homeric chieftains or kings (*basileis*) is appropriate for aristocrats who, like the Homeric heroes, squeezed their community for wealth in order to compete with other aristocrats in the various modes of elite display. Solon's poetry emphasizes that the leaders of the Athenian community, unable to satisfy their greed or control their extravagant expenditure, took to stealing from others and from the polis itself (frr. 4.7–13, 4c, 4b)—no doubt with a view to demonstrating their power and superiority over other aristocrats both inside and outside Athens.[56] Edward Harris has argued persuasively that Attic elites resembled the overlords of Homer and Hesiod, who "receive gifts from local inhabitants in exchange for protection against outside aggressors and for maintaining order internally."[57] The Athenian aristocrats were exploiting a protection

[53] Houby-Nielsen 1992, 357.

[54] For the specific vocabulary, see Nagy 1985, 59–60. On Solon's poetry as possibly Panhellenic, see n.64.

[55] By giving evidence of elite one-upmanship, the archaeological record corroborates our only other fleeting testimony to early Athenian politics—Cylon's attempted coup and Drakon's laws, which illustrate the importance of family rivalries and the violent backlash against individual families, such as the Alcmaeonids, as well as the lawgiver Drakon's attempt to provide some measure of elite self-regulation; Seaford (1994, 92–102, 106–9) offers a fascinating picture of violent elite rivalry in the Cylonian period, which was closely related to family loyalties; Osborne (1996, 186–90) argues convincingly that Drakon's code is, like the seventh-century law at Dreros (ML 2), an elite attempt at self-regulation, concerned primarily with procedure and with separating offices from individuals. Elite rivalries may well have been excited further by trade in wine and oil carried in Attic SOS amphorae, which appear in increasing numbers throughout the Aegean in the late seventh century: see Johnston and Jones 1978.

[56] Qviller (1981) makes a similar argument about the Homeric heroes.

[57] Harris 1997, 108.

racket: examples from the *Odyssey* (13.13–15, 19.194–98) show that aristocrats like Alcinous and Odysseus's lying Cretan king collect contributions from their communities in order to give lavish gifts to their guest friends (*xenoi*).[58] In Solon's Athens, the elites milked their dependents in order to compete with other aristocrats. As intra-elite competition intensified, so too did the economic difficulties of the dependent poor—a dynamic that led to social unrest and the appointment of Solon. Hence, Solon's reform grew out of circumstances in which elite greed and competition were threatening to destroy Athens altogether.

Solon's concern with elite greed is illustrated by his attention to the amount of land an individual could acquire (Arist. *Pol.* 1266b14–18)[59] and by his funeral legislation, which attempted to curb the elite competition that had generated greed in the first place.[60] Ironically, those Athenians who had more to begin with desired more and more in order to display superiority over their aristocratic rivals: "No limit of wealth [*ploutou d'ouden terma*] is clearly laid down for men; for those of us who now have the greatest livelihood [*pleiston . . . bion*] have twice as much eagerness [*diplasion speudousi*]; who could satisfy all [*tis an koreseien hapantas*]?" (fr. 13.71–73). At the same time, Solon also carefully avoided indulging the demos in its desire to get more. He did not carry out a full redistribution of land, but he did put the individual's ownership of land on a firmer basis and limited the possibility of elite encroachment.[61] Like Hesiod, Solon believed that land, and wealth in general, are the gifts of the gods and should be considered an aspect of *moira*, the individual's lot in life; consequently, the distribution of land should not be significantly altered either by the greedy rich or the greedy poor, or by the reformer himself.[62] Solon exempted himself from the partisan conflicts of elite and demos in an attempt to create solidarity in Athens and to educate Athenian citizens to identify with the polis.

What verdict did antiquity offer on Solon's reform? Plutarch (*Sol.* 5.2) preserves an anecdote in which the sage Anacharsis disparaged the law code: "Anacharsis . . . laughed at Solon for thinking that he could restrain the citizens' injustice and greed [*adikias kai pleonexias*] by means of written laws, which were very similar to spider's webs: he said that they would hold the weak who might get entangled, but would be torn to

[58] Harris 1997, 109.

[59] Ruschenbusch 1966, fr. 66; Manville (1990, 131) rightly points out that Solon's measures were not imposed retroactively: there is no evidence that Solon broke up preexisting large estates.

[60] Plutarch *Solon* 21; Diogenes Laertius 1.55; Parker (1996, 48–50) offers a judicious interpretation of Solon's regulation of private funerals; cf. Seaford 1994, 74–92.

[61] Manville 1990, 130–32.

[62] On Solon's view of divinely ordained distribution, see Vlastos 1946, 76–77.

pieces by the rich and the powerful." Anacharsis turned out to be right, but, more significantly for us, his reaction to Solon's law code suggests that something beyond a new law code is needed if political change is actually to be effected. Indeed, as Aristotle observes (*Pol.* 1294a3–8), good government (*eunomia*) requires not only well-made laws, but also the citizens' willingness to obey them. Willingness to accept the law can be won only if the law code captures widely shared sentiments within the community about politics, social hierarchy, and justice; that is, only if the laws express a prevailing, and shared, political ideology.[63] Enter Solon's poetry—which tried to encourage Athenians to accept a certain set of beliefs about the necessity of eliminating greed and injustice from Athens, in favor of civic solidarity. Solon's idealistic poetry failed to win acceptance in the short term, but it did provide a moralistic, oppositional language to Athenian greed that would remain important throughout the archaic and classical periods.[64]

Solon's Critique: The Problem of Acquisition and Unfairness

Solon's poetry sets the themes of the reform in high relief. In particular, Solon presents himself as responding to the Athenian crisis from an unaffiliated, impartial standpoint, which took the interests of the entire polis as its key criterion of value. In order to promote the interests of the polis, Solon criticized the greed and injustice of both rich and poor, and he urged that self-restraint and fair-mindedness were the central virtues of a political life in common. As in his reform, so too in his poetry: Solon emerges as a patriotic, non-partisan poet and legislator who criticizes the vices that threatened to destroy Athens altogether.

As a result, Solon's poetry occupies a number of points on the ideological spectrum and cannot be easily pinned down as "elitist" or "egalitar-

[63] The term "ideology" has been used in a variety of ways in recent scholarship. For discussion of its relevance in the present context, see Ober 1989, 38–40; Rose 1997, 155–66.

[64] Gregory Nagy has argued that "the figure of the Archaic poet represents a cumulative synthesis of a given city-state's poetic traditions. . . . If this theory is tantamount to calling the Archaic poet a 'myth,' then so be it, provided that *myth* can be understood as a given society's codification of its own traditional values in narrative and dramatic form." See Nagy 1990b, 436; cf. Nagy 1996, 207–225; Nagy 1985 applies the model to Theognis. The model suits Theognis's poetry well, but in my opinion Solon was a historical lawgiver who composed poetry in the context of a specific crisis. There may have been later accretions to his corpus, but the fragments that I consider are specific enough to link them to an actual poet and lawgiver. A separate but related question is the Panhellenism of archaic poetry, which Nagy (1990b, 52–115) argues for. Even if Solon's poetry attempted to suit itself to a Panhellenic audience, it inevitably had particular implications in the social crises of early sixth-century Athens.

ian."[65] Rather, it gives evidence of a continuing process of ideological negotiation in early sixth-century Athens. Kurke has argued that the poetry of Theognis represents "the synchronic reflection of a period of contestation or negotiation between the two [elitist and egalitarian] ideologies."[66] My contention is that Solon's poetry, like Theognis's, reflects an engagement with the multiple ideological stances available at the time of the reform.[67] Although Solon articulates ideas that variously support either elitist or egalitarian positions, his underlying focus is on enforcing the distribution of power and resources that will lead to stability.[68] In the process, Solon established the critique of one's opponents as the dominant mode of ideological discourse in Athens.

In the poem later known as "Eunomia" (fr. 4), Solon stresses that the greed and injustice of the city's leaders are responsible for the crisis. In contrast to the conflict between Achilles and Agamemnon, two heroic individuals, Solon's focus is on the civil dispute between the few and the many:

> The citizens themselves are willing to destroy a great city through their folly [*aphradiēisin*], persuaded by wealth [*chrēmasi*], and the intent of the leaders of the community [*dēmou . . . hēgemonōn*] is unjust,[69] since they are ready to suffer many pains because of their great hubris; for they do not know how to restrain

[65] I take these terms from Morris (1996; 2000, 155–91), who argues that archaic poetry in general is informed by competing "elitist" and "egalitarian" ideological viewpoints. On the one hand, he argues, elitist poets utilized luxury goods and contacts with the East in order to highlight their superiority to the average citizen; on the other hand, egalitarian poets rejected elite self-importance and insisted on the primacy of the polis. For further exploration of this view, see Kurke 1992, 1999; Mazzarino 1947.

[66] Kurke 1999, 28. Morris (2000, 157–61) refines his earlier model by observing that "Each poet might occupy not a point on this spectrum [from elitist to egalitarian] but a span of its length, overlapping with areas occupied by other poets."

[67] Cf. Bowie 1986, 20, who writes of fr. 4a: "This suggests an elegy in which, probably written within an expository framework where Solon *did* speak in his own person, one set of sentiments was encapsulated as the views of the rich addressed to the *mesoi* and another as the views of the *mesoi* addressed to the rich."

[68] This view contrasts with the argument of Kurke (1992, 94), who writes, "And as *nouveaux riches* non-aristocrats acquire the wealth to compete in the different arenas of display, money is no longer the distinguishing factor: style of expenditure becomes all-important." This type of issue does not arise in Solon's poetry, which does create distinctions according to possession of money (and power); this is the basis of the Solonian reform. Kurke does not deal with Solon in that article, but Solon's poetry illustrates the difficulties in making generalizations about "elitist" ideology. Solon's poetry shows that elitist ideology, as well as egalitarian ideology, could be deeply concerned with the polis itself, and that it too developed critiques of other classes as a central feature of its own discourse.

[69] Nagy (1985, 43), following Donlan 1970, 388–90, argues convincingly that "demos" here means simply "community," while the "leaders" are not champions of the demos or democracy, but rather the oligarchs in control of the community. The translation here is adapted from Nagy 1985, 59.

> their greed [*koron*][70] or to order their present merriment in the serenity of a feast; . . . and they become rich, swayed by deeds without justice . . . sparing neither sacred nor public property, they steal from one another by forcible seizure [*apharpagēi*], nor do they respect the holy institutions of Justice [*Dikēs*], who silently observes what is and what has been, and who will in the future come to exact retribution. (fr. 4.5–16)[71]

Anhalt has argued persuasively that the poem's opening lines suggest "an analogy between Athens with its internal troubles and a city at risk from external enemies."[72] The city's leaders treat Athens as if it were a foreign conquest, and as if the city's goods should be seen as spoils that justly belong to the victors. Solon presents civil strife as *polemos* (external war) rather than as *stasis* (internal conflict) and in doing so he recasts traditional, especially Homeric, treatments of city sacking by external enemies.[73]

In the Greek world, victors typically kill or enslave the vanquished; if they opt for the latter, then they either sell their captives for profit or take them back to their own countries as booty. Solon conjures up the possibility of enslavement of free Athenians by reporting that many of the city's poor "go as slaves into a foreign land, bound by shameful fetters" (fr. 4.23–25). According to Aristotle (*AP* 2.3), the poor felt that the potential for slavery was the bitterest aspect of their socioeconomic situation, although they also had other grounds of discontent; in Aristotle's words, "There was nothing, so to speak, in which they had a share [*oudenos . . . metechontes*]."[74] When Athenian elites sold Attica's poor into slavery, they implicitly rejected the idea that those they enslaved were full-bodied members of their own community, treating them rather as the vanquished. According to Solon's law code, however, this is a category mistake: no Athenian citizen should be treated as a foreign captive.[75] Solon therefore resists the overarching greed of Athens's leaders, who resemble Aristotle's tyrant in enslaving their fellow citizens in order to satisfy extravagant desires for power and wealth.

[70] In translating *koros* "greed," I follow the arguments of Anhalt 1993, 79–93; Helm 1993; see my subsequent discussion.

[71] In context Demosthenes cites this passage in order to vilify Aeschines for taking bribes from Philip in exchange for compromising Athenian interests. Demosthenes argues that the good of Athens as a whole depends on the demos's ability to supervise and restrict the greedy behavior of manipulative leaders. In the fourth century, democratic ideology used Solon's negative construction of elite behavior to reinforce the link between the good of the polis and the limitation and even punishment of elite greed (Cohen 1995, 112–14; Ober 1996b, 86–106).

[72] Anhalt 1993, 74.

[73] Anhalt 1993, 72–79; Loraux 1984, 199–214.

[74] The elite resembles Aristotle's tyrants in the *Politics*, whose greed drives them to plunder their own communities for all sorts of acquisition, both human and material.

[75] Ober 1989, 60–65; Manville 1990, 132–34.

By representing Athenian *stasis* (internal conflict) as *polemos* (external war), Solon frames the Athenian leaders' behavior as a threatening and destructive failure to occupy their appropriate roles as leaders of their community. Rather than protecting their city from external aggression, these perverse Athenian leaders have implicitly become the city's most dangerous enemy. According to traditional ethical viewpoints, it is the winners' prerogative to take home the spoils of victory, but when members of a group have legitimate claims on each other, as within a victorious army or in Solon's Athens, then an altogether different ethic applies. Principles of fair distribution must be observed in virtue of each individual's membership in the community. Thus, in order to underscore the Athenians' obligations to each other, Solon condemns the leaders' improper acquisition. By plundering Athens itself in order to satisfy their greed, the city's leaders behave according to an inappropriate, disruptive model of acquisition.

This interpretation gains strength when we see that seventh-century Athenian aristocrats tried to keep up with the many forms of extra-polis elite expression arising throughout Greece at this period. They participated in the Olympic games,[76] contracted marriage alliances with upper-class families of foreign cities (Cylon and Megacles),[77] forged ties of guest friendship (*xenia*) (Solon fr. 23), and held symposia.[78] Like Homeric heroes, they cultivated external connections as a source of prestige and legitimacy. Solon's polemic is directed against this elite's tendency to use Athens as a source of wealth from which it can draw in order to compete in the international arena. This is tantamount, Solon suggests, to acting like the foreign conqueror of one's own city! Solon's poetry makes a concerted attempt to teach all Athenians, including the elite, that their collective welfare depends on identification with the polis, rather than cultivation of extra-polis ties and rejection of the polis itself—or, differently, using the wealth of the polis in order to win international prestige.[79] Solon's "Eunomia" suggests that Athenian leaders abuse their power within the city for the sake of satisfying their insatiable desire to get more.[80]

[76] We hear of three Athenian Olympic victors in the seventh century: Cylon, Pantakles, and Stomas. For the latter two, see Moretti 1967, nos. 25–27, 54, with Morris 1984, 105.

[77] See Thucydides 1.126; Herodotus 6.126–30.

[78] Wallace 1997, 16; Murray 1993, 184–86.

[79] In his study of guest friendship (*xenia*), Herman (1987, 157) shows that the Greek elite often valued its extra-polis ties with other aristocrats over its loyalty to the polis: "Throughout Greek history, it was the community that arrayed itself against the one-time hero, against xenoi [elite guest friends] plotting its plundering, subjection and exploitation." Solon's poetry is in part aimed at combating this centrifugal tendency of the elite.

[80] As Nagy (1985, 43) has argued, "*hubris* and *stasis* are in the diction of Solon catchwords for the excesses of an oligarchy (fr. 3.8/34 GP [= frr. 4 and 6 W] and fr. 3.19 GP [= fr. 4

After securing citizen status for itself, however, the demos replicated the elite's abuse of power for the sake of destructive, self-interested advantage. After censuring the rich, Solon also criticizes the poor citizens, saying that, once they had identified a champion, they exhibited similar urges to take more than they deserve. Like the rich, the poor seek to plunder the state (fr. 34.1). If they had found a champion who mirrored their own acquisitive character, then they would have pursued every possible advantage under his leadership: "Had someone else taken the goad as I did, an unwise and greedy [*philoktēmōn*] man, he would not have restrained the demos" (fr. 36.20–22). Both rich and poor demonstrate the same potential to abuse power for the sake of satisfying their greed, but in Solon as in Aristotle the "greed" of the respective groups is conceived differently as one goes up the social scale. Whereas the poor are said to seek material goods primarily, the rich want to possess everything, including their fellow citizens. Both groups, however, are equally responsible for a failure to understand the proper role of power in politics. Whenever they have enough power to assert their will, both rich and poor alike take on the role of victors in war over Athens, rather than acting like responsible members of the Athenian political community.[81]

In his critique of the demos, Solon activates a strand of elitist thinking that can be fleshed out further by considering Theognis.[82] Because of the multiplicity of ideological stances found in Theognis, it is necessary in each case to elicit the particular viewpoint being voiced.[83] Like Solon, Theognis often concentrates on criticizing the excesses of particular groups within the state; Theognis tends to focus, however, specifically on people described as the "bad" or the "base" (*kakoi*). There is some blurring in Theognis's use of the term *kakos*, but in general his message is that greedy non-nobles have usurped the status and power once held by the Megarian aristocracy.[84] Theognis laments their suc-

W], respectively)"; cf. Donlan 1970; 1980, 68–74. For the view that these *hēgemones* are "popular leaders," see West 1974, 68.

[81] The *polemos* theme of fr. 4 is picked up in fr. 34: Solon says that because he restrained the acquisitive impulses of the poor, "all [of the poor] eye him askance as an enemy [*deion*]" (fr. 34.5).

[82] Nagy (1985, 33) has persuasively argued that Theognis is a persona that represents "a cumulative synthesis of Megarian poetic traditions." For problems of dating the Theognidea, see Cobb-Stevens, Figueira, and Nagy 1985. Contra West 1974, 65–71, who argues that Theognis's "career began in the 630's at the latest, and apparently extended over several decades" (70).

[83] Kurke 1999, 27–28.

[84] See, e.g., 53–60, 105–12, 145–48, 153–54, 183–96, 289–90, 315–18, 319–22, 383–87, 523–26, 667–79, 1117–18. The social identity of Theognis's *kakoi* is difficult to determine, and seems to shift depending on the passage in question. As Nagy (1985, 43–44) argues, the *kakoi* at 43–46 seem to be members of the aristocracy (the *hēgemones* [leaders] of line 41)

cess, and he persistently rebukes these non-aristocrats for their base striving after gain.

Theognis criticizes the greed of non-aristocrats by evoking the Homeric and Hesiodic conceptions of appropriate distribution. He rejects Megara's prevailing standard of distribution in his image of the *kakoi*'s seizure of control over the ship of state: "They have deposed the noble pilot, who skillfully kept watch, and they plunder the possessions by force [*chrēmata d' harpazousi biēi*]: and order [*kosmos*] is lost, and there is no longer a fair distribution [*dasmos . . . isos*] in the middle [*es to meson*]" (675–78). As we have seen, Detienne has shown that the notion of the "middle" (*es to meson*) had traditionally occupied a key role in communal institutions such as deliberative assemblies, booty distributions, and funerary games: "The significance of the center emerges clearly from the institutional forms operating both in the allocation of prizes and in the distribution of booty: the center means both 'that which is held in common' and 'that which is public.'"[85] Theognis's passage applies this traditional image to the division of goods within the political community, alleging that the *kakoi* (the "base") have seized power unjustly and now arbitrarily control both the deliberative process and the distribution of goods in Megara. Theognis's marked terminology of moral evaluation—plundering (*harpagē*), order (*kosmos*), fair distribution (*isos dasmos*), "the middle" (*es meson*)—provides insight into Solon's own conception of both demotic and elite greed.

Like Theognis, Solon adapts the older notions of distributive fairness and excessive acquisitiveness to fit them into the framework of his presentation of the Athenian political community.[86] Although Solon says that both rich and poor came forward in order to plunder their fatherland (frr. 4.13, 34.1), he adds that he himself observed fair standards of distribution in making his laws: "It gives me no pleasure to act by force of tyranny [*turannidos . . . biēi*], or that the base and noble should have an equal share of their rich fatherland [*oude pieirēs chthonos / patridos kakoisin esthlous isomoiriēn echein*]" (fr. 34.7–9). *Pieirēs* (fr. 34.8) literally means

who have fallen into *kakotēta* (depravity) (41–42), and hence do not uphold genuinely (and exclusively) aristocratic moral values. Their *hubris* will soon be punished by a corrector (*euthuntēr*), who perhaps should be identified with the tyrant Theagenes. On the other hand, at 53–60 and 1109–14, Theognis is clearly censuring non-nobles who have usurped the position of the nobility in the state by means of their acquisition of wealth, and this is surely the dominant "message" of Theognis's portrayal of the *kakoi*: cf. Donlan 1980, 77–82. On the fluctuation between the sociopolitical sense of these terms and the ethical sense, see Nagy 1985, 44n4; Donlan 1980, 78; Cobb-Stevens 1985, 159–65; Adkins 1972, 37–46.

[85] Detienne 1996, 95.

[86] On Solon's conception of justice, see further Vlastos 1946, but Vlastos does not bring his account into the intellectual framework of distributive justice in the archaic tradition, nor does he view Solon's conceptions as elements in ideological struggle.

"fat" and calls to mind the epithet *dēmoboros* (feeding fat on the people), which Achilles applied to Agamemnon. Solon exploits traditional poetic resources in order to point a connection between greed for wealth and gluttony, but in this poem he charges the demos rather than its leaders with possessing a ravenous hunger for more (cf. *AP* 12.3). According to Solon, the community's "fat" (*piar*) should be reserved for the rich, not mixed together with the rest of the milk (fr. 37.6–10). That different groups within the state should possess a certain differential level of the community's material resources is a matter of distributive justice. Solon does not explicitly describe the canons according to which he measures distributive fairness, but his language of "equal shares" and his commitment to unequal distributions for different classes prefigure the Aristotelian notion of proportional equality. As much as Solon disavows tyrannical ambitions, however, he himself is by implication uniquely capable of bringing just distribution to Athens—a trait characteristic of several tyrannical figures in the archaic period.[87]

Although the notion of fair distribution was deeply traditional, Solon frames the ideas of greed and injustice within an explicitly political, even humanistic context. By way of contrast, Hesiod envisions an unjust city that is destroyed by hubris, greed, and violence, which pervert true justice; but the agent of destruction is Zeus himself instead of civil strife (*WD* 238–47). As retribution for the wrongdoing of even a single person, Zeus visits famine, plague, and childlessness on the entire community (*WD* 242–45). Those who disregard justice are often motivated by the desire for wealth, but Hesiod warns that the watchful gods destroy those who acquire wealth unjustly: "Wealth [*chrēmata*] should not be plundered [*harpakta*]: that which is given by the gods is far better. For if someone takes great riches [*olbon*] violently [*chersi biēi*], or steals it with his tongue, which often happens when profit [*kerdos*] deceives the mind of men and shamelessness trampels down their shame, then the gods quickly make him powerless [*maurousi*], and make his house small, and wealth attends him only for a brief time" (*WD* 320–26).

Commentators have pointed out that whereas Hesiod emphasizes the watchfulness and retribution of the gods, Solon lays stress on the logical and human connections between greedy violations of justice and the destruction of the community by human agents themselves.[88] Solon, however, also retains features of Hesiod's divine framework within which justice is rendered as punishment: the long central section of his "Hymn to

[87] McGlew (1993, 87–123) insightfully analyzes Solon's position in comparison to other archaic lawgivers and to tyrants, especially Pittacus of Mytilene (94–98); compare the emphasis on straightness and impartiality in Theognis 331–32, 543–46, 805–10; cf. Nagy 1985, 37–38.

[88] See most recently Anhalt 1993, 32–33.

the Muses" (fr. 13.16–32) states emphatically that no wrongdoer escapes Zeus's notice (27) and that retribution always comes sooner or later (29–32). Solon has naturalized Hesiod's religious conception of justice as retribution, but his departure from the traditional religious conception should not be overestimated. In particular (and not surprisingly), he does not offer an altogether secular view of social justice like Aristotle's.

The major difference between Solon and Hesiod is rather that for Solon justice is a condition of social health within the polis that pertains to all citizens and is constituted by the relationships that exist between them. All Athenian citizens both owe their fellow citizens justice and are owed justice in virtue of their membership in the political community. This conception of justice further entails that any affront to the individual is also an affront to the entire community and that all citizens have a stake in the communal welfare.[89] This sentiment finds legal expression in Solon's law granting the right to any citizen to seek retribution on behalf of another (*AP* 9.1). Solon himself is responsible for determining fair standards of distribution by laying down the city's laws, but, as we shall see, he also stresses that each citizen is responsible for incorporating a sense of justice into his own self-image. Solon's conception of justice thus has a psychological depth and significance for political thought that cannot be found in earlier literature.[90]

For Hesiod, by contrast, justice is a gift from the gods to men; justice is something that Hesiod's kings receive from Zeus and then render unto others (*Theog.* 81–93). Human beings expect justice from the king because the king is Zeus's deputy and is responsible for enacting Zeus's justice on earth. This means that rather than being a defining feature of political identity, justice is for Hesiod a defining characteristic of humanity as opposed to animals: "For the son of Cronos has ordained this law for men [*anthrōpoisi*], that fish and wild beasts and winged birds eat one another, since justice [*dikē*] is not in them; but to human beings he gave justice [*dikēn*], which is by far the best" (*WD* 276–80).[91] Justice is owed to all alike, including strangers, in virtue of Zeus's ordinance, which serves our common humanity; it is by now predictable that, as Hesiod's unjust kings are "bribe-devouring," so too do his animals, lacking a sense of justice, eat one another as the most tangible sign of their injustice.[92] By

[89] The sentiment is captured by Plutarch's notice that Solon "wisely accustomed the citizens as members of one body to feel and sympathize with one another's wrongs" (*Sol.* 18). Advocates of modern philosophical liberalism will find this sentiment—and Solon's attempt to promote a primarily civic-based notion of identity—uncomfortable at best, because it appears to place serious constraints on individual self-determination. See Holmes 1979.

[90] Cf. Will 1958.

[91] Lamberton 1988, 121–24.

[92] As we will see in the next chapter, Herodotus also laid stress on Zeus's role in guaran-

contrast, Solon repeatedly emphasizes the notions of the city, citizens, demos and fatherland, and the destruction wrought by citizens on their community (frr. 4.5–6, 21, 32; 4a; 5.1; 6.1; 9.3–4; 32; 34.8–9; 36.25; 37.1). Although Solon retains Hesiod's religious framework to a certain extent, he has also begun to conceive of justice and injustice as features of the political relationship that pertains among citizens of Athens. Solon thus represents a bridge figure in the transition from poetry that imagines that justice, distribution, and social stability are divinely ordained to a specifically political mode of reflecting on precisely the same questions.[93]

Solon elsewhere expresses his conception of the appropriate distribution of goods in the language of booty distribution: "For I gave the demos as much privilege [*geras*] as is sufficient, neither adding to nor taking away from its honor; and those who had power and were admired for their wealth, I provided that these should suffer nothing shameful; and I stood with a strong shield thrown around both, and did not allow either to have an unjust victory [*nikan . . . adikōs*]" (fr. 5.1–6). Solon's mention of "unjust victory" presupposes a notion of fairness according to which each of the city's factions gets what it deserves. Solon's recognition of the just deserts of each group originates in acknowledgment of the demos's importance and power within the political community, but his resistance to elite oppression did not drive him to renounce his equally important aristocratic leanings.

The implications of Solon's statement can be drawn out more explicitly by examining the semantics of distributing prizes of honor in Homer. In Homer, the term *geras* means a "prize of honor, an honorific portion."[94] It refers to a material sign of recognition accorded an individual warrior (*Il.* 1.123, 276, 506–7; *Od.* 7.10, 11.534), such as a choice cut of meat, as at *Iliad* 7.319–22: "But when they had finished the work and prepared a feast, they feasted, nor was any man's hunger denied a fair portion [*daitos eïsēs*]; and Atreus's son, the hero wide-ruling Agamemnon, gave as *geras* [*gerairen*] to Ajax the long cuts of the chine's portion." It is widely accepted that Homer's notion of the *dais eïsē*, in the sense of fair apportionment at a feast, is emblematic of fair distribution in general. This connection is strengthened by the etymological associations between *dais* (banquet) and the verb *daiomai*, "to divide, apportion, distrib-

teeing distributive justice throughout the world, but Solon's more secular and specifically communal conception again becomes prominent in Thucydides and later political thinkers.

[93] Because coinage was introduced in Athens long after Solon's archonship (cf. Rhodes 1981, 167–68), it is possible to date this transition earlier than the introduction of coinage in Athens. Von Reden (1995) and Kurke (1999, 3–37) helpfully discuss the importance of coinage in the politics and social imaginary of archaic Greece.

[94] On *geras*, see Nagy 1979, 132–33; Anhalt 1993, 100–101.

ute."[95] Solon's use of the term *geras* shows both that he offers due recognition to the demos as a political force within Athens, and that he conceives of this due recognition as part of the distributive fairness that he tries to institute in settling Athenian strife.

If Solon's evocation of Homeric distribution lends the authority of tradition to his poetry, then his novel uses of the terms *dais* (banquet) and *koros* (satiety, greed) make his political redefinition of the relationship between greed and injustice explicit. As we have seen, Solon reproaches the leaders of Athens for their failure to check their greed (*koron*) and their inability to order the merriment (*euphrosunas*) of the banquet (*daitos*) in peace (fr. 4.9–10). Read in conjunction with the Homeric notion of *dais eïsē*, these lines indict the Athenian leaders' excessive greed, which violates the standards of distribution implicit in the *dais*; in this passage as elsewhere, the *dais* operates as a paradigm for civic distribution generally.[96] Scholars typically connect this passage with the parallels that Theognis draws between polis and symposium, but there is an important distinction between Solon's *dais* and Theognis's symposium as models of civic relations.[97] For one thing, as Anhalt observes, Solon implicitly criticizes the symposium paradigm for failing "to account for the fact that, in the polis, members of all levels of society will necessarily be present, not only the aristocrats."[98] This interpretation is strengthened by the archaeological evidence for elite use of incinerated banquet services at funerals, which were meant to call to mind the exclusionary banquets of the Homeric elite. Writing in a traditional, possibly Panhellenic idiom, Solon brings home to Athens the disruption caused by exclusive elite banqueting.

Moreover, and more importantly, as Theognis's lengthy description of proper comportment in the symposium reveals (467–96), immoderation in the symposium is censured because of the disruptive behavior it causes, rather than for its violation of justice. After drinking too much, people break cups, they say inappropriate things, they destroy tables by dancing on them. Nowhere in his description of symposiastic disruption does Theognis accuse the drunkard of injustice; excess in the symposium

[95] On *dais isē*, see Motto and Clark 1969; on the semantics of *dais* and *daiomai* in general, see Nagy 1979, 56–57, 123–39, 214–15. The image of fair apportionment at a banquet contrasts with the earlier accusations that Agamemnon gluttonously devours his own community, violating the custom of distributing spoils fairly.

[96] The use of the ceremonial banquet as a paradigm of civic equality is well known in the archaic period: see Nagy 1990a, 269–75; Schmitt-Pantel 1990, 14–15.

[97] On parallels between polis and symposium, see Levine 1985, 176–91; Anhalt 1993, 91–98.

[98] Anhalt 1993, 93.

is a violation of temperance and then of decorum, not a transgression of principles of fairness or justice.[99]

In Solon's new vision of the Athenian polis, on the other hand, goods belong to other citizens and, prior to that, to the community as a whole, and the aristocrats' excessive grasping violates the legitimate claims that others have on their own, and on the community's, possessions. The community's leaders have no respect for "possessions either sacred or private" (fr. 4.12). When placed in the civic context, as opposed to the symposium, immoderation and greed retain the shamefulness associated with lack of self-control, but elicit additional moral disapproval because these vices violate the just claims of other citizens, along with the prior commitments and obligations that pertain among political actors within a single polis. Hence Solon refers to *dais* rather than symposium because of the importance of distinguishing between contexts in which fair distribution occupies a place of ethical primacy, and contexts where the ethical focus is temperance and self-control rather than justice. Although Theognis elsewhere conceptualizes justice in the community in terms of fair distribution of the community's resources (e.g., 605–6), he does not connect the *isos dasmos*, or distributive fairness, with the explicit discussion of the ethics of the symposium.

Solon thus describes and condemns his fellow citizens' greed in the traditional language of distributive fairness. This language enables him to offer a compelling psychological analysis of Athenian greed, which will remain influential throughout Athenian political thought, and which sheds light on the solutions that Solon later proposes. The basis of this psychological analysis is a claim about human nature in general. Solon frames a well-known passage in fragment 13 by emphasizing the generality of his psychological analysis: "We mortal men [*thnētoi*], both noble [*agathos*] and common [*kakos*] alike, think this way" (fr. 13.33). In the framework provided by this generalization, Solon proposes that human beings are universally acquisitive and that possession of wealth actually

[99] In a discussion of the relative importance of the *dais* and the symposium as models for civic institutions, Schmitt-Pantel (1990) concludes that both *dais* and symposium play significant roles as paradigms for civic institutions in the archaic polis. The evidence cited by Schmitt-Pantel does, however, support the ethical distinctions between *dais* and symposium that I draw in the text. Book 1 of Plato's *Laws* also makes clear that self-control and the lack of self-control are the key ethical issues associated with the symposium, not justice and injustice. It is true that the elected symposiarch would determine the proportion and quantity of wine given to each guest (cf. Levine 1985, 176n1), but it is striking that surviving discussions of the ethics of the symposium from both archaic and classical periods focus on self control, not fairness. On the symposium in general, see Murray (1990), who emphasizes the symposium as an anti-polis, a place separated from the ordinary rules of the (egalitarian) polis ethos.

increases desire, rather than satisfying it:[100] "One hastens after one thing, another after something else; one man, desiring to bring home profit, wanders over the fishy sea in ships . . . another, whose concern is the curved plow, cleaves the thickly wooded land and slaves away for a year . . . but no limit of wealth [*ploutou d' ouden terma*] is clearly laid down for men; for those of us who now have the greatest livelihood [*pleiston . . . bion*], have twice the eagerness [*diplasion speudousi*]; who can satisfy [*ko-reseien*] all?" (fr. 13.43–45, 47–48, 71–73).

The key term in Solon's analysis is *koreseien*, a verb that means "to satisfy" or "to fill up to the limit"; but in these lines Solon claims that, because no limit is fixed for the acquisition of wealth, no satisfaction or sense of fullness (*koros*) can be achieved. Elsewhere, *koros* is a force of excess desire that needs to be checked or stopped before it destroys Athens (fr. 4.9, 34). Similarly, Theognis sometimes uses *koros* in a desiderative, and negative, sense to mean "greed, excessive desire for more" (605–6, 693–94).[101] These uses are distinctive within the tradition of archaic poetry.[102] In all other archaic poets, *koros* refers to the satisfaction of physical desires, such as the desire for food or sleep. But because the desire for wealth, with which Solon and Theognis are especially concerned, has no inherent physiological limits, the community itself must impose "objective" limits on this desire, rather than making the individual alone responsible for regulating his desires.[103] The communal regulation of acquisition sets limits to individual desire in a way that the self-interested individual's own perceptions and (often misguided) judgment cannot. In his discussion of acquisition in the *Politics* (1256b31–34), Aristotle contests Solon's verse by arguing that a limit *has* been fixed in the acquisition of wealth, because the proper art of acquisition is subordinate to the tasks of the householder and the statesman (1256b34–39; cf. chapter 2). Even so, Aristotle's subsequent discussion of the improper art of acquisition reveals that Solon's concern for the collective regulation or management of excessive individual desire is not out of place; indeed, Aristotle's own analysis shows that few if any historical agents actually recognized, much less abided by, the fixed limits that he himself sees as natural. Moreover, Aristotle fully supports Solon's acknowledgment that self-interested individuals and groups characteristically make unethical judgments in relation to other groups and the whole community—hence

[100] The idea that the possession of wealth actually increases greed is well known from fourth-century oratory: see, e.g., Demosthenes 45.

[101] Theognis does, however, also use the verb *korennumi* in the traditional sense "to satisfy"; see 229, 1249, 1269.

[102] Anhalt 1993, 79–93; Helm 1993.

[103] Anhalt 1993, 92–93.

the need for a Solon to instruct the Athenians on appropriate forms of self-restraint and suitable standards of distributive fairness.

Framing Solon's interests as a concern to limit desiderative *koros* correctly emphasizes his concern with individual insatiability and with the need to limit desire for the sake of communal well-being. In Solon's presentation, however, the community's welfare and stability also depend on the Athenian citizens' willingness to observe fair standards of distribution. For Solon, insatiability is a special form of communal evil because it drives the greedy to violate distributive justice. In terms of our earlier analysis of Aristotle, Solon has forged a connection between the two central "pillars" of greed: unchecked desire, the first pillar, drives those who lack self-control to commit violations of distributive fairness, the second pillar.

This point is significant because it is possible to misunderstand Solon's emphasis on moderation and self-restraint. Speaking of the transformation of *koros* between Homer and Solon, for example, Helm has argued as follows: "There is an increasing awareness of the dark side of abundance. This metamorphosis (of the noun *koros* in particular) mirrors a shift in perspective from the Homeric struggle for survival to an emphasis on limit and moderation in the face of relatively more abundant means. It anticipates the later Greek philosophical emphasis on moderation."[104] This is a plausible reading, but it does not adequately convey the significance of Solonian *koros* for the Athenian discourse on greed. Solon uses the language of *koros* in order to articulate the key insight that immoderation in the context of communal distribution is a violation of justice, and that this combination (later expressed by Aristotle's term *pleonexia*) is specifically the problem that plagues Athens. However prosperous Athens becomes, each citizen deserves a fair share of that prosperity in virtue of his membership in the political community. If citizens do not receive a fair share, then Athens will be destroyed by internal conflict.

These connections between acquisition and injustice are made explicit in the beginning of the so-called "Hymn to the Muses," where Solon prays for prosperity (*olbon*) and a good reputation (*doxan*) from the gods (fr. 13.1–4), emphasizing that genuine prosperity is necessarily acquired justly and from the gods: "I desire to have wealth [*chrēmata*], but I do not want to possess it unjustly; *Dikē* [Justice] comes assuredly afterward. Wealth which the gods give, remains with a man from the bottom to the top, whereas wealth which men honor with violence [*huph' hubrios*] does not come in order [*ou kata kosmon*], but follows unwillingly and persuaded by unjust deeds [*adikois ergmasi*]" (fr. 13.7–13). This passage illus-

[104] Helm 1993, 11; North 1966, 12–16.

trates the enduring religious background to Solon's thinking about acquisition, which involves the standard opposition between *hubris* and *dikē* in archaic poetry.[105] As in the later classical discourse on greed, *hubris* and greed (*koros*) are closely related but not identical: for Solon *hubris* is the offspring of *koros* (fr. 6.3–4; cf. Theog. 153–54) and denotes the lack of respect and attempt to dishonor that usually, though not always, attend the activity of taking more than one's share.[106] That these two concepts are conceptually distinguished by Solon is shown not only by the specific genealogical relationship he assigns to them, but also by Aristotle's quotation (or possibly paraphrasing) of the opening of another elegy in which Solon says he fears the greed (*philochreian*) and arrogance (*huperēphanian*) of the rich (fr. 4b).[107]

Although the relationship between *hubris* and *koros* has received considerable scholarly attention in recent years, two points have not received due consideration. First, although Solon uses *koros* in the desiderative sense of "greed" (e.g., fr. 4.9), he also uses it in the sense of "fullness, satiety," as in fragment 4c.1–2: "Calm the strong heart in your breast, you who have had more than your fill [*koron*] of many good things." *Koros* may also mean "satiety" in Solon's claim that "*Koros* breeds *hubris* whenever great wealth (*olbos*) comes to those whose mind is not sound" (fr. 6.3–4). If *koros* is the state reached when much prosperity has been won, then this fragment implies that those who possess more than they can handle typically become arrogant toward their less prosperous fellows.

Reading *koros* as "satiety" alongside *koros* as "greed," (fr. 4.8–10), we arrive at a seemingly unending cycle of *koros* and *hubris*: overabundance generates disrespect for others and contempt for what one already possesses, both of which inspire the individual to pursue greedy satisfactions;

[105] Recent critics have downplayed the importance of the gods in Solon's conception of justice, acquisition, and social relations, in an attempt to demonstrate Solon's "naturalism": see most recently Anhalt 1993, 57–65, 113–14, which develops lines of interpretation first laid down by Jaeger 1943–45, 1:135–49, and Vlastos 1946, 65–67. For the traditional opposition between *hubris* and *dikē*, see esp. Nagy 1985, 51–63. On the semantics of *hubris* and *koros*, see my subsequent discussion; on the relationship between *hubris* and greed in the later tradition, see chapter 4, where I argue that although the two terms are often related psychologically, their focus and context in moral thought become more and more distinct in the late fifth and fourth centuries, until we reach Aristotle's *Politics*, where they are clearly distinguished; for Aristotle's separation of the terms, see Cairns 1996, 5–6.

[106] See also frr. 4.8–10, 34; 4c for combinations of *hubris*, *koros*, and related terms. On the relations between *koros*, *hubris*, and *atē* in Solon and Theognis, see North 1966, 14–20; Fisher 1992, 70–74, 206–14; Nagy 1985, 59–61; Anhalt 1993, 79–96; for genealogies of these terms, see Doyle 1970; Michelini 1978, 36–40.

[107] Fr. 4.34–37 makes a similar link between *koros*, *hubris*, and *huperēphana . . . erga* (deeds of pride), but equally shows that these notions should be kept distinct at least in discussions of Solon. For discussion of the status of fr. 4b, see West's edition (1992, 143–44); Rhodes 1981, 125; Fisher 1992, 71.

but greed itself, if it successfully achieves its goal, leads in turn to further degrees of fullness, which sets the cycle in motion once again.[108] If successful, greed keeps reproducing itself through a specific psychological feedback loop. This psychological process explains why those with an abundance of wealth hasten to get more twice as eagerly as others (fr. 13.71–73).[109] Solon thus reformulates standard archaic moral terminology in order to provide a unique psychological analysis of the mechanisms by which greed is motivated and perpetuated within the Athenian community. This analysis deepens his claim that human beings are by nature acquisitive by explaining how human nature can be expected to play out in psychological processes and in behavior.

The second point I want to make is that Solon's use of *koros* terminology again demonstrates his impartiality in criticizing both rich and poor. Both rich and poor alike are equally prone to *koros* and equally guilty of behaving unjustly in the state. Aristotle says that Solon is explicitly warning of the dangers of giving the poor too much when he voices the sentiment that "*Koros* breeds *hubris* whenever great wealth [*olbos*] comes to those whose mind is not sound [*artios*]" (fr. 6.3–4).[110] Conversely, he also warns of the *koros* of the rich in senses of both "greed" (fr. 4.8–10) and "fullness" (fr. 4c). If these statements break down an ideological distinction between rich and poor by criticizing both groups for *koros*, then, through repetition of the key term *artios* (sound, exactly fitted, suitable), these lines also suggest a possible solution to the problem of *koros* that applies equally to rich and poor.

When the rich have "have had more than [their] fill [*koron*] of many good things," Solon says, they must become moderate, for "these things will not be suitable [*artia*] for you" (fr. 4c.1–4). When the rich have reached the point of overabundance and still want more, then their unjust, immoderate behavior does not sit well with themselves or the rest of

[108] Cf. Michelini 1978, who, through analyzing the use of *hubris* in relation to plants, illustrates that *koros* and *hubris* are causally connected at the physical, as well as the psychological, level.

[109] Hence, whereas some others (e.g., Michelini 1978, 36n5; Dickie 1984, 108–9) have tended to see a virtual equivalence or interchangeability in *hubris* and *koros*, I argue that attention to their specific uses in Solon and other authors might illuminate the complexities, and the differences, in these authors' presentations of psychological processes associated with these terms; my view thus shares certain elements with that of Anhalt 1993, 79–96.

[110] The sentiment may be compared with Theognis's claim that "*koros* begets *hubris* when prosperity [*olbos*] comes to a base [*kakōi*] man whose mind is not sound" (153–54). Again we see Solon expressing an anti-poor sentiment, which is then made more explicit in Theognis's vociferous attack on the *kakoi*. If Aristotle is to be trusted, then we should not distinguish too sharply between these two passages of Solon and Theognis; cf. Anhalt 1993, 95–97.

the citizen body, since their gains are ill-gotten. According to Solon, what makes everything in the state "well ordered" and "sound" (*eukosma kai artia*) is "good rule" [*Eunomiē*] (fr. 4.32). Social health, the condition in which political affairs are balanced in equilibrium, is the result of individual citizens' possession of an appropriate civic and ethical outlook, a well-ordered mind (*noos artios*, cf. fr. 6.3–4), especially in relation to the acquisition of wealth. The soundness of the political order, in short, depends on the soundness of the individual moral consciousness of citizens.

Solon's poetry thus maps out the social crisis in Athens by offering a compelling reformulation of traditional concepts of individual desire and distributive fairness. It sets these notions within a self-consciously political context, which "naturalizes" Solon's conception of justice and political relations. A proper understanding of the political situation is the precondition of Solon's attempt to alleviate social discord. Like his law code, however, Solon's poetry is meant to provide a solution to the city's problems, rather than to stop short with analysis. Solon explicitly understands his poetry as a means of civic education: "My heart orders me to teach [*didaxai*] the Athenians this, that bad government [*Dusnomiē*] brings many troubles to the polis, but good government [*Eunomiē*] makes everything orderly and sound [*eukosma kai artia*]" (fr. 4.30–32). Solon hopes to create the conditions of *eunomia* by educating Athenians to understand the benefits of social order and to appreciate more fully the consequences of their actions. Having citizenry with orderly and sound minds is the precondition for achieving a stable and well-governed society. In Solon's poetry, *eunomia* is less a goddess (as at Hesiod *Theogony* 902) than a condition in which civic justice and self-restraint prevail.[111] It is likely that the etymological connotations of *eunomia* would be felt in a poem concerned with justice: *eunomia* is derived from *eu-nemesthai*, "to distribute well," and hence refers to that condition of social health in which fair and equitable distribution is maintained.[112]

Solon's strategy for "teaching" the Athenians is to refashion the Athenian self-image in order to inculcate the values of self-restraint and respect for just distribution. Solon says that, in conditions of civil strife and unjust aggression, "The common evil [*dēmosion kakon*] comes into each man's house, and the doors of the courtyard will no longer keep it out, but it leaps over the high hedge and surely finds him, even if he hides himself in an innermost corner of his room" (fr. 4.26–29). Civic troubles break down traditional boundaries separating public and private.[113] But in

[111] Ostwald 1969, 64.

[112] Cf. Strabo 8.4.10c362 and Aristotle *Politics* 1306b40 on Tyrtaeus's poem "Eunomia"; see also Xenophanes 2.19; Aristotle *Politics* 1294a4–7; Adkins 1972, 52; Nagy 1990a, 270–71.

[113] Anhalt (1993, 108–10) usefully discusses this passage in connection with Iliadic paral-

this passage Solon also proposes another, even bolder, idea: that, try as they may, individuals cannot exist independently of the community, that the community is prior to the individual; that individual self-interest is to be equated with the interest of the community. With the appearance of this poem, the individual is no longer defined simply as an individual, but rather, first and foremost, as a citizen of Athens.[114]

Seen in this light, Solon's formulation of the relationship between individual and community has implications that reverberate throughout the history of Athenian political thought. As Ostwald has written of political thought in the classical period, "Citizenship was neither a right nor a matter of participation, but a matter of belonging, of knowing one's identity not in terms of one's own personal values but in terms of the community that was both one's possession and possessor."[115] The seeds of this later conception are found in Solon's poetry. This is Solon's most significant reaction against the elite's attempt to maintain a quasi-Homeric structure in which the rural peasantry, in danger of being enslaved, was dependent for protection and livelihood on the chieftainlike elite at the center of the community. Where earlier the community had depended on the individual hero for protection, it now depends on individual self-restraint and, if necessary, the imposition of restraint by the community in support of the law. Where earlier the individual had had few qualms in pursuing his own honor (*timē*) at the community's expense if necessary, even to the extent of treating community members as war captives, Solon proposes an altogether different model of individual glory, according to which individual success is to be identified with self-restraint and the ability to contribute to the communal welfare.[116]

In a fragment quoted by Plutarch, Solon imagines how "the many and the base" (*tous pollous kai phaulous*) deride him for shirking tyrannical power:

> Solon is not a deep-thinking [*bathuphrōn*] or wise [*boulēeis*] man; for when the god gave him good things, he did not take them; although he had cast his great net around his prey, he was too stupid to draw his net in, having lost courage and sense alike. If I had gained power [*kratēsas*], obtained vast wealth [*plouton*

lels (e.g., 9.470–77), suggesting that Solon presents barriers between public and private as irrelevant and insignificant in times of civic strife.

[114] Thus I find that the civic definition of the individual traced out for the fourth century in Holmes 1979 has identifiable roots in Solon's poetry.

[115] Ostwald 1996, 57; cf. Shaw (1991, 202–3), who judiciously presents another strand of political thinking according to which Athenian citizens could withdraw from political participation as a matter of democratic freedom; see Hansen 1991, 80–85, on Athenian concepts of public and private freedom.

[116] For Homeric ethics in contexts of conflict between individual and community, see Irwin 1989, 38; Adkins 1960; 1971; Long 1970.

> *aphthonon labōn*], and become tyrant [*turanneusas*] of Athens for only a single day, I'd be willing to be flayed into a wineskin afterward and to have my posterity destroyed. (fr. 33.1–7)[117]

In this fragment, Solon vividly imagines the psychology that motivates Athenian greed and injustice. To most Athenians, it is unimaginable that Solon, or anyone in Solon's position, would not use his power in order to gratify his base desires for wealth and tyrannical rule. Although Plutarch says that Solon is referring to the demos in these lines, these verses could also be directed against those aristocrats who unjustly exploited their power for the pleasures of rule and material advantages. Solon publicly articulates the acquisitive individual's attitudes in order to illustrate the selfishness, stupidity, and moral bankruptcy that such attitudes entail. Hard-core greed and self-interest imply a lack of regard for one's own descendants and even one's own humanity; greed makes the human body into a wineskin, a fitting outcome for those who greedily wish to consume more than their share of the community. As Aristotle saw, greed derives ultimately from insistent bodily urges. The fool with excessive desires is therefore ultimately self-destructive: as Theognis aptly puts it, "*Koros*, to be sure, destroys many fools; for it is difficult to know due measure when good things are at hand" (693–94).[118]

As a result, both the community and the individual have an interest in individual self-restraint. Although Solon uses traditional poetic language, he foreshadows the salient features of the psychology of greed, such as one finds in Plato's Callicles: the self-aggrandizing desire for power as a base and unenlightened pleasure in its own right and as a means to satisfy the lust for material possessions without regard for communal standards of fairness. Both Solon and Socrates agree that such desires violate justice and tend to disrupt or even destroy the community, but they also criticize their targets for the damage done to the individual self by unrestrained greed. For Solon, as for Socrates, self-restraint is a central constituent of individual well-being. Hence, for Solon, the tyrannical road to the ultimate satisfaction of greedy desires is a road that is open but not taken. Despite the similarities between Solon's position and that of (other) tyrants, such as Pittacus of Mytilene, Solon abjures the tyrannical greed that provided Plato and Aristotle with such compelling images of individual destructiveness.[119]

Solon provides no easy solution for the corruption of power, but after attempting to undermine the individualistic, self-seeking values exemplified by both groups in the ongoing civil discord, he offers a new un-

[117] Although Plutarch presumably had read more Solonian poetry than we can, there is no clear reason why this passage must refer to the demos rather than its leaders; after all, in fr. 4 Solon directs his criticisms against the greed of the rich.

[118] Cf. Solon (fr. 16) for a similar sentiment.

[119] McGlew 1993, 94–98.

derstanding of individual success according to which victory is won when the individual restrains his desires and uses power appropriately. "If I have spared my fatherland and did not grasp tyranny and implacable violence [*turannidos de kai biēs ameilichou / ou kathēpsamēn*] bringing stain and disgrace upon my reputation [*kleos*], I am not ashamed; for I think that in this way I will the more surpass [*pleon . . . nikēsein*] everyone" (fr. 32).[120] This statement pointedly reverses the victory envisioned by each side in the civic conflict: "I stood with a strong shield thrown around both sides, and would not allow either to have an unjust victory" (fr. 5.5–6). The implication is that the demos and the elite alike wrongly believe that genuine victory can be won in an intrastate competition for the greatest share of the community's limited store of resources. Solon's glory is something vastly different from the dishonorable greed pursued by the Athenians.

Solon rejects their conception of victory. Solon's own victory, by contrast, is not the acquisitive sort won by getting the better of his fellow citizens through unjust greed, but rather a firmly grounded civic success that is defined by his own self-restraint and love of country and that is proved also by his capacity to restrain others. Solon invokes the markedly Homeric term *kleos* (fame, glory) in order to emphasize his revaluation of the individualistic ethos; for Solon individual success can be equated with the act of saving one's country through self-mastery and, if necessary, through heroically imposing restraint upon one's wrongheaded fellow citizens. His investigation of his own and his fellow citizens' psychology adds significance to his portrayal of himself as saving the state through military action.[121] Through his poetry Solon becomes a model Athenian citizen who correctly understands the value of self-restraint, and gives priority to his country over his own self-interest. To put it more precisely, Solon redefines self-interest: the individual should conceive his own welfare and good name not in narrowly selfish terms, but rather in terms of the good of Athens. His behavior conveys what it means to be a genuine Athenian citizen, and what self-image is required, both morally and politically, of those who plan to live together in the Athenian political community.

Solon's self-presentation, finally, has implications for the appropriate use of power in the state. The analysis of conflict presented in Solon's poetry emphasizes the abuse of power for the sake of selfish, destructive goals, rather than for the promotion of fairness and self-restraint among all citizens. One key component of Solon's own self-mastery and concern for the common good is his proper understanding of the relationship between force and justice: Solon claims that he has "fit together might

[120] My analysis shares some elements with the discussion of Anhalt 1993, 104–6.

[121] Loraux 1984; frr. 5.5–6, 4a, 37.8–9.

and right" (*biēn te kai dikēn xunarmosas*, fr. 36.16) in freeing the earth from servitude, which means that he has exercised his power for the sake of the common good. In defining the appropriate relationship between power, the individual with the capacity to use power, and the community, Solon heralds an enduring theme of Athenian political thought, which later became not only the subject of reflection in work by theorists, historians, and orators, but also surfaces in dramatic reflections upon power's capacity to promote or destroy the civic good. Most notably, Aeschylus's *Eumenides* ends with a scene in which Athena persuades the former Erinyes, who had once been bent on destroying Athens, to become Eumenides (Kindly Ones)—that is, to use their avenging power to punish evildoers and to promote the collective welfare (881–987).

If Solon envisions using power in order to reduce intra-Athenian conflict, though, then he also imagines uses of power in which Athenians act as a unit to assert their claims in international politics. Here we begin to make a transition from intra-polis attacks on greed to assertions of power on the international scene. Solon experiences pain not only at the dishonorable slaying of Athens by its own citizens (fr. 4a), but also at the Athenian loss of Salamis after a war with Megara (Plut. *Sol.* 8; Diog. Laert. 1.2.2). Ridiculing his fellow Athenians as "those who let Salamis go" by coining the Aristophanic-sounding neologism *Salaminapheteōn* (fr. 2.4), he urges Athens to "thrust away grievous disgrace [*aischos*]" (fr. 3.2). It is possible to conjecture that Solon's focus on civic solidarity was also envisioned as a way to win back Salamis from the Megarians. As later theorists were quick to point out, a polis divided within itself cannot fight effectively against other, unified city-states. The tradition held that, thanks to Solon, Athens was successful in regaining Salamis (Diog. Laert. 1.2.2).

Solon's presentation of greed and injustice provides insight not only into Solon's own conception of the Athenian social and political crisis, but also into the key themes of Athenian political discourse: leadership and the abuse of power, the psychology of the tyrannical soul, and the relationship between individual and community—in particular, the emergence, or at least the full articulation, of a civic definition of the individual self. By presenting his own position as disconnected from partisan affiliations, Solon is able to critique the excesses of both demos and aristocrats and, therefore, to provide a language and conceptual framework that later authors, even those of radically different ideological persuasions, could employ in their own work. His promotion of civic solidarity paved the way for the Athenians' international politics of the late sixth and fifth centuries, when their collective harmony did indeed enable them to assert themselves in the rapidly changing world of Mediterranean politics.

4

Herodotus and the Greed of Imperialism

> If you capture Susa, you can confidently compete with Zeus himself for riches. You should stop fighting over a scrap of land—and poor land at that—with your rivals the Messenians and Arcadians and Argives, who possess no gold or silver which is worth fighting and dying for, since you are being offered the chance to conquer all of Asia easily. Is there really any choice between the two?
>
> *Aristogoras of Miletus to King Cleomenes of Sparta (Hdt. 5.49.8)*

THE history of Athenian greed begins again in earnest with the history of Athens just before and during the Persian Wars. In recounting that history (along with much else), Herodotus wants to provide a historical, but also an ethically evaluative, account of how individuals and cities establish cultural norms of action, such as imperialism, and how they view those norms as contributing to their general well-being. Within the framework of the Persian Wars, Aristagoras's question sets the key problem: what is really worth dying for, or, differently, what is worth living for? Herodotus offers a multifaceted and often ambivalent vision of the Athenian response to this central issue of political and ethical life. As we shall see, Solon's intention of creating unity within Athens was fulfilled in the early fifth century, but with perhaps different results from those anticipated in Solon's poetry itself. The formerly class-specific charge of greed, which Solon levels at both aristocrats and the demos, is, in Herodotus's vision, well on its way to becoming generalized into a characterization of Athens as a polis during the fifth century.

The classical discourse on greed, which is initiated by Herodotus, borrows language, concepts, and themes from Solon's attempt to articulate and resolve the problems posed by unjust acquisitiveness within the political community of archaic Athens. Fifth century political thinkers, however, elaborated the intra-polis discourse within the complex framework of international politics. Herodotus's treatment of greed in the context of the Persian Wars therefore leads to two related questions. First, how can the terminology and conceptualization of greed be reformulated in an international context, when Aristotle and Solon link their ideas closely to "sharing in" (*metechein*) an individual political community? To grapple with international greed, it will be useful to examine Herodotus's representation of the aggressive empires of the East, which, in his view, were the precursors to the Athenian Empire. Herodotus's emphasis on Persian imperialism enables his audience to understand in detail his elaboration of greed as a problem of human psychology and international justice. Furthermore, his vision of greed and unfairness within the Panhellenic league, which was created in order to resist Xerxes' invasion, enables his modern readers to view Herodotus as a bridge figure between archaic and classical evaluations of greed. Second, how are the competing social groups of Solon's poetry, the elite and the demos of Athens, reconfigured within the new Cleisthenic democracy? I argue that in Herodotus's account the peculiarly democratic interaction between these groups paved the way for the emergence of Athens as a spectacularly successful greedy polis.

Eastern Imperialism

In representing the Eastern empires, Herodotus focuses on lack of self-control and excessive desire for more territory and control over others. Here the story begins with Croesus's insatiable craving to add territory to his own kingdom: "He wanted, out of a craving for land, to add to his own territory" ([*gēs himerōi prosktēsasthai pros tēn heōutou moiran boulomenos*] 1.73.1; cf. 1.26.3–27.2).[1] Croesus's craving (*himeros*) is matched by the excessive desires of other Eastern despots, whose expansionist drives are played out in a strikingly repetitive pattern in the *Histories*.[2] Their excessive acquisitiveness is often associated with the desire for revenge (*tisis*, *timōria*), which constitutes either a useful pretext for invasion (e.g., 6.94.1, 7.138.1) or an actual motivation for imperial aggression (4.1.1, 7.1.1).[3] Herodotus offers a veritable catalog of the rich and evolving vocabulary for desiring more. Cyrus has desire (*epethumēse*, 1.201) and ea-

[1] On the character of Croesus, see Stahl 1975; Immerwahr 1966, 154–61. Nagy (1990b, 274–89) sets Croesus within the framework of *hubris* and *habrosunē* (luxury) in archaic Greek poetry.

[2] See King 1997; Lateiner 1989, 165–67; Immerwahr 1966, 148–88; Evans 1991, 23–28.

[3] Evans (1991, 15–23) underplays the significance of both greed for more and revenge, while overemphasizing the importance of *nomos* (custom, cultural norm). Derow (1994, 73–83) does precisely the reverse: "I think it can safely be said that, for Herodotus, the explanation of why something happened reduces to the explanation of why someone did something, and that this is achieved by the imputation of what are fundamentally personal motives" (79).

gerness (*prothumiēn*, 1.204.1) to conquer the Massagetae, and is said to be insatiable for blood (*aplēstos haimatos*, 1.212.2–3, *bis*),[4] Deioces is said to be in love with tyranny (*erastheis turannidos*, 1.96.1); Darius is insatiable for money (*aplēstos chrēmatōn*) and greedy (*aischrokerdēs*, 1.187.5; cf. 3.89.3, 3.134.1–3); Cambyses desired (*epethumēse*) someone else's kingdom (3.21.2).[5]

In the previous two chapters, we have seen that, for Aristotle and Solon, cultural norms—of competition, for example, or of overvaluing the role of wealth in one's conception of the good life—play a central role in encouraging the excessive desire to get more. For Herodotus, too, personal desires are shaped and strengthened by their social and cultural contexts. At the physician Democedes' request, for example, Atossa encouraged Darius to invade Greece on the grounds that the Persian king must show energy and aggressiveness if he hopes to win the respect of his subjects (3.134). According to Atossa, pursuing a policy of aggression will not only prove Darius's manliness but also wear down the Persians' strength and thereby reduce the possibility of revolt. Thus Darius's natural greed for gain (3.89.3) was expanded into a policy of imperialism through Atossa's suggestive explanation of the expectations of his Persian subjects. Cultural norms, in their turn, are in part the product of individual choices at specific times in history, which shape the self-image and identity of later individuals within the same culture. Originally individualistic desires and behavior are gradually institutionalized within the politics and culture of the wider society. This process of gradual institutionalization both explains the cultural norm of Persian imperialism and sheds light on Herodotus's telling remarks on Athens's own rise to dominance in the Aegean.

When Xerxes attains the throne, he immediately reflects that his royal predecessors have established a specific, aggressive image of the Persian monarch. In Xerxes' case, alongside the usual motives of greed and revenge, Herodotus stresses the cultural norm (*nomos*) of expansionism, which shapes individual desire and creates an ideal of behavior according to which Xerxes judges his own merits as a king (7.8a.1–2). Xerxes tries to emulate Cyrus, Cambyses, and Darius: "Ever since I took the throne," he says, "I have been thinking how not to fall short of the previous Persian kings and how to add as much power as they did to the Persian Empire [*mēde elassō prosktēsomai dunamin Persēisi*]" (7.8a.2). The cultural

[4] Fisher (1992, 356) rightly notes that the repeated use of the verb *korennumi* (to fill or glut), of Tomyris's giving Cyrus his fill of blood, is thematically linked with Cyrus's being "insatiable for blood" and with his insatiable desire for further conquest in general.

[5] On these kings and the terminology used to describe them, see Derow 1994, 76–83; Fornara 1971, 87; King 1997, 79–99; Immerwahr 1966, 148–76; Gould 1989, 63–67, 82–85.

norm, established by specific individual behavior in the past, reinforces Xerxes' own preexisting, fervent personal desires. Recent studies have emphasized the relationship between divine and human responsibility for Xerxes' decision to attack Greece, but these concerns are also influenced by the interplay between personal desires and wider social ideals.[6] It is within this complicated individual and social framework that Herodotus explores the psychological forces that drive Persian imperialism.[7]

Xerxes' own articulation of his acquisitive desires reveals his impiety and overweening *hubris*: "We shall extend the empire of Persia and make its boundary that of Zeus's sky [*gēn tēn Persida apodexomen tōi Dios aitheri homoureousan*], so that the sun will not look down upon any land beyond the boundaries of what is ours. Together with you, I shall pass through all of Europe and make it all one country" (7.8c.1–2). His desire to rule the entire world explicitly violates natural boundaries, which is a standard Herodotean topos in characterizing hubristic and sacrilegious individuals.[8] Opposing the planned attack on Greece, Xerxes' uncle Artabanus draws out the themes of impiety and excess when he warns the king that "the god does not allow anyone other than himself to think big [*phroneein mega*]" (7.10e). Reflecting on the war council later, Artabanus says that he is grieved not so much by Xerxes' abuse of him, but rather by the fact that "when we were offered a choice between two courses, one of them increasing our arrogance [*tēs men hubrin auxanousēs*] and the other checking it by pointing out how bad it is to teach the heart always to seek to have more than what is present [*pleon ti dizēsthai aiei echein tou pareontos*], you chose the one which is the more likely to lead both yourself and your country to disaster" (7.16a.2). The passage offers a unique opportunity to explore the interconnections between *hubris* and greed at a specific stage in their respective conceptual histories. Recent scholars have tended to argue that there is not much to choose between *hubris*, the desire to have more, and "thinking big" in Artabanus's account.[9] It is useful, however, to be more

[6] On divine and human responsibility in Xerxes' decision to invade Greece, see King 1997, 91–93; Lateiner 1989, 207; Luce 1997, 47–51; Gould 1989, 69–72; Fisher 1992, 368–74. On the episode in general, see Solmsen 1974.

[7] In Thucydides' treatment of Athens's imperialistic drive, the divine factor has all but dropped out, but the cultural and individual strands are still present in similar ways: in the Funeral Oration, Pericles specifically says that Athenian expansionism is an inherited ideal, and that success is measured against the achievements of one's ancestors (2.36.1–4). Conversely, Thucydides himself regards Athenians as motivated by their own greed apart from specifically cultural ideals. See chapter 5.

[8] Immerwahr 1956, 250; 1966, 166–67, 293–94; Lateiner 1989, 126–44; Gould 1989, 106–9.

[9] Dickie 1984, 104–9; Cairns 1996; contra, Fisher 1992, 367–85. Most commentators have interpreted *hubris* as no more than a form of overweening self-confidence: Pohlenz

precise about the interconnections between *hubris* and greed here, because their relationship undergoes significant changes depending on the social context and intellectual interests of the speaker or thinker concerned.[10]

A minimalist reading of Artabanus's key sentence (7.16a.2) is that those who teach their hearts to show self-restraint tend to check *hubris*, whereas those who give their desires free rein tend to increase *hubris*. Solon's psychological treatment of *hubris* and *koros* is reformulated in Artabanus's assertion that indulging in the desire to get more than one has, combined with contempt for what one already possesses, tends to increase arrogance and contempt for others. In other words, arrogance follows from excessive desire and contempt for one's present possessions. By checking one's desires, conversely, one checks one's attitudes of arrogance and impiety.

Herodotus's psychological explanation of *hubris* is therefore consistent with the one we have already encountered in Solon, who says that *koros* (greed for more) gives birth to *hubris* (fr. 6.3). According to the interpretation presented in chapter 3, this explicit statement should be seen against a wider Solonian horizon in which *koros* and *hubris* are involved in a cycle of perpetual mutual reproduction. A similar effect is achieved in Herodotus's text if we read Artabanus's sentiments alongside another presentation of the genealogy of *koros* and *hubris*. Later, Herodotus quotes an oracle predicting the Persian defeat at Salamis: "Bright Justice will quench strong Koros, the child of Hubris, fearful, eager, planning to swallow up everything [*dokeunt' ana panta pithesthai*]" (8.77).

Here the familiar image of *koros* as gluttonous hunger is applied to the Persian invasion; the grammar shows that *koros* specifically, rather than *hubris*, is being quenched by Justice and is characterized by gluttony. Gluttonous hunger is the child of *hubris*, which implies that arrogance and "thinking big" lead to greedy, materialistic drives that are unwholesome for the individual and harmful to those he attacks. In these two passages (7.16a.2, 8.77), Herodotus recreates Solon's mutually reinforcing cycle of *koros* and *hubris*. As we shall see, by using the marked fifth-century terminology of desiring to have more (*pleon echein*, 7.16a.2), he also establishes links between Xerxes' imperialism and Greek disputes over hegemony. Both are in turn related to Athens's own emergent imperialism, which is represented as an outgrowth of seeds planted already during the Persian Wars.

1937, 125–29; Redfield 1985; Dickie 1984, 104–9. This is surely correct: Fisher (1992, esp. 374–75n144, 377–78) creates too fine a distinction between *hubris* and *mega phronein*.

[10] On the significance of greed in this account, see Pohlenz 1937, 123; Raaflaub 1987, 229–31.

Because greed, in the Greek conception, usually implied taking from others what is rightly theirs, it is clear why Herodotus should conceive of greed as the offspring of *hubris*, which is an arrogant disregard for others, potentially including the gods, and which is rooted in a fundamental belief in one's own superiority to others. There is thus a *logical* connection between these two ideas, but, to the extent that we are concerned with intellectual history rather than analytic philosophy, our focus is on how different authors conceived and experienced conceptual relationships, rather than on how different concepts are logically, aprioristically related. In other words, it is crucial to understand how relationships between different ideas were experienced and reconfigured by those who lived over time with the concepts in question, instead of trying to posit a timeless, transcendent relationship between key cultural abstractions. Hence it is significant that later classical thinkers such as Aristotle emphasized the connection between *hubris* and greed far less than the associations between greed and distributive justice. For Herodotus, greed, at least in Artabanus's central formulations, fits securely within a framework of *hubris* and impiety, whereas for Plato and Aristotle greed is more at home in discussions of distributive justice among co-inhabitants of a polis. To illustrate this distinction, let us revisit Plato's presentation of Callicles in the *Gorgias*, because Callicles uses Xerxes' invasion as an example of greed. This coincidence in subject matter reveals how greed underwent conceptual development in the decades separating Herodotus and Plato.

Both morally and psychologically, Callicles understands Xerxes' imperialism in an altogether different way from Artabanus. His vision of "natural justice" is worth quoting at length:

> [The weak] frighten the stronger and those able to have more [*dunatous ontas pleon echein*], and in order that the strong do not have more than themselves [*hina mē autōn pleon echōsin*], they say that it is shameful [*aischron*] and unjust [*adikon*] to desire to have more [*to pleonektein*], and that injustice consists in seeking to have more than others [*to pleon tōn allōn zētein echein*]; for they, being inferior, would be content if they could have an equal share [*to ison*]. Therefore, this is called unjust and shameful by convention [*nomōi*], to seek to have more than the many [*to pleon zētein echein tōn pollōn*], and they call this injustice [*adikein*]; but nature herself, I think, makes it plain that it is just that the better man have more [*pleon echein*] than the worse, and the more powerful than the less powerful. And it is clear from much evidence that this is so, both among the other animals and in all the cities and races of human beings, that justice is judged thus, that the stronger rule over the weaker, and have more [*ton kreittō tou hēttonos archein kai pleon echein*]. By what right, for example, did Xerxes invade Greece, or his father Scythia, to take two of the myriad examples that

> present themselves? I think that they did these things according to natural right [*kata phusin tēn tou dikaiou*], and indeed by Zeus according to the law of nature [*kata nomon ge ton tēs phuseōs*], though not perhaps according to the law that we set down. (*Gorg.* 483c1–e4)

According to Callicles, Xerxes' invasion exemplifies the natural law that the stronger should use their strength in order to get more than the weaker. His understanding of the desire to get more is set within an explicit context of thinking about justice and injustice in the distribution of possessions, as these ideas relate to strength and to socially constructed equality as opposed to natural entitlement. His language and concepts therefore point the way directly to Aristotle's own conception of greed in the *Ethics* and *Politics*. Callicles' use of Xerxes as a paradigm of imperialistic greed shows that the same activity, Xerxes' imperialism, can be understood differently depending on the intellectual interests and milieu of the thinker who represents them. This means both that Herodotus's Artabanus and Plato's Callicles are interested in different aspects of Xerxes' attitudes and behavior, and that they conceptualize Xerxes in altogether different ways. Artabanus's emphasis is on impiety and arrogance, of which greed is at once the origin and the symptom, whereas Callicles emphasizes the *justice* of greed in the context of debates over political equality. Callicles does not comment particularly on the motivations for greed in this passage. For that, we must look to other passages in the dialogue, where it turns out that Callicles' strong man is driven by his own desires (*epithumiai*, e.g., 491e9, 492a2–3), which originate both in his own nature, and in his belief that true excellence (*aretē*) means conceiving, and then satisfying, the greatest possible number of desires.[11] Callicles, too, is an individual trying at once to fulfill personal desire and to emulate cultural ideals.

It is now possible to generalize about the evolving relationship between *hubris* and greed. In Homer, as we have seen, the language of greedy desire (e.g., *philokteanōtate*, *Il.* 1.122) is very tightly connected to Agamemnon's act of *hubris* and dishonoring, but the language of justice (*dikē*) has not yet taken center stage in the dispute between Achilles and Agamemnon. In other archaic poets, however, *hubris* and justice (*dikē*) are often opposed to one another in varying formulations, and it is Solon who specifies that greed (*koros*) is the particular behavior by which hubristic individuals violate justice within the Athenian political community. Flashing forward to the *Gorgias* and then to Aristotle, we can see that greed has become the opposite of distributive justice, according to conventional, non-Calliclean viewpoints, and *hubris*, though still a very

[11] On Callicles and *aretē*, see Adkins 1960, 244–46, 269–74.

important concept in fourth-century discourse, is distinguished from greed.[12] What later became greed thus begins, both psychologically and morally, as a facet of *hubris*, or at least as closely related to *hubris*. This particular desiring component was then conceptually differentiated from *hubris*, as political agents and thinkers began to connect it more closely to the idea of violating fair distribution within self-conscious communities. Within this large-scale conceptual evolution, Herodotus acts a bridge-figure between archaic and classical periods. In his treatment of Xerxes, *hubris* and greed are very tightly connected. In other Herodotean passages, though, a connection between the two seems less strongly felt, and greed is considered rather in terms of distributive unfairness and excessive acquisitiveness without any emphasis on *hubris*.[13] We shall return to this in examining the body of Greek states that united to resist Xerxes.

The acts of aggression perpetrated by Eastern despots (and their deputies) did not violate distributive justice in the specifically Aristotelian sense: that is, the justice that pertains among equals, who have prior obligations to act fairly with each other, in virtue of their commitment to living together in a polis. In Herodotus's presentation, however, Persian imperialism violates a broader notion of justice according to which it is wrong to take what belongs to another, regardless of any prior contact or preexisting mutual obligations. This notion of justice is exemplified in Herodotus's proem, where Herodotus explicitly indicates that he is cataloging a series of reciprocal injustices (*adikēmata* or *adikiai*) between Greeks and Phoenicians (1.2.1, 1.2.2, 1.4.2). This account leads directly to Herodotus's claim that it was Croesus the Lydian who first committed an injustice against the Greeks by exacting tribute from them (1.5.3–1.6.3).[14]

An unnamed Ethiopian king most clearly elucidates the concept of justice that underlies Herodotus's proem and his evaluation of Persian imperialism in general. The Ethiopian king rebukes Cambyses' envoys, who have traveled to Ethiopia in order to seek information for Cambyses' planned invasion: "You have come to get information about my kingdom; therefore, you are liars, and that king of yours is unjust (*oute . . . dikaios*). For if he were just (*dikaios*), then he would not have desired

[12] See chapter 2; Cairns 1996, 5–6.

[13] It is worth noting, in connection with the discussion of greed in Aristotle's *Nicomachean Ethics* in the chapter 2, that all of Herodotus's greedy agents actually want to possess the goods they are after, and are never said to be excited simply by the thrill of violating fairness for its own sake.

[14] For Herodotus's associations between *phoros* (tribute) and empire, see Stadter (1992, 795–98), who persuasively argues that Herodotus's notice that the Ionians have continued to pay tribute down to his own day (6.42) refers to tribute paid in his day to Athens; contra, Murray 1966.

(*epethumēse*) another land than his own, nor would he have enslaved men by whom he had been done no wrong [*mēden ēdikētai*]" (3.21.2). The speech clarifies both the salient characteristic of the Persian monarchs, excessive desire for more, and the sense in which that desire is unjust—that it involves taking what is not one's own without any provocation. If his proem itself is any indication, then Herodotus himself seems to have shared this basic view of justice as essentially embodying respect for the life, liberty, and private property of others.[15]

This Herodotean conception of justice also derives from the idea of appropriate "shares" in divisible goods but in a broader and vaguer sense than we have thus far observed. These "shares" are equivalent to "portions" (*moirai*), which have been dispensed to individuals and nations by fate and the gods, and which, to Herodotus, inhere in geographical boundaries such as rivers and (famously) the Hellespont.[16] For Herodotus, moral "facts" about the global distribution of goods are thus inscribed in the physical boundaries of the world. This geographical and religious framework for the global distribution of goods explains why characters throughout the *Histories*, as well as Herodotus himself, consistently use the terminology of injustice (*adikia*) to describe actions, such as Cambyses' planned invasion, which are aimed at taking what rightly belongs to another. This belief structure is similar to the divine "umbrella" found in both Homer and Hesiod.[17]

Herodotus explains this "umbrella" and its relation to global distribution when he describes the Pelasgians' method of sacrificing to the gods without any distinction of name or title (2.52.1). He says, "They called these [divinities] *theoi*, from the fact that they place [*thentes*] all things in order [*kosmōi*] and assign all distributions [*pasas nomas eichon*]."[18] Such a perception of the gods' control over distribution, which Herodotus himself seems to share, shows that the excessive desire for more that characterizes Eastern despots is intimately linked to injustice in distribution, but in a different way from the injustice in distribution that characterizes Aristotle's

[15] See Lateiner 1989, 140–44, for the primary sense in which Herodotus conceives of *dikē*: namely, as looking to one's own and not coveting another person's goods; cf. 1.130.3 (Croesus), 7.9.2; 4.119.4 (Scythians); 1.2.1; 6.119.1. In accordance with his key themes of retribution and revenge, Herodotus typically emphasizes the *beginning* of the *adikia*: cf. 1.5.3–4, 3.21, 4.1.1.

[16] The term *moira* in fact often means "territory" (e.g., 1.73.1, 1.75.2, 1.82.2, etc.)—which reveals that for Herodotus the territory that one in fact possesses before conquering others' territory is what is given by the gods.

[17] See chapter 3; Lloyd-Jones 1971, 58–60.

[18] Throughout the Egyptian logos, Herodotus is obsessed with the ideas of measuring, division, and distribution, both in property, occupation, and scientific discovery: see 2.3, 2.6–7, 2.41, 2.52, 2.82, 2.84, 2.86, 2.109, 2.147. In this, too, he is similar to Hesiod: see Slatkin 1996.

conception of greed. Aristotle's conception, by contrast, is firmly secular and reflects the belief that human beings themselves, not the gods, bear primary responsibility for distributing goods within communities of their own making. Aristotle's view, therefore, depends on concepts of prior commitments and obligations of the parties concerned, rather than on the subjection of human beings in general to the distributive standards established in advance by the gods. As we shall see, Thucydides dramatically transforms the terms of Herodotus's conceptualization and is the first thinker to point the way clearly to Aristotle's account.

Greed and Fairness in the Panhellenic League

Herodotus begins to transform his evaluation of greed in his account of the Greeks' response to news of Xerxes' invasion. One of Herodotus's central concerns in documenting the resistance is the degree to which the Greeks could present a unified, Panhellenic front against the invaders. Non-Medizing Greeks tried to create a Panhellenic league made up of individual Greek states, which resembled in many respects the polis communities of Greece made up of individual citizens.[19] In describing the first meeting of this league, Herodotus says, "At a conference of the Greek states who were loyal to the general cause guarantees were exchanged [*didontōn sphisi logon kai pistin*], and the decision was reached, first of all, to make up their own quarrels and to stop fighting among themselves" (7.145.1). Herodotus had already conjured up the idea of Panhellenism in the opening paragraphs of the *Histories*, and he generally treats Greeks as an internally consistent cultural and political community, which is defined in opposition to the cultures of the East.[20] It is within this Panhellenic community, rather than the individual polis community, that Herodotus evaluates the excessive desire to get more exhibited by individuals and by member states.

The abstraction *pleonexia* (greed), in fact, first appears in Greek literature in Herodotus's account of the Greek embassy to Argos, which sought to conclude an alliance with the Argives against the anticipated Persian invasion (7.148–52).[21] Immediately prior to this story, Herodotus

[19] This league is conventionally known as the Hellenic League; for the administration and principles of the league, see Brunt 1993a.

[20] Pelling 1997a shows that Herodotus's "national stereotypes" are subjected to scrutiny and evaluation by Herodotus himself, and that there are "internal others," such as the Spartans, who undermine our sense of the clear and stable contrasts Herodotus draws in the proem and in various passages in books 7–9. The now classic account is Hartog 1988; cf. Konstan 1987, Georges 1994, 115–66.

[21] Wickersham (1994, 4–6) usefully shows that the Argive disaster at Sepeia (6.76–84)

explains that the Greeks had hoped to unite the entire Greek world, if possible, in order to resist the invader with as much force as they could muster, because the danger threatened all Greeks alike (7.145.2). Herodotus offers three stories that purport to explain the Argives' subsequent refusal to join the league, the first of which, told by the Argives themselves, illustrates the uses to which allegations of greedy, grasping behavior could be put in the political rhetoric of the period. Despite Delphi's warning that they should remain neutral, the Argives agreed to join on two conditions: first, that they obtain a thirty years' truce with Sparta and, second, that "they lead the entire alliance on equal terms" (*hēgeomenoi kata to hēmisu pasēs tēs summachiēs*, 7.148.4). By right, the Argives contend, the hegemony is theirs (*kata ge to dikaion ginesthai tēn hēgemoniēn heōutōn*), but they are nevertheless content with equal terms (*kata to hēmisu*, 7.148.4). The Spartans promise to refer the truce to their people, adding, however, that it was impossible to deprive either of the two Spartan kings of leadership, but that the Argive king could have an "equal vote" (*homopsēphon*, 7.149.2), if he wished, with each of the two Spartan kings. This elicits the accusation of greed: "The Argives say that they could not endure the greed [*pleonexiēn*] of the Spartans, and that they would rather be ruled [*archesthai*] by foreigners than yield at all [*ti hupeixai*] to the Lacedaimonians" (7.149.3). Then follows the familiar demand that the envoys leave Argos before sunset or be treated as enemies.

This story strains to lay responsibility on the Spartans for Argos's reluctance to join the Greek cause and purports to show that, but for the Spartans' needless "grabbiness," the Argives would have defied even the Delphic oracle for the sake of Greece. Ironically, in the second story, the Argives receive a message from Xerxes to the effect that they are related by blood to the Persians through a joint ancestor, Perses, and therefore that they should refuse to join the Greek alliance. This anti-Argive tradition alleges that the Argives "demanded a share" (*metaiteein*, 7.150.3) in the command in order to provoke the Spartans, and thus to give themselves an excuse for not participating. The third story, perhaps the most believable of the three, says that the Argives invited in the Persians because their war with Sparta was going badly; if that is true, then all the talk of equality and proper shares is merely superficial rhetoric designed to win debating points over their rivals.

Whichever story is most plausible, three points about the Argives' accusation of greed emerge from this section. First, the Argives accuse the Spartans of having greed for power rather than greed for wealth. This

underlies the Spartan Argive negotiations. As Wickersham points out (ix), this episode, along with the Greek negotiations at Syracuse, have rarely received extended scholarly discussion.

illustrates that the ancient Greek notion of greed is broader and vaguer than our own restrictively economic conception of "greed." In contemporary usage, "greedy" usually designates a person with an excessive desire for a certain kind of material good, especially money and, less often, food. The Argives' conception of "greed," by contrast, is focused on leadership (*hēgemoniē*) and power within the group, rather than on the possession of material goods. As we shall see in discussing Thucydides, power and material acquisitiveness are often closely interconnected, but, given the modern use of "greed" as excessive acquisitiveness of material goods, it is important to recognize that both power and material goods are considered proper objects of ancient Greek greed in one of our earliest surviving prose texts.

Second, claims regarding greed arise in the context of the international community of Greek city-states that join together to fight the Persians. This community, though not in the strictest sense a political community, does exhibit the central features of such a community, such as deliberation in an assembly, collective decision making, and an underlying commitment to communal projects.[22] Thus the Panhellenic community of Greek states provides a clear international context for discussing greed and excess acquisitiveness as problems of distributive justice. The underlying moral framework for this dispute is the agreement that the leadership is divided up into different "shares" that should be distributed fairly; the disagreement is over what the Argives and Spartans, respectively, deserve as a matter of the fair distribution of power. Given this framework, the Argives imply that the Spartans' greed is unwholesome in the first instance for the Panhellenic community, but much less so for Sparta as an individual polis. Indeed, as later "immoralists" will recognize, greed seems actually to benefit the individual against the group.[23] By focusing on the well-defined Panhellenic league, Herodotus has made a coherent and plausible transition, from the perspective of greed and injustice, from the polis-centered world of Aristotle and Solon to the problematic international politics of fifth-century Greece.

Third, in this passage, Herodotus proves capable of breaking away

[22] In the *Republic* (470a-d), Socrates argues that Greeks as a whole form an international community in opposition to the "barbarians." Their sense of community, he says, should govern their military decisions: "Then when Greeks fight barbarians or barbarians Greeks, we'll say that they're natural enemies and that such hostilities must be called war. But when Greeks fight with Greeks, we'll say that they are natural friends and that in such circumstances Greece is sick and divided into factions [*nosein* . . . *stasiazein*] and that such hostilities are to be called civil conflict [*stasis*]" (470c5–d1). This sentiment underlies the presentations of the international Panhellenic community found in Herodotus and Thucydides and, as is well known, much fourth-century thinking about the opposition between Greeks and barbarians.

[23] For further discussion of late fifth-century "immoralism," see chapters 1, 6, and 7.

from the archaic tendency to link greed with *hubris*, asking rather what constitutes a "just desert" within a community of equals. Although his representation of Xerxes owes more to the archaic links between greed, gluttony, and *hubris*, his presentation of the Panhellenic community illustrates an early philosophical conception of greed as a problem of distributive fairness within a community of equals tied together by their commitment to shared goals. The disagreement between Argives and Spartans recalls the Iliadic dispute over the distribution of spoils by the army, but, rather than framing their conflict in terms of honor (*timē*) and *hubris*, the Argives and Spartans argue in terms of the fair (*dikaios*) distribution of hegemony, which is violated, according to the Argives, by the Spartans' excessive grasping for more. The undercurrents of *hubris* may be felt in this episode, but it is crucial that greed has diverged to some degree from the constellation of *hubris*, honor, and dishonor, and inhabits instead the conceptual space of injustice and unfair apportionment in an explicitly distributive context. Herodotus thus bridges archaic and philosophical senses of the semantic and conceptual field.

Many of the same themes are revisited in Herodotus's account of the Greek embassy to Gelon of Syracuse (7.153–62), which follows immediately upon the Argives' indignant rejection of the Greek request. Before detailing the negotiations, Herodotus establishes that Gelon is himself a ruthless tyrant, seizing power from the young sons of his former master (7.155.1), and then successfully acquiring much of Sicily through his crafty and forceful imperialism (7.155–56). Upon their arrival, the Greek envoys point out that Xerxes aims to dominate all of Greece and propose that, as Gelon possesses a considerable "share" (*moira*) of the Greek world, he should help maintain Greek freedom against the invader (7.157.2). Their rhetoric is calculated to persuade Gelon that the Greeks must unite if they are to defend their country successfully: "We ask you, therefore, to help us, and to add your strength to ours in our struggle to maintain our country's liberty. Greece united will be strong and a match for the invader" (7.157.2). Gelon replies angrily: "Men of Greece, you dare to come here with a greedy argument [*logon pleonektēn*] and urge me to help you resist a foreign invader!" (7.158.1). In contrast to the earlier episode, neither the envoys nor Gelon has thus far raised the issue of hegemony. Instead, Gelon is angry because, prior to this, when he had asked for Greek help against the Carthaginians, the other Greeks had unequivocally refused his request (7.158.2).

Gelon's unusual mention of the Greeks' "greedy argument" (*logon pleonektēn*) refers to his perception that the other Greeks want to get more than they deserve from him, considering their previous unwillingness to aid him. Even if he entertains the Greek rhetoric of community, he says, the mainland Greeks themselves had earlier failed to honor the principles of mutual obligation on which such a community must be based. The implication is that, if Gelon contributes to the confederacy, then he will be doing more than his fair share of the work to keep Greece—considered as a community of all Greek-speaking states, east and west—free.[24] Gelon thus manipulates the Greeks' mention of Panhellenism for his own rhetorical purposes and thereby takes hold of the moral high ground.

His next move is equally clever and follows on his first debating point. Because of his ability to contribute troops on a grand scale, Gelon proposes that he be given supreme command of the Greek forces. The Spartan envoy responds that Agamemnon would never abide by this—which apparently means that the Spartans are entitled to the leadership (*hēgemonia*) because of historical precedent: their king, Agamemnon, once led the united Greek forces against Troy. Gelon replies, "Surely, if you maintain so eagerly your right to the command [*tēs hēgemoniēs*], it is only reasonable that I should maintain my right more strongly than you, since I have a much bigger fleet and am the commander [*hēgemona*] of an army many times the size of yours" (7.160.2). By now, this is a familiar argument in debates over the fair distribution of goods and power—namely, that those with more to contribute to collective projects deserve a larger share of the divisible "goods" that the group has to offer. His argument extends the earlier rationale that greater contribution to group projects merits a larger share of power within the confederacy.[25] This is substantially the same argument that Achilles presents to Agamemnon, and one that Aristotle later systematized in his theory of proportional desert: those who give more should get more, in accordance with their merit or worth (*axia*). Gelon thus invokes the Panhellenic framework and the patterns of just distribution that it requires, along with traditional arguments about merit and just deserts, in order to represent the Greek envoys as selfish, unfair, and greedy.

This episode also helps characterize the Athenians in relation to the themes of self-sacrifice and self-aggrandizement. Gelon suggests that he be given command either on land or, if the Spartans refuse, then at sea. The Athenians take umbrage at this. They will gladly give Sparta com-

[24] Aristotle (*EN* 1130b2) says that "particular injustice" is "concerned with honor, money or safety." The inclusion of safety (*sōtēria*) in this group has often puzzled commentators: cf., e.g., Williams 1980. But this Herodotean passage shows that "safety," or at least "mutual defense," was also considered a corporate activity divided up into "shares" of work done for the common good.

[25] As Wickersham (1994, 6–9) points out, the other Greeks require further recommendations, such as past glory or antiquity of nationality, if they are to yield their claims to hegemony. Even so, the structure of Gelon's argument reformulates Achilles' own arguments (cf. chapter 3), and points the way directly to Aristotle's theory of proportional deserts.

mand on land and at sea, but why, the Athenians ask, should they have built up the finest navy in Greece if they are then to surrender command of the fleet to Gelon (7.161.3)? On the one hand, the Athenians freely subordinate themselves to the Spartans, which evokes Herodotus's own belief that the Athenians willingly waived their claim to leadership in the interest of Panhellenic unity: "When the allies resisted [giving Athens the naval command], the Athenians waived their claim in the interests of the survival of Greece, considering that if they quarreled about the command [*ei stasiasousi peri tēs hēgemoniēs*], Greece would be destroyed—and they were right" (8.3.1). Athens's virtue lay in its self-sacrifice for the sake of the Panhellenic cause.[26]

On the other hand, the Athenians are mindful of their own place in the pecking order, and they are far from abandoning their own self-interests. They will not give up second place in the Panhellenic community, even if that means giving up Gelon's support. In his response to the Athenian envoy, Gelon brings home the Athenians' excessive greed: "Because you yield nothing and wish to have it all [*ouden hupientes echein to pan ethelete*], you had better rush home and announce to Greece that the spring of the year is lost to her" (7.162.1). His specific terminology helps elucidate the distributive framework that underlies the arguments of each side. His accusation presupposes that the Greek forces have, at least theoretically, divided up the command into "shares" in hegemony; Gelon implies that, rather than duly sharing the leadership with their fellows, the Athenians want to have all the power at sea. The phrase "you wish to have it all" (*echein to pan ethelete*) echoes and extends the terminology of *pleonexia* that runs throughout these two episodes. In Gelon's view, the Athenians do not simply desire to have more than their fair share; they want to take it all. Gelon's terminology therefore reinforces his contention that, despite their rhetoric of Panhellenism, the mainland Greeks, and here especially the Athenians, do not honor the principles of distributive fairness, which (he realizes) is necessary to communal stability and success.

Furthermore, and more pointedly, Aristotle (*Rhet.* 1.7, 3.10) says that the phrase "the spring of the year is lost" was used by Pericles in a funeral oration of uncertain date to describe the loss of Athenian fighters. This verbal echo provides another link between Gelon's accusation and the aggressive militarism of imperial Athens.[27] Gelon's charge looks ahead to Herodotus's own connections between greed, injustice, and Athenian imperialism, aptly framing these ideas in terms of a dispute over naval

[26] Ironically, Herodotus also records a story (7.165.1), which is probably accurate, that Gelon could not send help in any event, because he was threatened at the time by the Carthaginians.

[27] Fornara 1971, 83–84.

power.[28] With Gelon's accusation, we are not far from the birth of Athenian imperialism, which commences, according to Herodotus, just after the Persian Wars: "When the Persians had been driven from Greece and the war had been carried to Persian territory, the Athenians made the arrogance [*hubrin*] of Pausanias their excuse for depriving the Lacedaimonians of the command [*tēn hēgemoniēn*]" (8.3.2). The Athenians came a long way quickly in transforming their courageous self-sacrifice into daring and greedy imperialism.

The Emergent Imperialism of Athens

With the Persian and Panhellenic backgrounds in mind, we are now in a position to understand Herodotus's account of the "prehistory" of Athenian imperialism, which looks forward to Thucydides' full-scale development of Athens as a tyrant-polis. Although Thucydides is usually represented as scornfully rejecting Herodotus's historical analyses, the history of Athenian imperialistic greed and its inextricable links to Athens's democratic politics enable us to see that Thucydides later developed his own version of what were originally Herodotean theses. Much of Herodotus's account of the Persian War period reflects later traditions about the war, which operated as "usable history" in conflicts both within and between Greek cities throughout the fifth century.[29] The focus of these later conflicts was, naturally, which states had resisted the Persians and which had "Medized," and, from the reverse angle, which individuals or states were most responsible for the Greek victory.[30] From the mass of often conflicting material preserved and presented by Herodotus, it is possible to elicit particular viewpoints on the Athenians' tremendous energy and capacity, as well as a vision of the nature and moral status of Athenian imperialism and its relation to Athens's democratic politics.

As Herodotus explained Eastern imperialism with reference to the cultural expectation of never-ending expansionism, so too does he reflect on the "prehistory" of Athens's own imperialism through his particular understanding of its elite and its demos. Herodotus suggests that the tremendous capacity and energy of Athens and its leaders keeps falling short of its own highest ideals, and that as a result Athenian power is increas-

[28] On Herodotus's emphasis on sea power in political history, see Shimron 1989, 89–100.

[29] As Osborne (1996, 329) puts it, "Too much was invested in antiquity in answering the question of how the Greeks beat the Persians for us to be able to disembed truth from partial tradition. What we can do is to exploit the tensions between competing traditions, and by doing so throw light on the nature of city-state politics in these years, and hence on the classical legacy left by the war."

[30] Osborne 1996, 337–43; Hornblower 1991, 25–34.

ingly dedicated to the satisfaction of greed rather than to the cultivation of glory. The opposition between greed and glory is evident in the earliest formulations of the Greek discourse on greed: for Achilles and Thersites, Agamemnon's insatiable greed undermines his capacity to be honorable. Herodotus's Athenians, similarly, reveal their capacity for self-sacrifice during the Persian Wars, and thus their ability to transcend their baser desires for the sake of glory, but in his reconstruction they also tend to pervert their capacities for the sake of morally reprehensible greed. Their perversion is the result, for Herodotus, of a uniquely democratic combination of elite and demotic collusion in pan-Athenian greed. Ultimately, then, Herodotus poses the question whether the goal of the new democracy is imperial domination, not freedom or equality.

Raaflaub has argued that no classical author provides a truly developmental account of the relationship between Athenian imperialism and democracy: "Thus in the late 430s the connection between democracy and imperialism was well-established and taken for granted. It is interesting that no ancient source provides an analysis of the cause and development of this connection. Rather, if Herodotus is representative, the assumption seems to have been that the two went together from the very beginning of the democracy in the days of Cleisthenes."[31] Herodotus, however, does provide a telling developmental perspective on the interconnections between Athenian democracy and imperialism, in particular by showing that elites and demos alike could be united politically around their shared greed. Herodotus's own narrative also offers insight into the perceptions of Athenian imperialism and democracy that were held by his contemporaries.[32]

First, two preliminaries. I assume that the narrative contains "proleptic" hints of Athens's later imperialism, which only emerges after the chronological conclusion of the *Histories*.[33] Given the surviving evidence, it is difficult, if not impossible, to know the identity of Herodotus's audiences, or to grasp fully how those audiences would have interpreted such prospective allusions within his narrative. It is likely that Herodotus presented his material orally throughout the Greek world, without consistently championing any polis in particular.[34] Readers should therefore expect a certain degree of ambivalence, and even internal "contestation,"

[31] Raaflaub 1994, 125; cf. 144–46, citing 5.66.1, 5.78, 6.109.3, 6.109.6.

[32] On contemporary perceptions of Athenian democracy, see Raaflaub 1989.

[33] The take-off point for the following discussion is primarily Fornara 1971, which has gained a great deal of currency in recent Herodotean scholarship: cf. Redfield 1985, 115; Raaflaub 1987; Stadter 1992; Moles 1996; Konstan 1987, 72; Nagy 1990b; contra, Gould 1989, 117–20; Pelling 1997a.

[34] Raaflaub 1987, Stadter 1992.

within the text.[35] In addition, Herodotus's audiences, living in the latter half of the fifth century, would have been acutely sensitive to the military and ideological conflicts between Athens and Sparta during that half century. As a result, these audiences would have interpreted Herodotus's narrative in terms of their own experience of that conflict. In particular, his language must have had special resonance for an audience aware of the Spartan-Athenian conflict, which was represented in terms of a characteristic moral terminology. Therein lies the significance of his characterization of pre-imperial Athenians as excessively greedy to get more. Although the Athenian Empire did not exist before 479, Herodotus's presentation of Athenian leaders and demos can provide insight into the workings of Athenian imperialism, which was later viewed in terms of injustice and greed.

Second, I argue that Herodotus has a complex and ambivalent view of the Athenian democracy.[36] He is neither an unambiguous supporter nor an unflinching critic of the democracy. In discussing this issue, scholars have tended to focus too narrowly on Otanes' praise of democracy in the so-called constitutional debate (3.80–82), equating Otanes' arguments with those of the author himself.[37] It is better to regard Otanes' abstract, theoretical claims as subject to revision and redefinition by the narrative as a whole. The narrative itself opens up a range of interpretive possibilities and then pushes readers in particular interpretive directions. In this sense, the text "constructs" the reader as much as the reader constructs the text.[38] As a result, readers must pay close attention not only to Otanes' speech, but also to Herodotus's explicit presentation of democracy and democratic process in action. If they are to be interpreted correctly, then Otanes' theoretical statements should be tested against the rest of the work in order to determine whether they are upheld or refuted.

Otanes spends most of his time criticizing monarchy, rather than praising democracy, but he does assert that "isonomiē," which probably

[35] In the contemporary academy, of course, readers normally expect dissonance in any text, but the internal conflicts in Herodotus may have been intensified by his changing contexts of performance. See Pelling 1997a for a discussion of the idea of "internal contestation" in connection with Herodotus's categories of "East" and "West."

[36] For the view that Herodotus is (to some extent) critical of democracy, see Strasburger 1955 and Fornara 1971; Raaflaub 1987; Stadter 1992; Flory 1987, 131, 143–45; Lateiner 1989, 181–86. For a subtle account of Herodotus's ambivalence, see Edelmann 1975, 319. Forrest 1984 develops a fascinating prosopographical argument to the effect that Herodotus opposed the political policies of Periclean Athens. Harvey 1966 argues that nothing in Herodotus's text proves he is critical of Athens.

[37] Kagan 1965, 69–70; cf. Harvey 1966.

[38] A perceptive treatment of the "construction" of the reader in Thucydides can be found in Connor 1984, 3–19; cf. Lateiner 1989, 165–81.

refers to democracy in this passage, has particular advantages over other forms of government.[39] These include the accountability of magistrates, open debate, and the coincidence of interests between the demos and the state as a whole (3.80). Herodotus himself seems to approve these sentiments in his famous statement at 5.78:

> This makes it clear that free and equal speech [*isēgoriē*] is a serious [*spoudaion*] thing not only in one respect but in all, if the Athenians under the tyranny [*turanneuomenoi*] were weaker in warfare than their neighbors, but having thrown off the yoke were first [*prōtoi*] by far. This shows that, held down by authority [*katechomenoi*], they shirked their duty in the field, because they were working for a master, but once free each man was eager to work for himself [*eleutherōthentōn de autos hekastos heōutōi proethumeeto katergazesthai*].[40]

The semantics of the Greek term *isēgoriē* are notoriously complicated, but a near consensus has emerged that the term emphasizes specifically democratic free speech.[41] Herodotus's praise of Athenian democracy is derived from the connections he draws between democracy and military potential. This is richly ironic, since Athenian military aggression also generates for Herodotus a great deal of moral ambivalence about Athens. Athenian democracy and imperialism play a key and closely related role throughout the latter books of the narrative. The theme of greed links the emergence of Athenian imperialism with the excessive desires of Persian despots and with the allegations of injustice that arise during the embassies to Gelon and the Argives. If Xerxes' imperialistic desire unites both his own intense personal acquisitiveness and his emulation of his predecessors, then it is plausible that the Persian culture of expansionism was gradually instituted by the specific actions of excessively grasping individuals, such as Cyrus and Darius. Herodotus provides a similar perspective on the forces, both cultural and individual, that inspired fifth-century Athenian imperialism.

Herodotus's focus on the greed of Themistocles and other members of the Athenian elite enables him to explain the Athenians' ability and desire to be imperialists.[42] In characterizing Themistocles, Herodotus emphasizes the excessive acquisitiveness that Thucydides later identifies as a

[39] That Otanes is speaking of democracy, although he uses the term *isonomiē* rather than *dēmokratiē*, is demonstrated by 6.43.3; cf. Vlastos 1964, 2–3; Ostwald 1969, 111–13.

[40] For further discussion of Herodotus's use of *prōtoi* to describe the Athenians, see my discussion in the conclusion of this chapter.

[41] On *isēgoriē*, see Vlastos 1953, 1964; Ostwald 1972, 1991; Raaflaub 1996; Hansen 1991, 83–84; Cartledge 1996, 178.

[42] Moles 1996 is valuable for theorizing the ways in which "prospective allusion" can be elicited from Herodotus's text. For the importance of Themistocles as a "prospective" figure within the narrative, that is, one that looks forward to Athens's later imperialism, see Fornara 1971, 66–73; Konstan 1987, 70–73.

defining characteristic of Athens as a whole. Herodotus capitalizes upon Themistocles' already legendary reputation for greed in order to make specific points about the development of Athenian imperialism.[43] Themistocles took advantage of the Hellenic League's decision to exact payment from Medizing states like Andros. According to Herodotus, he secretly demanded that several island-states pay him off in order to escape a visit from the Greek fleet (8.111–12): "Themistocles—for he never stopped being greedy [*ou gar epaueto pleonekteōn*]—sent threatening messages to the other islands and demanded money [*aitee chrēmata*], using the same messengers he had sent to the king, saying that if they did not give what he asked, he would bring the Greek fleet and besiege them into surrender" (8.112.1).[44] Herodotus makes a specific point about Themistocles' excessive acquisitiveness by indicating that he made his demands without the knowledge of the other commanders (8.112.3).[45]

Themistocles' secrecy is intelligible only if he believes that his behavior is unjust or shameful. The key is that he is cheating the other members of the league out of advantages that all members should hold in common, in virtue of their collective participation in resisting the Persians and in besieging Andros and Carystus (8.121.1). In other words, Themistocles' greed violates the canons of distributive fairness that operate within the league in view of their collective goals. This context of distribution within the league is made clear by the Greeks' traditional division of spoils after the devastation of Carystus. According to Herodotus, the fleet subsequently returned to Salamis, where a division of the spoils was conducted (*diedasanto tēn lēiēn*, 8.121.2; cf. *tēn diairesin tēs lēiēs*, 8.123.1). The specific terminology recalls the archaic institution of the military division of spoils (*dasmos*).[46] This division also extends to the gods: when the Greeks send thank offerings to Delphi, they ask the god if he has received his "full share" (*plērea*, 8.122). Although pleased with his gifts from everyone else, the god demands from the Aeginetans the prize of valor (*ta aristēia*) for the battle of Salamis (8.122). His claim on shares in the division of spoils results, like that of the individual city-states, from his participation in the victory: as Themistocles himself argues, "Indeed, it was not we who performed this exploit; it was the gods

[43] On Themistocles' reputation, see Barth 1965.

[44] Such a characterization of Themistocles remains consistent throughout the text: cf. 8.4–5, along with Herodotus's notice that Themistocles is the determined enemy of Aristides the Just (8.78–81), whom Herodotus calls *ariston . . . kai dikaiōtaton* (8.79.1); Herodotus's notice hints that Themistocles' greed is also a violation of justice.

[45] On Herodotus's moral evaluation of Themistocles, see Weber (1967, 26–41, esp. 28–32), who concludes that Herodotus evaluates Themistocles negatively. I believe that the systematic account of greed developed in chapter 1 helps us interpret Herodotus's evaluation more fully by enabling us to set it in the context of distributive justice.

[46] For discussion of the archaic *dasmos*, see chapter 3.

and the heroes, who were jealous that one man in his impious arrogance [*eonta anosion te kai atasthalon*] should be king of Asia and of Europe too" (8.109.3). Everyone who promoted the Greek cause deserves a share of the rewards of victory.

Herodotus has thus framed Themistocles' greed for gain within the most traditional of Greek distributive contexts—the distribution of spoils after a successful military campaign. The proceeds stolen by Themistocles rightly belong to the group as a whole and should have been distributed equally after the campaign. The traditional expectation of proportionally equal distribution is, by contrast, fulfilled after the battle of Plataea: "The rest of the booty—the Persians' women, pack animals, gold, silver, and so on—was divided [*diaireonto*] among the troops, each man taking the things he was worthy of [*elabon hekastoi tōn axioi ēsan*]. . . . Pausanias himself was granted ten of everything—women, horses, talents, camels, and everything else" (9.81.1–2).[47] Here Herodotus anticipates two ideas that Aristotle later theorized in detail: that distribution should be based on "worth" (*axia*) and that leaders, such as Pausanias, should receive a greater distributive share in accordance with their greater contributions. Themistocles preempts this entire array of ethical practices. By hoodwinking the process of collective distribution, Themistocles recalls Agamemnon's famous violation of distributive procedure in the first book of the *Iliad*. In light of this conception of Themistoclean greed, Athens's later institution of imperial tribute was appositely called *dasmophoros*, which literally means "the bringing in of the distribution," because its imperialistic greed similarly violated the canons of distributive fairness that should have informed relations among the Panhellenic community of equal, or proportionally equal, states.

Earlier in the narrative, Herodotus's characters had used the language of greed to describe the violation of distributive principles with regard to hegemony; now Herodotus himself explicitly embeds greedy desire within the framework of the collective Greek army's distribution of spoils. The two central elements of Aristotle's account of greed—acquisitiveness and distributive unfairness—are already in place, although Herodotus does not forge a tight connection between them in the way Aristotle himself does.

In hearing that Themistocles never stopped "being greedy for more," we should recall that Artabanus had once lamented Xerxes' acceptance of advice that "teaches the heart always to want to have more" (7.16a.2).[48]

[47] Miller (1997, 43–46) helpfully discusses the division and diffusion of the spoils from the Persian Wars, arguing for the likelihood that individual hoplites could have garnered significant portions because of their contribution to the victorious cause.

[48] In Themistocles' case, though, the psychological framework is subtly different, because he is motivated by excessive desire rather than by the arrogance that drives Xerxes' imperi-

Speaking of the failed expeditions of Xerxes' predecessors, Artabanus declares that he "knows how bad a thing it is to desire many things" (*epistamenos hōs kakon eiē to pollōn epithumeein*, 7.18.2). The terminology is pointed and ironic: Themistocles himself had once blamed Xerxes' defeat on divine jealousy (*phthonos*) and on the king's impiety and outrages (8.109.3). Despite sharing Artabanus's sentiments, however, Themistocles, like Xerxes, uses his control of military power in order to satisfy his greed. By falling into the trap of excess desire, Themistocles exhibits the characteristic moral failing of Persian kings. Unlike the Persian kings, however, he must rely on his ability to manipulate Xerxes and the other Greeks in order to achieve his own self-interested ends.

Although Themistocles can abuse the Panhellenic political process for ulterior motives, the Athenians as a collective body are usually complicit in their leaders' desire to attack other Greeks for the sake of material profit. The Athenians' practice of free democratic deliberation initiates a transition from individual elite greed to the pursuit of greed by the entire polis. Ultimately, the Athenian elite and the demos unite in exerting their shared acquisitiveness against their former allies. Repetition of the verb *diaballō*, which means "to deceive" or "to impose upon," links together two key passages in which Herodotus contrasts Sparta and Athens in order to emphasize the Athenian demos's willingness to follow the plans of acquisitive members of the elite, on the assumption that their self-interests are congruent. These passages illuminate how Herodotus constructs a contrast between Spartan self-restraint and Athenian greed, as well as between Spartan good judgment and Athenian gullibility.[49]

After establishing popular government (*isonomiēn*, 5.37.2) in Ionia, the Milesian Aristagoras attempted to persuade Cleomenes of Sparta to join the Ionian Revolt (5.49–51). Aristagoras argues not only that the Ionians' enslavement is shameful and that the Persians are weaklings, but also that "the inhabitants of that continent [Asia] have more good things [*agatha*] than all the rest put together—gold, silver, bronze, . . . and slaves" (5.49.4). Aristagoras urges the Spartans to give up fighting over a worthless scrap of land, and to set their minds on things that, he assumes, are actually worth fighting for, like gold and silver. He works his way carefully through the map he has brought, pointing out the particular and distinctive ways in which the individual countries are wealthy—Lydia in money, Phrygia in cattle and crops, and so on (5.49.5–8).[50] Cleomenes asks for two days to make his decision (5.49.9) and in that time thinks to

alism. Here again we see the beginnings of a new conceptualization of greed that is distinct from *hubris* and that points toward Aristotle.

[49] These are central points of comparison and contrast for Thucydides, too: see chapter 5.

[50] By using this argument, Aristagoras foreshadows the well-known Tritantaechmes episode (8.26), which I discuss below.

ask how far Susa is from the sea. Herodotus says, "But Aristagoras, though clever [*sophos*] and leading him on with success [*diaballōn ekeinon eu*], tripped up in this" (5.50.2). That is to say, Aristagoras eventually told the truth—that Susa is three months' journey from the sea—which made Cleomenes force him out of Sparta. Displaying admirable self restraint, Cleomenes then refused to be bribed, although even he had his limits; he ultimately succeeded in driving away Aristagoras only with his daughter's help (5.51.2–3). Aristagoras is forced to leave Sparta empty-handed. Whatever its historical merits, this story shows that, in Herodotus's Sparta, foreign policy is conducted by a single individual who takes his time to reflect on alternatives and to scrutinize relevant facts before making policy decisions. Because he is not greedy, gullible, or rash, Cleomenes makes the decision that seems to be in Sparta's best interest.[51] Especially noteworthy is his self-restraint in the face of Aristagoras's bribes, although the temptation almost becomes too much even for him.[52]

In Athens, by contrast, greed was becoming a way of life for all citizens, not only the clever Themistocles. When Aristagoras approaches the Athenian Assembly (5.97.1), he promises the same rewards—an easy conquest and all of Asia's riches. According to Herodotus, "He said the same things he had said at Sparta, about the good things [*tōn agathōn*] in Asia, and the Persian methods of warfare—how they used neither shields nor spears and were easy to beat" (5.97.1). The demos agrees to fight, whereupon Herodotus offers the following verdict: "For apparently it is easier to lead on [*diaballein*] a crowd [*pollous*] than an individual, because Aristagoras was not able to lead on [*diaballein*] Cleomenes, a single Lacedaimonian, but he succeeded with thirty thousand Athenians" (5.97.2).[53]

This passage provides a good opportunity to see how Herodotus shapes his narrative to make a specific and derogatory charge against the demos and Athenian democracy. By this point in the narrative, the Athenians had recently refused to accept the return of Hippias, which meant, according to Herodotus, that they were already openly hostile to Persia (5.96.2). If Herodotus had unambiguously admired free democratic deliberation, then he could have interpreted the Athenians' decision differently by affirming its merits. The Athenians, he could have said, took

[51] For a historical account of the Ionian revolt, its causes, and its consequences, see Murray 1988; Evans 1963. Murray (1988, 482) argues that Cleomenes "was perhaps too preoccupied with the Argive threat" to get Sparta involved.

[52] Some other Spartans, in fact, do give in to bribes: Leotychides was not above taking a magnificent bribe in Thessaly (6.72.1–2).

[53] Contra Harvey 1966, I believe that this passage does express a criticism of Athenian democracy. The figure of thirty thousand is, of course, too high: cf. Hansen 1991, 130–31. But it may show that Herodotus conceives of the demos in Assembly as the "capital-D Demos"—that is, as the imagined community of all Athenian citizens; cf. Ober 1996b, 107–22.

advantage of a good opportunity to ally themselves with the Ionians, thereby weakening the king's forces, creating a geographical buffer between Athens and the king, and, most importantly, showing the world that Athenians were freedom fighters. Instead, Herodotus interprets the Athenian decision as exemplifying the Athenian demos's imprudent, but all too characteristic, gullibility and instinctual drive to satisfy its greed. Both characteristics make the Athenians too quick to collude in the greedy projects of a self-interested speaker. Cleomenes will not sacrifice the interests of his country for money (*chrēmata*), but thirty thousand greedy Athenians will permit Aristagoras to lead them into an unwise decision. Herodotus's authorial comment challenges the prevailing democratic belief in the wisdom of the masses when gathered together in the Assembly.[54]

This passage takes on a wider thematic significance if read against Herodotus's well-known contrasts between Greeks and Persians, which are captured in Tritantaechmes' famous contrast between greed and glory.[55] Marching through Greece, Xerxes learns that the Greeks were celebrating the Olympic festival at that time, a competition dedicated to winning not money but an olive wreath (8.26.2). The festival elicits the following remark from Tritanaechmes, which Herodotus records approvingly: "Good heavens, Mardonius, what kind of men are these that you have brought us to fight against—men who compete with one another not for money [*peri chrēmatōn*] but for honor [*peri aretēs*]" (8.26.3).[56] As it appears to an observant outsider (who happens to be the son of the same Artabanus who discouraged Xerxes' expedition in the first place), Greeks are motivated by valor, not the desire for gain. The Athenian Assembly, by contrast, is persuaded not by considerations of nobility and honor, but by Aristagoras's promises of material wealth. It is not only Themistocles who embodies the traits of Persian imperialism but the Athenian citizenry as a whole.[57]

These characterizations of the Athenians and of their democratic process are confirmed by another episode that illustrates the Athenian demos's willingness to follow its leaders in order to satisfy its own greed,

[54] Ober (1989, 163–66) usefully analyzes this central tenet of Athenian democratic ideology.

[55] Konstan 1987; Pelling 1997a.

[56] Scholars have noted that *chrēmata* and *aretē* are not precisely parallel in this passage, because one cannot fight "for" *aretē* in the same way one can fight "for" *chrēmata*: see Macan 1908, ad loc. Konstan (1987, 62) offers an illuminating explanation of this difficulty: "Money, properly speaking, may be a goal; virtue is a quality that is manifested in the contest, not the object of it. . . . Because the Greeks do not, in Tritantaechmes' aphorism, fight for something extrinsic, but merely as a function of their commitment to valor, there is nothing short of death that will discourage them on the battlefield."

[57] Cf. Konstan 1987, 70–73; Fornara 1971, 66; Rosenbloom 1992.

even when, as Herodotus tells it, the demos has not fully considered the reasons for its military campaigns. Herodotus records that after Marathon, Miltiades persuaded the Athenians to sail against Paros (6.132–33); this story also takes an unfavorable view of democratic process. Miltiades, Herodotus says, "asked the Athenians for seventy ships with troops and money, not telling them against what region he was making the expedition, but saying that he would enrich them [*kataploutiein*] if they followed him: for he would lead them to a place from which they could easily take away unlimited gold [*hothen chruson eupeteōs aphthonon oisontai*]; saying this, he asked for the ships, and the Athenians, excited by what he said [*toutoisi eparthentes*], gave them to him" (6.132). According to Herodotus, Miltiades himself is not greedy; his motive is revenge (6.133.1).[58] Like Aristagoras, however, he can manipulate the greedy instincts of the demos and drive the Assembly to a hasty, unreflective decision. Excited by the prospect of getting more, the demos trusts its leaders too much and indulges its greed with potentially detrimental consequences. On the other hand, democratic leaders, relying on their military reputations, manipulate the demos in Assembly in order to promote an imperialistic agenda that often bears no relation to the welfare of Athens as a polis.

Herodotus provides a deep context for the Athenians' gullibility, which, as we have seen, is often combined with their greedy desires, with the result that they make rash, unwise political decisions. Even though Athenians are reputedly the most intelligent of the Greeks, Herodotus says, they had once been persuaded (*peithomenoi*) that the country girl Phye was the goddess Athena, and that Athena herself was welcoming the tyrant Peisistratus back to Athens (1.60.4–5). The freedom-loving Athenians, who achieve greatness only by eliminating tyranny (5.78), were foolish enough to embrace the tyrant when deceived by clever religious manipulation.[59] Just before the siege of Andros, moreover, Themistocles deceives the Athenians into allowing Xerxes to leave Europe without being harassed; he did this, Herodotus says, in order to win Xerxes' favor for the future (8.109.5). As Herodotus puts it, "In saying these things, Themistocles deceived [*dieballe*] them, and the Athenians

[58] On the character of Miltiades, see Hartog 1988, 335–36, who fits him into a typically tragic pattern of success followed by *hubris* and then failure.

[59] On the rise of Peisistratus and the Athenians' gullibility, see Gray 1997. Sinos (1993) reinterprets the ritual context that lies behind the Athenians' acceptance of Phye, while Thalmann (1998, 239–42) provides a helpful rereading of the Odyssean background of Peisistratus's ruse, but I am concerned with Herodotus's own explicit interpretation of the event as illustrating the Athenians' stupidity and gullibility. It is possible that Herodotus reflects a fifth century democratic tradition that asserted stupidity to avoid the anathema of having self-consciously chosen a tyrant, but nonetheless his story as it stands squares with other episodes that illuminate the Athenians' gullibility.

obeyed [*epeithonto*]; for they had always thought him clever [*sophos*], and now that he had proved beyond a doubt both clever and successful, they were willing to follow his lead in everything" (8.110.1). Themistocles hoodwinks the entire Panhellenic league for profit, but, Herodotus adds pointedly, the Athenians in particular are too foolish to see that Themistocles' narrow self-interest governs the advice he gives as their leader.

Thus, as Herodotus depicts it, the emergence of Athenian imperialism was a fitful process in which the Athenian elite and the Athenian people tended to pursue their own self-interests in the international arena, where, they discovered, their narrowly conceived self-interests could become at least temporarily congruent. Herodotus's account represents a transitional stage between Solon and Thucydides. The two classes of Athenians—mass and elite—still conceive of their own interests in narrowly personal (or group) terms, which, in Solon's poetry, had once created the conditions for civic disaster within Athens. The democratic process, however, enables Athenians to negotiate their own interests in the public realm of political speech. Although political language was a fragile and imperfect tool, and sometimes led to hasty, unwise decisions, at least Athens itself benefited from the capacity of political speech to harmonize elite and demotic interests by channeling the aggressive impulses of *all* Athenians outward against other Greek city-states. Athens had not yet become the fully greedy polis that we find in Thucydides, but an emerging congruence of self-interests among the elite and the demos was strongly pushing Athens to attempt to seize imperialistic power.

What do these diverse indications of elite greed, combined with demotic greed and gullibility, portend for Athens itself and, even more, for its Aegean neighbors? By Herodotean lights, the outlook is not very promising because, among Athenian leaders, Themistocles is not the exception but the rule. His deceptiveness and ulterior motives are matched by those of Miltiades; his greed, by that of the aristocrat Alcmaeon.[60] Having assisted the Lydian envoys at Delphi, Alcmaeon traveled to Sardis as Croesus's guest and was given as much gold as he could carry on his person at one time (6.125.2). Dressing up in a baggy tunic and tragic buskins (*kothornoi*), he loads himself down with so much gold that he can hardly walk. In Herodotus's telling expression, he looked, "with his bulging cheeks and swollen figure, like anything rather than a human being [*panti de teōi oikōs mallon ē anthrōpōi*]" (6.125.4). In Herodotean terms, Alcmaeon has transgressed the boundaries of his own humanity, which recalls the Persians' immoral transgression of natural boundaries such as

[60] On the oral traditions surrounding the Alcmaeonids in general, Thomas (1989, 238–82) is indispensable.

rivers.[61] Alcmaeon is a glutton for gold, not blood (cf. Cyrus, 1.201); his unquenchable greed recalls that of Xerxes, as well as the greed of Athenian aristocrats in Solon's poetry.[62] The image of a gluttonous Alcmaeon is Herodotus's reformulation of the archaic tendency to figure greed as a form of excessive bodily consumption.[63]

When Croesus sees Alcmaeon, he bursts out laughing, and gives him as much gold again in addition (6.125.5). On the face of it, this is a comic scene: the standard commentary on Herodotus says that the story "is obviously a comic version of the enrichment of the [Alcmaeonid] family by the Lydian king or by successful trade with Sardis."[64] Gluttony is, after all, a humorous topos in Attic comedy, and Croesus, who may be imagined as Herodotus's "internal audience," laughs when he sees the gold-laden Alcmaeon. But Croesus's laughter strikes a more ominous note within the *Histories*, because it echoes the tragic, hubristic laughter of other Eastern despots.[65] Greed, especially at an Eastern despot's court, is nothing to be proud of or laughed at. This story should rather be seen as tragic, or even "tragicomic": Alcmaeon rushes onto the stage in baggy Persian pants, wearing the buskins normally worn by tragic actors (6.125.3), while Croesus, the actor-cum-spectator, laughs foolishly, unaware that prosperity never lasts for long, and that wealth is not the same thing as genuine prosperity (*olbos*).[66] Croesus's laughter is the laughter of recognition, which acknowledges shared sentiments and mutual understanding; Croesus sees himself in Alcmaeon. If Croesus is an internal audience, then what does this story say to Herodotus's *external* audience, whether Athenians or other late fifth-century Greeks?[67]

[61] See n.8.

[62] For Herodotus's ambivalence toward the Alcmaeonids, particularly as expressed in this episode, see Waters 1985, 124–25; Strasburger 1962; Thomas 1989, 264–68; Georges 1994, 157–60.

[63] On Alcmaeon's grotesque body, see Kurke 1999, 144–46.

[64] How and Wells 1912, ad loc.

[65] On the laughter of despots, see Lateiner 1977; on non-verbal communication in general, see Lateiner 1987.

[66] This story may give evidence that Herodotus was even more deeply aware of, and influenced by, trends in late fifth-century Athenian dramatic production than has previously been thought. In particular, it evokes Euripides' and Aristophanes' persistent focus on defining and blurring the boundaries between tragedy and comedy. On Herodotus's relationship with tragedy, see Immerwahr 1966, 11–12, 238–39; Hall 1989; Rosenbloom 1992, esp. 222–51; for a different interpretation of Alcmaeon's clothes, see Kurke 1999, 145–46; Georges 1994, 158.

[67] Alcmaeon's story shows that, in the late archaic period, Athenian aristocrats were becoming infected with the greedy, immoral attitudes characteristic of Eastern despots. Would an audience of late fifth-century Athenians see themselves in such attitudes? Should they? They should at least see in themselves the historically ingrained Athenian tendency to take too much, and perhaps equally the light laughter of overconfidence. These points of

Alcmaeon has been corrupted through his contact with Croesus; his viewing of Croesus's treasury has triggered an unwholesome desire for more, which makes him fat, gluttonous, and even seemingly inhuman. Alcmaeon's corruption would have resonated all the more with an Athenian audience, because "Croesus" had become an Alcmaeonid family name in the late sixth and fifth centuries.[68] Alcmaeon's greed does not, of course, raise questions of taking more than one's share of divisible goods. As Aristagoras has pointed out, in the East there is always more, and Eastern overabundance tempts Alcmaeon to devour literally more than he, as a human being, can swallow. His greed therefore does not violate canons of distributive fairness within a polis. Still, Alcmaeon's acquisitiveness should be read prospectively, because Alcmaeon points ahead genetically to Pericles and to the Athenians' tyrannical polis; hence, his archaic greed (*koros*) will, in time, become Aristotelian greed within a distributive community. The Alcmaeonid excursus (6.125–31) concludes with the notice that Alcmaeon is the ancestor of Pericles, Xanthippus's son (6.131.2).[69]

This notice has two implications for fifth-century Athens: first, it looks forward to the conclusion of the *Histories*, where Xanthippus, the Athenian general at Sestos, barbarically crucifies the Persian governor Artaÿctes (9.120.4)—an act that resembles the Persian kings' tyrannical cruelty toward the bodies of their subjects. Second, Pericles, Xanthippus's son, is represented as a lion in his mother Agariste's dream (6.131.2), which recalls the use of lion imagery to describe Cypselus, the murderous and greedy tyrant of Corinth (5.92b.3).[70] Pericles is no tyrant

contact reduce the cultural disparity between Greeks and the barbarian "other"; see Rosenbloom 1992, Georges 1994, 130–57. On self and "other" in Herodotus, see Hartog 1988; Pelling 1997a; Hall 1989; Nagy 1990b; Rosenbloom 1992, 252–91.

[68] *IG* i^3 1183; 1240; Davies 1971, 370–71, 374.

[69] In the *Gorgias* (518e1–519a7), Socrates holds Pericles, Alcmaeon's descendant, responsible for Athens' imperial "gluttony": "You now, Callicles, are behaving in just the same way as these men; you are extolling men who have regaled the Athenians by giving them their fill of what they desired [*hoi toutous hestiakasin euōchountes hōn epethumoun*], and people say that they have made Athens great. They do not perceive that through the efforts of these earlier statesmen it is bloated [*oidei*] and rotten to the core [*hupoulos*]. They have glutted the state with harbors and dockyards and walls and tribute and rubbish of that sort, without self-control [*sōphrosunēs*] and justice [*dikaiosunēs*], and when the inevitable fit of weakness comes, the citizens will blame their current advisers and praise Themistocles and Cimon and Pericles, the real authors of their problems."

[70] In the oracle describing Cypselus as a lion, it is notable that the lion is said to be "strong, ravenous" (*karteron ōmēstēn*); the epithet "ravenous, eating raw meat" (*ōmēstēn*) recalls the well-known connections between greed and gluttony in the archaic period; cf. chapter 3. When Cypselus was tyrant, according to the Corinthian ambassador Socles, "He drove many Corinthians into exile [*ediōxe*], and many he deprived of their property [*chrēmatōn*], and many more of their life" (5.92e.2). Cypselus's greed, like Alcmaeon's, is suggestive in Herodotus's notice of Pericles' birth.

within Athens,[71] but, as an architect of Athenian imperialism, he is suitably portrayed as the leader of the "tyrannical polis" (*polis tyrannos*), Athens.[72] The tyrannical impulse is amply evident in the behavior of members of the Athenian elite, who work through the democratic process in order to satisfy their own desires for more by exploiting the demos's greed and gullibility.

Herodotus has integrated this array of ethically meaningful details, however apparently diverse, into a telling, proleptic composite. In Herodotus's presentation, the greed of the Athenian leadership matches that of the demos but with a stunning and original effect. As we have seen, Solon's poetry articulates and tries to resolve the conflict between these groups over power and material resources *within* Athens. Herodotus, on the other hand, suggests that after the Cleisthenic democracy was established, these groups formed a working compact that allowed them to transfer their desires for more outward against Persians, Medizers, and other Greek city-states in general. The Athenians were no longer troubled by domestic disputes over power, such as those found in the Peisistratus stories, nor did Athenians any longer waste their time producing goods for a tyrannical master. They were working for themselves and, indeed, in partnership with one another. This compact usually involved elite political maneuvering and demotic culpability, but, in Herodotus's presentation, both groups shared a basic greedy impulse. Greed glued together elites and demos in a powerful, dangerous military, and now political, coalition. Greed is already established as a distinctive, even defining, characteristic of Athens as a polis by the time the Athenians decide to besiege Sestos, the repository of Protesilaos's rich treasures (9.116.2).[73] To an audience educated in the language and practice of fifth-century Athenian imperialism, Herodotus's indications provide a perceptive developmental account of the diverse political, cultural, and individual factors through which the Athenian Empire came into existence.

The emerging tradition of thinking about greed as a fundamental feature of Athenian politics and sociology can be drawn together even more tightly when we interpret Alcmaeon's behavior against the background of

[71] Even so, Ehrenberg (1954, 84–91; cf. Tuplin 1985, 368) collects a number of comic fragments and passages from Plutarch's *Life of Pericles* that show that Pericles was lambasted as a tyrant, or as a new Peisistratid, even in his own time in Athens.

[72] Tuplin 1985 offers a recent examination of the "tyrannical polis" motif.

[73] Artaÿctes, "a clever and arrogant man [*deinos de kai atasthalos*], had deceived [*exēpatēse*] the king on his way to Athens, and had thus gotten hold of the treasures [*chrēmata*] of Protesilaos, son of Iphiclus, at Elaeus" (9.116.1). Artaÿctes' story therefore brings together the earlier themes of deception, gullibility, and greed; these characteristics are inherited by the later Athenian Empire, which gets its start by succeeding Artaÿctes in Sestos.

Herodotus's account of Solon's visit to the court of Croesus (1.29–33).[74] Herodotus makes a special point of characterizing Alcmaeon in contrast to Solon. This contrast says something important about Herodotus's perspective on the (future) fifth-century Athenian Empire. Like Alcmaeon, Solon tours the royal treasury, but the sight of wealth does not trigger a swarm of riotous desires within, nor does it compromise his moral integrity or his understanding of human happiness. Croesus, by contrast, is filled with desire (*himeros*) and hope (*elpis*) during Solon's visit (1.30.2): as he conceives passionate desires for conquest, so too does he conceive a craving for Solon to judge him the most prosperous (*olbiōtatos*) of human beings. According to Herodotus, Solon resists the impulse to flatter the king, urging Croesus not to mistake his present wealth and power for true happiness. Modest means, a family, health, life without reversal of fortune, and an honorable death: being "middling" in the polis is best, Solon suggests.[75] Herodotus almost completely ignores Solon's legal and social reforms, focusing instead on the image of Solon as moral sage. Herodotus utilizes that image in order to condemn the fanatical greed that characterizes both the Athenian elite and demos elsewhere in the text. Solon acts as an "in-house" critic of Athenian imperialism, and he is thereby established as all the more powerful an ethical authority.

Solon's ideals have often been understood as programmatic for the *Histories* as a whole, and as expressing moral views that Herodotus himself held. This seems right in general.[76] Still, his programmatic ethical statements must be tested and refined, or redefined, according to later statements and patterns in the narrative. Here two points are worth noting. First, Solon says that the rich man is better off than the poor in two ways only—"he is more able to satisfy his desire [*epithumiēn ektelesai*] and to bear great misfortune" (1.32.6)—but he is worse off in a variety of other respects. Herodotus's picture of Eastern despots and their greedy counterparts among the Greeks, including tyrants, Athenian elites, and Athens in general, must be understood to modify this general claim in one important way. Rich and powerful men tend to conceive elaborate desires for acquisition that even their extravagant wealth cannot help them satisfy; wealth gives rise to an insatiable greed, which it is then

[74] Moles 1996 offers a perceptive analysis of this episode both as paradigmatic for Herodotus's moral thinking and as prospective for his underlying evaluation of imperialism generally. Other useful treatments are King 1997; Shapiro 1996; Strasburger 1962, 598–99; Thomas 1989, 267.

[75] Kurke (1999, 146–51) offers a valuable reading of the comparison between Solon and Alcmaeon and of Solon's visit to Croesus's court; she emphasizes Solon's use of civic ideology to "short-circuit" the network of aristocratic gift exchange exemplified by Croesus's gift to Alcmaeon (147).

[76] See most recently Shapiro 1996, with How and Wells 1912, Jacoby 1913, cols. 487–88; Immerwahr 1966, 313; contra, Lang 1984, 61; Waters 1985.

helpless to satisfy. Because it creates outlandish desires to get more, extravagant wealth is usually self-defeating. Solon's case against excessive acquisitiveness and pride in one's own wealth is therefore even stronger than he himself seems to realize.

Second, Croesus has a basic conception of human well-being that, in Solon's opinion, is fundamentally misguided.[77] True happiness is altogether different from the possession of wealth and power; it is rather a matter of living a modest life in accordance with virtue, and having some measure of fortune in retaining basic human goods, such as health and fine children, until death. Alcmaeon does not see this; neither does Themistocles; nor, ultimately, do the Athenians. Herodotus's presentation of Solon therefore has far-reaching implications for his account of the Athenians, and for Athenian democracy in general. In light of this, his famous praise of free democratic deliberation must be reinterpreted: "This makes it clear that when they [the Athenians] were held down they shirked responsibility because they were working for a master, but once free each man was eager to work for himself (5.78)." In the "local" context, this comment is, of course, intended as praise: Herodotus is explaining why the Athenians became the finest fighters in the world once they had thrown off the yoke of tyranny. But do the Athenians know how to accomplish things for their own sake in a way that will lead to genuine human happiness, or do they, like Croesus, embody a deeply inadequate understanding of the gods, the moral universe, and their own nature and self-interest as human beings? For Herodotus, the Athenians' greed and stupidity become two sides of the same self-destructive coin.

Conclusion

Let us return to Tritantaechmes' comment on wealth (*chrēmata*) and virtue (*aretē*), taking a broader perspective that will elucidate the continuities and differences between Herodotus and his successor Thucydides. The point of Tritantaechmes' remark is that Greeks compete with one another, not for wealth, but rather in order to display their valor (*aretē*), an intrinsic personal, and sometimes moral, quality that (to Tritantaechmes) seems to entail disdain for cash rewards. The opposition between wealth and the rewards of valor evokes a number of topical, and long-standing, questions about the nature of Greek virtue or excellence (*aretē*) and its mediation of the relationship between individual and community.[78] Does "virtue" or "excellence" amount to being simply a sort of skill, such as athletic skill, that empowers its possessor to achieve his own

[77] For this formulation, I am indebted to King 1997, chap. 1.

[78] On *aretē*, see Adkins 1960, 6–7, 220–25, 232–40, 254–56.

ends successfully, regardless of what those ends happen to be? Or does true virtue, rather, place limitations on non-moral, potentially self-serving capacities? Are there virtues of character that both promote the genuine welfare of the individual *and* harm the interests of his wider community? Or does the kind of capacity that promotes the individual against the wider community lead to the merely apparent, but not genuine, welfare of the individual? In other words, does virtue by definition imply duly respecting the legitimate interests of others?

All these questions bring us back to our initial issue, posed by Aristagoras of Miletus in the epigraph, of what is truly worth living and dying for. At the time of the Persian Wars, the Athenians are in the process of decisively answering that question for themselves in a way that will govern their history throughout the fifth century. By the end of the wars, they have the power to go in many different directions: Herodotus says that, after shaking off their tyranny and becoming free, the Athenians became "first" (*prōtoi*) by far among the Greeks (5.78). But what will being "first" among the Greeks mean for them? Herodotus's use of *prōtoi* to describe the Athenians foreshadows Miltiades' later assertion to the polemarch Callimachus that if he fought the Persians bravely at Marathon, then he would make Athens free (*eleutheras*, 6.109.3) and possibly turn it into Greece's first (*prōtē*) city (6.109.3; cf. 6.109.6). By the end of the *Histories*, the political freedom praised so highly by Herodotus paves the way for Athens to dominate its Greek neighbors; this, ultimately, is what it means for Athens to become "first" among the Greek cities (cf. 5.66.1).

Individual desires and democratic decisions have come together to establish a cultural norm of expansionism that will define Athens throughout the century. That cultural norm culminates in nothing less than a national ethos of imperialism. In Thucydides' *History*, Alcibiades argued for a policy of international aggression by pointing to that very ethos: "In general, I believe that a city which is active [*polin mē apragmona*] will quickly be destroyed if it becomes idle; and the safest way for a people to live is to conduct civic affairs according to their present character and customs [*tois parousin ēthesi kai nomois*] for better or for worse, with the least possible change" (6.18.7). In his opinion, Athenians cannot "calculate like housekeepers" (*tamieuesthai*) how much empire they would like to have; instead, they are forced to plan new conquests or else fall under others' dominion.[79] Equally, Athens will have the greatest security if it accepts the character and customs (*ēthesi kai nomois*) that it actually has, even if they have faults, and tries to live up to them in the highest degree

[79] As Connor (1984, 176n45) has observed, Alcibiades persistently uses financial metaphors to describe Athenian domination of other Greeks.

(6.18.7). Thus Alcibiades says, in effect, that the paramount national characteristic of Athens, greed, should be taken as an ideal that guarantees future security and prosperity; if Athens abandons this ideal, then it will soon ruin itself.

For Herodotus, this development is especially regrettable because the Athenians had once used their overflowing energy and ability to save Greece: "One is surely right in saying that Greece was saved by the Athenians. It was the Athenians who held the balance: whichever side they joined was sure to prevail. It was the Athenians, too, who, having chosen that Greece should survive and be free [*helomenoi de tēn Hellada perieinai eleutherēn*], roused to battle the other Greek states that had not yet submitted. It was the Athenians who—after the gods—drove back the Persian king. Not even the terrifying warnings of oracles from Delphi could persuade them to abandon Greece; they stood firm and had the courage to meet the invader" (7.139.5–6). Herodotus announces this contention boldly, despite knowing that most people disagree with it (7.139.1). Like Themistocles, the Athenians fight brilliantly for Greece when necessary, thereby exemplifying a "cooperative" vision of their national excellence. The Athenians give up claims on leadership within the Hellenic League in order to strengthen the alliance. They will never forsake Greece in time of need; "there is not so much gold in the world," the Athenians say, "nor land of such beauty and excellence that we would take in return for medizing and enslaving Greece" (8.144.1). Exhibiting admirable self-restraint and an adherence to their perceived moral obligations, the Athenians used their military power in order to promote Greek liberty against the Persians.

But the Athenians' democratic freedom, which itself makes Athens strong, all too easily became the capacity to dominate others.[80] According to Herodotus, the Athenians had planned to seize power among the Greeks for quite some time and were only biding their time until they could do so (8.3.2). This startling charge immediately precedes the notice that Themistocles took bribes to stay at Artemisium and bribed his fellow commanders to do the same, making off with a healthy sum for himself (8.4–5). Herodotus's narrative juxtaposition memorably links the

[80] See Raaflaub (1994, 124–25), who carefully traces the idea that, to many contemporaries, the greatest goods were "'freedom and power over others,'" which had become virtually equivalent to one another in fifth-century Athens; Raaflaub cites Plato, *Gorgias* 452d, Thucydides 3.45.6. As we will see in chapter 5, Thucydides develops this equivalence at great length, and shapes his narrative to suggest that freedom is fully constituted by power over others; freedom cannot, in the terms of many Thucydidean speakers, exist in a vacuum apart from power. Gray 1997 has adduced several parallels showing that in Sparta, too, *eunomia* (good government), once instituted, was quickly transformed into an overarching will to dominate (cf. 1.65–1.67; cf. the shackles that Athenians put on their own neighbors at 5.76.3).

Athenians' seizure of power with the insatiable greed of Themistocles. By the end of the *Histories*, Herodotus has elaborated this link and applied it to Athens as a whole. As a corporate body, the Athenian polis has begun to embody a competitive, immoralist conception of its national virtues according to which Athenians are free to use their power not to fight for freedom and to win glory, but to satisfy their greed.

These issues are strikingly prominent in late fifth- and fourth-century discussions of justice, power, and greed—during the heyday of the Athenian Empire and probably when Herodotus was writing and reciting his inquiries. The late fifth-century discussion is conducted in terms of virtue (*aretē*), greed, power (*kratos*), and self-mastery (*enkrateia*), all of them terms that, as we shall see in chapter 6, assume a renewed significance in Xenophon's recollections of Socrates and his account of the oligarchic revolution of 404 in Athens.

To take one example among many, the Anonymus Iamblichi, a fifth-century political theorist, argues for a strong opposition between virtue and greed, proposing that greed leads to both immoral and imprudent behavior.[81] He exhorts his contemporaries, "We must not rush to pursue our greed [*pleonexian*], nor should we consider either that power [*kratos*] with a view to greed [*epi tēi pleonexiai*] is virtue (*aretēn*), or that obeying the laws is cowardice [*deilian*]" (6.1). Apparently, certain fifth-century philosophers, revaluing ordinary moral terminology,[82] had argued that genuine virtue or excellence consists in using one's power in order to satisfy the desire to get more. The Anonymus vigorously rejects this view: using power (*kratos*) for the sake of greed is precisely the opposite of virtue or excellence and must be condemned on both moral and prudential grounds.

As we have seen, the relationship between power (*kratos*) and excessive acquisitiveness is one that recurs repeatedly throughout the archaic and classical discourse on greed. Even if greed often aims at political power (*kratos*), one's power (*kratos*) over oneself (*enkrateia*) sets clear limits to excessive desire, thereby bringing individual desires to heel at the feet of distributive fairness. Like (both real and Herodotean) Solon, the Anonymus also emphasizes the need for self-mastery (*enkrateia*), particularly in matters of money: "He would be particularly self-disciplined [*malista* (*enkratestaton*)] if he should be superior to money [*tōn chrēmatōn kreissōn*], for it is in respect to this that all are corrupted [*diaphtheirontai*]" (4.1). At the level of individual character, *aretē*, an other-directed virtue expressed in

[81] Further consideration is given to this important but neglected political thinker in chapter 6. Citations are to DK 89.

[82] For further discussion of such reversals of terminology, see chapters 5 (Thucydides on Corcyra) and 7 (Plato's Thrasymachus). For discussion of reversals of moral terminology in earlier Greek literature, see Edmunds 1973.

self-conscious acts of self-restraint (*enkrateia*), ensures the possibility of Aristotelian distributive fairness. This kind of virtue, along with civic trust (*pistis*), is responsible for binding together political communities (7.1). The Anonymus's ethical and political sentiments resonate with the central themes of trust, political deception, and greed, which we have encountered in Herodotus's presentation of the Athenians' internal and external politics. Once their empire is in full swing, Herodotus's Athenians have managed to exhibit the Anonymus's central political virtues within the polis, while promoting the self-obsessed values of his immoralist interlocutors in their external relations.

Herodotus's status as an outsider to Athens and his stance as an impartial judge in Hellenic affairs makes this state of things highly problematic. If Solon is Herodotus's "in-house" critic of Athenian imperialism, then it is natural that Herodotus should evoke Solon's own poetry in creating and undermining the opposition between valor (*aretē*) and the desire for money (*chrēmata*).[83] The poetry of Solon is preeminently responsible for articulating for Athens the internal political benefits of justice and reciprocity. Central to Solon's vision of the healthy polis is an inviolable opposition between true virtue (*aretē*) and the wrongful acquisition of wealth (*ploutos*): "For many base men [*kakoi*] are rich, and many good men [*agathoi*] poor; but we will not exchange our virtue [*aretēs*] for riches, because the one lasts forever, but one man has wealth now, another tomorrow" (fr. 15). In this passage, virtue (*aretē*) acts as a general evaluative term implying both moral and "social" goodness: Solon claims that he and his peers will not commit injustice in order to get rich. In unsettled political and social conditions, the unjust are driven to take undue advantage because of their capacity to do so combined with their moral defects. By contrast, the just maintain moral integrity despite its far-reaching consequences.

Solon's stance finds good moral justification in the traditional value of reciprocity among those who mutually consent to form corporate associations, such as armies or political bodies. Still, his arguments do not solve the more complicated, international moral issues to which Herodotus's narrative draws attention. Indeed, although Solon figures his "heroism" *within* Athens as an ability to calm civic strife, he also promotes a different, competitive form of virtue in the conflict of Athens with Megara: "Let us go to Salamis, to fight for a lovely island, and thrust away bitter disgrace" (fr. 3). Even in Solon's poetry, and certainly in Solon's social and military milieu, there are indications that civic stability, a basic good in its own right, also strengthens Athens in its exter-

[83] For the relationship between the views of the Herodotean Solon and Solon's own poetry, see Chiasson 1986.

nal conflicts. At the roots of Solon's vision of internal justice, one can already find—if one is already unjust?—the seeds of external aggression. Perhaps the way was already open for fifth-century Athenians to believe that the positive good of "virtue" does not have to be exchanged for riches *within* the polis. Rather, political stability can be maintained, and even strengthened, by using collective power to satisfy greed *outside* the polis.

Adapting Solon's central themes and moral concerns, Herodotus offers a significant historical perspective on the Athenian democracy's constituents—leaders and demos—and on their dynamic cooperation, which is potentially dangerous to their neighbors. In his presentation of the relationship between the elite and the demos, Herodotus reformulates Solon's own analysis of that relationship in a newly democratic and international context. Like Solon, Herodotus is a non-partisan critic of both elite and demotic greed. His concern, however, is not with justice within Athens, but rather with the potential of Athens to satisfy its greed internationally, once it has achieved internal stability. As Herodotus inherits Solon's interest in greed, injustice, and the relationship between leaders and demos, so too does he set the stage for Thucydides' own treatment of democratic politics and Athens's international greed. Thucydides refines and expands Herodotus's basic insight that Athenian democratic process harmonizes and habitually reinforces the ingrained greed of both elites and demos. Moreover, Thucydides brings together the two conceptual strands of greed that run throughout this discussion—excessive acquisitiveness and distributive injustice. In a radical synthesis, he presents Athenian greed as the excessive acquisitiveness conceived by the democratic Assembly, which violates canons of fairness that now pertain within the Panhellenic community. The Greeks' joint effort in defeating the Persians highlighted an ethics of reciprocity and mutual obligation among all Greeks, which the Athenian Empire is intent on violating.

In Gelon's language, Athenians "want to have it all" in a community that values the fair distribution of power (and then resources) among mutually consenting equals. Thucydides' synthesis paves the way for a further conceptual transition back to the polis, where a two-pronged notion of greed, such as we find in Aristotle, is reinvigorated by a complex history of application in the international arena.

Although Herodotus presents imperialism as immoral and doomed to failure, one amazing fact will have confronted his audience, namely the imperialistic success of Athens. Despite the greed and hasty decisions of the demos, the ulterior motives and greed of the Athenian leaders, the nemesis of the gods—despite everything, Athens, and no other "free" Greek state, was, uncontroversially, an imperialistic success. Herodotus may have been "warning" the Athenians that the gods' day of wrath was near to hand, but did they have any good reason to listen?[84] Thucydides, writing after a new set of historical facts has changed the international situation, tries to answer this question in a radical reformulation of the Herodotean treatment of virtue, greed, power, and justice.

[84] For the argument that Herodotus himself was a "warner" figure akin to those familiar throughout his text, see most recently Moles 1996, which develops suggestions of Raaflaub 1987. On warners in general, the fundamental study is Bischoff 1962.

5

Thucydides, Greed, and the Breakdown of Political Community

Rejecting the divine framework of Herodotean morality, Thucydides creates a secular paradigm in order to investigate the constituents of political corruption and stability. In his excursus on the Corcyraean stasis, which I examine in the first section, Thucydides draws attention to the elements of political dissolution: greed, mistrust, narrow self-interest, and vicious leadership. These concepts, or rather their opposites, underlie Thucydides' picture of Athenian political stability under Pericles, which I analyze in the second section. By focusing on the relationship between intra-polis cohesion and international greed, Thucydides shows how Athenian democracy created an innovative and energetic model of imperial success. Thucydides' representation of human nature, in combination with his treatment of democratic politics, encourages his readers to consider whether Athens's well-known greed has a historical explanation itself. If Athenian greed is at least partly a product of history, rather than simply an expression of human nature, then Thucydides' account of Athenian imperialism will turn out to be more complex than has previously been thought. I consider these possibilities in the third section. In the fourth section, I argue that, toward the end of Thucydides' work, Athenian greed tears apart the fabric of Periclean unity in a distinctively democratic way—or so Thucydides would have us believe. Finally, I consider the deep moral ambiguities associated with the Athenian Empire, and the ways in which Thucydides' account of Athens reformulates and develops Herodotus's own explanation.

First, several general points. Thucydides provides a complex reading of the political mechanics of greed in Athenian culture and draws attention to the moral and prudential ambiguities of the Athenian Empire. As an honest historian *and* a normative political thinker, Thucydides offers a powerful contemporary perspective on, and window into, the fifth-century discourse on greed. Sometimes his normative agenda—his biases, so to speak—conflicted with his efforts to achieve historical accuracy, famously in his overly sharp division between Pericles and the post-Periclean successors, but also in other important sections of the work.[1] I

[1] On Thucydides' shaping of his narrative, and the relationship between this shaping and

remain attuned to these sorts of tensions throughout. Moreover, I argue that Thucydides, like Herodotus, had a highly ambivalent attitude toward Athenian democracy: under the right leaders, he believed, it could achieve outstanding success, but without the guidance of a Pericles or a Themistocles, it quickly created the conditions for its own failure.[2] His opinions about democracy, however, are themselves open to question. Ultimately, Thucydides' critical vision seems unable to account for the remarkable resilience of the Athenian democracy, both in the late fifth century and throughout the fourth century. Contrary to tendencies in Thucydides' text, the Sicilian expedition did not destroy Athens altogether, nor even did losing the Peloponnesian War prove to be a lasting and final disaster.

Revolution at Corcyra: Greed, Leadership, and Civic Trust

Thucydides' treatment of Corcyra begins long before his famous excursus on civic strife (*stasis*) in book 3 (3.82–84). Already in book 1, Corcyra's character and behavior, as a polis, make the Corcyraeans' eventual *stasis* predictable. Thucydides says that Corcyra, a powerful naval democracy, prided itself on its financial resources, power, and preparedness for war, and consequently looked down on its mother city, Corinth (1.25.4).[3] His interpretation is developed in the debate between Corcyra and Corinth at Athens. These two cities found themselves in a bitter conflict over Epidamnus; Corcyra sought an alliance with Athens, and the Corinthians made every effort to block it. In their speech before the Athenian Assembly, the Corinthians emphasized the Corcyraeans' arrogance (1.38.5), and they underscored Corcyra's greed, which is disguised by the city's

the historical record, see Connor 1984, 3–19; Ober 1985; Strauss 1964, 139–45; Woodman 1988, 1–69; Hornblower 1987, 43–47. All these works in different ways reassess the older and, in my view, untenable belief in Thucydides' historical "objectivity" (e.g., Cochrane 1929); and they render largely meaningless the attempt to criticize Thucydides for not being objective (e.g., Badian 1993). On the difficult question of the status of Thucydides' speeches, see the judicious comments of Hornblower 1987, 45–72; Yunis (1996, 61–66) adds persuasive considerations that "the speeches are fictitious and serve Thucydides' own artistic and didactic ends" (63).

[2] As Thucydides often criticized democracy for its evident failures, so too did he criticize oligarchy: once in a while, one of his contemporaries got it right: on these ambiguities, see Connor 1984, 237–42. For other helpful discussions, see Dover *HCT* 5:335–39; Hornblower 1987, 155–74; Pope 1988. Hornblower (1987, 163–64) quite usefully distinguishes carefully between Thucydides' own opinions, insofar as they can be elicited from the text, and the opinions put in the mouths of various speakers throughout the *History*.

[3] Most commentators strikingly avoid the question of Corcyra's "constitution." That it is a democracy before the revolutions is implicit in Thucydides' account: cf. 3.69–71; Lintott 1982, 106.

posture of neutrality (1.37.4), and which they twice designate as *pleonexia* (1.37.4, 1.40.1). The Corcyraeans themselves advanced a thesis of cold self-interest (1.32.1, 1.33.1–2)—a thesis referred to by political theorists as the "Athenian thesis" because it captures the Athenian justification for imperialism.[4] Corcyra's national attributes, as we see in book 3, are brought home in destructive ways during its civic strife.

In Thucydides' view, war is a "violent teacher" (*biaios didaskalos*, 3.82.2), and accordingly Thucydides advertises its lessons in Corcyra, a polis whose citizens are, according to the Corinthians, "violent and greedy" (*biaioi kai pleonektai*, 1.40.1). Civil war in Corcyra was the result of a conflict between democratic and oligarchic factions over control of the state and, in particular, over the state's relationship with Athens.[5] Viewing Corcyra's alliance with Athens as tantamount to enslaving the state, oligarchs knew that their own political power depended on allying with the Corinthians; democrats, by contrast, saw a possible alliance with Athens as an opportunity to assert political superiority over their rivals. The ideological conflict broke down along class lines: the rich were oligarchic, and the poor, democratic. According to Thucydides, the entire civic convulsion can be traced back to a single causal nexus: "Power [*archē*], for the sake of greed and ambition [*dia pleonexian kai philotimian*], was the cause of all this" (3.82.8).[6] Thucydides' reconfiguration of these terms in different theoretical "equations" is the key to understanding his analysis of Corcyra and then of Athens, but his cryptic formulation makes it desirable to unpack the central terms in detail.

The most prominent of the three grammatically is *archē* ("power" or, according to the scholiast, "the love of power"), which refers especially to control of the institutional apparatus of the polis. Rather than understanding power in itself as the object of illegitimate desire, however, Thucydides says that desire for power originated in desire for objects other than power, namely material goods and honor (*timē*). In this statement, and throughout the section, power is the instrumental means whereby certain material goods and psychic satisfactions are acquired, such things as property (3.84.1), the pleasures of revenge (3.82.7), and the prizes of public competition (cf. 3.82.8).[7] As a result, the conceptual

[4] As Johnson (1993, 35) formulates it, the "Athenian thesis" is the claim that "the strong do what they will by compelling urges of human nature"; cf. Crane 1998, 64–65, 274–76; Orwin 1994, 123–25, 155–57.

[5] The Corcyra episode has been dealt with helpfully by Orwin 1994, 175–182; Euben 1990, 167–202; Connor 1984, 95–105; Edmunds 1973; Finley 1942, 183–87.

[6] On the complex syntax of this sentence, see Gomme *HCT* 2:379; Hornblower 1991, 485.

[7] Although 3.84 has long been suspected of interpolation, the sentiments expressed in the

work of this sentence is done by the terms "greed" (*pleonexia*) and "ambition" (*philotimia*), which together describe the psychological factors that drive Corcyra's citizens to lust after power. Thucydides' claim suggests that greed is distinct equally from the competitive love of honor and from the love of power.[8] Hence, in this sentence greed refers to the desire to possess more than one's share of material goods. This suggestion must, however, remain subject to reevaluation in light of later narrative and authorial interpretation. Thucydides' unusual compression here as elsewhere leaves open much room for debate, and requires the reader to work through the narrative carefully in order to understand both the meaning and the complex interrelationship of key abstractions. Looking ahead briefly, we can say that the sentence carries a wide-ranging implication. Thucydides' emphasis on greed (*pleonexia*) and power (*archē*), which are typically used to describe the Athenians and the Athenian Empire, suggests that the work as a whole will reflect on the possibility that the Athenians have transformed the entire Greek world into the divisive world of Corcyra.

Greed and ambition drive Corcyra's citizens to seek power at any cost. Under its influence, they care nothing for the traditional norms that had once united them in a stable political community. By definition, greed implies a lack of concern for preexisting intuitions or laws about the distribution of power and wealth. Thucydides brings this point home in an analytic statement that recalls the Hesiodic, and then Solonian, categories of just and unjust wealth getting: "These parties were not formed to enjoy the benefit [*ōphelias*] of the established laws, but for the sake of greed [*pleonexiai*] in violation of established law" (3.82.6). In Thucydides' mind, there are appropriate ways to earn wealth according to the law, but, by pursuing their greed to the full, the Corcyraeans transgressed preexisting boundaries in the act of grasping too much. This conception foreshadows Thucydides' treatment of Athenian greed within an imagined Panhellenic community. If Corcyra's stability depends on its established laws and customs, then the disregard for these preexisting norms,

chapter are arguably Thucydidean. For arguments for its authenticity, see Connor 1984, 102; Wenzel 1968, 18–27; contra, Hornblower 1991: 488–89; Gomme *HCT* 2:382–86. The conception of power as instrumentality has a long history in Greek political thought: cf. Callicles in the *Gorgias* (cf. esp. 484b9–c3, 491a7–b4); Aristotle *Politics* 1302a16–1302b4. The importance of power as instrumentality is enduring but is nowhere more central than in political thinking about cases, like Corcyra, where material goods are scarce (3.82.1–2) and where competition for them becomes a zero-sum game.

[8] On these distinctions, see Huart (1968, 388), who argues that greed (*pleonexia*) is directed toward material profit, while ambition (*philotimia*) is a loftier, more elevated motive—at least, he says, in appearance.

inspired by greed and carried out by political factions, severely restricts Corcyra's ability to function at all.[9] Such a startling breakdown of established law is merely symptomatic of certain deeper forces that are destroying the community, which Thucydides describes in terms of factionalism, mistrust, and deception.

The powerful political factions that effectively ruled Corcyra during the revolution represent a class-centered notion of self-interest that replaced central human ties, such as patriotism and kinship.[10] Citizens identified more strongly with their political parties than with their own families (3.82.6). The very possibility of identifying with the polis as a whole was lost; once the revolution is underway, Corcyra hardly has any claim to being a political community at all. Within his narrative of the revolution, Thucydides reformulates Solon's vision of the proper citizen as one who identifies broadly with the interests of the polis rather than narrowly focusing on his own selfish desires. In a healthier polis, the individual would at least take into account the welfare of his fellow citizens, even if he did not pursue polis interests aggressively—as Solon had desired. In Thucydides' representation, instead, the Corcyraeans came to define their own individual interests much more narrowly and diversely than a healthy political community could permit. For them patriotism was not a state-centered conception of self-interest, such as we see in Solon's poetry and in Periclean Athens, but rather a propagandistic banner waved by those who sought advantage for themselves exclusively.

For Thucydides the revolution meant a release of certain primal human energies like greed, violence, revenge, and the lust for power.[11] The appearance of these forces within the polis created a lack of trust among citizens—and not unnaturally, because individuals realized that others, perhaps like themselves, were pursuing narrow policies of self-interest.[12] The loss of confidence and trust (*pistis*) signaled the end of all genuine political relationships. Only the violent and aggressive were trustworthy

[9] Hornblower (1987, 119, 131, 154, 174–78, 188–90; and 1991, 484–85) is one of the few critics who recognize the importance of greed in this episode and the significance of greed's reverberations throughout the work; cf. also Macleod 1983, 128–29, 138–9n40; Grene 1965, 5–6, 29–30, 92. On *pleonexia*, see de Romilly 1963, 322–43; and for criticisms of de Romilly's schematic treatment, see Fisher 1992, 397n51.

[10] On political factions, see generally Calhoun 1913; Sinclair 1988, 141–42. On the concepts of "groups" and "factions" and their use in ancient history, see Strauss 1986, 15–31.

[11] The literature on Thucydides' treatment of human nature (*anthrōpeia phusis*) is enormous, but I have found the remarks of Immerwahr (1973, 19) especially helpful. See also Kateb 1964, 486–90; Orwin 1994, 44–50; Cogan 1981, 233–54; Johnson 1993, 27–71; Finley 1942, 54–60, 98–99, 100–109, 293–94; Hornblower 1987, 76–77.

[12] For brief but trenchant remarks on trust in Thucydides, see Orwin 1994, 180. I am currently developing these themes in a piece on trust in fifth- and fourth-century political thought.

(*pistos*, 3.82.5); individuals could trust one another only if they were partners in crime (3.82.6); and revenge, if it came through breaking faith, was all the more pleasurable because it also involved treachery (3.82.7). Oaths were meaningless and non-binding because no one feared breaking an oath if it meant personal advantage.[13] In short, "Society had become divided into two hostile camps, and each side viewed the other with mistrust [*apistōs*]" (3.83.1). Ironically, the Corcyraeans had once suggested to the Athenians that the greatest source of trust (*pistis*) between two international powers is having the same enemies (1.35.5), a principle that returns with a vengeance to Corcyra's domestic politics. The breakdown of trust, which had once tied the community together, resulted directly from the willingness of individuals to use any means whatever to acquire advantages for themselves, in flagrant disregard of preexisting notions of what belonged to others or to the community as a whole. In particular, individuals and groups made preemptive strikes against their opponents (3.82.5, 3.82.7), which is precisely what the Corcyraeans had earlier recommended that the Athenians do in relation to their own potential enemies (1.33.3–4). The Corcyraeans' lack of trust encouraged them to ferret out conspiracies at home where there were none (3.82.5), just as they had earlier persuaded the Athenians that war with Sparta had almost broken out already, when it certainly had not (1.36.1).[14]

Political leaders were the guiltiest of all. They advanced programs of reform that claimed to have the state's interests at heart and promised to serve both the masses and the aristocracy. Thucydides regards all their claims as unfounded propaganda, intended to reserve political prizes for the few who came out on top (3.82.8). Leadership, perversely used for self-aggrandizement, generated further mistrust and disintegration. Thucydides emphasizes the leaders' competitiveness throughout the section, using the language of the "contest" (*agōnisma* 3.82.7; *athla*, 3.82.8; *agōnizomenoi*, 3.82.8). His language therefore recalls Corinth's accusation that the Corcyraeans' offer of arbitration over Epidamnus was a sham, because arbitration is suitable only when one has not already engaged in a contest (*diagōnizesthai*, 1.39.1) and won a position of superiority. Thucydides has foreshadowed the behavior of individual Corcyraeans by characterizing Corcyra as a whole as pleonectic, hubristic, and thoroughly self-interested. Greed, self-aggrandizement, and ambition: for Thucydides these are the origins of civic breakdown, which lead in their turn to mistrust, the pursuit of narrow self-interest, and the failure of genuine political leadership.

[13] On language as an instrument of disruption, see Connor 1984, esp. 96–102; Euben 1990, 189; White 1984, 59–92.

[14] On the Corcyraeans and the Corinthians as "inadequate instructors" (77) of the Athenian assembly, see Ober 1998, 72–79.

Periclean Athens: Greedy Success

Does Athens itself exhibit similar possibilities for civic division? There are two sides to the answer—the domestic and the international.

Domestic Politics

Even as early as his "Archaeology," Thucydides isolates unity as a defining Athenian characteristic. Whereas the rest of Greece experienced a succession of forced migrations, as one invader took over from another, Attica was always inhabited by the same people and hence remained free from civic strife (*astasiaston*, 1.2.6). The political unity exemplified by Athens is a key feature of the Archaeology's anatomy of power (1.3.1–4, 1.18.1): internal factionalism severely limits a city's capacity to achieve greatness.[15] Internally divided as it is, Corcyra cannot become a leading imperialistic state, but Athens managed to build an empire despite the Athenians' reputation for greed and self-aggrandizement.[16] In order to see how this is possible, we must come to a clearer understanding of Athens's stability during the early fifth century and under Pericles. Its stability both made possible and was strengthened by the Athenians' success at pursuing greed internationally.

Athens's cohesiveness in the fifth century reflects its early history of unity. During the Persian Wars, Athens was not only internally cohesive, but, according to Thucydides, was also the force that united all Greeks in a collective effort against Persia. Abandoning their own city, the Athenians became a people of sailors in order to unite with the Spartans and their allies (1.18.2). By sacrificing their own possessions, the Athenians saved Greece as a whole and won lasting glory and, in the process, laid the foundations for empire. Self-sacrifice of both individual and polis self-interest is the first key to Athenian success: in the end it is contempt for their own possessions that allows the Athenians to satisfy their desire for acquisition on a grand scale. When Pericles encourages the Athenians to imagine themselves as islanders (1.143.5), or to despise their land (2.62.3), he is only recreating the facts of Athens's own history during the Persian Wars (1.18.2, 1.73.4; Hdt. 8.41). In their relations with one another, Athenians reject the individual and class-centered greed found in Corcyra. If Athens as a city-state sacrificed its own property for the sake of Greece, then its citizens too showed the same concern for their polis.

[15] On the Archaeology's emphasis on political unification, see Finley 1942, 78–94; Farrar 1988, 140; Ober 1998, 63–67; Kallett-Marx 1993, 21–36; Connor 1984, 20–32.

[16] On the Athenians' reputation for greed, see Raaflaub 1987, 227, 229.

In Thucydides' account, Athenian self-sacrifice resulted from a broadly defined notion of Athenian self-interest at least before the death of Pericles.

The Athenians' collective ethic is reinforced under the leadership of Themistocles and fully elaborated under Pericles.[17] Immediately after the Persian Wars, Themistocles persuaded the Athenian demos to erect walls around the city, removing Spartan obstruction through a clever diplomatic stratagem. Thucydides emphasizes the unity of the demos and its willingness to follow Themistocles' directions: "Themistocles ordered them to send him as an envoy to Sparta at once . . . and the whole population of the city, the entire demos all together [*pandēmei*], to build the wall, sparing no private house or public building which was of any use [*ōphelia*] to the work, but razing everything to the ground. So Themistocles set off, leaving these instructions behind him [*tauta didaxas*] and indicating that he himself would arrange the other affairs in Sparta" (1.90.3–4). The act of destroying private homes parallels the destruction of homes before the Persian invasion (1.18.2) and foreshadows the losses suffered by Athenians during the Peloponnesian invasions, while the term *pandēmei* echoes the speech of the Athenians at Sparta, which emphasizes Athenian unity and self-sacrifice in abandoning Athens during the Persian invasion (1.73.4).

Moreover, after demonstrating the military importance of sea power in "ancient" history, Thucydides alludes to Themistocles' proposal, which the Athenians accept, to build ships in preparation for the expected invasion of the Persians (1.14.3). His plan was to use the money from the silver mines at Laureion for the common defense, rather than for a single distribution of cash to each citizen (Hdt. 7.144; *AP* 22.7). Alluding to another act of demotic self-denial for the common good, Thucydides emphasizes the farsighted leadership of Themistocles, which translates into military glory for the polis as a whole. For Thucydides, the democracy has set up a stable, effective hierarchy: Themistocles counsels the state with foresight, ordinary citizens trust his advice and good faith, and the demos as a whole acts for the good of Athens. This pattern will be repeated under Pericles but (regrettably in Thucydides' view) not under Pericles' successors.

Internally, pre-war Athens presents a mirror image of Corcyra. Individual Athenians saw their own advantage as depending on the good of the polis as a whole, with the result that patriotism and individual inter-

[17] On Themistocles and his place within Athenian history more generally, see Forde 1989, 69–70, 106. Compare Thucydides' positive evaluation of Themistocles (1.134–38) with that of Herodotus, who emphasizes the Athenian leader's greed: see Herodotus 8.111–12 and chapter 4.

est genuinely coincided.[18] Although we are given no explicit account of Athenian attitudes during the Pentekontaetia, Pericles formulates a concept of self-interest that seems to underlie Athenian stability: "I myself think that when the city as a whole is sound, it profits [*ōphelein*] private citizens more than when individual interests are satisfied but, taken all together, the city falters" (2.60.2). This sentiment echoes Solon's ideology of civic unity, which was based on the notion of a broad, polis-centered notion of self-interest. The fragility of a broad, civic self-conception, however, especially in times of internal crisis or war, is abundantly demonstrated by Athens's historical need for courageous, articulate leaders, such as Solon or Pericles, to step forward and maintain a coherent civic ideology through their powerful use of language. If language is a tool of disruption in Corcyra, then it is equally a tool of civic formation for Solon, Themistocles, and Pericles.

The themes of wise and reliable leadership, changing concepts of self-interest, and communal trust, which structure Thucydides' account of the Corcyraean *stasis*, are positively elaborated in Thucydides' representation of Periclean Athens. In strife-ridden Corcyra, trust was perverted and exploited, so that citizens relished murdering each other through breaking shared compacts and leaders manipulated their followers by false propaganda. Similarly, at the beginning of the Funeral Oration, Pericles is aware of the possibility of envy and conflict among the citizens (1.35.1–2). He stresses the difficulties involved in justly distributing glory to the dead (2.35.2); every Athenian is concerned with having his own fair share and with giving a fair share to his friends and relatives. Pericles solves the problem by focusing not on the particular glory of the dead but on the collective glory of the city, thereby transforming the narrow individual concern for a fair share into an interest in the communal welfare of Athens. This focus allows him to praise the Athenians for being free of mutual suspicion (*hupopsian*, 2.37.2). According to Pericles, the Athenians should trust in their own courage (2.39.1) and rely on themselves (2.42.4) in confronting the hazards of the future. Their good judgment and that of their leaders provide ample reason for confidence (2.62.4). In eulogizing these characteristics, Pericles is helping to create and maintain well-founded mutual trust among citizens, who, in his ideal, unite themselves around a broad, civic model of self-interest. Even if the speech does not describe democratic Athens accurately, it articulates a vision of Athenian democracy at its best and offers an explanation

[18] Edmunds (1975, 82–88) neatly captures Pericles' civic conception of the individual: "In Athens, citizenship means, or should mean, the individual's choice of the city's ends" (Edmunds 1975, 84).

for the city's ability to maintain internal cohesion, while channeling its acknowledged pleonectic impulses outward.[19]

Under Pericles the identification of self-interest with the good of the state takes on an unusual cast. In his Funeral Oration Pericles transforms patriotism into a type of erotic commitment: "I could tell you," he says, "a long story . . . about what is to be gained by beating the enemy back, but I prefer that you look upon the actual power [*dunamin*] of the polis each day and become lovers [*erastas*] of it" (2.43.1). In Corcyra party commitments replaced natural family affections; in Athens sexual union is sublimated in love of the state. Pericles challenges Athenians to become not responsible heads of their households, or committed parents of their children, but fully invested lovers of their country, who concern themselves not with the material rewards of military victory but rather with developing their affections for the state. This sentiment represents a far-reaching reinterpretation of Solon's polis-centered vision of the individual. Now, not only do the city's disasters leap over the walls of the individual household, touching everyone's private interests (Solon fr. 4.27–30); instead, the most intense, personal feelings of the individual are subsumed within a wider polis-oriented framework of values. Pericles' reinvention of the citizen male is possible only because of a democratic system, which ensures a due return of rewards for those willing to direct their innermost convictions to the common good.[20]

The Athenians' lateral trust between citizens is also, and more importantly, a product of the vertical trust that pertains between citizens and their leaders. The creation of trust is an essential requirement for a leader of democratic Athens, because it encourages the demos to stand behind a single individual over a period of time, despite the absence of institutional controls that would require such constancy. In Thucydides' eyes the mob was fickle (2.65.4), which could be disastrous if it led to facile reversals of decisions once made.[21] Trust between the demos and an individual leader meant belief in the leader's foresight but, even more so, it meant belief in the leader's moral character—in particular, the belief that a leader was not abusing his rhetorical power for the sake of private advantage.

[19] On the Funeral Oration, see Kateb 1964, 485; Loraux 1986, esp. 116–23; Orwin 1994, 15–29; Ober 1998, 89; Edmunds 1975, 44–70; Saxonhouse 1996, 61–71. Pericles offers an idealized vision of Athens that does not represent the ordinary workings of the democracy.

[20] For the primacy of the city in Pericles' speech, cf. Edmunds 1975, 84–87; on the erotic metaphor, see Monoson 1994.

[21] Roberts 1994, 54–58. For Thucydides' negative views of the demos, see also 4.28.3, 4.65.3–4, and de Romilly 1963, 102.

In order to characterize Pericles specifically in this regard, Thucydides points out that when the Peloponnesians first invaded Attica, Pericles realized that his guest friend, the Spartan king Archidamus, might leave Pericles' own estates undamaged in order to create suspicion (*hupopsia*) against him (2.13.1). As a result, Pericles proposed to make his own estates public property. This private sacrifice later put moral muscle behind his recommendation that the demos move into the city, thereby allowing all the country estates to be ravaged; he later pointed out, speaking of sending one's own children into battle, that it is fair for a leader to give advice to the city only when his own personal interests are at stake (2.44.3). Pericles is fair in his expectations: he himself will undergo the same sacrifices he demands of the Athenians.[22] The demos accepted Pericles' exacting policy, even though most Athenians still resided in the country (2.14–16). The story aligns Pericles both with Themistocles and with the legendary king of Athens, Theseus, who effected the so-called Union of Attica (2.15). The contrast with Corcyra could not be clearer. Rather than pursuing profits at the expense of the state, the Athenians, acting out of deference to Pericles, relinquish their possessions in order to serve the common interest, while Pericles himself makes a telling display of his own superiority to venality.

As the plague reveals, however, Athenians are also prey to pursuing momentary pleasures whenever disaster strikes, even if that means violating sacred and civic laws (2.53.1–4). In this they anticipate the Corcyraeans: explaining the disaster at Corcyra, Thucydides says, "War likens the passions of the many to their present circumstances" [*kai pros ta paronta tas orgas tōn pollōn homoioi*] (3.82.2). Pericles had once pointed out that people change their minds in accordance with circumstance (1.140.1). His remark turned out to be accurate; already by 430, war difficulties had inflicted unforeseen suffering on all social sectors and divided the Athenians among themselves, because they began to attend more to their present sufferings than to the possibility of future glory. Both Pericles (2.61.2) and Thucydides (2.65.2) note regretfully that the experience of pain fragmented the Athenians, who begin to view themselves as individuals and members of class groups rather than as patriotic lovers of their polis.[23] This is yet another way in which war is a cruel teacher. As a socially divisive force, war counteracts the "teachings" of

[22] Thucydides does emphasize Pericles' superiority to venality but does not explain why Pericles was fined in 430 (2.65.3). Both Plato *Gorgias* 515e10–516a3, and Plutarch *Pericles* 32.3–4, suggest that Pericles may himself have been involved in some form of embezzlement; cf. Yunis 1991, 193–94.

[23] Saxonhouse 1996, 61–71.

Pericles, which are meant to unify the Athenians by elevating their gaze from their present circumstances to the renown of the city.[24]

Through his powerful oratory, Pericles wards off the forces of civic disruption. He enables the Athenians' intelligence and courage to work in unison for the common good.[25] He thereby countervails the Corcyraeans' belief that "an intelligence that could grasp the whole" (*to pros hapan xuneton*) was utterly lazy (3.82.4), and their empirical observation that the more intelligent among them were likely to be victimized by their inferiors (3.83.3–4). Pericles' Athenians combine rational calculation with a courage (*andreia*) that comes to them naturally, rather than through education (2.39.1, 2.39.4). The Corcyraeans, by contrast, pursue a corrupted, rash masculinity (*alogistos andreia*, 3.82.4). Thucydides' emphasis on *andreia* in the Corcyraean episode shows that the Corcyraean "politics of masculinity" knows no limits in its perversion of ethical values and its pursuit of private satisfaction. George Kateb offers a clear formulation of the issue: "to desire to possess more than one's share, as if true satisfaction exists beyond mere satisfaction; to see in one's power not so much a stake to defend as a precondition for transgressive adventure; and to thrive on risk, especially to one's continued existence—all this is the project of individual and group masculinity."[26] Although Pericles directs the Athenians' aggressive masculinity toward the common good, the seeds of civic corruption are present in their collective and individual psyche and will flourish once Pericles is dead. Athens needs a Pericles to make its intelligence and courage work in unison.

The political organization described by Pericles is justified later by the Syracusan demagogue Athenagoras, who says that the intelligent counsel best, but the many are best at listening to arguments and then judging them (6.39.2).[27] Contrary to the elitist view that the many are unfit to serve the state politically, Athenagoras voices a democratic argument that shows evidence of some staying power in political theory.[28] For Pericles, the judgment of the demos is so wise that Athenian democracy becomes a form of meritocracy; individuals attain positions of leadership through their acknowledged accomplishments and abilities (2.37.1).

[24] On Pericles as a teacher of Athenians, see Yunis 1991; 1996, 72–86.

[25] Thucydides of course would disagree with the notion that the Athenians are intelligent, but that does not stop Pericles from thinking (and saying) that they are; see my subsequent discussion for Thucydides' disagreement with Pericles on this point.

[26] Kateb 1998, 86.

[27] Athenagoras is introduced in language that recalls Cleon, whom Thucydides maligns as a violent, thoroughly "demagogic" leader of the Athenian Assembly: see *HCT* 4:301. On Cleon and Pericles, see Yunis 1996, 89–92; Ober 1998, 98–100; Hornblower 1991, 334–35, 420–22; Tuplin 1985, 355–56.

[28] See, e.g., Aristotle *Politics* 1281a43–1281b2, 1281b34–37.

At this stage, however, Thucydides parts company with Pericles, because the text as a whole raises the question of whether the demos's judgment is good enough to sustain the conception of democracy as meritocracy—or, more pointedly, whether the demos can reliably choose good leaders and make decisions that are genuinely in its own interests.[29] To this question Thucydides' answer is clearly negative: the demos can hardly envision its own narrow self-interests properly, much less those of the entire community. As the rest of his *History* shows, Thucydides' indictment extends outward from the demos itself to include the political system that favors the demos, democracy.[30] For Thucydides, Pericles' democratic idealism is fundamentally mistaken in its analysis of how politics works. In Pericles' conception, it is the democratic system and democratic culture that is responsible for Athenian greatness (2.36.4); in Thucydides' presentation, it is rather the particular leadership at any given time that determines Athens's fortune.[31] And this is why Periclean Athens is the thing it is: "In name there was a democracy, but power was really held by the first citizen [Pericles]" (2.65.9). If that is the only kind of democracy Thucydides can admire, then it might as well not be democracy at all.[32] Pericles' creation of civic trust, collective pride and responsibility, and total identification with the good of the polis holds true—under Pericles, not necessarily under democracy in general. Once Pericles is gone, Athens begins to experience the problems of Corcyra, as its formerly "democratic" virtues quickly reveal their destructive underbellies.[33]

[29] See the disparaging presentation of the Athenian demos (often called an *ochlos*, a "crowd" or "mob") and the democratic process at 2.65.4, 4.28.3, 8.1.1, along with Dover *HCT* 5:337 and Roberts 1994, 54–58.

[30] Some aspects of this point are treated in Ober 1993.

[31] Contra Yunis (1991), who suggests that through the "instructional" rhetoric of Pericles the demos is able to make politically responsible decisions. In my reading this fails to account for Thucydides' strong suggestion (2.65.8–9) that the demos subordinated itself to Pericles and needed a Pericles to make wise decisions.

[32] Although Hobbes's "monarchical" view of Thucydides certainly goes too far, it is at this point that one might justifiably view Hobbes's reading of Thucydides with some sympathy; in Leo Strauss's words, "History too then conveys precepts; to take the most important example, according to Hobbes, Thucydides' work teaches the superiority of monarchy to any other form of government but especially to democracy": Strauss 1964, 144.

[33] The accuracy of Thucydides' sharp distinction between the Periclean "Golden Age" and the degenerate period of his successors is a subject of considerable scholarly controversy: Connor 1971, esp. 87–136, is a classic defense of the ancient derogatory view of the "new politicians"; Connor is in essentials followed by Henderson 1990, 279–84. The skeptical position is lucidly sketched out by Finley 1962, who argues that our sources do not identify changes in political policy toward the end of the century; for a helpful critique of Connor 1971, see Davies 1975. I tend to side with the more skeptical critics of the traditional picture.

This analysis explains an important nuance in Thucydides' portrayal of Pericles because it illuminates an apparent conflict in his eulogy of the leader after his third speech (2.65). If Pericles had the outstanding political acumen Thucydides ascribes to him, then why was Pericles himself unaware of his own all-important role in the success of Athenian democracy? It is plausible to suppose that, like the rest of the Athenians, he had accepted Athenian ideology. Rather than maintaining a critical distance from democracy, Pericles too was fully subsumed within the framework of democratic thinking and wholeheartedly endorsed the Athenians' self-confidence in the democratic process. Thucydides stands out against this endorsement. It was precisely in order to destroy the political blinkers created by democratic ideology that Thucydides turned to history as a form of critical analysis in the first place. For Thucydides the careful reader of and even participant in democracy will thus become not another Pericles, but rather an enlightened Pericles who reflects critically upon his own position in the system.[34] Thus, Pericles' tragedy is that he is sincere in his own evocation and praise of democracy in the Funeral Oration but is fatefully blinded to democracy's limitations.

International Politics

Periclean Athens enjoyed civic trust, a generous conception of self-interest, and outstanding leadership—a nearly precise reversal of the elements of corruption in Corcyra. Those aware of Corcyra's eventual self-destruction might wonder, however, where Athenian greed has gone. Why has Pericles' redefinition of self-interest been possible? Thucydides suggests an extraordinary answer. The city of Athens is safe because Athenians as a group channel their greed outward against other Greeks. Athenians had by this time acquired the reputation throughout Greece of being selfish and greedy: Athenian greed was a topos.[35] However reprehensible it may be, there is no doubt that Athens was a fantastically successful imperialist polis, which prosecuted its greed on a grand, international scale against other Greek states.[36]

[34] Contra Finley (1942, 309–10), who argues that the *History*'s didactic function aims to produce men like Pericles in the future.

[35] See Raaflaub 1987, 227, 229; 1994, 107–9.

[36] Galpin (1983–84) asks an important question about the coherence of the ethical stances and behavior of Athens: how can Athenians value freedom and equality within the city and yet focus their foreign policy on the de facto enslavement of other Greeks? Here again the problem of impartiality arises in the gap between internal and external politics. In the Greek conception, freedom and equality were not "rights" that inhered in individual human beings, but rather privileges granted to each individual by the political community of which

Thucydides' telescoped vision of Corcyra provides a provocative background against which to view Athens's international politics also. Throughout the first three books, Corcyra is characterized by specific attributes that also, and even more deeply, apply to the Athenians as a unified group. Corcyra's financial health at the beginning of the war prefigures that of Athens, as documented by Pericles (e.g., 2.13.2–9). Like Athens, Corcyra is a naval democracy. The Corcyraeans' failure to attend to customary relations between polis and metropolis illustrates their unwillingness to be bound by convention (1.25.3–4, 1.38.1)—a hallmark of Thucydides' Athenians. Most important, the same *pleonexia* attributed to the Corcyraeans, both in international and domestic politics, is also one of the Athenians' paramount national attributes. Unlike Corcyra, however, Athens experienced a period of great success before its greed came back to haunt its domestic politics.

Thucydides represents the Athenian national character first in the debate between Corcyra and Corinth, and then in the debate between Athens and Corinth at Sparta. When the Corcyraeans, in their speech at Athens, insist that self-interest should guide political decisions (1.32–36), the Athenians accept their advice. Rather than abiding by their treaty with the Peloponnesians, the Athenians show that they too embrace a thesis of cold self-interest. In response to this, the Corinthians warn Athens not to be drawn in by the prospect of a naval alliance with Corcyra: "For not to commit an injustice [*to . . . mē adikein*] against one's equals provides more security than to take advantage [*to pleon echein*] by running risks, excited by the appearance of an immediate gain" (1.42.4). Here the Corinthians already invoke Athens's *pleonexia*—its willingness to run risks in order to "take advantage" (*pleon echein*)—and they elaborate the theme in more detail in their speech at Sparta. The Athenians, for their part, accept the advice but quite rightly regard the Corcyraeans as more "equal" (*homoious*, 1.42.4) to themselves than the Corinthians.

At Sparta, the Corinthians characterize the Athenians as energetic, innovative, and greedy. Their characterization of Athens (1.68–71) was substantiated by Athenian activities during the Pentecontaetia.[37] Having come into conflict with Athens over both Corcyra and Potidaea, the Corinthians try to convince Sparta to declare war by demonstrating the threat posed by the aggressive, imperialistic Athenians:

---

he was a part. It is not strange, in the ancient context, that the Athenians would not extend these privileges to those whom they had conquered. In the ancient world, the conquered were considered the property of conquerors, because they were held to owe their very lives to the goodwill of their conquerors. On these issues, see Ostwald 1996 and Garlan 1988.

[37] Connor 1984, 36–47; Rawlings 1981, 80–85.

> While you stay at home, they are always abroad, for they think that they will acquire something [*ti ktasthai*] by being abroad. . . . They use their bodies on behalf of their city as if they belonged to someone else, while they keep total possession of their minds when they do anything for its sake. When they aim for something and do not get it, they consider themselves deprived of their own property [*oikeiōn steresthai hēgountai*], and when they do get [*ktēsōntai*] what they are after, they consider it nothing compared with what they will get next. . . . For they alone get what they hope for as soon as they think of it, through the speed with which they execute their plans. And they toil throughout their lives in hardship and danger, and they least of all enjoy their current possessions because they are always acquiring more [*dia to aiei ktasthai*]. (1.70.4–8)

The Corinthians explain that one notorious Athenian characteristic, *polupragmosunē* ("restlessness"), served the interests of another, greed, because the Athenians' hyperactivity drives them to undertake further conquests incessantly. Admittedly, this characterization comes from an interested party, a city that had recently felt the Athenian pinch at Potidaea. But it coincides with other speakers' impressions of the Athenians as well as with Thucydides' own statements (6.93.1, 8.96.5; cf. 4.21.2, 4.65.4). Moreover, the Corinthians' attitudes must have had purchase in the wider Greek world, or otherwise their speech would have been politically useless. Even if the Corinthians do not always persuade their audiences, they are adept at accurately identifying the core characteristics of both Corcyra and Athens.

What do the Athenians themselves make of this? Some unnamed (and therefore perhaps characteristic) Athenian envoys conveniently happened to be in Sparta on other business and spoke in response. Surprisingly, the Athenians themselves embrace their rampant acquisitiveness, using it to convince Sparta to think carefully before going to war. In this, too, they follow the Corcyraeans, who had suggested that the Athenians would frighten Sparta if they accepted the proffered alliance (1.36.1). The beginning of the Athenians' speech is standard. Invoking their self-sacrifice during the Persian Wars, they suggest that they deserve gratitude from the Greeks instead of hostility. But then they make the claim, unusual in Greek diplomatic exchanges, that although they were originally compelled to take on a hegemonic position through fear of Persia, they afterward acted out of concern for their own honor and profit (1.75.3, 1.76.2).[38] This is the first formulation of the three key constituents—fear, honor, and profit—of

[38] White (1984, 68) convincingly argues that the debate at Sparta signals a deterioration of a certain Greek "culture of argument" that had previously held together international relations; for him "Athens and her empire presented a problem that the language of this community could not contain or manage." For further elaboration of this view, especially in relation to Pericles, see my concluding remarks in this chapter.

the "Athenian thesis." They say that they were "conquered" (*nikēthentes*, 1.76.2) by these three motives, which implies that the Athenian discipline grudgingly praised by the Corinthians is accompanied by weakness of will (*akrasia*); the Athenians' hunger for more is an unrestrained appetite that acts as the directing principle of their hyperdisciplined fighting power.[39]

The argument does not present a genuine moral justification for empire. If self-interest (among other things) justifies empire, then it is difficult to see what types of activity would lie outside the realm of the justifiable.[40] For these speakers, though, the Athenians have done nothing unusual or contrary to human nature, by accepting an empire when it was there for the taking (1.76.2). Thus they adopt a posture of ethical impartiality, not so much in order to justify their own actions, as to show that the Spartans are at their level: "You Spartans, in your leadership of the Peloponnese, have arranged the Peloponnesian cities with a view to your own advantage (*epi to humin ōphelimon*)" (1.76.1). This method of "debunking" the Spartans' self-righteousness is effective because it implies that the Spartans, self-proclaimed liberators of Greece, are hypocrites. The Athenians present themselves as impartially observing widely acknowledged standards of behavior—as if they would be happy enough to accept a subordinate position if they happened to be weaker than another state! Ironically, the Athenians maintain the structure of impartial argument even as they self-consciously abandon ordinary moral discourse in favor of self-interest.

Here, as elsewhere, the Athenians argue that their treatment of their subjects is less severe than it could conceivably be, and that they deserve praise for their self-restraint. They argue that their willingness to go to trial in Athens with their allies illustrates generosity and fairness rather than forcible greed (1.77.1); this echoes the Corinthians' charge that the Corcyraeans cheat citizens of other *poleis* by forcing them to appear in court in Corcyra (1.37.3). As if in response to the Corinthians' warnings against taking advantage (*to pleon echein*, 1.42.4), the Athenians argue that no one has ever refused to take advantage (*tou mē pleon echein*) rather than simply acquiring something by force when it is available (1.76.3). According to the Athenians, their subject states feel more burdened by general equality conjoined with minor aggression than they would be if the Athenians openly aggrandized themselves at the subjects' expense

[39] It is important to see that the Athenians argue not for Callicles' immoralist view that one ought to do the same; instead they suggest that, human nature being what it is, they have done only what anyone else in their position would have done (1.76.2); cf. Andrewes in *HCT* 4:183–85. Pericles' *own* justification for Athenian imperialism, however, does resemble the arguments of Callicles and Thrasymachus: see my conclusion in this chapter.

[40] Bolotin 1986, 13; Strauss 1964, 183.

(1.77.3–4). The Athenians do not deny that they try to satisfy their greed in relation to their subject states. They simply reject the accusations that they are *excessively* greedy, given their hegemonic position, and that they use unnecessary force in dealing with their subjects. Rather, they pursue their greed systematically, with a legal apparatus in place, rather than brutishly and forcibly (1.77.3–4).

Thucydides paves the way for his analysis of international greed by making use of an analogy between cities and individuals.[41] We have already grappled with this analogy in the Corcyra episode and seen that it had wider implications for the Athenian Empire. Other examples of the analogy are found in two speeches of Pericles. In his first speech in the *History*, Pericles encourages the Athenians not to yield to Spartan demands, declaring the necessity of seeing "that the greatest danger gives rise to the greatest glory for a city and an individual" (1.144.3). Despite the differences between Thucydides' own views and those of his character Pericles, it is plausible to suppose that Thucydides did have the city-individual analogy in mind throughout the work. Pericles also commented on strength in the face of adversity in similar terms: "The most powerful cities and individuals are the ones that are the least distressed in their minds about misfortune and the firmest in their actions to resist it" (2.64.6). Thucydides' tendency to make such an analogy returns with critical implications in the debate before the Sicilian expedition. In terms of intellectual history, Thucydides applied to the Athenian greed for empire certain formulations that normally specified an individual's excessive desire for material goods within the polis.

Following Herodotus, Thucydides extends Solon's analysis of Athens's intra-polis problems to the relations between Greek states in general. By using similar conceptual language to describe international politics, Thucydides suggests that greed is still present within the individual Athenian soul, but that Athenians have effectively solved the problem of greed's self-interested character within the polis by collectively turning the impulse outward onto other Greek states. The Athenian "solution" will have implications for Thucydides' own verdict on Athenian imperialism. To anticipate, it is greed to acquire further empire (*archē*) that drives Athens to behave imperialistically, but this impulse played itself out in radically different ways in the Periclean period, on the one hand, and in the period of leadership by Pericles' successors, on the other. Up to and including the period of Periclean leadership, this drive was properly restrained by the moderation (*sōphrosunē*) of Pericles and others and was christened by Pericles as a way to bring Athens glory. After Pericles, by

[41] See Grene 1965; Hornblower 1987, 178–79 and 1991, 231; Strauss 1964, 193–94.

contrast, individual leaders indulged their greedy impulses and tried to use the city's power to gratify their own personal desires.[42]

In other words, after the Persian Wars and until Pericles' death, Athenians desired money in order to increase power and power in order to acquire glory. Hence the bizarre compression that had linked greed (*pleonexia*), power (*archē*), and ambition (*philotimia*) (3.82.8) is here unpacked, but in a way that the grammar of the original sentence does not lead us to expect. Under Pericles, greed is conceived as driving the Athenians toward empire (*archē*), which in turn exists for the sake of *philotimia*, the "love of honor." Thus the relationship envisioned in book 3 represents a deep perversion of the proper relationship between the three terms. By contrast, the Athenian lust to acquire more was shaped by great men and reenvisioned as a means to glory. Athenians collectively reinvested the financial dividends of imperialism into a mutual fund of empire that kept expanding and hence kept winning glory. In the pre-war period, Athenian power was commensurate with Athenian desire, by virtue of wise leadership that kept in check the potential excesses of desire. The balance between power and desire meant success and communal glory for the polis. By contrast, after Pericles' death, the demos and its corrupt leaders mutually eroded the Athenians' sense of restraint. Desire was swollen and outstripped their capacity to fulfill it. And greed, the greed that had made Athens great, was reconfigured as the individual lust for gain that destroyed the ability of Athens to exert its collective desires onto other Greek states.[43]

Human Nature, Democracy, and Greed

Because of its centrality in Corcyra and Athens, it is useful to look for an account of greed's origins, its relation to democracy, and its connection with other abstractions such as arrogance (*hubris*), hope (*elpis*), and desire (*erōs*). In the Corcyra passage, greed, like other irrational psychological urges, is understood as a part of human nature unleashed when war or other forces make it difficult to acquire the necessities of life easily (3.82.2). In Cogan's analysis of the passage, "Human nature is again con-

[42] This way of reading Thucydides is encouraged by his treatment of the Corcyra episode, which directs the reader to ask what empire (*archē*) is "for"; cf. 3.82.8. On my account the text offers different answers to this question depending on the leadership of Athens at any given time: cf. Hornblower 1987, 188–90.

[43] Hornblower (1987, 173–75, 188–90) rightly criticizes Thucydides for not overtly acknowledging the external greed of the Periclean and pre-Periclean democracy, while over-emphasizing the greed of the generation after Pericles; Finley (1978a) persuasively argues that such a view wrongly emphasizes the harshness of Cleon, without seeing that Athenian imperialism had been "harsh" for the entire century.

ceived of as a particularly amoral (if not immoral), selfish, often cruel manner of acting attributable to appetite, and, therefore, ultimately to our animal or biological nature."[44] In Thucydides, as in the prior tradition, greed derives from our physicality as human beings, and it is therefore a passion that potentially affects all human beings.

At the same time, the expression of greed in action was influenced by cultural practices and conventions—by the "national character" invoked by the Corinthians (1.68–71). Even though presumably greed was a latent feature of individual Spartans, Thucydides credits Sparta as a polis with extraordinary restraint and moderation (*sōphrosunē*).[45] Sparta's internal cohesion is demonstrated by its observance of the same constitution for four hundred years (1.18.1). No doubt this internal stability was further explained by the Spartans' strict institutions, their rigorous tradition of education (*agōgē*), their system of dining clubs (*sussitia*), their regulation of property ownership, and so on. Sparta's specific cultural practices encouraged individual Spartans to restrain their greed. Sparta's characteristic restraint, it should be stressed, seems to undermine the "Athenian thesis."[46] If the Spartans share the same human nature as Athenians, then Spartan culture played a key role in limiting the expression of Spartan greed. Still, when an opportunity for empire presented itself in 403, the Spartans took advantage of it.[47]

In Thucydides' several democracies, on the other hand, a very different political culture prevailed. According to the Corinthians (1.68–71), the Athenians as a unified body were always focused on acquiring more from sources outside the polis. Democratic politics and culture conspired to liberate human energy in such a way as to promote Athenian greed internationally, while maintaining the stability of the political community. Democracy is, for Thucydides, specifically energetic and characteristically greedy.[48] Even outside Athens, other democracies are widely acknowledged to be acquisitive: for example, the Corinthians call the Corcyraeans "violent and grasping" (*biaioi kai pleonektai*, 1.40.1). As we will see, Hermocrates, the vocal leader of the Syracusan democracy, becomes, for Thucydides, the second great advocate and theorist of greed

[44] Cogan 1981, 187. Thucydides was deeply pessimistic about human nature in general, and his view that human nature is constant over time must have added to that pessimism: Cogan 1981; Kateb 1964.

[45] See, among others, Strauss 1964, 146.

[46] On the Athenian thesis, see n. 4.

[47] Still, it was only through the energy of exceptional Spartans, that is the most un-Spartan of the Spartans, namely Lysander and Agesilaos, that empire building became a focus of Spartan attention.

[48] On democracy's unique capacity to liberate human energy in the public sphere, see Kateb 1964. For Thucydides' view of the similarities between democratic Syracuse and democratic Athens, as opposed to Sparta, see 7.55.2, 8.96.5.

after the Athenians (cf. 8.96.5). Hearing of the Athenians' proposed Sicilian expedition, for example, he insists that the Athenians "are not attacking Sicily because of ethnic loyalties" but rather "because they lust after [*ephiemenoi*] the good things Sicily has, which we possess in common. . . . It is understandable that the Athenians desire to have more [*pleonektein*] of these things and that they make their plans accordingly. I do not find fault with those who want to rule [*boulomenois archein*]" (4.61.3–5). He understands the Athenians' motives because he himself shares their generally positive attitude toward taking risks in the pursuit of greed. Syracuse is similar to Athens in more than one way (cf. 7.55.2, 8.96.5).

Why are democracies especially greedy? Thucydides answers this question in his extended representation of Athens after the death of Pericles, which I consider in the next section. To anticipate my argument, democracy is by definition rule by the demos, and for Thucydides the demos is by nature irrational and greedy (2.65.4, 2.65.10–11, 4.21.2, 4.65.4; cf. 4.28.3).[49] Democracies like Athens can only be successful in pursuing greed when they are governed by self-restrained and politically wise leaders. Athens's obsessive acquisitiveness depends on the cycle of greed created by the unhealthy relationships between its democratic leaders and the demos—relationships that are themselves distinctively democratic in Thucydides' view. Moreover, history and cultural practice in Athens influenced the raw expression of human nature in several other ways.

First of all, by abandoning Athens during the Persian Wars, the Athenians demonstrated their capacity to refashion their own self-conceptions in accordance with circumstances. They were willing and able to make themselves into islanders in order to ward off the Persian threat. Their capacity for innovation enabled them to break free from traditional norms and strictures; in this case, they abandoned the precinct of the Acropolis, among other sacred regions of the city, for pragmatic human purposes (1.18.2; cf. 1.73.4).[50] By so doing they became the innovative, anti-traditional Athenians that we hear described, with a certain grudging admiration, by the Corinthians. The success of this innovation made the Athenians confident enough to construct innovative arguments about human nature and justice, which permitted them to pursue their own aggressively greedy instincts to the hilt. When they abandoned their own polis, they also abandoned the standard morality of international relations, which the Corinthians invoke in their debate with the Athenians at

[49] See, n. 29.

[50] Forde 1986a; 1989, 22–25.

Sparta. The Athenians were willing to take on a different and unexpected role in the Greek world.

Second, their success in the Persian Wars also gave rise to hope and to *hubris*, the psychological conditions most conducive to producing and unleashing the greedy desire for more that characterizes Athenians. Their victory over the Persians not only provided an opportunity for the Athenians to exert their acquisitive urges on other Greeks but also inspired confidence that the Athenians could exert their greed with lasting success. In Thucydides' presentation, Athenian greed often followed on Athenian success, which led to high spirits and hopefulness (4.41.4); at times, one imagines, these attitudes are justified, but Thucydides often suggests that they are not (e.g., 4.17.4, 4.41.4, 4.65.4), and that they have the potential to lead Athens to catastrophe. Athens's unorthodox behavior and resulting success during the Persian Wars were key factors in shaping Athenian psychology and therefore in enabling Athenian imperialism.

Finally, given this history of psychological formation, later Athenian leaders could invoke a tradition of aggression and successful acquisitiveness in stirring up the demos for war. To inspire the Athenians, Pericles frequently refers to their glorious ancestors (2.36.1–4, 2.62.3), who not only acquired an empire but handed it on intact. By the beginning of the Peloponnesian War, imperialism had become an established part of the Athenian national character, asserted through reference to the immediate past. Pericles challenges his contemporaries by forcing them into an implicit competition with their fathers. Pericles' challenges capture the paradoxical nature of the continuing Athenian capacity for innovation, which derives strength from an ability to look to the past. Apart from being interested simply in the mechanics of empire, as several recent studies suggest,[51] Thucydides analyzes the Athenian national soul—its fundamental impulses, its characteristic weaknesses and strengths, its formation in Athenian history and democratic politics.[52] Thucydides wanted to know not only why the Athenian Empire worked, but also what history of psychological and political formation made the Athenian Empire possible.

Moving outward conceptually, we find that Thucydides embeds his psychological analysis of greed in a framework of other characteristically

[51] Esp. Kallet-Marx 1993; Allison 1989.

[52] Thus my account differs fundamentally from that of Cogan (1981, 252), who writes, "More recently, we have expanded our notion of the originating and shaping factors of action to include social, psychological, and cultural forces whose content and influence are still being debated, but whose operation is now felt to be significant. To all of these factors Thucydides, as we have said, pays only fitful attention, and then only as they appear in rhetorical shapes."

Greek abstractions. A central passage here is Diodotus's speech in the Mytilenean debate in which Diodotus argues, against Cleon, that law, and specifically the threat of capital punishment, is not an adequate deterrent from crime in the face of the human passions:

> Poverty [*penia*] forces men to be daring, whereas wealth [*exousia*] leads the powerful, through pride and arrogance, into taking more than their share [*hē d'exousia hubrei tēn pleonexian kai phronēmati (parechousa)*]. Each human condition is dominated by some great and incurable passion that impels people to danger. Hope [*elpis*] and passionate desire [*erōs*], however, dominate every situation: with desire as the leader and hope as the companion, desire thinking out a plan, and hope promising a wealth of good fortune, these two cause the greatest mischief. (3.45.4–5)

The generality of the claim strongly suggests that it should be read against the unfolding narrative of the Athenian Empire, but again careful attention is needed in order to see how this should be done.[53] In the first place, Diodotus says that the necessities of poverty will drive men to try to get more than they have, which seems to hold out a possibility that there can be a good and justifiable sort of grasping. After this single mention, however, little is made of this possibility in other sections. Alongside this, Diodotus mentions the familiar belief that greed results from an abundance of means (*exousia*), which apparently provides confidence that the relentless pursuit of acquisitiveness will be successful. Earlier in the speech (3.45.1), in fact, Diodotus had stressed the importance of belief in future success as an essential precondition for any act of daring.

Specifically, he argues that abundance of means creates greed through pride and arrogance.[54] As we have seen in Solon and Herodotus, *hubris* had had long-standing connections with greed, but it is essential to discuss each individual author's contextually specific conception of their relationship. Diodotus distinguishes clearly between *hubris* and greed: where greed is the desire to get more, *hubris* is a psychological attitude virtually synonymous with *phronēmati*, both of which accompany greed but are not its equivalent—just as necessity explained why poverty leads to daring.[55] In the next sentence, greed is opposed, but linked, to *hubris* and *phronēmati*, this time in the form of an opposition between *erōs* and *elpis*. If it is correct to see this second sentence as an elaboration of the first, then an interesting point about the connections between *hubris* and greed is disclosed. For the second sentence states explicitly that desire is

[53] On this sentence, see Fisher 1992, 392–93.

[54] For telling criticisms of the use of *hubris* as a cover-all umbrella term, see Fisher 1992, 390–92, criticizing de Romilly 1963.

[55] For comparable Thucydidean uses of *hubris* as "arrogance," "high spirits," see also 1.38.2–5, 1.84.2, 2.65.9, 4.18.2, 6.28.1, 8.45.2.

primary and itself conceives enterprises such as acquiring more empire (cf. 3.45.6), whereas hope or high spirits provides an encouraging psychological framework within which desire is approved, expanded, and urged to move ahead with its plans. If in earlier Greek thought greed had been dependent on and subsidiary to *hubris*, and even sometimes included within it, as for example in Solon, then in Thucydides at least the desiderative component of greed has become primary, and *hubris* has become an attendant psychological force.

It would be wrong to develop an entire theory about Thucydides on the basis of a single passage, but two factors make this passage central. First, its generality strongly suggests that it should be read as a significant proposition that the rest of the text can confirm, refute, or modify. Second, it is the only sentence in the whole work in which greed and *hubris* occur in the same passage. Generally speaking, Thucydides emphasizes the Athenians' *desire* to have more than they already possess, be it wealth, land, and other material benefits, or control over others, or some combination of these that was rarely made explicit in the Athenian political consciousness. For Thucydides what is primary is the desire to have more, as a conceptual category in its own right. This desire was associated with other ideas, notably hope and overconfidence after success, but in itself desire was the fundamental drive behind Athenian imperialism.[56] Thucydides provides a highly complex and plausible account of how this desire derived from human nature and was implicated in Athenian history and cultural practices.

Post-Periclean Disintegration

Eventually the monumental Athenian edifice, erected on foundations of greed, crumbled. The factors that led to this disintegration are present, ironically, both in the image of strength offered by Pericles and in the image of decay offered by the Corcyraeans. It is precisely the greed that Periclean Athens organized out of the political community that returns to haunt it.[57] In the post-Periclean period, Thucydides brings the analysis of greed back to its more familiar context—inside the polis. The arrival of greed within the polis, he shows, has devastating consequences both for Athens's externally directed greed and for the Athenian political com-

[56] Fisher's attempt (1992, 401–11) to view the Sicilian expedition as an act of *hubris* can be justified in that the expedition would not have been undertaken without feelings of overconfidence and without a desire to inflict humiliation on the Sicilians in order to demonstrate Athenian superiority, but, as I will show, the primary thrust driving the expedition was Athenian desire to get more.

[57] See Strauss 1964, 193–94; Orwin 1994, 123–26.

munity itself. If Athens's domestic politics and acquisitive foreign policy had once been mutually supportive, then these two facets of the city's political structure now become mutually destructive. In contrast to the earlier Solonian account of aristocratic greed, and also to Xenophon's later account of the Thirty's greed, both of which are primarily disruptive within the city, Thucydides' own picture is complicated by the copresence of greed within Athens, and the continuation of its outwardly focused imperialistic greed.

Thucydides himself is clear about the reasons for the breakdown,[58] but the straightforward reflections offered in the eulogy of Pericles can be enriched by paying attention to the narrative as a whole. The same cluster of political concepts that operated in Corcyra and in Athens "before the fall" can be used to analyze post-Periclean Athenian politics: greed, trust, self-interest, and leadership. Thucydides' own comments after Pericles' third speech (2.65) are especially important for understanding his analysis of Athenian disintegration, along with his critique of democracy. After giving notice of Pericles' death, Thucydides says that in contrast to Pericles' restraint, his political successors "did the opposite, and in other matters that apparently had no connection with the war they conducted politics badly both for Athenians and the allies, by looking to their own ambition [*philotimias*] and their private profit [*idia kerdē*]; when successful, their policies meant honor [*timē*] and profit [*ōphelia*] for private individuals alone, but when they failed the whole war potential of the city was impaired" (2.65.7). Reversing the key components of the city's internal strength, Pericles' successors seek private advantage over the public good, with the result that they rob the polis not only of resources but, more importantly, of the trust that Thucydides had marked out as the cement of political community. In part, then, Thucydides blames the greed of the city's leaders for its dissolution. His fundamental criticism, however, is reserved for the democratic process itself, precisely because of the freedom that its advocates claim as its foremost virtue.

According to Thucydides, because Pericles was above venality, and because he never sought power from ulterior motives, he was able to lead the people without flattering them. Instead of simply mirroring the demos's own unwise political views in order to win public approval, Pericles genuinely directs the state's policies according to his own political vision (2.65.8). His successors, on the other hand, who could not win unrivaled ascendancy among themselves, were forced to curry the people's favor in order to win political advantage, which led to disastrous

[58] Again I would stress that Thucydides' division of Athenian history into periods of Periclean success and post-Periclean breakdown is too neat and illustrates the historian's critical theoretical agenda, rather than a plausible picture of history as we can reconstruct it.

policies for the polis. For Thucydides, the agonistic ethic that animated post-Periclean leadership was detrimental to the interests of the whole and yet was a central element in democratic process.

For Thucydides, then, democracy tends to bring about its own downfall through a disastrous cycle of greed and personal ambition. Athenian leaders saw in their political position the opportunity to make profits; the demos also wanted to take a share in the profits for themselves; the leaders, in turn, perceived the greed of the demos and offered policies that would satisfy it, in order to secure their own positions of leadership, which would then pay out in personal profits for themselves, and so on. This cycle of greed is authorized by the democratic process, whose very structure encourages too much freedom in the exchange of attitudes between leaders and demos. Thucydides' analysis anticipates that found in Aristotle's *Politics* 5.[59] Rather than harmoniously directing their greed outward against other Greeks, and using the city's power for the sake of collective glory, Athenians began to see the city's power as something to use instrumentally for their own private profit. The cycle of greed would not exist, one imagines, in a more properly constituted political order. But democracy is for Thucydides an excessively porous filter in which cultural currents move too freely between mass and elite, with the result that leaders and demos both actively encourage the greedy impulses of one another.

Through his portrayal of the Athenian Assembly, Thucydides illuminates his view of the democratic condition. He rejects the idea, espoused by Athenagoras (6.39.1), that the demos deserves a leading political role because of its good judgment. For him, democratic debate fails miserably on several counts, especially that of possessing accurate information and using it intelligently.[60] Moreover, elite greed creates suspicion in the Assembly, which results in deception, irresponsibility, and policies that lack foresight. In order to function effectively, the democracy needs a democratic leader whose superiority to greedy self-interest creates trust and confidence among the people. Granted a leader with integrity, democracy also needs a leader who can restrain the greed of the masses; for Thucydides the demos, being what it is, will always lust after more than it has.[61] But if no leader with the character and charisma of a Pericles emerges, then the people have to decide which ones to choose, basing their choices on partial information, limited political vision, and their own acquisitive desires.[62] This amounts to saying that the discovery of

[59] On Aristotle's analysis of greed in democracy, see chapter 2.

[60] Ober 1993 explores this facet of decision making in the Assembly in detail; cf. Ober 1998, 72–79.

[61] See Roberts 1994, 48–70.

[62] This is a theory-laden view of Athenian democracy: for more generous historical accounts of the democracy, see Ober 1989, Hansen 1991.

good democratic leaders is a matter of luck rather than political process. Democracy can guarantee no succession of good leaders.[63] As a result, all the democratic virtues that used to cohere under Pericles' leadership are destroyed once self-interested or imprudent leaders come to prominence.

Thucydides develops these criticisms in Diodotus's speech during the Mytilenian Debate. After regaining control of the insurgent city Mytilene, the Athenians publicly debate the sort of punishment the rebels deserve. At first they decide on a universal death penalty but then, on the next day, they reopen the case because of a sudden change of heart. Thucydides shows us the debate on each side between Cleon and Diodotus. The details of their arguments are less important than several remarks that give insight into democratic process. Diodotus makes a set of telling criticisms of the Assembly: accused of being bribed, Diodotus says,

> Besides, if someone gives the best possible advice but is under the slightest suspicion of being influenced by his own private profit [*kerdous*], we are so resentful of the profits we think he is making (though this is uncertain), that we rob the city of the certain benefit of his good advice. So it has become the rule that good advice honestly put forward is just as suspect as bad, so that just as the speaker who advocates some monstrous measure has to win over the people by deceiving them, so also a man with good advice to give has to tell lies in order to be believed. (3.43.1–2)

The later narrative substantiates these criticisms. This does not, of course, necessarily mean that they are "true," in the sense that they or Thucydides' narrative reports democratic process "objectively," but rather that Thucydides took pains to prove them and believed in their underlying accuracy.[64] Infighting among Pericles' political successors, which is encouraged by the agonistic process of democratic debate, creates mutual suspicion and mistrust between leaders and demos, as the demos comes to believe that individual leaders are concerned more for their own selfish profit than for the welfare of the polis. As a result, leaders must flatter and deceive the demos—which at once furthers communal mistrust and leads to the imprudent gratification of the demos's own desires. Through his emphasis on deception and imprudent gratification, Thucydides elaborates themes that were central to Herodotus's own representation of democracy. These themes are expanded in his por-

[63] Johnson 1993, 191–94.

[64] Helpful treatments of the Mytilenean debate include Yunis 1996, 87–101; Cogan 1981, 50–65; Hornblower 1991, 420–22; Connor 1984, 79–91. On the question of Thucydides' "objectivity," Connor (1984, 3–19) is the fundamental account, showing that Thucydides' ostensible detachment is an authorial stance and that the modern critic of Thucydides must engage with the ways the author shapes the responses of his readership.

trayal of the Sicilian debate, which captures Thucydides' formidable critique of post-Periclean Athens.

Sicily is depicted as an object of Athenian craving throughout the work, and the desire to control the island constitutes a paramount example of outwardly directed greed. In his description of the first Athenian forays into Sicily, Thucydides makes it plain that, whatever the ostensible reasons for sailing west, the Athenians' real aim was to gain control over Sicily (3.86.4; cf. 4.1.2, 4.24–25). His conception of their desire is variable and complex, but all of his formulations cluster around a wide-ranging lust to get more. For Thucydides, their greed meant the desire for money or land or both; sometimes excessive desire for power in its own right, or, perhaps even more vaguely, for "empire" (*archē*); sometimes desire for power as the instrumental means to acquire further goods. But sometimes it is simply impossible to make these distinctions in any individual case purely on the basis of Thucydides' language. Taken together as a conceptual system, however, the lust for empire envisioned in his text includes both frankly material aspects, as well a general desire to experience the irresistible joys of power over others. The conceptual vagueness of the desire to get more is what we should expect after examining the compressed relationship between power, greed, and honor in Thucydides' explanation of the Corcyraean stasis. At the beginning of book 6, for example, Thucydides says that the Athenians aimed at ruling (*ephiemenoi . . . arxai*) Sicily (6.6.1) and that they aimed at or desired (*ephiesthai*) Sicily itself (6.8.4; cf. 6.11.5). Within certain parameters Thucydides' conception of the Athenians' greed for more is more wide-ranging and imprecise than simple greed for money.[65]

The Syracusan leader Hermocrates began to entertain the possibility of an Athenian attack by the summer of 424. As we have seen, Hermocrates is the second great theorist of international greed in the work. He plays an integral role in saving Syracuse and in annihilating the Athenian troops in Sicily, in part because of his understanding of the psychology of greed. Presaging the eventual Athenian disaster, Hermocrates says, "Nor is strength [*ischus*] secure simply because it is confident [*euelpi*]" (4.62.4). Precisely this error in reasoning plagued the Athenians: Thucydides reports, again connecting strength with hope, that the Athenians' good fortune made them think that "nothing could stand in their way; that the possible and the more difficult were equally attainable by both a strong

[65] Thucydides often uses the periphrasis *ephiesthai [tōn pleōn]*—"to aim at, to desire, more things"—in regard to *archē* (empire or rule over territory), on which cf. 1.128.3, 4.87.4, 6.6.1, 6.8.4, 6.11.5, 6.33.4, 6.85.3; and in regard to material possessions, cf. 1.8.7, 4.92.4, 4.61.3. His uses convey a broad notion of greed that targets excessive acquisitiveness of material goods as well as power, conceived as the instrumental capacity to acquire those goods. See further Huart 1968, 402.

and an insufficient force; the reason for this was their surprising success in most directions, which suggested to them that their strength was equal with their hopes [*aitia d' ēn hē para logon tōn pleonōn eupragia autois hupotitheisa ischun tēs elpidos*]" (4.65.4). Moreover, and more important, Hermocrates says that those who hope (*elpisantes*) that they will gain an advantage (*pleonektēsein*) through their power (*dunamei*) often must leave behind what they already have, instead of getting more (*anti tou pleon echein*, 4.62.3). He later uses this sentiment to encourage the Syracusans to believe that they will win glory when they send the Athenians home without having accomplished what they wanted (*apraktous hōn ephientai*, 6.33.4).

Hermocrates clearly understands both the psychic motivations and the practical pitfalls associated with the Athenians' greed. As Syracuse is a colonial foundation of Corinth (6.3.2), so too is Hermocrates the heir to the Corinthians of book 1, who sensitively and accurately characterize the Athenians as the greedy and ambitious imperialists that they are. If it takes a naval democracy like Syracuse to defeat the premier naval democracy, Athens, then perhaps the key to Syracuse's success is Hermocrates, who understands the psychology and ambitions underlying Athenian greed. By contrast to Athenagoras, who fails to understand the power and excitement of Athenian greed (6.37.2, 6.38.1), Hermocrates sees, already in the 420s, that the Athenians' ambitions are driving them to attack, despite the lack of prudence involved in the expedition (4.61.7). He uses this insight to unite the Sicilians around the concept of national self-defense.

Under Pericles, we imagine, the Athenians would not have indulged their greedy desires for acquisition in Sicily; it would take a Pericles to match up to Hermocrates. But a new ethos altogether has entered Athenian politics by the time of the Sicilian debate. Pericles had once exerted a force of restraint, or *sōphrosunē*, upon Athenian desire (*epithumia*, *erōs*). His rational calculations coordinated Athens's international strategy with its real capacity (*dunamis*) to accomplish its purposes. Now, however, Athenian leaders began to reflect the demos's greed in their proposals, or even to magnify it, with the result that Athenian desire quickly overreached the capabilities of Athenian power.

In the Assembly debate before the Sicilian expedition, the rival orators are Nicias, an older and well-respected general, and Alcibiades, a young man whose sexy unconventionality alarmed even the Athenians. Roughly speaking, Nicias represented the Periclean force of moderation on Athenian desire, while Alcibiades, virtually the incarnation of desire itself, proposes policies aimed at gratifying his own and the demos's excessive acquisitiveness.[66] Although Nicias possesses Periclean foresight, he has

[66] On Nicias and Alcibiades, and in particular their place within the structure of the work

none of that leader's strength; Alcibiades, on the other hand, has charisma but lacks foresight, and in addition lacks the ability to build genuine consensus around his policies. It is up to the demos, witless as it is in Thucydides' account, to choose between these unpalatable alternatives. Its choice is not surprising: the demos stands behind the "leader" who catalyzes into action its own self-destructive desires.

Although Nicias is in some sense a stand-in for Pericles, he represents important thematic variations, which tell a great deal about the corruption of politics in post-Periclean Athens. Discussing self-interest, for example, Nicias argues that individuals should be concerned for the welfare of the polis because of their prior concern for their own safety and property (6.9.2). For Nicias the polis does not come first; instead, concern for the state is a second effect of narrow self-interest. If Nicias values his own safety and possessions above the interests of the polis, then he must also think that the polis is not worth dying for. Thus his attitude undermines the patriotic ideals of self-sacrifice envisioned in the Funeral Oration.

Unlike Pericles, Nicias does not feel contempt for his own possessions and therefore cannot command the Athenians' respect. He begins his speech, in fact, by pointing out his weakness: "My speech would be too weak to prevail over your character [*tropous tous humeterous*], if I advised you to safeguard your present possessions and not to run a risk with what you have for the sake of unseen and future gains" (6.9.3). Nicias's weakness makes his argument, however sound on prudential grounds, unconvincing;[67] as a result, he is forced to use the ploy of denigrating his opponent for selfish greed for gain. The Athenian Assembly cannot see the value of a Nicias, because it cannot fully understand its own prudential interests. In accordance with Diodotus's prediction, Nicias must rely on deception, and he thereby loses his moderating Periclean influence and effectively stirs up demotic desire for more.[68] Arguing that Alcibiades is in favor of the expedition for purely selfish reasons, Nicias says that "He wants to be admired for his horsebreeding, and because of the great expense involved, he hopes to make a profit from the command [*ōphelēthēi*

as a whole, see Rawlings 1981, 126–60; Tompkins (1972) analyzes the language used by each figure, concluding that Nicias's language characterizes him as self-absorbed, unconfident, and ineffectual, while Alcibiades' language characterizes him as forthright, uncomplicated, and strong. On Nicias, see also Finley 1942, 216–21; Edmunds 1975, 109–42; Strauss 1964, 200–209.

[67] Stahl (1973), suggests, rightly I think, that Nicias's reservations about the expedition are shown to be justified by Thucydides' narrative statements about the expedition once in progress, especially his statements concerning money and cavalry.

[68] See also Edmunds 1975, 110: "Thematically, un-Athenian Nicias is the foil to an Athens bent on its own ruination, while factually he is in large part the cause of this ruination." On moderation in Thucydides, see North 1966, 100–115.

ti ek tēs archēs]" (6.12.2). Nicias's speech contributes to the atmosphere of mistrust that surrounds the debate, a spirit that again is the direct consequence of greed and allegations of greed within the community. Whether or not the allegations are true, greed has become a powerful rhetorical weapon for speakers who want to gain advantages over their political rivals.

For Thucydides the implications of greed for Athenian society have by this time undergone a remarkable change. Earlier in the century, greed had driven Athens to acquire an empire and, because it was properly managed and understood in the exalted Periclean terms of glory, it had resulted in success and greatness and had helped solve the problem of narrow self-interest within the polis. After a period of restraint at the beginning of the war, greed entered the city's internal politics in two ways. First, it became a key ideological weapon in public debate and thereby created a mood of suspicion. Greed thus infected a central pillar of democratic process and destroyed the sense of civic trust on which Athenian vitality depended. Second, greed operated as an individual motivation, Thucydides says, and was characterized by attempts to use the city's power, not for further imperialistic acquisition and its concomitant glory, but for personal profit. Both the appearance and the reality of greed structure his presentation of Alcibiades.

Thucydides introduces Alcibiades' speech by saying that the young man had ulterior motives for urging the expedition against Sicily. Alcibiades inserts his personal self-interest into the public domain to an unprecedented extent in Thucydides, but he is different only in degree from his post-Periclean colleagues. As for his motives, he did want to oppose Nicias, a political rival; but "most of all he wanted to have a command and hoped that Sicily and Carthage would be conquered through him, and that if he were successful, he would profit his own interests with both money and glory [*ta idia hama eutuchēsas chrēmasi te kai doxēi ōphelēsein*]" (6.15.2). In this pointed statement, Thucydides affirms his belief that oratorical charges of greed were justified and that Alcibiades was using the city as his instrument for private wealth and glory.[69] In addition, he reconfigures, albeit in slightly different language, a familiar triad of concepts—empire, greed, and ambition. The echoes of Corcyra intimate that Alcibiades' behavior within the polis will be responsible for a political breakdown in Athens. Gone are the days when nameless individuals gave up their lives in a single collective effort for the good of the whole; the narrow self-interest of Alcibiades takes Nicias's

[69] Finley (1942, 218) emphasizes the contrast between Alcibiades and Pericles on this account. For an account that emphasizes the Periclean characteristics of Alcibiades, see Edmunds 1975, 124–28.

moderate expression of selfish concern to its logical, and dangerous, conclusion. But his greed drives him to seek not only personal profit and aggrandizement; equally it makes him ambitious for further conquest on a grand scale. Operating as it does with a dual focus both on himself and on further conquest, his greed will in the end jeopardize the continued existence of Athens.

Alcibiades holds an extremely narrow view of self-interest. For him, self-interest is the acquisition of goods and glory for oneself, regardless of the consequences for other citizens or the state as a whole. Instead of regarding the state's welfare as primary, like Pericles, Alcibiades believes that the state's good is secondary to his own. In the Assembly he argues that his magnificent display at Olympia, which won glory for himself and his family, also profited Athens by providing the other Greeks with a symbol of Athenian strength (6.16.1–3). But Thucydides' own remarks make it clear that whatever rhetorical strategies Alcibiades offers in public, Alcibiades himself clearly comes first in his own mind (6.15.2–4). What this means for his own democratic leadership is obvious: by his public rhetoric he legitimizes and even promotes the pursuit of narrow self-interest, even when it conflicts with the interest of the state. He positions himself even farther from Pericles' idealistic vision than the moderately self-interested Nicias.

Such extravagance alarms the Athenians because they take it to express an inordinate feeling of superiority and an excessive desire to acquire more for himself. According to Thucydides, most people recognized that Alcibiades' desires outran his means (compare Athens as a whole), which "later contributed importantly to the destruction of Athens. For most people became frightened at a quality in him which was beyond the normal and showed itself both in the lawlessness of his private life and habits and in the spirit in which he acted on all occasions. They thought that he was aiming at the tyranny [*turannidos epithumounti*], and so they turned against him" (6.15.3–4). In essence Alcibiades becomes Thucydides' own version of Callicles. The Athenians are alarmed precisely because his excessive desire for more threatens their own possessions and, more important, their secure hold on the state. Thucydides' language of desire (*epithumia*) is intensified as soon as Alcibiades appears on the scene (6.15.2, 6.15.3, 6.15.4),[70] linking international imperialistic policies with the central ideas of trust and equality in domestic politics. When Alcibiades brings his own greed within the Athenian political community, he disrupts the central values on which Periclean order was founded. He embodies the Athenian national character but has the capacity to turn his

[70] For comparable instances of *epithumia* and *erōs*, see too 4.108.4, 6.13.1, 6.78.2; 3.45.5, 6.13.1.

greed inward against the Athenians themselves.[71] Like Callicles, he is ambitious both to control the state and thereby to acquire all the material possessions and psychological gratification he desires.[72]

Through his own extravagance, Alcibiades destroys the trust that had united Athens under Pericles.[73] Athenians despise Nicias's weakness but fear Alcibiades' self-aggrandizement. Athens, however heroic as a polis, cannot tolerate the same heroic self-centeredness in one of its own citizens: the foundations of its successful policy of externally directed greed depended on equality and fairness within the citizen community. These central features of democracy had sustained Athenian aggressiveness against other Greeks. Once the cement of community is gone, however, then Athens is well on its way to experiencing the same difficulties as Corcyra. Although Athens does not quite reach this level of disintegration yet, Alcibiades puts his own polis on the brink. By rejecting the Periclean model of democratic leadership altogether, Alcibiades reverses the democratic norms that had once held Athens together as a political community.

In his speech before the expedition, Alcibiades ridicules equality and creates an intimidating atmosphere in which free speech is impossible. In his mind individuals are not equal, and inequalities in ability and accomplishment should be publicly acknowledged. In his own words, "It is not unjust for a person who thinks highly of himself not to be equal to others. . . . But just as we are not spoken to if we are unfortunate, by the same token one has to put up with it if one is despised by the successful" (6.16.4). Whereas Pericles had taken pains in the Funeral Oration to preserve at least the appearance of equality, for Alcibiades this appearance is false and even unjust to the superior sort of individual who deserves more recognition than he typically gets in a democracy. If his overreaching desires have created mistrust among Athenians, then his public rejection of the Athenian ideal of equality could only strengthen that mistrust.

By encouraging fragmentation within the polis, Alcibiades is only furthering a process already begun by Nicias, who divisively called upon the older men in the Assembly to smarten up and oppose the proposals made by Alcibiades and his group of young followers (6.13.1). Dividing the Athenians into groups sets a precedent whose dangerous implications are not fully realized until the revolutions of 411 and 404, when class warfare led the city close to disintegration. Nicias urges his older, more moderate followers "not to have a morbid craving [*duserōtas einai*] for what is out of

[71] Orwin 1994, 123–26.

[72] On Alcibiades' ambition generally, see Forde 1989.

[73] On the importance of trust in this episode, see Strauss 1964, 199.

reach, knowing that success is won least of all by desire [*epithumiai*], but mostly by foresight [*pronoiai*]" (6.13.1). Like Pericles, Nicias sees the need to restrict Athenian desire in order to maintain a proper balance between desire and power, but he is too weak to create this balance through the strength of his own character. Being in a position to make policy now depends on gratifying the demos, which is Alcibiades' own trademark.

His rhetorical strategy is simple but to the point: Alcibiades argues that greed, far from leading to the city's demise, as Nicias would have it, actually coincides with national security interests. As we saw in the conclusion of chapter 4, Alcibiades maintains that a policy of idleness will wear the city down, accustomed as it is to the aggressive pursuit of imperialistic desires: "Recognize that the city, if it stays inactive (*ean men hēsuchazēi*), will wear out of its own accord, like anything else, and that every sort of knowledge will decay (*engērasesthai*); but if it wages war it will continually gain experience and become more used to defending itself in action rather than through making speeches" (*to amunesthai ou logōi all' ergōi mallon xunēthes hexein*, 6.18.6).[74] Like Callicles, he hopes to expand desire as much as possible and to acquire the power to satisfy it. He subtly and persuasively insists that, given the city's recent history and its national character, pursuing the Calliclean ideal of limitless expansion is the only hope of survival and success.

In Alcibiades' view, everyone should believe this, but everyone conceived as representatives of private group interests, rather than as unified Athenians. According to Alcibiades, the city is strongest when "the simple people and the middle sort and those who make the most exact judgments are all mixed together" (6.18.6). The problem is that all these individual ingredients of the Athenian polis must constitute something new and different when they are mixed together, if the city is genuinely to be strong. The various individuals and groups must all be refashioned into a unified Athenian citizen body, and they must make policy on the basis of their shared Athenian identity, instead of private rivalries and narrow self-interest. That is the lesson of both Solon and Pericles. However much Alcibiades imitates Periclean language and appears to promote a politics of unity, his own life-style and his manner of debate make it clear that he cannot reinvent Athenian greed as a drive for acquisition that results in glory for the city as a whole. Instead, under Alcibiades, Athenian greed remains greed flat-footedly—greed, moreover, with an eye to individual profit rather than the common welfare.

According to Thucydides, different sectors of the population con

[74] On Alcibiades' rhetorical use of decay and old age (cf. *engērasesthai*) to disparage and undermine Nicias, see Tompkins 1972, 212.

ceived their aims differently. The old wanted to conquer; the young, to see new places; the masses, to get pay for the time being, and to add to the empire in order to secure permanent paid employment in the future (6.24.3). All these can unite around Athenian greed: but one group, ominously, refuses to do so.[75] Thucydides says that "because of the excessive desire for more [*dia tēn agan tōn pleonōn epithumian*], if someone opposed the decision, he kept quiet, fearing that he would seem disloyal to the city if he voted against the expedition" (6.24.4). This statement provides the first real hints of fragmentation beneath the mirage of consensus, which, as we will see in the next chapter, destroys Athens from within once the rivalries between different groups become too deep and oppressive for political unity to be maintained.

This passage richly evokes Thucydides' central concerns in the scene. The phrase *tōn pleonōn epithumian* is ambiguous: it can mean either "desire for more things" or "the desire of the majority." The ambiguity emphasizes that the majority of Athenians, not just Alcibiades or other leaders, conceive excessive and destructive desires to get more.[76] It rounds out Thucydides' vivid evocation of Athenian desire throughout the passage: the Athenians' desire to sail (*to men epithumoun tou plou*) was not diminished by the difficulty of preparation (6.24.2); they were inspired much more (*polu de mallon hōrmēnto*) by Nicias's second speech (6.24.2), and a passionate desire (*erōs*) to sail fell upon them all (*erōs enepese tois pasin homoiōs ekpleusai*, 6.24.3). Pericles' civic *erōs* has been transformed into a destructive urge to acquire more. The Athenians themselves, imagined in his speech as the lovers (*erastas*) of Athens, now became uncontrollably impassioned in their pursuit of further goods and further empire. The irony of this connection is abundant: did the Athenians still feel passionate about the good of their polis once they became, in Nicias's words, "ill-starred in their passionate desire for things far away" (*duserōtas . . . tōn apontōn*, 6.13.1)?[77]

Moreover, the ambiguous phrase *tōn pleonōn epithumian* may imply, more darkly, the tyranny of the majority, which limited the free expression of ideas in Assembly.[78] If Alcibiades' own greed has matched and even expanded that of the demos, then the Assembly has effectively turned into a Panathenaic festival of greed in which opposing voices are literally muted. Alcibiades has not only rejected the democratic ideal of equality; he has also in effect eliminated free speech, which was a hall-

[75] On Alcibiades' creation of a false consensus, and on the debate in general, see Ober 1994.

[76] Connor 1984, 168n25.

[77] For discussion of *erōs* as a central characteristic of Thucydides' Athenians, see Forde 1986; Immerwahr 1973, 28; Monoson 1994.

[78] See Ober 1998, 82–89; Saxonhouse 1996, 61–71.

mark of democracy.[79] The consensus effected by Alcibiades' gratification of his own and the demos's desires is thus shown to be false. But its consequences are all too real.

Alcibiades and the demos alike have miscalculated the Athenian capacity to effect those desires, and similarly have misjudged the Sicilians' own ability to repulse their military assault. They do not yet know that Hermocrates, another theorist of international greed, will be too strong an opponent for them. If power is now viewed as the coefficient force that allows desires to be fulfilled, then the Athenians have made a huge mistake. Their swollen desires (*epithumiai*) have outstripped their capacity (*dunamis*) by a long way, and their craving for conquest leads them to a serious, and almost fatal, disaster. For Thucydides this mistaken calculation is not set against a background of divine intervention, nor does it follow the traditional religious pattern, in which destruction and revenge follow upon excessive arrogance, that one sees, for example, in Homer and Aeschylus.[80] Rather, it is purely a pragmatic matter for Thucydides: lack of foresight, which originates in the Athenian democratic process, brought Athens to the brink of its Sicilian disaster.

But Thucydides suggests another way of looking at the Sicilian expedition that coexists with his condemnation of its imprudence. These two explanations exist side by side and ambiguously, without any real resolution. Thucydides had suggested earlier that the demos was mistaken to entrust its affairs to anyone other than Alcibiades, who was conducting the war in excellent fashion (6.15.3). This claim introduces some complexity into his view of the Sicilian expedition. Thucydides had once seemed to endorse Pericles' policy of restraint but now praises Alcibiades' policy of endless expansion. Was Periclean restraint valuable for a period of time but, given the thoroughgoing greed of the Athenian demos, not for too long? Would the Athenians "wear themselves out" internally, as Alcibiades suggests (6.18.6–7), if they went too long without conquest? Thucydides gives no clear answer. But his narrative of the Sicilian campaign does suggest that if Alcibiades had been allowed to continue as general for the duration of the war, then Athens could have won.[81] Thus there is a glimmer of the idea that Athens could have sustained a policy of ever expanding greed. This would fit in well with Thucydides' claim (2.65.11–12) that what ruined the Sicilian expedition was in fact the internally directed greed of the Athenian leaders while the expedition was underway. On this view, their greed removed Alcibiades from the campaign and therefore destroyed the expedition. Democratic

[79] Raaflaub 1980.

[80] On this point, see Finley 1942, 323–84, who argues against Cornford 1907; cf. Fisher 1992.

[81] Orwin 1994, 118–26.

greed could have survived the excesses of Alcibiades, if only the demos had had the capacity to follow his outlandishly greedy instincts to the hilt. An ineffective democratic process, however, which permitted other, less capable leaders to pursue their own greed and ambition in public affairs, destroyed even that tenuous possibility.

Conclusion: The Ethics of Athenian Imperialism

Because talk about greed was loaded with moral, social, and political implications, the Athenians were often harshly censured for their imperialistic activities, but they themselves had little moral compunction about their empire. Greed implies breaking preexisting moral boundaries and exceeding due limits, and consequently each use of "greedy" as a label involves an ethical judgment about the rights and obligations of an individual or community. Such ethical judgments are persistently contested throughout Thucydides' text by both Athenians and their opponents. At a pragmatic level, the excess of Athenian acquisitiveness concerns Thucydides because it challenges the stability of the political community. Because of his interest in explaining Athens's success and downfall, Thucydides often shows more concern with the prudential than the ethical implications of greed. Still, he was also deeply interested in the ethics of the Athenians' global prosecution of greed.

We saw above that the Athenians' justification for empire in their speech at Sparta—fear, honor, and profit—was empty. Thucydides' potentially conflicting interests in Athenian imperial success and in the morality of empire receive focus in his presentation of Pericles. Pericles is famous for advocating a defensive policy during the war, which Thucydides himself seems to endorse (2.65.7). In essence Pericles urged the Athenians to remain within the city, not to fight the Peloponnesians on land, and not to extend the empire during the war. He effectively confronted the problem of a hugely swollen Athenian power (*dunamis*) that had to be squared with the need to restrict national desire. In Thucydides' scheme, Pericles acts as the highly un-Athenian force of moderation (*sōphrosunē*) within the powerful and desirous national soul, and is in fact able to suppress the Athenians' desire to acquire, by force of his own character. For Thucydides, Periclean restraint was the only way to keep Athens secure during the war, although, as we have seen, Thucydides qualifies his analysis by envisioning the ever expanding Athenian Empire of Alcibiades' dreams.[82]

[82] For the idea that Pericles represents an un-Athenian force of moderation, see Connor 1984, 62; cf. Edmunds 1975, 92–93; North 1966, 104–6, 109. See also MacIntyre (1988,

Pericles' policy is nonetheless chronologically limited: he recommends it only for the duration of the war (2.65.7).[83] Furthermore, he advocates it solely on the basis of prudence. Pericles is concerned only with the city's safety, not justice or what is right. In fact, although Pericles is usually (and rightly) regarded as a restraining force on Athenian greed, he had also been involved in Athenian imperialism prior to the war and in some passages comes across as its foremost exponent. Far from being the opponent of imperialistic greed, Pericles is a purely prudential leader who believes that imperialistic greed, if properly managed, can lead to glory for the polis.[84] Pericles' own comments on Athenian greed provide an original perspective that illustrates his liberation from the standard vocabulary of Greek social relations.

As a general in the period before the Peloponnesian War, Pericles had led Athenian forces against the Acarnanian town of Oeniadae (1.111.2–3). He had also led troops against Euboea, when it revolted from the Athenian Empire, and against Samos, where oligarchs had joined with the Persian governor Pissuthnes to overthrow the Athenian garrison (1.114–116). Pericles is presented as simply another cog (albeit a very important one) in the turbinelike machine of Athenian greed. Thucydides passes no direct comment on this machine, and, it appears, the Athenians themselves had no afterthoughts. Pericles, though aware of the brutality of imperialism, does not stand out against it for that reason.[85]

However much violence and injustice Pericles sees in Athenian acquisitiveness, he consistently praises prior generations for acquiring the empire, which has made Athens great and Athenians happy. He begins the Funeral Oration by honoring "our ancestors" for what they have done, and even more so "our fathers," because, "in addition to what they received, they acquired as much empire as we now have, not without toil, and left it to us who live now" (2.36.2). He also praises the present generation for adding to the power of the empire (2.36.3). The pleonectic spirit denigrated by the Corinthians is here praised for its promotion of Athenian expansion. As if responding to the Corinthians directly, Pericles says that expansion is the greatest possible goal of the state and much more important than international popularity. In his words, "Who-

---

48), who, on the basis of Isocrates and, apparently, Thucydides, argues that in Periclean Athens, *sōphrosunē* "had become the virtue, not of setting constraints upon one's goals, but of moving with due and deliberate caution in one's choice of means." I consider Periclean *sōphrosunē* to be a virtue of somewhat wider application.

[83] On Pericles' strategy during the war, see Powell 1988, 145–54.

[84] See de Romilly 1963, 140–41, Grene 1965, 91. On Pericles' own role in building the empire, see Hornblower 1987, 172–75.

[85] Cf. 2.13 and *HCT* 4:183–85.

ever incurs odium for aiming at the highest ends, counsels rightly. For hatred does not last for a long time, but present brilliance is left behind as future glory in everlasting memory" (2.64.5).[86] For Pericles, obsessive greed for more pays out in universal glory, so long as it is properly managed; never mind the other Greeks.

Positioned on the brink of something unusual within the tradition of Greek ethical thought, Pericles openly admits that the Athenians have done wrong in acquiring their empire and, what is more, he believes that their acknowledged injustice, their openly confessed imperialistic greed, has been glorious. He does so despite feeling that the empire seems to have been "wrong [*adikon*] to take" (2.63.2). Furthermore, he holds out the prospect of universal dominion in the future, which is within reach, he says, because of Athenian control of the sea (2.62.2–3). The prospect of gratifying their desire to acquire more after the war is meant to encourage the Athenians to endure their present suffering with resolution. In fact, Pericles suggests that Athens has taken some strides toward acquiring a universal empire: "By our daring," he declares, "we have forced an entry into every sea and every land, and everywhere we have established everlasting memorials of our evil and our good [*mnēmeia kakōn te kagathōn*]" (2.41.4). "Memorials of evil": what can this mean?

Although attempts have been made to emend the text or to construe the phrase differently, this passage conveys meaningful ambiguities in Thucydides' own thought on Athens and empire.[87] This passage casts Pericles as a moral revisionist. He proposes that Athens's outstanding level of achievement renders moot the other Greeks' expression of moral opprobrium.

Thus, he advances an entirely individualistic ethic according to which the city's glory, however achieved and however condemned by the wider community, transcends the question of moral justification. For Pericles, Athens is not responsible to the wider Greek community, and the city's pursuit and then attainment of glory is "self-justifying."[88] This can only suggest that, within the context of the wider Greek world, Periclean Athens reexpresses a heroic ethic that existed, indeed could exist, only

[86] This quotation comes from Pericles' second Assembly speech, rather than the Funeral Oration. But I take his position to be essentially similar in the three speeches he delivers in the *History*.

[87] This problem has long puzzled critics. For arguments on behalf of emendation, see Mueller 1958. See also Connor 1984, 74n54, with which my account is in sympathy. *Kaka* ("evils") is the manuscript reading, and there is no reason to suspect the passage on stylistic grounds. The only reason for suspicion has been that the reading causes moral discomfort among modern readers of Thucydides.

[88] Connor 1984, 74.

before the polis was established as the social and political norm.[89] Heroes cannot exist within the polis; their greatness cannot bear its limitations. If we accept Thucydides' own view that the Athenian Empire was driven by the impulse of greed within the Athenian national soul, then we should see Pericles as brilliantly reimagining that characteristic as, now, no longer greed but glory. In Pericles' vision Athenian greed before the Peloponnesian War was christened as Athenian glory, as the collective achievement of greatness. One might compare the Platonic Thrasymachus's remarks to the effect that people are vilified socially and morally for being petty thieves, whereas the tyrant becomes an object of unadulterated admiration because of his success, however immoral, on a grand scale (*Rep.* 344a1–344c2).

How does Thucydides' text push the reader to evaluate this moral stance? Although Pericles has often been regarded as the mouthpiece of the author within the text, the situation is more complicated than that. The historian's own views are notoriously difficult to extract, but several of his comments, along with sections of the narrative that pass by without explicit judgment, suggest a deep ambiguity in his own thought.[90] For Thucydides, Athens was at its greatest "under" Pericles, who represents, at least in wartime, the force of moderation on Athenian greed, which, Thucydides knew, could readily lead the demos to overextend itself. In his eulogy of the leader, for example, Thucydides says that Pericles' foresight with regard to the war became even more evident after his death: he recommended that Athens avoid trying to add to the empire during the war, but his successors did the opposite, and seriously impaired its war potential (2.65.5–7). Thus Thucydides agreed that further expansion during the war was detrimental to Athenian interests.

Moreover, Thucydides certainly suggests that Athenian acquisitiveness, in its capacity as greed instead of glory, led to the city's dissolution, but readers of the Funeral Oration may well conclude that Thucydides there reveals an almost unqualified admiration for Athenian greatness and for the vision of glory evoked by Pericles. This is another sense in which Athens was at its greatest under Pericles: that by the time of his ascendancy it had fully reaped the fruits of its obsessive acquisitiveness and had achieved glory because of its successful greed. Pericles' speeches, read together with the Pentecontaetia, suggest that this greatness was motivated and sustained by a successful policy of imperialistic greed. Clearly

[89] For this conception of Periclean Athens, see also MacIntyre 1988, 47–50. Immerwahr (1973, 28) also sees in Athenian commitment to *dunamis* a "certain heroic quality."

[90] This problem has generated an enormous body of work, but I have found two treatments by Andrewes most helpful: Andrewes 1960; *HCT* 4:183–85. The most provocative view is that of Grene 1965.

Thucydides regretted Athens's increasing lack of prudence, but he also admired the products of its well-managed imperialism. His *History* is in some sense a memorial to the glorious edifice whose foundations were Athenian greed.

At the same time, the text raises questions about the manner in which that edifice was built. In the Corcyra episode, for example, Thucydides saw greed as at least partly responsible for a moral breakdown, and for Thucydides this breakdown is morally lamentable in itself and in its consequences for the individual. The analogy between city and individual suggests that Thucydides also regretted the moral costs of internationally directed greed. Unlike his own Athenian speakers, Thucydides does have some sense of the integrity of the international Greek political community.[91] The praise of Athens is put into Pericles', not Thucydides', mouth. In the Funeral Oration Thucydides puts on display the moral attitudes that enabled Athens to achieve its imperial greatness: Pericles believes that Athenian glory transcends any question of ethical responsibility. However much Thucydides himself was attracted to Athenian greatness, and however far he entertained Pericles' beatification of Athenian greed, though, he also understood and regretted the moral burdens incurred in pursuing a policy, even a successful policy, of international greed. If Pericles reinvents Athenian greed as a feature of the heroic ethic, then Thucydides has assumed a stance akin to that of Homer himself: success in war is glorious, but is it really worth the human costs involved? Those who believe it is, like the Athenian imperialists, may achieve everlasting renown, but lose something humanly valuable in the process, whether this is Patroclus, the Athenian troops destroyed in Sicily, or, more important, one's own sense of human decency.

Thucydides regrets that the Athenians' frightfully successful technologies of power have eroded a sense of honor and shame as guiding moral principles within the Greek world.[92] This erosion is especially clear in their advice to the Melians (5.100–101, 5.111.3). If Thucydides regrets the destruction of Athenian greatness after Pericles, then he also wants to know whether the Athenians have, in the process of acquiring an empire, become as barbaric as the booty-hungry, bloodthirsty Thracians who murder a schoolhouse full of young boys at Mycalessus (7.29–30). Is this barbarous image, and not Periclean glory, the real meaning of Athenian greed? Perhaps the Athenians have merely perfected and systematized

[91] Farrar (1988, 141, 151–52) accepts the existence of an international community, but treats it as the context within which Athenian decisions should be considered prudentially rather than morally. The other Greek states' consistent emphasis on the Athenians' injustice, however, suggests that the international community of Greeks was importantly a moral community.

[92] Crane 1998, esp. 294–325.

the destructive booty raids characteristic of utter barbarians. The tragedy of Athenian imperialism, in Thucydides' eyes, is that because of their success, Athenians lose moral self-consciousness and come to accept the purely amoral, utilitarian views expressed by their agents throughout the work, most famously in the Melian Dialogue.[93]

This tension is inherent in Thucydides' view of Athenian greed. On the one hand, it has led Athens to incur sizable moral burdens. On the other hand, Thucydides admires the Athenians for organizing greed out of domestic politics, which ultimately is a kind of self-overcoming: it was only by restraining human urges within their own community that Athenians could begin to solve the long-standing problem of greed-driven stasis within the Greek polis. Solving that problem meant that the Athenians were able to, almost had to, acquire an enormous empire that underwrites the city's own greatness and glory. In Pericles' powerful formulation the empire provided the conditions in which every day at Athens is a festival and every Athenian strives to become the best human being he can possibly be. This is the closest any ancient author comes to saying that greed is good; that greed is responsible for human progress; in sum, that greed motivates men to transcend their human condition and nearly transcend their own sense of right and wrong.

Reading Herodotus and Thucydides together, we derive a startling image of the transformation from hegemony to empire, as democracy harmonizes and enables the acquisitive impulses of both leaders and demos in Athens. Taking over what are originally Herodotean theses, Thucydides shows that Athens has found a "solution" to the long-standing problem of internal class conflict driven by greed: by turning their greed outward against other city-states, Athenians resolve the problems of *stasis*. Despite their affinities, however, Herodotus and Thucydides use different tools of historical analysis, make different philosophical claims about the past, and disagree sharply on the future of Athens as an imperial power. It will suffice to make only two points about these differences.[94]

First, Herodotus, unlike his successor, makes no claim about human nature: for him, historical process is, beyond the occasional divine intervention, the result of individual choices, which establish and reinforce cultural norms. Even if states rise and fall in organic regularity for Herodotus, it is still unclear that human nature as such, given the right circumstances, will repeat itself in predictable ways, even when favorable circumstances are present. Greed is a feature of particular unrestrained individuals, who then encourage, sometimes successfully, acquisitive im-

[93] Crane 1998, 237–57; for a different interpretation of the Melian dialogue, see Andrewes 1960.

[94] Hornblower (1987, 26–33) usefully charts several other continuities and differences between Herodotus and Thucydides.

pulses in the state; Herodotus never makes greed a universal facet of human nature. For Thucydides, on the other hand, human nature plays a key role in explaining the pleonectic impulse that drives Athenian imperialism. Greed is displayed not only by particularly greedy individuals or poleis, but emerges whenever resources become great enough to enable it and laws become powerless to restrain it (3.82–84). While Thucydides could write a work for all time as he thought (1.22.4), because of his belief in the predictability of human nature, Herodotus concentrates rather on the specificity of the Greek and Persian past, because that past has special significance for his contemporaries.

The second relevant difference is that, for Herodotus, imperialism is immoral and imprudent because it is unjust and dangerous to take something that belongs to another. In time, therefore, imperialism will be revealed as both a prudential and a moral disaster and, indeed, the two are scarcely distinguished by Herodotus. In his moral universe, the Athenians set themselves up for disaster as soon as they enter into patterns of *hubris* and greed visible in the rise and fall of Persia. All states, in Herodotus's view, undergo quasi-organic transformations from greatness to humility, and vice-versa; prosperity never abides long (1.5.3). For Herodotus, this nearly becomes a moral law of the universe, which states would be (prudentially) wise to remember. For Thucydides, on the other hand, Athens's ultimate failure is the result not of organic process, or of moral defects, but rather of the weakness of good judgment (*gnōmē*) and moderation (*sōphrosunē*) in the face of imperialistic greed. At the same time, however, there are glimmers in Thucydides' text that the best "cure" for greed is simply further greed, as long as it is managed by capable, energetic leaders.

Thucydides' view of Alcibiades, who represents the best possibility of such a "cure," is complicated. But it can be read meaningfully against other passages that suggest the importance of a few central concepts in Thucydidean political thought: greed, trust, self-interest, and leadership. Alcibiades is in some sense novel in his attitudes toward all these factors. However one understands his place in Thucydides' text, it is clear that the Sicilian expedition, which is authorized by his own greed and ambition, and by his own rhetoric of greed, is responsible for an increasing fragmentation of interests within Athens, and therefore for pushing the polis further down the road to revolution. Once Alcibiades is removed from a position of leadership, the centrifugal tendencies of the democracy spiral outward in an increasing display of civic mistrust and divisiveness. The democratic process can no longer coalesce successfully around Alcibiades' compelling personality and vision. The revolutionary unraveling of competing strands of self-interest, which had been united in the Athens of Pericles, is the subject of my next chapter.

6

"Revolution Matters"? Oligarchic Rebellion and Democratic Hegemony in Athens

In the late fifth century, a unified discourse on greed arose in response to changing social, economic, and military conditions in Athens. Focusing on fragmentation and factionalism within Athens, this discourse expressed deep tensions in Athenian culture that date back at least to the Solonian period. At the same time, it is thoroughly enmeshed in the setting of the Peloponnesian War, when disputes over distributive resources in Athens became especially acute. In the intellectual controversies of the time, as well as in the two oligarchic revolutions at the end of the century, Athenians played out conflicts between rich and poor and between individual self-interest and collective responsibility. Although having firm roots in Athenian culture, these conflicts were also deepened by the Athenians' experience of imperialism and by the ethical language that they and others employed to describe their imperialism.

My argument is that ethical language of this sort is not simply an epiphenomenon of events or an ethereal superstructure of ideology built on or explained by a solid economic and material base. The Athenians' notions of greed and injustice conspired with economic and military changes to produce widespread social fragmentation and internal divisiveness at Athens. The events of the late fifth century, especially the two oligarchic revolutions, can be closely linked to socially divisive self-perceptions and perceptions of others, as members of the Athenian elite engaged in revolutionary activity at least in part because of the way they saw themselves and their fellow citizens. In particular, members of the elite resentfully accused the demos of being greedy and of habitually taking more than its fair share of the city's collective resources. Other members of the elite, moreover, embraced greed as a positive ideal of political behavior, according to which those with power should use their positions to get as much as they can for themselves. As a result, the late fifth-century discourse on greed played a major role in causing the oligarchic revolutions through its capacity to shape, transform, and invigorate divisive ways of thinking about the individual, the group, and the polis.[1] Equally, the effects of revolutionary action contributed to the fur-

[1] My discussion is informed by modern intellectual historians' efforts to theorize the

ther development of ideas about greed. Hence, as I argue, ideas about greed are neither unitary causes nor mere by-products, but are at once causes and effects of a rapidly evolving social and political environment.[2]

Athenian Culture in the Late Fifth Century: Unity and Division

Athenians were embroiled in two conflicts in the late fifth century. One they fought against the Peloponnesians, one against each other. Athenians had begun to drift away from the Solonian and Periclean ideals of unifying all classes.[3] To explain this, it is helpful to think in terms of competing ideologies of unity and division, which shift continually depending on individuals' self-conceptions and perceptions of their own self-interests. At the two extremes, individual Athenians could identify their self-interests entirely with those of the polis, or view themselves as narrowly self-interested, and even anti-Athenian, revolutionaries. In practice most people probably did what seemed like a good idea at the moment. Consequently, ideological consensus can be imagined, not as a framework within which rigorously developed theoretical commitments were expressed, but rather as a makeshift agreement in which different groups formed mutual compacts that seemed to serve their self-interests at the time, whatever their self-interests were. Any apparent "consensus" may mask the victory of one ideological standpoint, which, for all practical purposes, silences views to the contrary. Our evidence for the early to middle fifth century does not allow us to determine whether that happened in Athens. Whether or not the Athenian elite willingly and self-consciously integrated itself into the prevailing democratic ideology, though, it probably participated in the democracy in order to attain for itself the material and psychological benefits of empire.[4]

---

relationship between ideas and political behavior; see esp. Skinner 1988a, 1988b; Minogue 1988; Walzer 1988. One line of approach is well captured in the following quotation (Skinner 1988a, 117): "The general conclusion derives from the fact that any cause of action is inhibited from occurring if it cannot be legitimated. It follows that any principle which helps to legitimate a cause of action must also be amongst the enabling conditions of its occurrence." I argue that such legitimating principles not only enable but also inspire actions. For further discussion, see chapter 1.

[2] Morris (1998, 5–6) successfully applies the methods of the "new cultural history" (cf. Chartier 1990, Hunt 1989) to archaeology and ancient history. As Morris argues, "Our understanding of the world is always discursively constituted, through the manipulation of words and things, and through competing interpretations of what such manipulations mean" (5).

[3] On Solon's influence on Thucydides' representation of Pericles, see Szegedy-Maszak 1993.

[4] If so, then such participation minimizes the distinction between "social contract" and

By offering a powerful solution to the problem of reconciling individual self-interest with wider polis interests, the developed empire sustained domestic harmony within the polis for half a century. Athenians of all socioeconomic groups had come to believe that their own ambitions could best be fulfilled if they joined together to create a powerful, amoral polis capable of seemingly endless expansion, desire, and satisfaction. As long as the empire was successful, there was no conflict between the good of the polis and the good of the individual. Imperialistic success made it easy for individuals to identify themselves first and foremost as Athenian citizens.[5]

Even when political unity seems most secure, however, division is usually latent. Political unity is constantly under threat of dissipation.[6] Pericles himself, for example, was continually called upon to recreate unity in the face of the centrifugal forces of individual suffering: "Put away your private grief and and take up instead the cause of our common safety" (*apalgēsantas de ta idia tou koinou tēs sōtērias antilambanesthai*, Thuc. 2.61.4). As Saxonhouse has put it, "The unexpected suffering that the war has brought divides the city into individuals who care about their private welfare, . . . who see themselves as private rather than communal beings, who do not accept the Funeral Oration's identification between themselves and the city."[7] The Athenians' suffering made it increasingly difficult to envision a unified national policy that could serve the individual self-interests of all equally.

The Athenians' suffering was in part economic. By turning Athens into an island and prohibiting Athenians from going out to fight the ravaging Peloponnesians, Pericles caused material and psychological suffering for all classes.[8] Moreover, Athens found itself in a particularly bleak financial situation in the period following Pericles' death. The property tax (*eisphora*) of 428/7 both attests to the city's straitened circumstances and illustrates that the financial burdens of warfare fell most heavily on the rich.[9] Increasing taxation of the allies, and an increasing effort to collect

"democratic hegemony," which I have drawn in this paragraph. The "social contract" in which the elite may have willingly participated becomes a hegemonic condition only if the elite were not receiving due benefits from participation, but the apparent lack of political divisiveness earlier in the century suggests that the elite felt that it was receiving its due.

[5] I am grateful to Robin Osborne for discussion of several points in this and the following paragraphs.

[6] On the divisive cracks underlying Pericles' memorable vision of unity, as this is presented in Thucydides, see Saxonhouse 1996, 59–86.

[7] Saxonhouse 1996, 69.

[8] For Pericles' strategy of creating an "island mentality" for Athenians, see Thucydides 1.143.4–5, with Powell 1988, 149–50; Ober 1985, 174–75. For the difficulties and consequences of gathering all Athenians into the city proper during the war, see Thucydides 2.16. On the cavalry forces sent out to limit Peloponnesian ravaging, see Ober 1985.

[9] In 428 the Athenians increased this tax ("an extraordinary levy on capital": Hornblower

allied contributions, fit securely in this period.[10] The Spartans fortified Decelea with devastating effect to Athenian properties, and some twenty thousand slaves had escaped.[11] There was a renewed economic crunch after the Sicilian disaster. Properties abroad were in jeopardy or lost.[12] If the rich had grown differentially richer than the poor before the war, then they also suffered differentially greater losses from both Spartan raids and reclamation of cleruchies.[13] A number of cities on the coast of Asia Minor withdrew from the alliance by 412. The threat of further desertion was always present.[14]

In addition, Athens experienced a breakdown of communal norms in the plague of 429 (Thuc. 2.47–54).[15] Whatever other effects it had, the plague introduced divisiveness into many facets of Athenian life; it provided a shared experience of mistrust and internal competition. In this state of lawlessness (*anomia*) (2.53.1), Thucydides says, the pleasure of the moment became the individual's deepest concern: "It was generally agreed that what was both honorable and useful was the pleasure of the moment and whatever might conceivably contribute to it" (2.53.3). As in Corcyra, in Athens difficult economic circumstances liberated the aggressive elements in human nature, producing lawlessness, hunger for more, and a further breakdown of communal sentiments (3.82–83, 2.53).

Along with economic and social changes, political thought also encouraged division within the body politic. Athens became increasingly polarized as members of the elite leveled systematic criticisms against the Athenian democracy. Their response did not follow in any necessary way from the city's various war-time stresses; rather it was the result of a particular interpretation of the Athenian demos as greedy and unjust. To be sure, political criticism as such does not spell the end of unity. As long as the empire was successful, political criticism could be innocuously directed at individual politicians, rather than at the democratic system as a whole, which seemed on the face of it to succeed in satisfying all citizens'

1991, 403) and subsequently attempted to increase the tribute assessments of their subject states during the 420s: see Thucydides 3.19.1; Aristophanes *Knights* 773–75; with Sealey 1976, 334–36; Meiggs 1972; Gomme *HCT* 2:278–79; ML 68, 69; Hornblower 1991, 403–4.

[10] See, e.g., ML 45 (= Fornara 97), ML 46 (= Fornara 98), ML 47 (= Fornara 99); for the downdating of these documents to the 420s and the famous "tri-bar sigma" controversy, see Mattingly 1996, 281–314.

[11] Thucydides 7.27.3–5; for the economic consequences of this, see Sealey 1976, 356–57.

[12] Thucydides 8.2, 8.5, and passim; Lintott 1982, 148.

[13] For the background to this complex issue, see Finley 1978a.

[14] On the threat of secession, see Sealey 1986, 133; Sealey 1976, 356–57.

[15] For the dramatic juxtaposition of the plague and Pericles' Funeral Oration, see Connor 1984, 64–65. On the course of the plague, see Powell 1988, 157–59; Hornblower 1991, 316–27; Gomme *HCT* 2:145–62. Although we do not hear of the plague in other sources, Thucydides' presentation is believable; cf. Hornblower 1991, 318.

desires. Indeed, such criticism can be a revitalizing force that maintains preexisting frameworks and institutions, whether it operates in the mode of a "safety valve" mechanism, or as a positive, responsive adaptation to circumstances that are perceived to have changed.[16] Far from being harmed by political critique, Athens itself and Athenian democracy had once been sustained by it.

But late fifth-century political theory raised criticisms of (other) politicians to the level of a systematic critique of democracy as a political system.[17] In archaic Greek history, rebellious activity tended to be directed against the tyrant or ruling family and was therefore easily personalized; there was little or no need for theory, which identifies a regime as such rather than a person or familial unit as "the problem" demanding a solution. It may be easy to move from criticism of a tyrant to criticism of a democratic leader, but it is more difficult to criticize the demos in the abstract, much less the institutions and ideals that constitute Athenian democracy. Systematic political thought enabled Athenian elites, if they so chose, to articulate their reasons for discontent, and to place those reasons within a wider theoretical frame, which provoked further resentment, discontent, and, most important, desire for systemic change.[18] If some individuals or groups had once been resentful of democracy on elitist or prejudicial grounds, then they could now explain to themselves, using the powerful tools of new social theory, why democracy was immoral and ineffective.[19] It is plausible to suppose that such theories played an active role in shaping history, so long as we believe that consumers of them took political thought seriously and modified their beliefs and behaviors accordingly.[20]

[16] Ober 1996a; 1998, 3–13; on the relationship between Athenian democracy and political thought written in Athens, see Farrar 1988; on the concept of a "safety-valve mechanism" as applied to public festivals in the Renaissance, see Mitchell 1986.

[17] Cf. Forrest 1966, 224; 1975.

[18] When offering accounts of social and political process, historians have always tended to relegate intellectual and cultural currents to the sidelines, e.g., Lintott 1982, 125–84; Sealey 1976, 348–95; but for a useful attempt to integrate political thought into an account of the period, see Forrest 1966, 224–28. For an altogether different approach from the one taken in the text, see Ostwald 1986, 237–50. On the connection between the sophistic movement and Athens, see Kerferd 1981, 15–23. As will become clear, my focus is on a wider group of thinkers than the "sophists" in a narrow sense, for which see Kerferd 1981, 24–41.

[19] As shown by a variety of other Greek *poleis* in the period, oligarchic revolutions could occur without political theory, but Athens had had a long and successful tradition of democracy. It required peculiar efforts of the imagination to think oneself out of that tradition and into solid oligarchic frameworks.

[20] At least in the case of sophists, the willingness of certain members of the elite to pay large sums for their teaching makes this point clear. On the costliness of sophistic education, see, e.g., Plato *Apology* 20b9; Xenophon *Symposium* 4.62 with Ostwald 1986, 242, 278; Kerferd 1981, 26–28.

Earlier in the century, Athenians had embraced their greed within the international community as a psychological characteristic that won them glory. Reconceived as a core problem of Athenian domestic politics, however, the notion of greed was newly deployed in arguments over the fair distribution of imperial profits and over the appropriate correlation between political authority and the possession of wealth. To put it bluntly, and to adopt the elitist viewpoint, are democratic norms simply the most powerful tool of gratification that the demos had yet discovered?

Thucydides represents these issues as urgent matters of public consideration in 415, albeit in democratic Syracuse rather than Athens. Athenagoras's anti-oligarchic speech provides a clear entry to the rhetoric and theory of class conflict. Couching his speech in terms of fairness and equality (6.38.5, 6.39.1), Athenagoras says, "Oligarchy gives the many its share [*metadidōsi*] of dangers, but it does not only take more than its share [*pleonektei*] of the benefits—rather, it makes off with them all together" (6.39.2).[21] According to Athenagoras, the rich (*dunamenoi*) and the young (*neoi*) eagerly desire (*prothumountai*) everything for themselves (6.39.2). The speech incorporates all the traditional associations of greed: unfairness in the distribution of labor and benefits, excessive acquisitiveness, and vilification of one's ideological opponents. Greed and allegations of greed were firmly entrenched as a feature of class conflict between the rich and the poor.

Although criticisms of greed were usually directed in this period against the demos and its leaders, democrats and oligarchs alike could articulate their criticisms of ideological opponents at an abstract level and in terms of greed and injustice. According to Athenagoras, democracy is the best and most just form of government because the demos is the whole state, while the few (*oligoi*) are merely part of it: "Some say that democracy is neither intelligent [*xuneton*] nor fair [*ison*], but that those with money are the best rulers. But I say first that what is meant by the 'demos' is the whole state, whereas an oligarchy is only a part of it" (6.39.1). Athenagoras trades on the traditional ambiguity between two senses of "demos"—which can mean either "the entire people" or "the lower classes"—in order to suggest that democracy serves not only the interests of the poor but also the interests of the entire polis. This is a key ideological move, because it exploits the rhetoric of community for the sake of supporting the political claims of the lower classes against those of the rich. This is the kind of compelling democratic argument that most of our surviving Athenian texts argue against.

[21] Compare Herodotus's description of Gelon's indignant reaction to the Athenians at Syracuse: "Because you yield nothing and wish to have it all, you had better rush home and announce to Greece that the spring of the year is lost to her" (7.162.1).

In the early to middle fifth century, there are few indications that the Athenian elite tried to change Athens's basic democratic institutions for ideological reasons.[22] During the Peloponnesian War, however, rich and poor began to view themselves as competing for increasingly scarce resources and to identify themselves with narrowly self-interested factions within Athens, rather than with the polis as a whole. There was a growing belief that government serves the interests of the rulers and that not all truly shared in the democratic regime. A newly systematic form of social commentary provoked antidemocratic sentiments and helped to strengthen an oppositional group within the elite that seized its opportunity, in 411, to attack Athenian democracy. This oppositional group included both those who had opted out of democratic politics and, more generally, those who had come to believe that the Athenian demos was greedy and unjust in its governance of Athens and the empire.[23]

Increasingly systematic discussions of democracy were conducted in terms of greed and the unfair distribution of power and resources. The "Old Oligarch," author of a treatise called the *Constitution of the Athenians*, focuses on greed and injustice in his critique of the way Athens governed its empire and distributed its imperial profits.[24] As a theoretical analysis of why democracy works, the treatise is, contrary to traditional scholarly opinion, wide-ranging and insightful, but it does illustrate the

[22] Our sources mention two attempts to overthrow the democracy earlier in the fifth century: Plutarch *Aristides* 13.1, just before the battle of Plataea; Thucydides 1.107.4–6, just before the battle of Tanagra in 458/7. Neither necessarily gives evidence of aristocratic opposition to democracy on ideological grounds: see the arguments of Ostwald 1986, 176–81. Plutarch (*Per.* 11.1) mentions the opposition of Thucydides son of Melesias to Pericles, but again this need not imply opposition to democracy as such, even though later sources such as Plutarch interpret it that way; cf. Ostwald 1986, 186–87.

[23] Carter 1986 charts the growth of an antidemocratic opposition whose members opted out of the democratic system and were called *apragmones*; for the identities of those who joined the aristocratic opposition in 411 and 404, see my subsequent discussion.

[24] "Old Oligarch" is the nineteenth-century nickname for this author, whose manuscript was attributed in antiquity to Xenophon. Scholars have dated and sought a context for his essay in a variety of ways, but no consensus has been reached. Bowersock (1968, 465) dates it ca. 443 because of its failure to mention the Samian Revolt, but cf. Bowersock 1966; Gomme (1962, 50–54) gives an excellent overview of the multiple possibilities suggested by the text, ultimately dating it to between 420 and 415 (68); Ostwald (1986, 182n23) dates it between 431 and 424 on the grounds that it reflects the conditions of the early part of the Peloponnesian War; Forrest (1975, 44) suggests 424; cf. also Frisch 1942, 47–62, for discussion of various conjectures. Cole (1991, 102–4) offers a survey of recent opinions on the nature of the treatise and concludes that it represents a rhetorical exercise, while Ober (1998, 14–27) locates the piece within broader currents of antidemocratic criticism during the late fifth century. On the date, I suggest the 420s because of the author's tendency to use arguments that must have had currency in the conditions of the Archidamian War, such as the Athenians' decision to remove their property to Euboea (2.14–16) and the analysis of advantages that would accrue to Athens if it were an island: cf. Bowersock 1968, 464–65.

failure of a traditionally minded elite to reconcile democratic success with his ingrained prejudice against the demos. Ironically, in view of the author's standpoint, his analysis points up philosophical weaknesses in the antidemocratic position, instead of undermining democratic ideology. In the course of his analysis, he gives evidence of spectacular efforts to think himself out of central democratic tenets about acquisition, distribution, and empire.

The author begins his treatise with an explicit association between distributive justice and political stability, returning to this same equation at the end of the treatise. After proposing to show how the Athenians preserve their constitution (1.1), he says, "First I will say this, that it is just that the poor and the demos have more [*pleon echein*] than the well-born [*gennaiōn*] and rich [*plousiōn*] for this reason, that it is the demos that mans the ships and that gives power to the city" (1.2).[25] This is a highly traditional argument: the demos deserves a greater share in the profits of empire and power within the city because of its differentially greater contribution to the city's military strength.[26] The demos's fair distribution promotes political stability, a point that Aristotle appreciated fully in his analysis of revolution. The Old Oligarch's argument does not, as it happens, support his antidemocratic standpoint, because it provides a powerful moral backing for the democratic system, based on values that all Athenians, rich and poor, share. The Old Oligarch believes, somewhat awkwardly, that the demos's distribution of power and resources within Athens is indecent and yet just, socially unacceptable and yet highly successful. This awkwardness pervades his essay and ultimately leads to a failure to offer any moral grounds for opposing democracy.

The Old Oligarch conducts his analysis of Athenian democracy by examining the demos's distribution of power and resources both within the city and in allied cities. Mixed in with his recognition of the demos's essential justice in distribution is a belief in the inherent greed of the impoverished lower classes. In our author's view, the demos dominates Athens primarily in order to get more, independent of any considerations of taste, learning, or morality. Thus, to qualify his vision of fairness within the city, he argues that the people's control of the courts is concerned not with justice (*tou dikaiou*) so much as profit (*tou . . . sumphorou*) (1.13). In general, he proposes, the demos rules both Athens and the empire in order to satisfy its greed: the people are anxious to hold salaried magistracies (1.3); they are obsequious to their own slaves in order to take a portion of the slaves' earnings (1.11); they force the allies

[25] For the further language of justice and "shares" in a political sense, see 1.2: "It seems just for all to have a share in the magistracies" (*dokei dikaion einai pasi tōn archōn meteinai*).

[26] For the traditionality of this argument, see chapters 2 and 3.

to conduct judicial trials at Athens, which brings in revenue from tax and tourism (1.17); and they are prone to taking bribes (3.3). The Old Oligarch provides a veritable catalog of methods by which the Athenian demos successfully satisfies its extravagant desires to get more.

Most important, though, the demos's greed drives it to wage an immoral class war against the rich. Within the city, our author says, the demos violates decency by perversely taking more than its share and impoverishing all intelligent and well-to-do men (1.13–14). He resentfully points out, for example, that the demos redistributes wealth through a system of public liturgies, in which the rich provide financial backing for dramatic choruses, athletic contests, and triremes. As he declares, "The demos thinks itself worthy [*axioi*] of taking money for singing, running, dancing, and sailing in ships, so that the demos itself can grow wealthy while the rich grow poorer [*penesteroi*]" (1.13). The demos's assault on the wealth of the rich, however, is not confined to Athens. Arguing that "like is always loyal to like" (3.10), the author suggests that the demos unjustly distributes differentially greater shares of goods within allied states to the allied poor, rather than to the rich few. In order to promote their own interests, the Athenian people "disfranchise the aristocrats [*chrēstous*], take away their money, expel and kill them, whereas they promote the interests of the lower class [*ponērous*]" (1.14). The money they take away from the rich, they evidently give to the poor. "Everywhere," he claims, "the Athenian people distribute more [*pleon nemousi*] to the worst persons [*ponērois*], to the poor [*penēsi*], and to the demotic people [*dēmotikois*] rather than to good men [*chrēstois*]" (1.4). Both within Athens and throughout the empire, the Athenian demos oppresses the rich in order to satisfy its greed for more and in order to advance its own hold on power.

The similarity that our author evokes between external and internal aggression represents a critical change in the theoretical analysis of Athenian success at home and abroad. Now, rather than seeing internal harmony as complemented by external greed, as we found in Thucydides, the Old Oligarch argues that the demos follows a consistent policy of greed and aggression against the upper classes whether in Athens or in allied cities.[27] In other words, the demos has not co-opted aristocrats in a project that mutually benefits both classes within Athens.[28] Instead, the

[27] Of course, he recognizes also that the allied poor have just enough to live on, and that they too are in effect enslaved to the Athenian demos (1.19). But in his mind slavery to Athens and mastery at home is, to the allied demos, preferable to being enslaved by the rich few at home.

[28] In fact, his argument is hard to sustain: both rich and poor benefited from the democracy, but perhaps not in the ratios that would satisfy the Old Oligarch; for the seminal discussion of the profits of empire, see Finley 1978a.

ordinary citizens of Athens govern both their own city and their empire in such a way as to prosecute their greed on a grand scale, even when their excessive desires obviously, in the author's view, drive them to violate standards of justice.

In order to maintain conditions of systematic greed within Athens, the demos must employ mechanisms of social control that rule out any excessive acquisitiveness within its own ranks. In a digression on Athenian comedy, he writes:

> They do not allow the demos to be ridiculed in comedy, so that they may not have a bad reputation; but if anyone wants to attack private persons, they encourage it, knowing perfectly well that the person abused in comedy does not generally come from the populace and mass of people but is either rich, wellborn, or powerful. A few of the poor demotic types are abused in comedy, but only if they act like busybodies [*dia polupragmosunēn*] and try to get more than [*dia to zētein pleon ti echein*] the demos. (2.18)[29]

Harmony and fairness are to prevail within the demotic faction, because the demos places a premium on equality of respect for all its members; conversely, the demos permits comic writers to abuse those of its number who try to take more than their fair share. On the other hand, the demos readily permits abuse of the rich and, as we have seen, it characteristically considers the rich a prime target for its aggressive greed. In order to retain control of the polis as a whole, then, the demos attempts to secure trust and equality within its own faction, channeling its acquisitive urges outward against the rich, with whom it competes for shares in the city's power and resources. By combining intrafactional harmony with extrafactional greed, the demos has created an enclave within Athens whose behavior resembles that of imperial Athens within the Panhellenic community. To put it differently, the demos has acquired enough power to treat the wealthy elite of Athens as a subject state under the control of the Athenian demos; it has created two cities within the city of Athens, in which the demos has become a "micro-Athens" within Athens itself. The demos thus puts an innovative spin on the traditional symbiosis between foreign and domestic politics, which we have traced in Thucydides. Now the framework of "internal harmony, external greed" is applied to two competing factions within the city itself.

The workings of the empire provided a dangerous but effective model for the demos's stance within the polis. According to the Old Oligarch,

[29] Henderson (1990, 285–88) argues that the Old Oligarch is accurate in saying that in extant Old Comedy the demos is not ridiculed, and that Aristophanes blames the demos only to exhort it to recapture its own highest ideals; but Aristophanes' *Knights*, with its ridiculing of Demos as a personified character, shows that this needs qualification. On the other hand, extant comedy certainly does show that the bulk of comic abuse was reserved for the rich elite.

"It is necessary for the ruler to be hated by the ruled" (1.14).[30] For him, this is a necessary truth that explains why aristocrats hate their demotic overlords in the first place, and why the demos in turn mistrusts aristocrats everywhere (1.14).[31] If the ruler is hated, then he must hate in return (1.14). Our author has learned this "necessary truth" through empirical observation of the Athenian Empire and through listening to the moral attacks made on Athens by its subject states. In Thucydides, for example, Pericles declares, "All who resolve to rule over others are hated and offensive for a time" (2.64.5). In context, Pericles is encouraging the Athenians to view their empire as a means to win glory, in spite of the opprobrium they incur from their subjects. Thus the Old Oligarch applies the rhetoric of adversarial interstate relations both to the internal politics of Athens and to the relationship between demos and aristocrats in general. All the more striking, he employs this rhetoric despite the Athenians' long experience of successfully building coalitions between mass and elite during the fifth century.

By the late fifth century, the Athenian democracy was firmly entrenched as the system that best promotes the common good, particularly through its unique capacity to satisfy the acquisitive desires of both the elite and the demos. Moreover, as Thucydides' character Athenagoras urges, democracy promotes a fair, and even more than fair, distribution of goods and power within the polis (6.40.1). In this context, the Old Oligarch stunningly views Athens as the site of a desperate conflict over the distribution of power and resources. For him, this conflict results from the radical, albeit understandable, pursuit of self-interest: "It is understandable that everyone looks after his own interests" (2.20). It turns out that these self-interests are not defined individually, but rather with reference to group affiliations. In describing the demos's choice of its leaders, he says,

> I think that the Athenian demos knows which citizens are good [*chrēstoi*] and which bad [*ponēroi*], but the people nevertheless cultivate those who are useful and profitable [*epitēdeious kai sumphorous*] to themselves, even if they are bad [*ponēroi*], and they tend to hate the good [*chrēstous*]; for they believe that the natural virtue of good men will harm rather than benefit them [*ou gar nomizousi tēn aretēn autois pros tōi spheterōi agathōi pephukenai, all' epi tōi kakōi*]. On the

[30] The terms he uses for "rule" (*archē*) and "necessity" (*anankē*) are the same as those found in Thucydides, and both reflect the prevailing ideology of opposition to Athens among the allies, which was usually expressed in the terminology of freedom and slavery. On *ananke* in Thucydides, see Strauss 1964, 182–92. On debates over the "popularity" of the Athenian Empire, see de Ste. Croix 1954, Bradeen 1960.

[31] Although he applies this analysis specifically to allied aristocrats, his own resentment toward the demos shows that it is equally true of Athenian aristocrats.

other hand, some people are not by nature [*phusin*] democratic although they indeed favor the demos. (2.19)

The underlying premise of this argument is that class-based division is scripted into human nature and that, as a result, it is exceptional for a member of the elite to behave cooperatively with the demos. Some are by nature democratic, others by nature antidemocratic; nature promotes an irreducible identification of the individual with a particular socio-economic group. According to the Old Oligarch, one cannot avoid class affiliations, except in the case of a great wrongdoer, who lives by choice under a democracy only to escape notice (2.20).[32] The great wrongdoer, a wayward, unnatural aristocrat, typically teams up with the demos to oppress the elite, specifically in order to further his own material well-being.

This is an extremely powerful statement of class division, because its reference to what is true by nature suggests that there is no real hope of achieving city-wide consensus in Athens. Based as it is on a belief in the natural conflict between elite and demos, the author's position forecloses several possibilities that might have been advantageous to him and his group. If self-interest is really his concern, for example, then why should he not become a member of a different group that satisfies his self-interest even better than the small oppositional group of aristocrats within Athens? Or, conversely, why should he not work to unite that group with the demos in order to promote the mutual interests of both?[33] That these possibilities do not occur to the author results from the deep entrenchment in his mind of class-based interests, attachments, and identifications.

His vision of the polis as a site of class-based conflict is illustrated in his conception of "good government" (*eunomia*): "If you seek good government [*eunomian*], you will first see the cleverest men [*tous dexiōtatous*] establishing the laws in their own interest. Then the good men [*hoi chrēstoi*] will punish the bad [*tous ponērous*]. . . . As a result of these excellent measures, the demos would swiftly fall into slavery" (1.9). Unlike Solon, the Old Oligarch has no conception of "good government" as a system that institutes a fair division of power and resources among all citizens. As a result, he cannot articulate a genuine moral basis for the oligarchic regime he so fervently desires. Rather, he leaves his reader with an amoral vision of the polis—a polis that provides the context for power struggles but renders impossible the capacity for citizens to debate

[32] Compare Plato's picture of democratic apathy about lawbreakers (*Rep.* 558a4–8); cf. Saxonhouse 1996, 103–11.

[33] We should recall, after all, that this is the Thucydidean ideal, expressed in Pericles' three speeches; cf. chapter 4.

the merits of various standards of fair distribution. If the polis is by nature a site of competition and hatred, and does not admit the possibility of genuine moral dialogue, then there is no reason why any particular standpoint should be morally preferable to another.[34] The author thus must recognize that the democracy has acquired all the goods and privileges that he himself and his fellow aristocrats value—and that he cannot think of good moral arguments to the effect that the situation should be any different. The polis can at best achieve a condition of stability in which one class greedily wins all the goods for itself at the expense of another class that is powerless to resist. If Thucydides encourages us to ask whether Athens could become like Corcyra, then the Old Oligarch's answer is clearly affirmative.

His theory of natural class attachments leads him inevitably to make normative suggestions about an appropriate elite response to the demos. In particular, if the demos and its leaders have become a "little Athens" within Athens, then so too should the rich few become a united front of opposition against that bullying, greedy, demotic faction. Revolution is all that is left for the elite. This is the logical conclusion of the author's pessimistic vision of the polis as a site of conflict. If at least some upper-class Athenians accepted the author's view, then the revolution of 411 is all the more predictable, since revolutionary behavior will merely carry natural, preexisting conflicts to their logical conclusions. Ironically, though, the author misunderstands why people become revolutionaries in the first place: for him, only those unjustly disenfranchised pose a threat to the democracy, and at Athens very few have been victimized in this way (3.12–13). He cannot conceive that anyone will promote a revolution as long as he is a shareholder in the existing constitution, even if that constitution is, as he asserts, an unfair one. His attitude demonstrates that it took an imaginative leap for "shareholding" elites to think themselves out of the prevailing democratic system enough to participate in a revolution. But it is precisely texts like this that helped galvanize dissent even among shareholding citizens. Systematic political analyses enabled antidemocrats to justify their hatred of the demos even though they remained citizens of Athens.

The Old Oligarch's perceptions that the profits of empire are distributed unfairly and that the Athenian demos oppresses aristocrats for its own advantage have deep roots in the culture of the period. The full force of the treatise can only be appreciated in light of the many wide-ranging contemporary discussions of greed and injustice in a variety of

[34] The author would have to claim, in response, that, for him, some people are innately "better," and so, when they rule, the state that arises will reflect their innate superiority and thus will be "well governed." But this is weak, especially in the retrospective light of the oligarchic revolutions at the end of the century, discussed later in this chapter.

genres and contexts. In particular, both comedy and tragedy participate in the discourse on greed, but they must be understood, unlike the Old Oligarch, as part of a system of civic ritual enacted within a self-consciously democratic performance context.[35]

I deal first with comedy. In the view of many critics, this democratic context constrained the comic playwright to express and endorse tenets of democratic ideology, along with educating the Athenian demos in the proper ways of living up to its own highest ideals.[36] My emphasis, by contrast, is on the ambiguities of comic poetry itself—ambiguities that were themselves interpreted by a large, diverse, and far from monolithic audience. On the one hand, drama is, as many critics have argued, the polyvalent medium par excellence and manages to explore and engage with a wide variety of possible viewpoints even as it maintains a coherent theatrical economy. Hence, the democratic context is crucial but not determinative of how Aristophanic comedy (for example) could be interpreted. On the other hand, as the Old Oligarch and others show, Athens was experiencing dramatic internal division at precisely the period in which most of the extant comedies were produced. As we have seen, in the Sicilian debate, Thucydides depicts the Athenian Assembly as an internally divided body of citizens; groups within that body developed individual self-interests, self-images, and commitments, which often conflicted with those of other groups. As a result, Aristophanic plays were probably interpreted differently by members of different factions within Athens in the late fifth century. In particular, the oppositional and potentially revolutionary group to which the Old Oligarch appealed was dis-

[35] The literature on Athenian drama in its civic and religious context is vast: see the collection of essays in Winkler and Zeitlin 1990, Sommerstein et al. 1993. Henderson 1990, which argues that comedy has a serious political function and offers good evidence for the demos's attitudes to social problems, is fundamental. Nightingale 1995, 180–85; Edmunds 1987b, 59–66; and de Ste. Croix 1972, 231–44, 355–76, also argue that comedy has the potential to convey a serious political message. For the opposite view, see Gomme 1938, Reckford 1987, and Heath 1987. The opposition between a political and a non-political Aristophanes has tended to obscure discussion of the nature of Aristophanes' political commitments, as those in favor of a "political" Aristophanes tend to see him as sympathetically conveying democratic ideology.

[36] The Old Oligarch (2.18) initiated the tradition of viewing comedy as a vehicle of democratic ideology. As Henderson (1993, 308) says, "Anyone, orator, litigant, or comic hero, who for any reason admonished the collectivity of citizens had to persuade its members that he was still somehow in conformity with collective norms and with the democratic notion that collective norms must always control decision-making." Ober (1998, 122–26, 154–55) argues that Aristophanes was an internal critic of democracy who sought "amelioration of the existing society" rather than a rejectionist critic "who advocates fundamental changes in existing values and institutions" (155). Carey (1994) argues that comedy had a diversity of functions, but suggests, with some reservations, that it had little impact on political decisions or events.

posed to view Aristophanes' political criticisms of the demos and its leaders as criticisms of democracy as a political system.[37]

Reading Athenian tragedy in its civic and ritual context presents many similar difficulties, but with tragedy, in contrast to comedy, it is even more dangerous for the critic to attempt to establish direct connections with specific historical events, because tragedy maintains its dramatic fiction and treats issues of contemporary importance by projecting them onto a larger mythical backdrop.[38] Recent political criticism, which continues to add texture to our understanding of this complex genre, has ranged from viewing tragedy as "political art," to reading tragedy as evidence for the audience's mentality, to understanding it as a form of potentially subversive engagement with Athenian democratic experience.[39] For our purposes the current critical fragmentation is not so important as the potential for fragmentation of responses within the audience.[40] Speaking of the collective identity of the Athenian audience, for example, Cartledge has argued that "the discourse of tragedy as often fractured as it confirmed that comforting corporate identity."[41] Hence, as with comedy, it is best to allow the possibility of significant and legitimate divergences in audience sympathy and in the interpretation of both individual passages and plots as a whole.[42]

[37] My interpretation of tragedy and comedy thus relies on a version of "reader response" theory; for a helpful application of such theories to the audience of the *Odyssey*, see Thalmann 1998. Carey (1994, 69) has observed that "Ridicule includes and excludes, by defining a group (speaker and audience) as distinct from the target. . . . Its target may be selected according to the views of the communicator or the views of the audience or both." This view of Aristophanic ridicule works particularly well if we view the Athenian audience as potentially divisive and even revolutionary. De Ste. Croix (1972, 358–59) provides an excellent comparison between the political vocabulary found in Aristophanes and that of the Old Oligarch, which indeed suggests that Aristophanes "clearly resented the political power the demos was beginning [*sic*] to exercise" (357). Even if this is an overstatement of Aristophanes' hostility toward the demos, an antidemocratic member of the audience could easily have found in Aristophanes' plays useful theoretical objections to the Athenian democracy.

[38] For discussion of the difficulties in connecting tragedy with particular events, see Pelling 1997b, 216–18; Bowie 1997, 40–45.

[39] Political art: Meier 1990; 1993; mentality: Pelling 1997b, 218–19; civic engagement: Goldhill 1990; 1997; Cartledge 1997.

[40] On the potential for multivalent audience responses, see Pelling 1997b, 220–22.

[41] Cartledge 1997, 17. Goldhill (1990) suggests that both tragedy and comedy are "genres of transgression" (126), which question the terms of civic discourse.

[42] On the problems with viewing the Athenian audience as a homogenous interpretive community, see Goldhill 1990, 115. Pelling (1997b, 220–21) offers a fascinating reading of the interpretive possibilities of Medea's speech on the troubles of women (Euripides *Medea* 214–66); my analysis adds a class dimension to Pelling's exemplary treatment. For other attempts to read class as a key category in understanding audience response, see Sommerstein 1997, 68–73; Griffith 1995; Rose 1992.

While the Old Oligarch criticizes the greed and unfairness of the Athenian demos, and raises his critique into a systematic analysis of the democracy, other works offer alternative constructions of the sociology of greed. In Euripides' *Suppliants*, which was produced in about 420,[43] Theseus, the legendary king of Athens, criticizes Adrastus, the king of Argos, for leading his city to attack Thebes:

> You destroyed your city, led on by young men, who delight in being honored and stir up wars without justice [*aneu dikēs*], harming the citizens, one in order to lead an army, another in order to act arrogantly once he's taken power into his hands [*hōs hubrizēi dunamin eis cheiras labōn*], another for the sake of gain [*kerdous hounek'*], not considering whether the people [*to plēthos*] will be harmed by this. For there are three classes of citizens: the rich are useless [*anōpheleis*] and always lust after more [*pleionōn t'erōsi aei*]: those with nothing, who live in want, are dangerous [*deinoi*]; assigning too great a place to envy [*nemontes tōi phthonōi pleon meros*] and fooled by their wicked leaders, they sting the wealthy; of the three parts, the one in the middle saves cities, preserving the order established by the city. (232–45)[44]

Theseus's sociology differs from the Old Oligarch's in detail, but he too divides the city into classes based on the possession of wealth, and he rests his assumptions about character on basic economic divisions—rich, poor, and those in between. For him, however, greed characterizes the rich, who always lust after more, and resentment (*phthonos*), the poor. Rich and poor are pitted against one another within the polis because of the envy of the poor. But these groups can episodically unite in military expeditions, which are driven by elite greed and ambition and are pursued through the gullibility, and at the expense, of the poor, even if they are moderated by the presence of a "middling" element.[45] Since the time of Solon, Greek political thought had usually conceived of class interests as conflicting and mutually exclusive. Toward the end of the fifth century, specific but variable taxonomies of class and status had emerged and were more or less systematically inserted into theories about political stability, class relations, and group psychology.

The class discourse of late fifth-century Athens crystallized around the

[43] For a recent treatment of the dating of the play that puts it in the late 420s, see Bowie 1997, 45. For political interpretations, see Zeitlin 1990, 146–47; Burian 1985; Raaflaub 1989. Bowie (1997, 45–56) argues forcefully that the play engages with the religious problems and themes associated with the refusal of Thebes to return the Athenian dead for burial after the battle of Delium in 424.

[44] In his edition and translation, Kovacs (1998, 36–39) brackets this passage; Burian (1985, 133), rightly in my view, regards it as an "integral part of Theseus' answer to Adrastos."

[45] See Hanson 1996 for a fascinating discussion of the "metrios" ideology and political behavior of the "moderating" and "moderate" Athenian hoplite-farmers and their changing position in Athens during the revolutionary period.

idea of greed in ways that developed earlier critiques of the demos's relationship with its leaders. Often this took the form of attacks on the democratic leadership in general—attacks that were then transformed into criticisms of the demos. Later in the *Suppliants*, the Theban herald challenges Theseus's "democratic" government of Athens by leveling now familiar criticisms against the demos's gullible and self-defeating support of greedy, sophistical politicians. According to the herald, his city is better governed by a single individual than by a rabble (*ochlōi*, 411). The worthless masses, he asserts, are deceived by a clever rhetorician who "turns the city this way and that for his own gain [*pros kerdos idion*]" (413). "How," he asks, "can the common people [*dēmos*], if they cannot make a speech properly, know the right way to guide a city?" (417–18). These criticisms of the demos and its leaders show that the political schism was waged in terms of highly abstract arguments about democracy as a system.

Theseus, of course, rejects these derogatory views and praises freedom and equality, the trademarks of democracy (429–41). The debate as a whole, however, ends inconclusively with the herald saying, "As regards our debate, you keep your opinions and I will believe the opposite" (465–66). The play itself does not fully resolve the theoretical questions raised. Even if the herald is an unappealing character, his critique of Athenian democracy stands unrefuted and must have had strong resonance with at least some elements of an Athenian audience. As in others texts we shall consider, defenders of democracy articulate high-minded ideals, such as freedom and equality, without showing that their ideals can be achieved in practice. By contrast, antidemocratic thinking often assumes that democracy's high-minded ideology is both practically naive and, more cynically, geared toward securing power for the demos.[46] Elitist audience members might well have been disgusted by the unsympathetic portrait of the Theban herald, while finding his speech insightful and accurate. Whichever way members of the audience were disposed, their views of democracy were framed in terms of greed and fair distribution within the political community.

A remarkably similar allegation of greed against democratic leadership

[46] Pelling (1997b, 226) importantly brings out the possibility of "ideology as question": the notion that a set of collective values often includes questions by which a group can measure experience against its ideals, and vice-versa. For Pelling, such questioning does not necessarily imply that anything is wrong with the ideal as such, even if experience fails to match up to it. I would add, with Pelling (1997b, 227–30), that hard-core comparison between ideals and experience can sometimes lead to the conviction that certain ideals are simply impossible or wrongly articulated and that experience itself constitutes a higher form of "truth" than ideals. In particular, the Old Oligarch shows that democratic ideals of fairness could be attacked by those who found them unachievable in reality because of the demos's historically evident greed to get more.

appears in Andocides' speech *Against Alcibiades*.[47] According to the speaker, Alcibiades manipulated his role as tribute assessor in order to procure the revenues of empire for himself (11–12). The demos could have predicted Alcibiades' lack of concern for democracy, community and equality if it had just looked to his excessive greed (*pleonexian*) and arrogance (*huperēphanian*) in private life (13–17). After cataloging Alcibiades' rapacious behavior toward his father-in-law (13–15) and his ready abuse of his fellow citizens (20–21), the speaker condemns Alcibiades for his obvious contempt for equality: "He doesn't treat even his fellow citizens as equals [*ouk ex isou chrētai*]: he robs some, hits others, shuts others up, gets money out of others, and shows that democracy is worth nothing, speaking like a demagogue and acting like a tyrant, because he has learned that you care only about the name and not about the thing itself" (27). Alcibiades' greed is inextricably linked with his failure to respect equality among citizens. More important, the demos is stupid and inconsistent in its admiration for a bully who fails to honor key democratic principles (21). The speaker's critique of Alcibiades is verging on a critique of the democratic system that supports Alcibiades.

As his other speeches make clear, this author had strong oligarchic sympathies. Plutarch (*Them.* 32.3) records that "The people of Magnesia have a splendid tomb of Themistocles in their agora. As to his remains Andocides deserves no attention when he says in his speech, To His Associates [*Pros tous hetairous*], 'The Athenians removed his remains by stealth and scattered them to the winds.' He is lying in order to incite the oligarchs against the demos."[48] His words were meant to stir up enthusiasm among antidemocrats by criticizing the demos and its leaders. He agrees with the Theban herald: the demos foolishly supports clever politicians, such as Alcibiades, who manipulate the system in order to satisfy their own greed at the expense of the demos itself.

This double-edged criticism is the thrust of the argument made by the character Anticleon in Aristophanes' *Wasps* of 422.[49] Offering a comic

[47] The date and authorship of this work are disputed, but I follow the persuasive arguments of Furley 1989 that the work is a political pamphlet, composed in the summer of 415 by Andocides, which purported to be a speech written for Alcibiades' rival Phaeax. MacDowell (in Gagarin and MacDowell 1998, 159–61) argues that the speech is a literary exercise, composed after the fifth century, by "someone trying to imagine what a speech at an Athenian ostracism might have been like" (160). For further arguments, see Edwards 1995, 131–36.

[48] The speech to which Plutarch refers should be dated to 420–418; see Missiou 1992, 23. For Andocides' oligarchic sympathies, see Furley 1989, 154–55; Missiou 15–49, with ffr. 3–5 Blass, all of which abundantly illustrate Andocides' contempt for the Athenian demos and its leaders. Hints of Andocides' pro-oligarchic stance can be found in *Against Alcibiades* 11–12, 28, 32. On the antidemocratic "political clubs" of Athens, see Calhoun 1913.

[49] On the criticism of demagogues found in the *Wasps*, see Allen 2000, 130–33; Olson

balance sheet of the empire, Anticleon shows his demotic, jury-crazed father that the demagogues are making off with the profits of empire, while the demos itself gets mere scraps from their tables (655–724). This is all the more galling because the demos is responsible, through its own toil and daring, for acquiring the empire in the first place (672, 678). Such an argument conjures up very old debates, familiar already in the first book of the *Iliad*, over merit, contribution to group projects, and just deserts. In its zeal to support the paymaster, the demos is simply too stupid to recognize the underlying unfairness of the city's system of distributing the rewards of empire (695).

In several texts, then, such as the *Suppliants*, *Against Alcibiades*, and the *Wasps*, political criticism stops with express objections against the greed of the democratic leadership and the gullibility of the demos, without following the Old Oligarch in resentfully attacking the demos's own greed. Aristocrats found it intolerable that the demos stupidly and unjustly benefited certain members of the elite without in the least understanding the true character of their own demotic self-interest, much less the interests of the city as a whole. As the Theban herald in *Suppliants* puts it, "It really plagues the better sort of people [*tois ameinosin*] when a bad man [*ponēros*] is honored because, by his tongue, he has a hold on the people [*dēmon*], though he was nothing before" (423–25).

The reasons for elite resentment were further elaborated in other texts, like Aristophanes' *Knights* (424 B.C.), which makes a different and more cynical allegation against the demos.[50] First, the chorus of Athenian knights, along with the other slaves of Demos (a character who represents the Athenian demos), charges that the Paphlagonian (the politician Cleon) takes more than his share of the imperial revenue, flatters the demos for his own advantage, and has a keen eye on rich Athenians who want to avoid trouble with the demos (46–54, 65–68, 103–4, 222–24, 258–65, etc.). This is standard comic invective against democratic leadership and develops the line of thinking we have traced in the Old Oligarch, Andocides, and Euripides. Before the final contest between the Paphlagonian and the Sausage-Seller, however, the knights bluntly accuse the demos of being stupid: "O Demos, your power is a great thing; all men fear you like a tyrant. But you're easy to lead astray, and you love to be flattered and deceived, and you gape at everyone who makes a speech. You have a mind, but it is never at home" (1111–20). The ensuing con-

1996, 134–36. On the political ideology of *Wasps*, see Konstan (1985), who illuminates the deep structure of the play as an antidemocratic comment on the evolving character of the Athenian courts.

[50] See Forrest 1966, 226–29; 1975. Contra Edmunds (1987a, 1987b), who argues that Aristophanes tries to weaken the class attributes of knights and demos, thereby associating the two as one group; on the Demos as a tyrant, see Tuplin 1985, 357–58.

versation elevates the comic criticism of democracy to a new theoretical level:

> Demos: You have no mind in your long hair, if you suppose that I'm a fool; I play the fool this way for a purpose. For I myself love to drink every day, and I want to make a politician fat by stealing; I lift him up and, when he's full, I knock him out.
>
> Knights: In that case you'll be successful, and your character really does contain, as you say, very deep cunning, if you deliberately fatten these men, like public victims, on the Pnyx, and then when you happen to lack dinner, you sacrifice a fat one and have a meal.
>
> Demos: Watch me and see if I don't ingeniously trick them, those who think they're smart and that they are cheating me. I watch them all the time, pretending not to see them, as they steal; and then I force them to spit up whatever they've stolen from me, using a verdict tube as a probe. (1131–50).

The demos's response is a genuine epiphany for the knights, who now see that the demos dupes its politicians rather than the opposite. Whenever it wants, Demos simply forces its greedy politicians to regurgitate all the public goods they have swallowed.[51] Indeed, contrary to later sections of the play in which the demos publicly insists that it has simply forgotten or failed to notice or been deceived (1218–25, 1344–55), here the demos privately admits that it knowingly collaborates in the abuses of the democratic system.[52] This admission puts the lie to the demos's typical way of excusing itself from responsibility—by saying that it was deceived by greedy leaders.[53] Here the demos manipulates the system from behind the scenes in order to satisfy its own cravings for money, food, and power. It is possible, as Henderson has suggested, that some members of the audience interpreted this passage as an exhortation to the demos: "Could this be a fact, a reminder to the demos of its actual power, and not mere wishful thinking on the part of Aristophanes? If so, comedy after 429 would indicate to what extent the *dēmos* was hedging its bet on

[51] Aristophanes' political plays thus also revive the association, which is familiar from archaic poetry, of greed for money and power and improper, excessive consumption of food: see esp. my discussion in chapter 3. But we must note that Aristophanes preserves Solon's idea that political and economic "food" is importantly a zero-sum commodity, which must be distributed justly to all deserving members of a community. On the consumption motif in classical Athens, and its relation to revolution, see Davidson 1997, 278–308.

[52] Dover (1972, 33–34) denies that any criticism of democracy as a system can be found in Aristophanes, but if we read his plays together with the Old Oligarch's assaults on democracy, then it is legitimate to suppose that certain groups in the audience would interpret criticisms of the demos and its leaders as criticisms of the democratic system as such.

[53] Henderson (1990, 310) takes this as a typical form of Aristophanic criticism of the demos.

the new politicians who were winning the votes."[54] But antidemocratic listeners might equally have taken this exchange to represent a "debunking" of the demos's abdication of responsibility, and a rejection of its habit of blaming its leaders for failures in morality or judgment.[55] Both responses are possible, and the antidemocratic response fits coherently into the cultural framework provided by texts like that of the Old Oligarch.

Like the Old Oligarch, Aristophanes' *Knights* suggests a cynical view of the demos: behind its well-known rhetoric of freedom, equality, and community of interests, the demos and its leaders know that they are getting more than their share, and they relish putting one over on the aristocrats. The demos is itself a crafty manipulator of rhetoric and self-presentation, whose most effective mechanism of exerting its deep-seated greed on others is, perhaps, the appearance of gullibility. Seeming gullible allows the demos to claim that it actually promotes the common good, and that the source of corruption is clever, deceptive leadership. If the demos is too stupid to recognize that its politicians have hoodwinked it, then it can still participate unabashedly in the rhetoric of community, according to which its interests are allied with those of the aristocrats. Or, as Athenagoras puts it, it can assert that "demos" means the entire state, not just a part of it. It is this legitimizing ideology that the Old Oligarch and Aristophanes' *Knights* self-consciously try to unmask.

This view of democracy as an alliance between the demos and its leaders, both of whom abuse the political process for their own gain, recalls the Old Oligarch's vision of the demos as a "little Athens" within Athens, and it looks forward to Aristotle's criticism of democracy on the basis of greed. In *Politics* 5, we should recall, Aristotle finds that in democracies the greed of the demagogues is underwritten and promoted by the greed of the demos itself. The alliance they create engenders a politically unhealthy feedback system in which the greed of the one reinforces the greed of the other. Aristophanes' *Knights* points in that direction, but, in this conversation between Demos and the Knights, the demos itself is the primary mover and beneficiary in a process of greedy political manipulation—and, ironically, its own leaders have become unwitting pawns in the demos's deceitful strategy of getting more for itself. Aristophanes' *Wasps* and *Knights* complement the picture of class division found in the Old Oligarch and Euripides, while elaborating an image of demotic

[54] Henderson 1990, 299.

[55] On elite frustration with the demos's abdication of responsibility, see Thucydides' critical comments on the Athenians' anger at their orators for proposing the Sicilian expedition (8.1.1), along with his presentation of Nicias's inability to tell the demos the truth about his situation in Sicily (7.48.3–4); and see Diodotus's complaint about the demos's unwillingness to accept responsibility (3.43.4–5).

greed for more, which is successfully satisfied through knowing, self-conscious cooperation between the demos and its leaders. The "little Athens" within Athens effectively oppresses both the allies and the Athenian aristocrats.

Such a view of contemporary culture is given strong reinforcement at a systematic theoretical level from Plato's Callicles and Thrasymachus.[56] I have discussed Callicles at length in the introduction, but I emphasize again that in my view he was a real person living in the last decades of the fifth century. He helped theorize and justify a widespread desire among elites to try to get more social and material advantages than they then enjoyed under the democracy, and thus he fits clearly into the political divisions I am charting.

By the late 420s, people had begun to ask what kind of system it takes in the first place to support such inveterate, systemic corruption as one finds in democracy. The only plausible answer has seemed to be that "corruption" under the democracy is not accidental, or the result of wicked leaders; it is rather a conspiracy of demos and traitorous elites to promote an ideology of Athenian unity while hoarding the city's profits for themselves. Thrasymachus offers a powerful sociological critique of existing governments that develops the Old Oligarch's analysis of democracy, but equally he articulates a prescriptive statement of the "immoralist" ideal of greed. By doing so, he carries the sociological analysis of the Old Oligarch to its logical normative conclusion.

In *Republic* 1, Thrasymachus defines justice cynically as "the advantage of the stronger" (*to tou kreittonos sumpheron*) (338c2), "the advantage of the established government" (*to tēs kathestēkuias archēs sumpheron*) (339a1–2), and as "another's good" (*allotrion agathon*) (343c3).[57] Both in his sociological and normative claims, Thrasymachus is concerned with injustice at a broad, systemic level (338e1–339a4, 343e7–344c8), which links his arguments to those presented by the Old Oligarch, Euripides, and Aristophanes. Like the Old Oligarch, he believes that governments have set up laws in order to promote the interests of those who rule against those

[56] On the basic accuracy of Plato's portrayal of Thrasymachus, see Guthrie *HGP* 3:294–98. Whether or not the real Thrasymachus held the views attributed to him by Plato, it is reasonable to conclude that Plato is portraying problems and issues that had currency in the period immediately before the revolutions. On the dramatic date of *Gorgias*, Dodds (1959, 17–18) points out various indications for a date between 429 and 405; the dramatic date of the *Republic* is usually taken to be an unspecified time in the late fifth century. I note, too, that these characters' viewpoints are similar to the ones attacked by the Anonymus Iamblichi, who also probably wrote in the late fifth century, see my discussion later in the chapter.

[57] For arguments that the formulations are essentially incompatible, see Everson 1998; contra, Annas 1981, 45–46. I tend to think, with Annas, that Thrasymachus's basic position is comprehensible and unified, if muddled.

of the ruled. Hence the thing that we call "justice" is actually a serviceable ideological tool that constrains the simpleminded to serve the interests of the stronger, which usually means the interests of those who run the government.[58]

In his great speech (343b1–344c8) Thrasymachus transforms his sociological analysis into an immoralist recommendation. Socrates had argued that each craft encourages its practitioners to look to the advantage of their subjects, rather than themselves (342c1–9). Turning this argument around, Thrasymachus proposes that the art of herding does not promote the welfare of sheep but rather the profit of their owner. In human affairs, this means that the just man always "has less" (*elatton echei*, 343d3) than the unjust man—for example, in observing fairness in contractual arrangements or in paying state taxes. Thrasymachus explains, however, that he is really speaking of the tyrant: "For I mean the one I was speaking of just now, who can satisfy his greed [*pleonektein*] on a grand scale; look at that one if you want to judge how much more profitable it is for a man to be unjust rather than just" (343e7–344a3). Throughout the *Republic*, the term *pleonexia* (greed) is specifically used to characterize the tyrant.[59] Hence, in Plato's representation, greed has become associated with the normative prescriptions of immoralists, who explicitly recommend violating distributive justice in order to pursue one's own advantage as far as possible, whether as a matter of manliness (*andreia*), "natural" as opposed to conventional justice, or simply as a form of self-gratification. Thrasymachus seems to recommend injustice simply as a form of gratification, because he does not bother to argue that tyranny and *pleonexia* are actually just: "But when someone, in addition to taking their possessions, kidnaps and enslaves the citizens as well [*pros tois tōn politōn chrēmasin kai autous andrapodisamenos doulōsētai*], instead of these shameful names he is called happy and fortunate not only by the citizens themselves, but also by all others who learn that he has done the whole of injustice [*tēn holēn adikian ēdikēkota*]" (344b5–344c2). Thrasymachus advocates the grand-scale greed of the Aristotelian tyrant. He concurs with Callicles in his boundless desires to get more and in his disregard for the conventional restraints of justice.

Against such immoralists, the Anonymus Iamblichi, an Athenian political thinker of the late fifth century, offers a defense of ordinary polis morality.[60] His rejection of greed (*pleonexia*) as a source of human fulfill-

[58] As Schofield (2000, 204) points out, Thrasymachus is, at least here, offering a commentary on the language of morality.

[59] On *pleonexia* and tyrants in the *Republic*, see Algra 1996.

[60] The Greek text of the Anonymus is DK 89; accordingly, I cite him by chapter and subsection of DK 89. The date of the Anonymus is controversial: Cole 1961 dates him to approximately 400; Guthrie *HGP* 3:71: late fifth or early fourth century; Dodds 1963,

ment helps to refine conventional ideals, but his arguments are unlikely to convince immoralists on their own terms. Whatever its validity, however, his assault on greed implies the existence of a set of immoralist interlocutors, who—like Thucydides' Athenians, Thrasymachus, Callicles, and Eteocles (see my subsequent discussion)—had embraced greed as a positive ideal of political and ethical behavior. In essence, the Anonymus tries to solve what may be called the "Gyges ring" problem. In book 2 of the *Republic* (359c7–360d7), one of Socrates' interlocutors, Glaucon, asks for further justification of Socrates' view that the just life is best and most advantageous. In order to construct the strongest possible case for the opposition, Glaucon supposes hypothetically that the shepherd Gyges is given a ring that can make him invisible. He then proposes that all men, even the conventionally just, would naturally pursue greed if they could get away with it by making themselves invisible: "We would catch the just man red-handed doing the same things as the unjust, led on by greed [*pleonexian*], which all nature [*pasa phusis*], encourages him to pursue as good, but he is forcibly restrained by the law and made to respect equality [*epi tēn tou isou timēn*]" (359c3–6). This possibility is a live and problematic issue for Glaucon, because, as he says, he is constantly dinned with the immoralists' recommendation of greed (*Republic* 358c7–8). Judging by the late fifth-century evidence, Plato's representation of this debate, whose dramatic setting is the late fifth century, has a basic historical accuracy: at this period, members of the Athenian elite were seriously debating the merits and demerits of greed as an ideal of behavior. What sort of response do those who subscribe to conventional morality have to hand?

This is where the Anonymus earns his place in the late fifth-century discourse on greed. First, he seeks to wipe out the opposition, especially through defusing the Calliclean argument (see chapter 1) that the conventional rejection of greed as an ideal implies weakness and cowardice. The Anonymus argues that greed itself is often a sign of weakness rather than strength, and additionally that greed embodies a misdirected view of human goodness. In part the weakness of the greedy is simply a matter of lacking self-mastery (*enkrateia*) (4.1), but the Anonymus also offers a psychological etiology according to which greed is based on fear: "They love possessions [*philochrēmatousi*] because of the things that frighten them—sickness, old age, sudden penalties or losses" (4.2). Thus greed is merely

197n27: later years of Peloponnesian War; de Romilly 1992, 168–69: "it is unanimously agreed that he must have been writing during the Peloponnesian War." Because of his moral concerns and his language, I locate him within the late fifth-century controversies over greed (*pleonexia*) and social justice in Athens. Like Cole, I believe that the Anonymus was an Athenian, but I am more skeptical than Cole about his Democritean roots.

a reactive desire that results from anxiety about the future and self-defeatingly pits the individual against a community that could, indeed, be of service to him in time of need (7.2). This is why greed is not only an unambiguous sign of failing courage, but also ignorant and dishonorable (5.1–2). The Anonymus persuasively contradicts Callicles' belief that the grand-scale pursuit of greed, and nothing else, embodies manly virtue.

Second, he explains, ambition, envy, and the desire for political power drive men to be greedy for money, since money helps them satisfy their other desires (4.5). By explaining the instrumental capacities of money, the Anonymus clearly outlines the "social meaning" of excessive acquisitiveness in particular political contexts and socioeconomic groups (see chapter 1). The Anonymus argues that the truly good man rejects such competitive desires and seeks a reputation through his own virtue (*aretēi*) (4.6). The goods ordinarily won through public competition are sought under the wrong description and through the wrong means: the only good genuinely worth having is that which the individual acquires through developing his own moral character. What is the evidence for this?

In order to account for his non-competitive, socially cohesive vision of human virtue, the Anonymus turns, like many of his immoralist interlocutors, to nature:

> If men were given such a nature [*ephusan*] that they were not able to live alone, but formed an association with one another under pressure of necessity, and found out our general way of life and the skills related to it, and cannot associate and live with one another without observance of law (for this would be a greater punishment than living alone), we can conclude then that because of these necessities [*anankas*] law [*ton . . . nomon*] and justice [*to dikaion*] are kings among men, and that they could in no way change, for by nature [*phusei*] they have been firmly fixed. (6.1)

The human nature of single individuals forces men to live together in communities, while the nature of communities is such that they operate successfully only when law and justice are honored within them. Thus, contrary to Glaucon, who reports the immoralist belief that nature encourages individuals to pursue greed as a basic good, the Anonymus offers an account of nature that leads to respect for law and conventional morality. Law and justice, a familiar dyad in these fragments (cf. 3.6, 6.5), are responsible for the welfare of both communities and individuals (3.6, 7.1–16). Because of his arguments from nature, the Anonymus sees no necessary conflict between the good of the individual and the good of the polis; on the contrary, the (properly understood) interests of individual and community are necessarily compatible and even congruent. The full and proper development of the self leads not to competitive desires to take more than one's fair share but rather to a concern for the fairness and equality derided by Callicles and other immoralists, who constantly din their precepts into Glaucon's head.

Hence, individual acquisitiveness, which sets the individual against his community, gives rise to all that is the opposite of good, namely immorality (*kakia*) and injury (*blabē*) (6.1). To the Anonymus, these considerations lead to a straightforward moral injunction: "We must not rush to pursue our greed [*pleonexian*], nor should we consider either that power [*kratos*] with a view to greed [*epi tēi pleonexiai*] is virtue [*aretēn*], or that obeying the laws is cowardice [*deilian*]" (6.1). The Anonymus thus seeks to defuse Callicles' arguments (see chapter 1) that the successful pursuit of greed is the natural right of the strong man. He also vigorously rejects the Old Oligarch's vision of the polis as being by nature a divisive battleground between oligarchs and democrats.

Despite these arguments, however, hard-core immoralists might not accept the Anonymus's vision of human nature or his conception of human flourishing. Hence, they might still ask the following question: why is the possession of "genuine" (read: ordinary and conventional) virtue a good thing for the *individual*? Individual greed may lead to immorality and injury, granted, but aren't those evils bad only for others, and not for the greedy individual himself? To be sure, in the unlikely event that an immoralist should accept that human nature requires the individual to live considerately with others in a community, then naturally his self-seeking would be cut short. But why shouldn't the immoralist live in a society where everyone else observes the law, and he alone does not? The Anonymus has no moral response to these questions.[61] His response is, rather, practical. First of all, only a completely invulnerable individual—one made of adamant—could believe that power used for the sake of greed (*kratos epi tēi pleonexiai*, an expression repeated from 6.1) would be sufficient even if he does not abide by the law (6.2). Such a man could not exist (6.3). Even if he did, however, then all men would be hostile to him and, in their numbers, they would find the power to suppress him (6.4).[62]

As it stands, this argument fails to convince: what about historical examples of tyrants? What about oligarchs? This argument is precisely the one that Glaucon's hypothetical example of Gyges' ring is meant to refute: what happens if someone is, indeed, powerful enough to override collective restraints? In practice, threats to the political community came from a variety of sources, sometimes from coalitions of discontented citi-

[61] It is possible that there is no way at all to convince the immoralist of the rightness of morality through rational argument; see Williams 1985, 22–74.

[62] For a useful reading of this argument alongside those of Protagoras in Plato's *Protagoras*, see de Romilly 1992, 169–70.

zens. Events of the late fifth century convict the Anonymus of over-optimism about the possibility of containing the extravagantly aggressive and greedy. As we will see during the revolutions, the strong man often tries to manipulate conflicts between factions within a state in order to serve his own advantage, rather than pursuing his desires through brute force alone.

To some extent, the Anonymus himself had anticipated this objection by explaining the rise of a tyrant differently: he argues, quite strikingly, that in practice tyranny arises from a community's failure to observe the law rather than from the tyrant's strength itself:

> Tyranny, an evil of such proportions and so monstrous, arises from nothing other than lawlessness (*anomias*). Some men think, although they are wrong, that a tyrant is established from some other cause, and that men who are deprived of their freedom are not themselves responsible, since they have been overpowered by the tyrant who has been established. In this they are wrong. For whoever thinks that a king or a tyrant is established from any other cause than lawlessness [*anomias*] and greed [*pleonexias*] is stupid [*mōros*]. (7.12–13)

The Anonymus makes this argument in a catalog of the evils resulting from a failure to observe the law (7.7). The "greed" he mentions is the greed, not of the tyrant, but rather of individuals within the populace, whose mistrust and divisiveness pave the way for a tyrannical destruction of the political community altogether. This theory of the tyrant's rise to power, however sophisticated, does not show that *any and every* healthy community is too powerful to be overpowered by a Calliclean "strong man." Nor does it respond effectively to Glaucon's hypothetical. It does show, however, that the idealized community imagined by the Anonymus might be strong enough to resist the tyrant. What features of that community make it strong?

According to the Anonymus, the ideally healthy polis, first and foremost, is characterized by a strong degree of civic trust that guarantees collective safety against neighboring states and individual security against being harmed by fellow citizens (7.1–2, 6). Civic trust (*pistis*) is a basic requirement of all communities that have a serious chance of fulfilling the goals for which human communities were created in the first place. Trust allows individuals to enjoy the goods that they already possess, while offering security and even mutual charity in times of individual misfortune (7.1–5). This conception of civic trust recalls the Periclean ideal represented in the Funeral Oration and leads, like that ideal, to a socially integrated community whose power is directed toward preserving the basic goods of collective life. In short, the Anonymus generates a new conception of power that he sets against Callicles' instrumental power and the invisibility of Gyges' ring: "It appears that power itself, *that which really is power* [*hoper dē kratos esti*], is preserved through law and through justice" (6.5, my emphasis). The Anonymus has thus claimed to redefine what power really is—the power of interdependent individuals to enjoy a life in common, free of mutual suspicion, safely guarded by each other against individual changes in fortune, and united in war. Power is not the ability to violate one's fellow citizens' just claims for the sake of satisfying greed. It is rather a form of creative social energy that rejects the individual's greed and the claim that the polis is by nature a site of conflict, in favor of the positive goods that can be created through social cohesion.

As appealing as this vision of the healthy polis is, though, it is unlikely to persuade immoralists by arguing from premises they already accept, and of course it gives no reason to the immoralist individual not at least to try to become a tyrant. Rather, the Anonymus's treatise is an attempt to educate the ethical sensibility of Athenians by proposing a truer and healthier way of thinking about polis life and individual satisfaction. In its redefinition of fundamental terms of the current debate, this treatise is reminiscent of Solon's redefinition of glory and power within the strife-ridden Athens of the sixth century.

Where it is perhaps most convincing to the immoralist is its suggestion that even under the assumption that the greedy agent could wrongfully acquire goods on a grand scale, then he would still not be able to enjoy the goods he has acquired. He would hold his possessions precariously, because the greed that procured the goods in the first place has generated an atmosphere of civic divisiveness and mistrust: "When they are awake their thoughts are not pleasant, and when they have gone to sleep they do not find a pleasant place of refuge but one that is filled with fear. An awakening which is full of fear and dread leads them to a sudden recollection of their troubles; these and all other evils which I have mentioned result from a failure to observe law [*anomias*]" (7.11). Because of the nature of social groupings, the Anonymus claims, the immoralists' recommendation of greed defeats itself in that even when the greedy tyrant acquires his premised goals of getting wealth and power, his very act of immoral acquisition deprives him of the possibility of enjoying those goods. The Anonymus advances the thesis, as if to both oligarchs and democrats of his time, that their greed will not do them any good as long as discontented groups envy their success and look for every opportunity to undermine their good fortune. He even suggests that the attempt to hoard money in such circumstances makes money scarce, even if it exists in large quantities (7.8)—a consequence that undoubtedly sets the cycle of greed and mistrust in motion all over again. Thucydides' connections between greed and civic mistrust, as in his analysis of Corcyra (3.82–83), clearly had currency in the wider political culture of the time.[63]

[63] See chapter 5.

The Anonymus wrote his treatise in a culture that struggled with the morality of greed and injustice, with intensified political division, and with the burdens of war. His passionate rejection of greed as an ideal speaks to the existence of an oppositional group that was waiting for the chance to stage a coup. But does any of this theorizing even matter to real-life Athenian political agents? My contention is that more-or-less systematic political thinking was significant for real-life behavior because, on the one hand, it enabled those so disposed to explain to themselves and others why they felt resentful toward the Athenian democracy on the grounds of systematic injustice and greed at all levels. But another group, exemplified by Callicles or Thucydides' Athenians, advocated greed as a positive ideal, invoking new frames of reference, such as the opposition between nature and convention, or theories about the right of the stronger in international politics. Traveling down the spectrum, one arrives at the unabashedly greedy, who want more of a variety of divisible goods just because they consider those goods necessary constituents of the best possible life. They too are enacting ideals and principles of behavior by pursuing a particular conception of the good life that has some cultural basis in their positive valuation of goods such as wealth and power. But they have been driven lamentably too far, forgetful even of Thrasymachus's hope that they should be called blessed by commemorative poets. Their greed is based neither on sociological observations about politics as a game of power nor on speculative theories about what is right according to nature. Their greed is the crassest and basest sort, although it is hard to say whether the crassly greedy are worse than immoralists with a theory. In the *Gorgias*, as we saw in the introduction, Socrates tries to suggest that even those with a theory, like Callicles, in reality fit into the category of the crassly and basely greedy.

One example of such a coarsely greedy figure can be found in Euripides' *Phoenissae*, which was probably produced in 409.[64] Although the play engages a variety of characters and story lines, it serves our purposes best to examine one of its primary themes, the conflict between Eteocles and Polyneices over the Theban throne once held by their father Oedipus.[65] Euripides' treatment of this conflict is a near contemporary reflection on the ideological tensions that led up to the revolution of 411. Jocasta orients the audience to the importance of "fair shares" by ex-

[64] Mastronarde (1994, 11–14) argues that it was performed in one of the years from 411 to 409. My arguments support this dating.

[65] On the "open" texture of the play and the variety of themes and mythological figures it explores, see Mastronarde 1994, 3–11. For older allegorical interpretations, see Delebecque 1951; for a forceful rebuttal of such views, see de Romilly 1967, 108–12 (followed by Mastronarde 1994, 12). De Romilly 1967 emphasizes ambition (*philotimia*) as the ideological keynote of the play; Rawson 1970 focuses on familial relations; for a political interpretation, see Raaflaub 1989.

plaining that Polyneices has returned home and "seeks his father's scepter and shares in the fatherland [*merē chthonos*]" (80). The language of the just distribution of "shares" in the fatherland and in the royal house pervades the play and structures Polyneices' accusations against his brother.[66] During his exchange with Jocasta and Eteocles, Polyneices insists, "I have done everything justly, but without justice I am robbed of my fatherland in the most unholy way" (492–93)—and later he accuses Eteocles explicitly of "having more than [his] share" (*tou merous echōn ta pleiō*, 603).

The violation of fair distribution helps to conflate standard oppositions between friend or family and enemy. Antigone, Polyneices' sister, prays to Artemis to destroy those who come in order to sack her fatherland (151–53),[67] while Polyneices, although returning to claim his paternal inheritance, exclaims, "For all things seem terrible to those who dare when they cross into enemy land" (270–71). Although Thebes is Polyneices' fatherland (295, cf. 406), he has come among his enemies (*echthrous . . . andras*, 358). In short, through the wrongdoing of his brother Eteocles, Polyneices has been put in the dreadful position of having to plunder his own fatherland (488, 570–77), because he had earlier been exiled like a slave (626–30). Indeed, Jocasta reproaches Polyneices for attacking his own land, because even a victory in the coming war will be tantamount to failure (568–83). This blurring of categories between friend and foe, citizen and enemy, city-saver and plunderer recalls Solon's own potent imagery of aristocrats plundering Athens and enslaving their fellow citizens in order to satisfy their lust for gain. Now, however, Polyneices is motivated not so much by his own greed as by his resentment and indignation at Eteocles' attempt to take more than his fair share of their fatherland.[68] Even so, he is blinded by his own self-righteousness and is unaffected, at least in practical terms, by the problems raised by attacking his own country. The polis has literally become a battleground of competing forces that view their participation in civic

[66] Cf. lines 482–83, where Polyneices blames his brother for wrongfully holding on to his, Polyneices', share (*meros*) of the house. For other language of "sharing in" the divisible goods of Thebes, see 601–5. For the original division of the house and the plan to rule in sequence, see 69–73. The language of "ruling in succession," of course, looks forward to Aristotle's analysis of democracy, where fairness in the distribution of power is achieved through having equals hold office in succession; cf. *Politics* 1291b30–1292a38.

[67] As Mastronarde (1994, 194) points out, however, the servant continues to emphasize Polyneices' justice and Eteocles' injustice, and this opposition becomes a "leitmotif" of the first third of the play; cf. 258, 319, 369, 452, etc.

[68] Although Polyneices says "Men honor property above all else; it has the greatest power in human life" (439–40), I agree with Mastronarde (1994, 270–71) that this passage does not indict Polyneices as "motivated by greed rather than a sense of justice," but rather illustrates the "tragic entrapment of a character in his or her own system of beliefs."

strife as an irreconcilable conflict over the distribution of shares in wealth and power.[69]

By contrast to his brother, Eteocles is the dramatic embodiment of late fifth-century immoralism: sophistical, unconventional, and unabashedly greedy, he rejects Polyneices' talk of justice and "fair shares" in favor of his Calliclean pursuit of extravagant satisfactions. In his view, "If the same thing were by nature [*ephu*] fine and wise [*kalon . . . sophon*] for all, then men would not have debaters' double strife. But in actual fact there is nothing that is like [*homoion*] or equal [*ison*] for men except in their use of words. The reality [*to ergon*] is not that (sc. like or equal)" (499–502). His point is that terms like "fairness" and "equality" do not have a firm grounding in nature or reality and are therefore always open to dispute by those who disagree. The standards of fairness in any particular case are open to negotiation, rather than established in advance by an external authority. But, as we saw in chapter 1, arguments about standards of fairness must be made within a generally shared framework of values, or they lose all authority and are shown to be mere disguises for self-interest. This is what we find in the case of Eteocles.

Having made his self-interested and sophistical point about language, Eteocles shows that, like Callicles, he considers it a matter of manliness to take more than his share whenever possible: "For it is cowardice [*an-andria*] when someone loses the greater share [*to pleon*] and takes the lesser [*toulasson*]" (509–10). The hypermasculine ideology of greed that drives Athenian imperialism is brought home within individual psychology along with the language of greater and lesser shares in divisible goods.[70] By 409, this language was firmly related to political thinking about greed (especially expressed by the Greek term *pleonexia* and its etymological relative *to pleon*) and injustice. The political schism in Athens is nowhere more forcefully expressed than in Eteocles' belief, which echoes that of Thucydides' Athenians, that there are no options available other than ruling and being enslaved: "When it is possible for me to rule, shall I be his slave?" (519–20). His assumption is that cooperation within the polis is simply impossible, because one's opponents will always seize the opportunity to take more than their share whenever possible. This seems untrue of Polyneices, but Eteocles suspects the worst. The social fragmentation of the late fifth century involved not only individual or factional greed, but also the trap of interpreting others' psychology in the least charitable way possible. The tendency to interpret others in the worst possible light is a lesson that the Athenians have

[69] It is important to see here that wealth and power are interrelated in complicated ways, as they are throughout the discourse on greed: wealth is both the means to power (439–40) and the natural result of having power (552–53, 555–58, 566–67).

[70] For the "hypermasculinity" of Athens's imperial project, see Kateb 1998.

taught themselves in their own self-seeking pursuit of empire. Hence, in a self-fulfilling prophecy, the truly shrewd, canny strong man unmasks the self-interested ideology that lies behind his opponents' use of terms like "an equal share" (*to ison*), which is really only a name. Hence, Eteocles concludes, he might as well be virtuous unless his acts of injustice win him the tyranny (524–25); but if they do, then they are worth it. If names really do not matter, then he might as well simply call himself what he really is—an unjust, greedy, tyrannical bastard.

Jocasta picks up on Eteocles' comments about language, fairness, and tyrannical ambition in an effort to reproach his destructive greed and avert catastrophe. Her great speech is a reprise of the themes we have considered:

> Why do you seek after the goddess Ambition [*Philotimias*], son? Don't do it; this goddess is unjust [*adikos*]. Often she comes to happy homes and cities, and when she leaves, she has destroyed their owners, she after whom you rave. It's better, child, to honor Equality [*Isotēta*], who ties friends to friends, cities to cities, allies to allies. For equality [*to ison*] is by nature the law among men [*nomimon anthrōpois ephu*], and the lesser share [*toulasson*] has always made war against the greater [*tōi pleoni*] and ushers in hostile days. . . . Why do you honor tyrannical power so much and think that unjust happiness [*adikian eudaimona*] is great? . . . You want to have much wealth within your halls, but much trouble with it? And what is "the greater share" [*to pleon*]? It's nothing but the name. . . . If I ask you a double question, whether you wish to rule, or to save the city, will you choose to be its tyrant? (531–561)

Jocasta imitates the language of her son in order to cast doubt on the validity of his ideals. If Eteocles accepts that "an equal share" (*to ison*) is nothing but a name, then what justifies his belief that "a greater share" (*to pleon*) is anything more than a name? In a clever rhetorical move, Jocasta quotes from Eteocles but also from the wider Athenian culture, where greed has become, for some at least, an immoralist ideal: what is this *to pleon* that one hears so much about? What are its effects, if we look beyond the facile rhetoric of immoralism? Like the Anonymus, Jocasta points out that tyrannical greed usually brings trouble in its wake, now in the form of the invading Argive army. For Jocasta, *to pleon* may superficially resemble its once honorable cousin "ambition" (*philotimia*), but in a climate of factional conflict, even seeking after honor has become a crass, unjust, materialistic enterprise. It has become, in short, unabashed greed. Greed, masquerading under more honorable names, destroys the polis for the sake of shortsighted, narrowly self-interested gratification. Thus Jocasta, for her part, also unmasks the psychological motives of those who oppose her own vision of the city, but she, unlike Eteocles and his cohort, does so out of a genuine interest in preserving her family and her fatherland.

In 411, aristocrats' decisions to participate in revolution were based on resentment, greed, and especially the perception that the demos was unfairly, greedily benefiting from its control of the polis. Even so, aristocrats had to wait for the right opportunity. With a number of lower-class thetes serving in the fleet during the Ionian War, and with the large numbers lost throughout the war and in Sicily, an unusual opportunity presented itself. With the benefit of hindsight, we might think it almost predictable that in such circumstances aristocrats, whether former participants in democracy or those who had opted out of the system, would identify strongly with class-based resentment and join the camp of hard-core oligarchs.[71] In the event, however, the revolutions brought to light contradictions between the traditional aristocratic claim to benefit the polis and the belief, increasingly common among elites, that those in power do, and even should, rule in order to satisfy their own greed. While supporting the view that those in power do rule in their own interests, the revolutions apparently discredit the value of aristocratic rule for the flourishing of the polis. The role of violence and greed in the revolutions discredited aristocratic claims to control the state, because during their tenure in office the oligarchs provided positive proof that aristocrats were not necessarily morally superior to or more deserving than their social inferiors. By the end of a decade or so of political turmoil (411–403), it seemed positively just that the demos should apply to itself the formerly aristocratic value terms "noble" (*agathos*) and "well born" (*gennaios*).[72]

The Revolution of 411: Speech, Mistrust, and Violence

In 411, a group of Athenian oligarchs staged a revolution, establishing a regime that lasted approximately four months; then a counterrevolution led to a more moderate oligarchy, the so-called mixed constitution.[73] The revolution had a variety of causes: personal, demographic, ideological, and economic.[74] Roughly speaking, however, the revolution was driven by the greed of individuals and by elite resentment at the perceived greed of

[71] On those who had kept clear of politics (the *apragmones*), see Carter 1986.

[72] For the demos's growing application of these value terms to itself rather than to aristocrats in the late fifth and fourth centuries, see Whitehead 1993 on Athens's epigraphic "cardinal virtues."

[73] Key sources for the revolution are Thucydides 8.47.3–8.98; *AP* 29–33; Diodorus 13.34.1–3, 13.36, 13.38.1–2; ps.-Lysias 20 (*pro Polystrato*) (For Polystratus).

[74] Among the many treatments of the revolution, I have found the following works most useful: Hignett 1952, chap. 10; Lintott 1982, 135–84; Finley 1971; Calhoun 1913; Rhodes 1972, 115–27; de Ste. Croix 1956; Ostwald 1986, 337–411; Sealey 1976, 358–68; Lang 1967, 176–87; Gomme, Andrewes, and Dover *HCT*, vol. 5; Rhodes 1981, 362–415.

the demos. Naturally, we must keep in mind that human motivation is more complex than this rough schema suggests. In reconstructing the revolution, we should recall Thucydides' analysis of the crazy quilt of motivations at strife-ridden Corcyra.[75]

To contemporaries, the revolution was psychologically bewildering. The inability of Athenian citizens to interpret the motivations and political allegiances of their fellows led to a flourishing of fragmentation and mistrust among citizens—both within Athens and between Athenian oligarchs and the democratic fleet at Samos. Athens literally became two cities in 411, one democratic and stationed at Samos, the other oligarchic within the polis. As we will see, the power of false representations and public manipulation took center stage in a process in which individuals enacted ideals of greed and reacted against the perception that others were greedy and unfair. Now within the polis, rather than in their empire, the Athenians seemed, on observation, to demonstrate that rulers tend to rule in their own interests. The empirical observation became an ideal vision for the oligarchs, who embraced greed for their own part and struggled to take control of the political battleground that Athens had become.

Without offering a full narrative, I argue that the revolution exemplifies, in particular, three key elements of the contemporary discourse on greed: mistrust; social and economic fragmentation; and self-seeking manipulation of public speech and ideological representation.[76] Late fifth-century thinkers analyzed these elements of civic breakdown as both causes and effects of greed; all of them are, in turn, brought to light in the events of the revolution. Hence, the revolution provides an example of ideas in action. Whether self-consciously or not, political agents played out the themes of ideological thinking about greed, while our literary sources interpreted the revolutionaries as carrying into practice principles that were all too familiar from the divisive antidemocratic literature of the period.

The revolutionaries within the city of Athens were constrained by the powerful democratic leanings of the navy at Samos. Athens did not yet experience the chaos of revolutionary Corcyra because of this external check: the oligarchs always wanted to appear legitimate in the eyes of the

[75] On Coreyra, see Thycydides 3.82–83 with chapter 5; on the revolutionaries of 411, see Thucydides 8.47.1, 8.48–49, 8.53.1; the best analysis of the motives of different members of the oligarchic camp is that of Ostwald 1986, 344–68; cf. also Sealey 1976, 366–67.

[76] The events of this revolution are well known, and there is widespread agreement on the relationship between our two main sources, Thucydides and *AP*. On the chronology and relationship between Thucydides and the *AP*, see Sommerstein 1977; Lang 1967; Rhodes 1981, 364–65; Andrewes in *HCT* 5:212–40; Hignett 1952, 268–80, 356–78; Lintott 1982, 135–52.

fleet (Thuc. 8.72.1; cf. 8.74.2). For example, the delegates of the Four Hundred reassured the fleet that their relatives had not been treated badly, and still had control over their own property (8.86.3).[77] Once this check was removed, in 404, the oligarchic revolutionaries fully exhibited the greedy drives that contemporaries such as Euripides believed were present also in 411. In Calliclean terms, the revolutionaries of 411 had extraordinary desires without the full power to satisfy them, whereas the revolutionaries of 404 had enough power to turn their advantages into the full-scale satisfaction of greed.

According to Thucydides, the revolution began with Alcibiades' overtures to the Athenian fleet at Samos (8.47.3). At the beginning, Thucydides distinguishes two basic groups at Samos. On the one hand, "The most powerful [*hoi dunatōtatoi*] of the citizens, who were also suffering most from the war, now began to have great hopes on their own account of seizing power for themselves and defeating their enemies" (8.48.1). The so-called mob (*ochlos*), on the other hand, was attracted to the prospect of getting pay from the king (8.48.3).[78] Thucydides represents the "most powerful" of Athenians as motivated by a long-standing bitterness over paying for the war without receiving a corresponding share in the power to make decisions. Even after the oligarchs at Samos parted company with Tissaphernes, they went ahead with the revolution: "They would continue to hold out against the enemy in the war and would willingly contribute money and whatever else was necessary from their private estates, since they were now suffering not for other people but for themselves" (8.63.4). Their private estates (*tōn idiōn oikōn*; cf. 2.65.1–2) are a leitmotif of resistant, antidemocratic literature: the demos as a naval, unpropertied faction makes decisions in its own interests, willingly sacrificing the estates of the rich by leaving them undefended.[79] Thus, the rich sought oligarchy in order to establish a closer and, in their minds, more just correlation between their expenditures for the city and their political power within it.

Their methods were violence and the control of free speech, both of

[77] The Athenian fleet at Samos may have had recent experience of oligarchs who had staged a coup and then confiscated property from their fellow citizens in the way that the Thirty Tyrants were later to do in Athens: see ML 83 (with commentary). This recent experience would help explain the Athenians' worry over their families and their property now that the Four Hundred were in control of Athens.

[78] In this contrast, we can detect the first glimmers of Aristotle's ideologically conditioned view that great men conceive grand-scale ambitions, whereas ordinary people are pleased just to have a guarantee of material sufficiency. For Aristotle's views on the subject, see chapter 1.

[79] See Old Oligarch 2.14–15. Gomme (*HCT* 2:181–82) points out the inaccuracy of the belief that only the rich suffered during the war; cf. Ober 1985 on Pericles' attempts to limit Peloponnesian ravaging of the Athenian countryside.

them pushed through by the political clubs (8.54.4, 8.66). The democratic leader Androcles was promptly and secretly killed (8.65). According to Thucydides, if anyone spoke against them, he was soon killed, and the murder was left uninvestigated (8.66). The democratic process ended immediately when the members of these clubs, instituting a reign of terror, began to regulate the Council and Assembly (8.65–66). Throughout all this, the oligarchs mobilized a massive propaganda campaign that played on hoplites' resentment over democratic greed, and that publicly promoted the ideology of the common good (e.g., 8.86.3). Thucydides calls the oligarchic program merely "propaganda for the general public, since the revolutionaries themselves intended to take over the city" (8.66.1). The *Constitution of the Athenians* (*AP* 30–32.1) provides an excellent example of this oligarchic propaganda.[80] The documents preserved in chapters 30–32—essentially false constitutions—show how ideologues could manipulate antidemocratic sentiment in order to promote the narrow group of four hundred oligarchs, who considered even a "hoplite democracy" of five thousand citizens to be too democratic a regime (Thuc. 8.92.11). Although Aristotle records that the regime of the Four Hundred was instituted constitutionally (*AP* 29.1–2, 30.1, 32.1),[81] Thucydides' account discredits him.[82]

What was the nature of these propagandistic "constitutions," and what would their appeal have been? One key provision (*AP* 29.5) states, "The whole control of the state should be entrusted to the Athenians best able to serve with their persons and their wealth, not less than five thousand in number, for the duration of the war; they shall have full power to make treaties with whomever they wish." In all likelihood, the "five thousand" refers to the hoplite class and above; the measure apparently intends to exclude lower-class thetes from the franchise.[83] The details of

[80] I believe, with most scholars, that the *AP* accepts the veracity of documents that were, in all probability, issued as propaganda at approximately the time of the revolution (cf. Rhodes 1981, 365). The *AP* (29.2) is probably right that there were thirty *probouloi* rather than ten (as Thuc. 8.67.1 says); see Rhodes 1981, 366–67, 373.

[81] This is basically the picture one gets from Diodorus Siculus, who says, "Consequently [because of allied revolts and the Sicilian disaster], the demos, being disheartened, willingly [*hekousiōs*] renounced the democracy and, choosing four hundred men, turned over to them the administration of the state" (13.34.2). At 13.36.2, Diodorus says that the demos chose four hundred men to run the government because they thought oligarchy was more suitable (*euthetōteran*) than democracy in situations of crisis.

[82] Aristotle's view that the oligarchic constitutions were commissioned by the Five Thousand is also contradicted by his own later contention (no doubt derived from Thucydides) that "the Five Thousand were appointed only in name" (32.3).

[83] There is a big question over the nature of the eventual Five Thousand instituted after the overthrow of the Four Hundred, and over the relationship of this real group of Five Thousand with the fictional one imagined in these theorists' constitutions; neither question is precisely relevant to my account, but I basically follow the "traditional" view, stated most

the constitutions show a concern to limit expenditure (e.g., *AP* 30.2; Thuc. 8.65.3) and a desire to place a limited body of citizens in control of the government—specifically one *not* chosen by lot (*AP* 30.5; Thuc. 8.65.3). Judging by its restriction of the franchise and its close, direct correlation between wealth and political power, Draco's law code (mistakenly inserted at *AP* 4) was probably "reinvented" in precisely this period in order to provide further legitimacy for proposals to institute a limited franchise based on wealth.

For the purposes of cloaking the oligarchs' moves in august "democratic" tradition, a certain Cleitophon appealed to the "ancestral constitution" (*patrios politeia*) of Cleisthenes, which Aristotle considered to be "not populist [*dēmotikēn*] but similar to Solon's" (*AP* 29.3, 31.1).[84] In book 1 of Plato's *Republic* (340a3–b8), an interlocutor called Cleitophon introduces an amendment to Thrasymachus's arguments about the meaning and content of justice. It is possible that these are the same individual and that Cleitophon helped advance the oligarchic movement because he believed in, or at least entertained, views of government similar to those of Thrasymachus.[85] At any rate, by invoking one of the founding fathers of democracy, Cleisthenes, the hard-core oligarchs meant to cloak their narrow oligarchy in terms that might be more acceptable to Athenian democrats. Oligarchic propaganda everywhere promoted the idea of "saving the city" (*AP* 29.4; Thuc. 8.53.2–3), but, even if this well-known ideology prevailed in popular forums, Thucydides saw that the masterminds behind the revolution were interested only in their own political power and narrow gains (8.63.4, 68.1–4).

The alleged "constitutions" preserved by the *Constitution of the Athenians* offer a picture of the hoplites' dissatisfaction with the "radical" democracy; of a desire to limit decision making to a comparatively broad group of oligarchs; of the need to cut back on expenditures (*AP* 29.5); and, most importantly, of the significance for many Athenians of creating a tight, direct correlation between wealth and political power.[86] If thetic

recently in Rhodes 1972, that the thetes were excluded not only from holding office, but also from the franchise in general: contra, de Ste. Croix 1956, Sealey 1976, 368. Ps.-Lysias 20.13 shows that lists of the "Five Thousand" were being drawn up, but this does not mean that such lists were ever published or that the Five Thousand (or the nine thousand quoted in this speech) ever played a role in decision making before the counterrevolution.

[84] For the view that talk of *patrios politeia* (the "ancestral constitution") is pure but effective propaganda, see Finley 1971; contra, Fuks 1953.

[85] For the identity of Cleitophon, see Rhodes 1981, 375; on Cleitophon and Thrasymachus, see de Romilly (1992, 215–16), who points out that one of the extant fragments of Thrasymachus is a speech advocating the ancestral constitution.

[86] Cf. ps.-Herodes *Peri Politeias* (*On the Constitution*) 31 with Morrison 1942, 68–74, for a related argument. Other motives: unabashed opportunism, e.g., that alleged of Eratosthenes (Lys. 12.42); compulsion, e.g., Polystratus, ps.-Lysias 20.14 (alleged), perhaps

losses in the war were significant, then this type of constitution had broad appeal to those who were left in Athens: the hoplites and members of the cavalry, who were not the masterminds behind the revolution but who nonetheless desired change. The documents show that hoplite-class supporters of the revolution were motivated by a diversity of interests that Thucydides' focus on individual characters such as Alcibiades, Antiphon, and Phrynichus, or on a presumed elite faction, has the tendency to obscure. At least until the counterrevolution, though, these Athenians had no constitutional power, because the Five Thousand did not exist under the regime of the Four Hundred.

Whether or not some of these hoplites saw themselves as rectifying democratic injustices, such as those alleged by the Old Oligarch, the protagonists of Thucydides' account were motivated in the first instance by greed of their own. Such men were self-consciously enacting the ideals of those who promoted the politics of greed and self-interest, such as Thrasymachus and Callicles. If government was simply the rule of the stronger in their own interest, and if political agents took such a view as their ethical ideal, then in 411 certain masterminds of public attitudes and historical conditions took their chances and set the revolution in motion. Thucydides thought it predictable that the revolution would succeed, because it was undertaken by so many intelligent men, primary among whom was Antiphon (8.68). The staunchest oligarchs, according to Thucydides, were Phrynichus, Aristarchus, Pisander, Antiphon, and "others belonging to the most powerful families" (8.90). They did not act unreflectively in accordance with class interests; rather, armed with sophisticated antidemocratic theories, they thought themselves out of democratic ideology and into the Calliclean ethics of greed.[87]

To Thucydides Antiphon was the mastermind behind the scenes.[88] The small number of preserved fragments of his work show that he was capable of justifying his opposition to democracy through appeals to nature and self-interest. In a fragment of his *Truth*, he explained that

> Justice is not violating the laws of the city in which one is a citizen. Thus a person would best use justice to his own advantage [*chrōit' an oun anthrōpos*

combined with resentment over the demos's apparent lack of concern for elite property; cf. ps.-Lysias 20.33.

[87] Missiou (1992, 1) proposes a more straightforward and, to my mind, simplistic connection between class and political action: "Political groups in all periods of history attempt in various ways to promote the interests and achieve the goals of the classes they represent."

[88] With Gagarin (in Gagarin and MacDowell 1998, 4–5), I view Antiphon the orator and Antiphon the sophist as the same individual; for further discussion, see Guthrie *HGP* 3:292–94; Kerferd 1981, 49–51, 115–17; Pendrick 1987 argues vigorously for two Antiphons; Avery 1982 has convinced me of the unitarian position, though I cannot agree with all of his conclusions on DK 87 B44 A.

malista heautōi xumpherontōs dikaiosunēi] if he considered the laws important when witnesses are present, but the consequences of nature important in the absence of witnesses. . . . The requirements of the laws are by agreement, whereas the requirements of nature are unavoidable. Thus someone who violates the laws avoids shame and punishment if he escapes the notice of those who have joined in agreement, but not if he does not. But if someone tries to violate one of the inherent requirements of nature, which is impossible, the harm he suffers is no less if he is seen by no one. (DK 87 B44 A1)

By contrast with the Anonymus Iamblichi, Antiphon opposes nature to law and gives priority to nature. His recommendations on using justice for one's own advantage mark him out as an immoralist. Antiphon helped explain to his fellow conspirators why they should abandon the democratic rat race in favor of setting up a government that would act in their genuine, natural interests. Even in the single fragment preserved from his defense speech, Antiphon self-servingly argues that, as a speech writer, he could best serve his own self-interest under democracy; therefore, he asks, why should he of all people have wanted to overthrow the democracy in favor of oligarchy (Antiphon fr. 1)? Like Thrasymachus, he assumes, and expects others to agree, that satisfying self-interest is the primary motivation for political action. This was a fine argument to make in his defense speech before a newly restored democratic court.

Equally ironic is the charge, mooted roughly seven years later by the oligarch Critias, that Theramenes, another member of the Four Hundred, had always been a turncoat for the sake of satisfying his greed. As we shall see, Critias himself was lambasted on precisely the same account in the post-revolutionary period. After detailing Theramenes' activities in 411, and describing his prosecution of the generals after Arginousae, Critias says, "How, can it possibly be right to spare this man who so obviously is always concerned to satisfy his greed [*tou men pleonektein aei epimelomenos*] without any care for honor [*tou . . . kalou*] or for his own friends?" (Xen. *Hell.* 2.3.33).[89] Theramenes' chameleon-like ability both to anticipate and to manipulate public sentiment, which was demonstrated in his leadership in destroying the wall in Eetionia (Thuc. 8.90–92, cf. Xen. *Hell.* 2.3.30, 2.3.46), lends credence to Critias's charge that during the entire revolutionary decade, he enacted the Calliclean ethics of greed. His case shows that the Calliclean "strong man" is not necessarily stronger than the demos in brute strength but rather in his ability to exploit public conventions of speaking and behavior for his own advantage. He thus provides an empirical refutation of the Anonymus Iamblichi and of Socrates in the *Gorgias* (488d5–489b6), both of whom stress the demos's capacity to limit a single strong man's aggression.

[89] Here again we can see the opposition between greed and honor in the critical discourse on greed.

The revolution expresses in practice the themes of mistrust, fragmentation, and propaganda, all of which cluster around greed in late fifth-century political discourse in Athens. The resentment of some, combined with the acquisitiveness of others, inspired violence and manipulative propaganda, which worked together to create mistrust: the alleged existence of the Five Thousand was one of the Four Hundred's most powerful weapons in the ensuing campaign of terror. The Four Hundred did not want the Five Thousand either to exist or to be known to exist, since keeping the matter uncertain would make everyone afraid of each other (Thuc. 8.92.11). Democrats were suspicious of each other and fearful of getting into trouble if they spoke confidentially to someone who might turn out to be a participant in the revolution (8.66.1–5). As the Anonymus Iamblichi had theorized, the revolution flourished on the basis of collective mistrust (*apistia*). The Four Hundred oligarchs came to terrorize a large city because the people—primarily the hoplites—could not speak freely. By destroying a central democratic value, free speech (*parrhēsia*), the oligarchs reconfirmed their power over the city. Words did not lose their usual content or significance, as in Corcyra; they simply could not be spoken at all.

Mutual suspicions were enhanced by the oligarchs' repeated attempts to make treaties with the Spartans. Immediately upon assuming power within Athens, for example, the oligarchs attempted to make an agreement with the Spartan king Agis (8.70.2–71.3). Thucydides says that they wanted above all to preserve the oligarchy and maintain control over the allies; next to retain an independent Athens under oligarchic control; and, if all else failed, to save their own lives even if it meant betraying the city (8.91.3). Like Eteocles, they would sell out the city's interests for their own; like the Thirty Tyrants, their oligarchic successors in 404, they would try to use Spartan power in order to strengthen their own positions at the expense of their fellow citizens'.[90] Despite their propaganda, they rejected the Solonian ideal of the common good. If, as the fifth-century theorists suggested, government is and should be conducted in the self-interest of the rulers, then the Four Hundred exemplified the theorists' ideals in practice.

Before that happened, however, the hoplites' reappropriation of public speech overwhelmed the oligarchs' hold on the city. This led to the reunification of a broad group of hoplites, who instituted Thucydides' notoriously problematic "moderate blending" (*metria . . . xunkrasis*) of the few and the many (8.97.2). To democrats of the following decades, the oligarchs seemed to give clear evidence of the unwholesome effects of

[90] On the use of the phrase "Thirty Tyrants" to designate the thirty oligarchs of the later revolution, see Tuplin 1985, 369.

oligarchic rule altogether. The revolution rendered problematic the notion that wealth should have any significant connection to political power, because it provided ample empirical evidence that possessing wealth is no guarantee of reliability in a ruling class. Moreover, the claims made by the Old Oligarch and the like that aristocrats are ethically refined because of their birth and education were utterly discredited by the revolution. The revolutionaries showed, if anything, that the theorists and ideologues of greed considered in the first section were right that rulers usually do rule in their own interests; that greed creates mistrust; that greed causes social and economic fragmentation. The revolutionaries did not see, perhaps, that their greed for power over others and control of the city would ultimately redound to the moral and ideological benefit of the demos.

The Revolution of 404: Greed and the Thirty

> Do not obey those wicked men, the Thirty, who, just for their own private profit [*idiōn kerdeōn heneka*], have in eight months come close to killing more Athenians than all the Peloponnesians did in ten years of war. These men, when there is nothing to prevent our living peaceably together in our city [*exon d' hēmin en eirēnēi politeuesthai*], have brought on us war [*polemon*] among ourselves, and there can be nothing more shameful than this, nothing more unbearable, more unholy and more hateful to gods and men alike.
>
> *The herald Cleocritus, speaking to the army of the Thirty (Xen.* Hell. *2.4.21–22)*

After a brief period of rule by the Five Thousand, the demos again took control of the state (*AP* 34.1).[91] The second oligarchic revolution at Athens followed upon the Athenians' loss at Aegospotami and Lysander's siege of the city (Xen. *Hell.* 2.2.7–16).[92] The revolutionaries were enacting the prominent themes of contemporary political thought, which, as we have seen, either expressed resentment at the greed and injustice of

[91] Diodorus Siculus (13.38.1) gives a brief, though garbled, account that confuses the Five Thousand with the restored democracy.

[92] I have consulted the following modern treatments of the revolution. Ostwald 1986, 460–96; Hignett 1952; Lintott 1982, 158–68; Krentz 1982; Rhodes 1981, 415–82; Whitehead 1982–83; Fuks 1953, Loening 1987.

the demos, or incited aristocrats to embrace greed as an ideal of behavior. By reporting the events of the revolution in terms of greed and injustice, contemporary writers transformed the revolution into a key "intellectual event" within the Athenians' collective memory in the fourth century. Contemporaries sought a *moral* interpretation of events that would either vilify the Thirty or exonerate individuals thought to be their associates. Whether oligarch or democrat, everyone agreed that the Thirty, driven by greed for power and wealth, had committed serious crimes against their fellow citizens.[93] Hence, democrats used the revolution to seize the moral high ground against oligarchy in general, while antidemocratic thinkers were forced to explain away the behavior of the Thirty, in a desperate attempt to rehabilitate the aristocratic ideal.

A veritable chorus of ancient sources—Xenophon, Lysias, the *Constitution of the Athenians*, Diodorus—emphasized the revolutionaries' greed, which the oligarchs exemplified in its fullest tyrannical form. Like Callicles, Eteocles, and Thucydides' Athenians, they conceived an excessive acquisitiveness for wealth and power that drove them to bloodshed and tyranny. The Thirty were greedy for material possessions, to be sure, but they wanted all the city's divisible goods, especially power (*kratos*), which they understood as the capacity to ensure that they would continue to enjoy choiceworthy goods and psychic pleasures in the future.[94] They were paradigmatic Aristotelian tyrants. Indeed, as their significance in fourth-century ideological literature shows, the Thirty fostered a distinctive image of the omnivorous tyrant, usually as a negative exemplum. Moreover, like tyrants throughout the tradition, their position was precarious. Ultimately, like the Athenians on the eve of the Sicilian expedition, their excessive acquisitiveness outstripped their capacity to defend themselves militarily.[95] Their depredations, lack of political legitimacy,

[93] On the importance of this revolution in popular memory, and on the simplicity of the narratives usually told about it, see Dillery 1995, 139–44.

[94] See the comments of Frankfurt (1999, 180), who argues, "Like loving and like working, the possession of power derives inherent value from the fact that it is instrumental for the attainment of outcomes that are valued for their own sakes." Consequently, power is an essential constituent of *eudaimonia* (human flourishing) because power is instrumentally valuable in acquiring other goods, while the continued possession of power ensures that those other inherently valuable goods will always be available.

[95] There is no question that the Thirty had motives other than greed, such as suppressing dissident voices and activity (cf. Lysias 30.13). Consequently, Krentz (1982, 80–81) creates an unusual "straw man" when he argues that "to view all their convictions and executions as stemming from personal greed is to be overly gullible." In fact, the behavior of the Thirty fits more clearly into the wider notion of greed that I have proposed: the tyrannical desire for all sorts of material satisfactions, including the means, such as money and power, to obtain them.

and exclusion of large numbers of Athenians from political power caused resentment and finally successful resistance.

As in 411, the "political clubs" (*hetaireiai*) played an instrumental role in overthrowing the democracy (Lys. 12.43). First they killed Cleophon, the strongest voice of opposition to peace (Lys. 13.12). This act, which clearly aimed to undermine the people's role in politics, vitiated the moral self-justifications of the oligarchs. After being besieged to the point of starvation by the Spartans (Xen. *Hell.* 2.2.11, 2.2.14), the Athenians, represented by Theramenes among others, negotiated peace (Lys. 13.9; Xen. *Hell.* 2.2.16–24; cf. Diod. Sic. 14.3.4). Despite their allies' demands that Athens be destroyed, the Spartans called only for the dismantling of the Long Walls and the Peiraeus fortifications, along with a reduction of the Athenian navy to twelve ships. Lysander presided over the Assembly meeting that established the oligarchy of the Thirty, which was meant both to govern the city and to frame a constitution in accordance with the ancient laws of Solon and Cleisthenes.[96]

What were the aims of the revolutionaries?[97] Did they have any positive political program other than satisfying their greed on a grand scale? For their part, the revolutionaries self-consciously publicized the idea that their regime was founded on virtue (*aretē*) and justice (*dikaiosunē*) and enacted in accordance with its members' aristocratic values (*kalokagathia*).[98] This traditional ideology, however, came into sharp conflict with the new elitist views on power and self-interest, which encouraged the oligarchs to see Athens as a site of inevitable conflict, where the individual or his faction must struggle against others for scarce resources. The revolutionaries' aims must in large part be inferred from their behavior, but Critias, one of the junta's leaders, wrote a satyr-play called *Sisyphus*, in which Sisyphus explains that the gods were invented by a

[96] Krentz (1982, 50) argues, rightly in my view, that the Thirty were established as a government, not simply as a group of legislators; see also Hignett 1952, 383; Ostwald 1986, 478. Our sources disagree over the role of Theramenes in these proceedings. To give an overview of the source difficulties, Lysias 12 disparages Theramenes in order to defame Eratosthenes by association; the so-called Theramenes papyrus (Michigan Papyrus 5982; see Merkelbach and Youtie 1968) apparently responds to Lysias 12.69, recording that Theramenes had argued that the Athenians should not insist on different terms, to which the Spartans would inevitably add further clauses; *AP* 34, 36.1–2 and Diodorus 14.3.2–4.1 whitewash Theramenes; Xenophon's *Hellenica* 2.2.16 charges that Theramenes purposefully stayed with Lysander for three months in order to starve the Athenians further and make them pliant to any terms of peace whatever, while later in the narrative (2.3.15, 22) Xenophon rehabilitates Theramenes as an anti-Critian moderate.

[97] For detailed discussion of the identities of the revolutionaries, see Ostwald 1986, 460–68; Krentz 1982, 50–56.

[98] Lysias 12.5; Diodorus Siculus 14.4.1; Xenophon *Hellenica* 2.3.18, 2.3.22.

clever man in order to frighten his fellow citizens into obeying the law even when they could commit injustice without being detected. Through a clever lie, this trailblazer offered a practical solution to the problem of Gyges' ring. Whatever Critias' own relationship to this speech, he and his fellows carried into practice a thoroughgoing rejection of conventional morality, once they acquired sufficient power to pursue their acquisitive desires.[99] In particular, they carried into practice Sisyphus's insight that the law is a human construct, nothing more, which could prove useful to those who devised it and, above all, need not restrain those who understood its true origin.[100]

Their behavior suggests a strong proclivity toward violence and greed. Immediately after assuming office, the Thirty executed the generals and taxiarchs who had once opposed the peace treaty with Sparta, even though they would have been tried, under the democracy, before a panel of two thousand jurors (Lys. 13.35–38). Contrary to the demos's desire to grant due process, the oligarchs summarily dispatched these high-ranking democratic leaders in order to consolidate their power. They also brought to trial and executed those who had been informers under the democracy (Xen. *Hell.* 2.3.12; *AP* 35.3; Diod. Sic. 14.4.2). In criticizing the Thirty, Theramenes later evoked the hypocrisy of their attacks on these informers: "In my view it is dishonorable [*ou* . . . *kalon*] for those who call themselves the best to act more unjustly than the informers did [*adikōtera tōn sukophantōn poiein*]. The informers took money from their victims, but at least allowed them to stay alive. Are we, in order to get money, going to kill people who have done nothing wrong? Is this not more unjust [*adikōtera*] in every way?" (Xen. *Hell.* 2.3.22). Moreover, the oligarchs' legislation was violence carried on by other means: for example, they passed a law giving themselves "full authority to execute any citizens who were not included in the register of the Three Thousand" (*AP* 37.1). This law served the purpose only of legalizing the Thirty's murder of Theramenes and anyone else the oligarchs wanted, because they themselves drew up the register of the three thousand. In short, the Thirty were constantly about to revise the laws (Diod. Sic. 14.4.2; Xen. *Hell.* 2.3.11), but their only laws on record are shortsighted measures to provide some legal basis, however illegitimate, for their arbitrary exercise of force.

[99] For Critias's career before 404 and for his political sympathies, see Krentz 1982, 45–46; Ostwald 1986, 462–66, 542–43. On the controversies over the authorship of the *Sisyphus*, see Davies 1989, who concludes that "the issue of enjambment may be the least unreliable index of non-Euripidean authorship" (28); cf. Guthrie *HGP* 3:243–44.

[100] For other attempts to connect Critias's fantastic and self-avowed greed (cf. Xen. *Hell.* 2.3.16) with this fragment, see Dillery 1995, 149; Tuplin 1993, 43–44.

The Thirty often turned to violence in order to satisfy greed. As Lysias says, despite their rhetoric of virtue and justice, the oligarchs began to execute metics for the sake of their money: "those men thought nothing of putting people to death, but a great deal of getting money" (Lys. 12.5–7); he later exclaimed, "To what extremes of insatiable greed for gain [*aplēstian kai aischrokerdeian*] did they go!" (12.19). All our sources are agreed on the motive of greed. For Xenophon, the Thirty "put many people to death out of personal enmity, and many also for their property" (*Hell.* 2.3.21). Finally, as Critias revealingly explains to Theramenes, "It is impossible for those who want to satisfy their greed [*tois pleonektein boulomenois*] to avoid getting rid of those people who are most likely to form an opposition. And you are naive if you think that, just because we are thirty and not one, we have to keep a less close watch on the government than is done by a tyrant" (2.3.16).[101]

Examples could be multiplied.[102] Our sources record uniformly unfavorable interpretations of the Thirty, but those interpretations correspond closely to the Thirty's behavior, as far as we are aware, and generally come from contemporary, and even eyewitness, sources. After the revolution, indeed, Lysias was prosecuted by a certain Hippotherses, apparently because they disagreed over the terms on which Lysias's property, confiscated by the Thirty and sold to Hippotherses, should be returned (Lysias fr. 1). Once the Thirty oligarchs had acquired sufficient force to satisfy their desires, however, their greed for material goods led to greed for the state as a whole. The Thirty were carrying out a full-scale robbery of the city (Xen. *Hell.*. 2.4.13). Thus, contrary to recent arguments that the Thirty tried to imitate the Spartan constitution, the evidence of their behavior points to their acting out the ideas and ideals of the discourse on greed.[103] They were happy enough to be the quislings of Lysander and the Spartans so long as they had power (*kratos*) and

[101] On this important passage, see Dillery 1995, 149; Tuplin 1993, 43–44.

[102] See *AP* 35.4, Diodorus Siculus 14.4.4–5, 14.5.5–7, Xenophon *Hellenica* 2.3.39, 2.3.43; Lysias fr. 1. Rhodes 1981, 446, collects a large number of ancient references to the Thirty's confiscation of property.

[103] For "Spartan imitation," see Krentz 1982, 64–68; Whitehead 1982–83; Ostwald 1986, 484–90. The similarities between the oligarchic regime and the Spartan constitution are vague, and no ancient source draws this conclusion. Because we must, for the most part, infer the oligarchs' aims from their activities, it is most economical to suppose that they were driven by the greed for wealth and power that our sources continually emphasize. Lintott (1982, 163) accepts greed as a primary motive, but argues that the oligarchic movement can be explained without any reference to the philosophical and ideological background. I would argue that the philosophical justifications found in the literature of the preceding decades enabled and inspired the grand-scale depredations of the Thirty.

money (*chrēmata*), the two persistent ideals of acquisitive individuals from the sixth century through the fourth.

For military support within the city, the Thirty relied on the Spartan garrison commanded by the harmost Callibius.[104] This garrison seemed to enable the oligarchs to achieve the Calliclean ideal of ever expanding desire and the power to satisfy it. Among other things, the Spartan presence enabled the Thirty to seize Eleusis and kill its inhabitants: in Xenophon's view, "These things were pleasing to those citizens who cared only about satisfying their greed [*hois to pleonektein monon emelen*]" (*Hell.* 2.4.10). However much they could gratify their desires for more, though, they also demonstrated the difficulty, at least within Athens, of sustaining the Calliclean ideal. In order to acquire the physical force needed to satisfy their desires, they had to give up their freedom: only Sparta could support their grandiose self-seeking schemes. On the other hand, as Theramenes points out, the Thirty could never survive on their own, without the Spartan garrison, unless they broadened the franchise. Otherwise, they would be weaker than their subjects (*Hell.* 2.3.19). The Thirty had involved themselves in a vicious Calliclean circle: they needed to spend the money they plundered from others in order to pay the garrison, which was present in the first place to put muscle behind their acquisitive desires. As a result, the Thirty never truly achieved the Calliclean ideal of having the power to satisfy one's enlarged appetites freely and without answering to anyone.

Plato, however, was still worried by their example. True, the Anonymus may be right that Callicles' "strong man" can never exist for as long as he wishes, but what if he could? There is something else, even deeper, wrong with the Calliclean model, and Plato set himself the task of figuring out what that was. At a political rather than moral level, Plato's dilemma was that, by observation at least, aristocrats lost their vaunted civic and moral superiority whenever they controlled the state without democratic supervision. And yet limiting political participation to the elite could be justified only by appealing to aristocratic excellence. Hence Plato was forced to rehabilitate aristocratic claims to excellence in such a way as to justify elite control of the ideal state. It took a Plato to realize how closely intertwined the moral and political issues must be if one is unwilling to accept the claims of democracy to be the best we can hope for.

[104] On the chronological disputes surrounding the request for the garrison, the execution of Theramenes, and Thrasybulus's occupation of Phyle, I follow Rhodes (1981, 422, 454) in preferring Xenophon's account, in which the garrison was called in early in the oligarchs' regime: Xenophon *Hellenica* 2.3.11–12, Diodorus Siculus 14.3.7–4.2, Justin 5.8.8–10; cf. *AP* 37.2. For other views, see Ostwald 1986, 483–84.

Responding to the Revolutions: Lysias and Xenophon

The revolutionary period had deep roots in the history of Athenian thought about greed and injustice. Given the opportunity provided by the military failures in 413 and 405, the oligarchs' behavior was almost predictable. What was not predictable was democratic moderation in observing the amnesty of 403.[105] Contrary to elitist accusations of demotic greed, the demos responded with generosity and public-spiritedness in an effort to refound the political community. Strikingly, even though the agreement between the factions stipulated that oligarchs and democrats were to repay their debts separately, the newly restored democrats repaid Sparta for money the Thirty had borrowed (*AP* 40.3). Aristotle remarks that in other cities democracies usually redistribute the land, rather than making payments from their own property (*AP* 40.3). A cynic might claim that the demos acted moderately simply in order to ensure the stability of the future democracy (cf. Old Oligarch 3.12). The author of Plato's *Seventh Letter*, however, complimented the returning exiles on their great moderation (325b4–5).[106] The democrats had won a moral victory. Contrary to the allegations of the Old Oligarch, the democracy showed that its ideals went beyond self-interest and narrow partisanship. Democratic thinkers thus had an extremely effective ideological weapon against elitists. As Xenophon's Thrasybulus shows (Xen. *Hell.* 2.4.40–42), democrats quite reasonably felt justified in stripping terms of moral value from the elite and applying them to all members of the citizen body. As he says:

> Men of the city, I advise you to know yourselves. And you will best be able to do so if you consider what right you have to be so arrogant as to attempt to rule over us. Are you more just? Then why is it that the demos, though poorer than you are, never did you any harm for the sake of money, whereas you, who are richer than all of them, have committed many disgraceful crimes for the sake of your own profit?

Elitist authors were confronted with a powerful ideological challenge as they attempted to rehabilitate the antidemocratic position.

As these were "live" issues in the late fifth-century discourse on greed, so too did they feature in the short-term ideological reactions to the revolution. Lysias, writing in the early fourth century, cultivated popular

[105] For a persuasive account of democratic moderation, see Ostwald 1986, 500–509; see also Rhodes 1981, 464–65, 471–72; Loening 1987. On the inevitable difficulties in the transition back to democracy, see Hignett 1952, 294–97; Murphy 1992, 557–58; Todd 2000, 367–69.

[106] For arguments for the authenticity of this letter, see Morrow 1962, 3–16; Brunt 1993b, 313–25.

memory of the oligarchs' greed in order to affirm the superiority of democracy and to control antidemocratic discourse. In more specific cases, he vividly recalled the oligarchs' abuses in his speech against Eratosthenes (Lys. 12). He invoked the injuries done to Athens by the oligarchs in suggesting that the Athenians' formal scrutiny of potential magistrates (*dokimasia*) was really a way to weed out former oligarchs (26.9). But he also theorized at a more abstract level about democracy as a political system. In particular, by knitting culture into nature, he argues that democracy is not simply any alternative political regime but the best possible pragmatic choice of all.[107]

In his *Funeral Oration*, for example, Lysias recalls the events of the past purportedly in order to glorify Athenian casualties in the Corinthian War.[108] Turning to the events of 404, he praises not Athenian laws and conventions but the ineradicable nature of the demos as such. He recalls "those men who, shunning slavery, fighting for justice, and rallying to the cause of democracy, incurred the hostility of all and returned to the Peiraeus, compelled by no law, but induced by their nature [*ouch hupo nomou anankasthentes, all' hupo tēs phuseōs peisthentes*]" (61). This is a stunning reversal of the standard picture of human nature. In Thucydides' presentation, for example, human nature, especially when reinforced by democratic convention, is an amorphous mass of raw destructive energy, which surfaces in greed, violence, and revolution. According to Lysias, however, it is human nature (*phusis*) that drives the Athenian demos to resist the revolutionaries' injustice. This speaker is the intellectual heir of the Anonymus Iamblichi, who views human nature as a positive force of justice and social cohesion. Later in the oration, the speaker proposes that the people, after the events of 404, applied themselves "not to vengeance upon their enemies, but to the preservation of the city; and being men who at once could not be taken advantage of [*elattousthai*] and would not seek to get more [*pleon echein deomenoi*], they shared their own freedom even with those who wished to be slaves, and declined for themselves a share in that slavery" (64). The demos deserves moral congratulation for preserving the city by observing the terms of the amnesty. Above all, however, the demos is both powerful enough and sufficiently self-restrained to enforce democratic equality. As the demos will not accept less than its share (*elattousthai*), so too will it refrain from taking more than its share (*pleon echein*). In Lysias's powerful construction, it is simply the demos's nature to respect the fair distribution of goods and power.

[107] I owe this formulation to Brent Shaw.

[108] On the authenticity of the speech, see Snell 1979, who, rightly in my opinion, attributes it to Lysias; cf. Todd 2000, 25–27. Dover (1968, 61–68, 193–95) remains strongly agnostic.

The oligarchs, by contrast, were driven by greed to violate the fair distribution characteristic of democracy. In a pamphlet written in 403, "Against the Subversion of the Ancestral Constitution at Athens" (Lys. 34), Lysias argues against a proposal that Athenian citizenship should be restricted to property owners.[109] The speaker first urges that the recent disasters (*sumphoras*, 34.1) should have provided sufficient reminders (*mnēmeia*) of the dangers involved in changing from democracy to oligarchy (34.1), but apparently, he observes, they have not, since a proposal to restrict the democracy is again being mooted. Through the agency of popular memory, the revolution provides ideological "evidence" for the speaker's derogation of oligarchy and his praise of democracy. The revolutionaries, moreover, offered him a rhetorically effective negative exemplum with which to whip his opponents. Advocates of the current legislation, he says, share the attitudes of the oligarchic faction in the city, even if by chance they happened to return to Athens with the democrats (34.2). Seizing the moral high ground, the speaker asserts that democrats are the true saviors of their polis because they have always guaranteed security to those who own property (34.5). In previous oligarchies, on the other hand, property owners were killed or expelled (34.4)—presumably, one imagines, because men like the Thirty were greedy for their property. All of this rhetorical use of the past is somehow a preamble to the speaker's crowning touch, which confirms the democrats' trustworthiness and reliability and denigrates the oligarchs' false rhetoric and underlying greed. He urges his listeners to bring their views of oligarchy into accord with the historical evidence of their own city, which shows that oligarchs are clever propagandists and greedy plunderers of the state, while democrats are the state's benefactors: "If you take my advice, you will not be depriving your benefactors, so far as you are able, of their fatherland, nor be placing more confidence in words than in deeds, or in the future than in the past, especially if you remember those who fought for oligarchy, who in speech make war on the demos, but in fact desire your property" (34.5). The speaker has successfully transformed his understanding of Athenian history into an ideological vision of the ways oligarchs and democrats behave when in power.

Lysias 25, "Defense against a Charge of Subverting the Democracy," reprises the prerevolutionary discourse on greed and political division and looks forward to Aristotle's theory of revolution. It differs, however, from the other works we have considered because it is not straightforwardly democratic, but concentrates rather on the political abuses of

[109] This speech is quoted by Dionysius of Halicarnassus (*Lysias* 33) as an example of Lysias's deliberative oratory, but Dionysius is uncertain whether the speech was actually given. As Dionysius points out, the speaker is of high status, and the speech composed as if for a real debate.

those in power, be they ruthless oligarchs or greedy democratic informers. Using the "evidence" of the revolutions, the speaker makes unusually abstract points about the success and failure of democracy and oligarchy as political systems. As in Lysias 34, the speaker refers immediately to the "events of the past" (25.1; cf. 25.5), namely the revolutions, but here, during what is apparently his scrutiny before holding office (*dokimasia*), he must dissociate himself from crimes perpetrated by the Thirty.[110] As a citizen who remained in the city under the Thirty (25.2), he is now exposed to the same allegations of misconduct as the Thirty. But if the revolutions loomed large in the moral evaluations placed on suspect individuals, then they also occupied a key position in the more or less systematic political thinking embedded in popular genres.

Instead of using the revolutions to confirm the moral superiority of democracy, the speaker argues, with the Old Oligarch and Thrasymachus, that political allegiances derive from a calculation of personal advantage. No citizen is naturally either an oligarch or a democrat, but chooses whichever form of government he himself finds most personally advantageous (25.8).[111] This rhetorical stance is unusual, especially because the evidence adduced, "Phrynichus, Peisander, and their fellow demagogues" (25.9), seems to align the speaker with highly unsavory, antidemocratic characters. This may have been the only stance available, though, to a temporizing citizen whose best defense is that he did no serious damage to the democrats, and that he stayed in the city merely to protect his property. At least in hindsight, the ambiguities of his position illustrate that, during the revolution, the only morally appropriate behavior was to resist the oligarchs with all one's might. In the post-revolutionary period, democracy was the only viable political option in Athens, and the temporizing oligarchic sympathizer digs himself in deeper and deeper.

The speech illustrates special anxiety over oligarchic greed during the revolution: "Again you will find that I did not place the name of a single Athenian on the black list, or obtain a decree of arbitration against anyone, or enrich myself by means of your misfortunes [*oude plousiōteros ek tōn humeterōn gegonōs sumphorōn*]" (25.16). The most important move was to distance oneself from the violence and greed of the Thirty. His feeble

[110] Date: probably around 400; see Murphy 1992, 545–46. Dover (1968, 189) argues that this is "a hypothetical defence of a man against whom the charge is made at a *dokimasia* that he remained in the city during the rule of the Thirty Tyrants." Todd (2000, 261) sees it as a real speech meant to defend the speaker and other former supporters of the Thirty; see, similarly, Murphy 1992, for whom the speaker defends the policy of expediency of the city faction. Because of the tone, which criticizes democracy as well as oligarchy, I am inclined to believe that the speech was not delivered.

[111] This sort of defense also recalls Antiphon's celebrated, but unsuccessful, defense speech (fr. 1).

principle, as he puts it, was "under an oligarchy, not to covet the property of others [*me epithumein tōn allotriōn*], and under a democracy, to spend my own eagerly on your behalf" (25.17). This is not much in the way of defense, and the speaker's attempt at self-exoneration quickly became an attack on his opponents, which led to him to theorize about revolution and the character of oligarchies as opposed to democracies.

Anticipating Aristotle's discussion of revolution in *Politics* 5, the speaker argues, "It is clear now to all that democracy arises because of those who exercise power unjustly under oligarchy, whereas oligarchy has been established twice because of slanderers [*sukophantountas*] in the democracy" (25.27). What do slanderers do in a democracy? They prevail on the demos to condemn their fellow citizens unjustly, in order to make off with their property (25.26). That is, they commit the specific acts of unjust greed under the democracy, for which oligarchs are themselves well known (cf. 25.17). Revolutions and political instability, the speaker argues, result from the greed of those in power. Thus, his own accusers are just like the greedy Thirty, and their unjust slander holds out the danger of further political instability: "As for my opponents, it is legitimate to wonder what they would have done if they had been allowed to join the Thirty since now, in a democracy, they are doing the same things as the Thirty did; they have made a rapid advance from poverty to wealth, and they hold a number of offices without rendering an account of any; instead of concord [*homonoias*], they have created mutual suspicion [*hupopsian pros allēlous*]; and they have declared war instead of peace" (25.30). The Athenians' collective memory of the Thirty is used to denigrate the speaker's accusers. The experience of the oligarchs' greed is never far from the Athenian imagination in the post-revolutionary period.

The underlying assumption of the time was that democracy was a more just form of government than oligarchy, because oligarchs had been proved to be the plunderers, rather than the benefactors, of their community. If elites could be counted on to destroy the community, then it was the demos as a whole, put in a position of political power, that could save it. The demos had the power to enact its desire for satisfaction, revenge, and access to other men's goods, but instead democrats bound themselves by means of an amnesty to refound the polis on the premise of self-restraint. The amnesty of 403 legally required that all Athenians publicly, in assembly and courtroom, forget the events of the recent past. But the amnesty also acted as an opportunity for democrats to point to further evidence of the generosity and temperateness of the demos with regard to aristocrats.[112] If aristocrats had once asserted that

[112] For the consequences of the amnesty, see esp. Loening 1987, 147–49; Krentz (1982, 102–24) seems to me too generous to the oligarchs in his discussion of the aftermath of the revolutions.

the demos was unjust in pillaging them for money, then democrats could now quite credibly claim exactly the opposite. And claim it they did, both on inscriptions and in public oratory. The demos itself—the anti-pleonectic, anti-revolutionary demos—maintains just distribution of power and wealth within the community. Only a Callicles could disagree.

In such a highly charged political climate, in which recent events placed heavy constraints on the ideological claims that could be made for or against democracy and oligarchy, how could would-be traditional aristocrats respond? Conditioned to understand the power of history and its role in popular memory and ideology, they too turned to the past in order to rehabilitate specifically aristocratic claims to civic worth and moral excellence. There is an almost seamless continuity between Xenophon's historical account of the revolution of 404 and his "recollections" of Socrates, the *Memorabilia*, as well as other, more directly "moralizing" or ideological works such as the *Oeconomicus* (*On estate management*) and the *Cynegeticus* (*On hunting*).[113]

For Xenophon, the revolutions pose a central issue, which leads outward in several directions: what does it mean to possess true aristocratic nobility (*kalokagathia*) (cf. *Hell.* 2.3.21–22, 2.4.40–43)?[114] Are aristocrats, as egalitarians have long alleged, truly greedy at heart? Or is there a model of aristocratic virtue that does not entail excessive greed for more within the political community? Such concerns are pervasive in the *Memorabilia*.[115] Of particular interest for our purposes is that Xenophon's discussion of Socrates and his former pupils Critias and Alcibiades directly links these concerns to the revolution of 404. The greed and destructive ambition exemplified by both men were at the center of the accusations made at Socrates' trial (*Mem.* 1.2.12). As Xenophon explains,

> His accuser alleged that he selected from the most famous poets the most immoral passages and used them as evidence in teaching his companions to be evildoers and tyrants [*kakourgous te einai kai turannikous*]: for example, Hesiod's line: "No work is a disgrace, but idleness is a disgrace." He was charged with claiming that the poet encouraged people to refrain from no work, whether

[113] For an excellent reading of the *Hellenica* and its relation to other, larger themes in Xenophon, see Dillery 1995.

[114] For a useful treatment of Xenophon's *Oeconomicus* and *Cynegetica* as specifically aristocratic texts, see Johnstone 1994; Johnstone, however, argues that Xenophon is primarily concerned with aristocratic style, whereas I argue that Xenophon is much more deeply engaged with the proper aristocratic role in politics and the state, and with problems in the sociology of wealth that stem from the revolution of 404.

[115] For other perspectives on the *Memorabilia*, I have found Wellman 1976, 307–18 helpful.

unjust [*adikou*] or shameful [*aischrou*], but to do anything for gain [*epi tōi kerdei*]." (*Mem.* 1.2.56)[116]

In framing the charge this way, Xenophon picks up the themes, such as greed and injustice, he used in describing the protagonists of the revolution of 404. His "recollections" are directed at least in part at distancing Socrates from the charge that he encouraged revolutionary greed by his teaching. Contemporaries viewed ideology, philosophical thought, and political behavior as closely intertwined, which makes sense if we believe that moral agents of whatever sort act on the basis of particular beliefs about themselves and others and in order to exemplify or promote principles to which they are either self-consciously or unreflectively committed.

Arguing against Socrates' accusers, Xenophon attempts to show that Critias behaved as he did *despite* Socrates' teachings and personal example, which stressed self-mastery (*enkrateia*) and temperance (*sōphrosunē*) as the core features of nobility (*kalokagathia*) (*Mem.* 1.2.2).[117] Focusing on the need to check desire, Socrates specifically avoided making his companions "lovers of money" (*erasichrēmatous*, 1.2.5).[118] Even so, "Critias in the days of the oligarchy was the most thieving [*kleptistatos*] and violent [*biaiotatos*] and murderous [*phonikōtatos*] of all" (1.2.12). Despite Socrates' deep concern for Critias and Alcibiades, both men were out of sympathy with Socrates' ethical, self-examined, and self-controlled life (1.2.39). Even though Xenophon accepts the assumption that education plays a crucial role in shaping individual character, he argues that both Critias and Alcibiades first approached Socrates merely in order to become persuasive orators rather than good men, which colored their entire experience of Socrates' teaching.[119] In spite of everything, while these staunchly greedy and selfish individuals were with Socrates, they showed some measure of prudence (1.2.17–18) and were able to master their evil passions (1.2.24).

In terms of the late fifth-century discourse on greed, Xenophon takes

[116] Here again we find the opposition between honor and greed. On the importance of clearing Socrates of any charges resulting from his association with Critias, see Dillery 1995, 142–43.

[117] For *sōphrosunē* in Xenophon's presentation of Socrates, especially in his relationship with Alcibiades and Critias, see North 1966, 124–26; for the shape of the aristocratic ideal and its evolution in archaic and classical periods, see Donlan 1980.

[118] As Gray (1998, 42–43) shows, this argument starts off with Socrates' healthy suppression of bodily desires and then moves to self-control in the area of money (cf. *Mem.* 1.2.1–8 for the progression); on the connection between greed for money and bodily urges, see chapters 1–4.

[119] Xenophon himself comes down heavily on the side of "nurture" as opposed to "nature" in the creation of human character; cf. *Memorabilia* 1.2.23. On Xenophon's attempt to distance Socrates from Alcibiades and Critias, see Gray 1998, 46–47.

us full circle from Callicles' assertion of the value of increasing desire and the capacity to satisfy it. Rather than providing a philosophical argument for limiting desire, however, Xenophon attempts to show that, as a matter of historical fact, Socrates himself provided a model of aristocratic self-restraint that countervailed the images of aristocrats fostered by the oligarchic revolutions. His goal in doing so was twofold. First, he wanted to rehabilitate the moral reputation of his friend and teacher Socrates. Second, by reappropriating the values of self-restraint and prudence for the elite, he wanted to provide a paradigm for contemporary aristocrats that recreated the aristocratic self-image in the face of the newly energized democratic ideology.

Briefly put, this paradigm consisted both in the rejection of greed, which harms the greedy agent even more than those whose possessions are seized, and in the cultivation of lasting ties of mutually beneficial friendship. For Socrates, the acquisitive agent, like any wrongdoer, merely seems to make gains through acting unjustly, but his behavior damages his soul, the most precious possession of all (1.5.3). Similarly, Socrates himself considers that true happiness, which partakes of divinity, consists in having no wants (*to men mēdenos deisthai theion einai*, 1.6.10). Like Plato, Xenophon himself was deeply influenced by the language, concepts, and events of the revolutions, which inform his ethical concerns and reinvention of the aristocratic political ideal. Later in the work, the sophist Antiphon credits Socrates with being a just (*dikaios*) man who does not cheat people for the sake of his own gain (*epi pleonexiai*), but he is mystified by Socrates' unwillingness to accept money for his teaching, which seems to show, on the face of it, that his teaching is worth nothing at all (1.6.12). To Socrates, however, Antiphon's lack of comprehension reveals a fundamentally wrongheaded conception of the human good, which consists in living one's life morally and helping one's friends to do the same by searching for the truth together (1.6.13–14). This is Socrates' true goal in educating competent politicians (1.6.15),[120] not that of teaching them to seize power in order to satisfy their misguided greed. Throughout his portrait of Socrates, Xenophon is influenced by his own and his culture's experience of the revolutions, and by his perceived need to rehabilitate Socrates and aristocrats generally in the terms specified by the culture's collective memory of the revolutions.

The positive benefits of avoiding greed, on the other hand, are illustrated in Socrates' conversation with Critobulus (2.6.1–39).[121] While the man who constantly pursues selfish gain is a troublesome friend (2.6.3–4), the self-controlled man is likely to be a benefactor to both himself

[120] North 1966, 127.

[121] On this conversation and its emphasis on friendship, see Gray 1998, 132–36, 188–89.

and others. Because of human nature it is difficult to avoid greed (2.6.21, 23),[122] but it is necessary to master one's own desires if the aristocrats as a group are to become friends and work together for the benefit of the state (2.6.25–27). Xenophon's reinvented aristocratic ethic is not simply a personal ethical ideal but also an attempt to show how his new formulation of the virtues, and his rejection of greed, can lead aristocrats to make a contribution to the good of the polis as a whole.

Xenophon's attempt to rehabilitate the aristocratic ideal illustrates his deep engagement with Athenian cultural currents both before and after the oligarchic revolutions. On the one hand, Xenophon was a traditional aristocrat devoted to ideals of public munificence and polis leadership and to an underlying belief in the preeminent civic worth of the elite. His aristocratic attitudes, however, are complicated by his obvious embarrassment over the recent history of aristocrats in Athens, who lived up to all the accusations of excess and greed leveled against them by democratic ideology. In the only recent attempt to understand Xenophon specifically as an aristocratic writer, Johnstone has argued that Xenophon tries to demonstrate the value and importance of aristocrats by elaborating a certain model of aristocratic "style": a style of life to which only the wealthy have access.[123] As we have seen, however, Xenophon's rehabilitation of aristocratic worth proceeds primarily on the basis of claims about aristocratic civic value and moral character. This was an extremely awkward project in context. While accepting the democracy's accusations of greed against some aristocrats, Xenophon develops a counter-image of the morally virtuous aristocratic leader, the leader who deserves political prominence because of his appropriate relationship to wealth. Xenophon is concerned to educate the upper classes to become responsible and effective leaders; to make the upper classes unified to ward off the destructive effects of aristocratic competition; and, above all, to create an aristocratic moral character that repudiates the historically grounded picture of aristocratic greed constructed by the democracy. His project is comprehensible only if we see him as deeply enmeshed in the ideological struggle created in part by the legacy of aristocratic greed in ideology and history.

[122] The relevant Greek expressions are *ho tou pleonektein erōs* (the passionate desire to get more) (2.6.21) and *tou pleonektein apechomenoi* (keeping away from greed) (2.6.23).

[123] Johnstone 1994.

7

Epilogue: Plato's *Republic* in Context

In a vivid recollection of the Thirty Tyrants, Plato once wrote, "I thought that they would administer the city by leading it from an unjust way of life to a just way. . . . I saw that these men in a short time made the former government look like an age of gold."[1] Plato's personal and familial connections with several leading oligarchs, to which he draws attention in the course of his recollection (324d1–3), must have left a deep imprint on his moral consciousness. Plato praises the restraint of those who overthrew the Thirty and reestablished democracy, and he uncharacteristically finds something positive about democracy in comparison with the oligarchic junta. Elsewhere he is an outspoken critic of democracy, which, in his view, corrupts talented youth and gives power to the wrong people and priority to the wrong desires (e.g., *Rep.* 488a2–489a2, 492b5–c8, 555b3–562a2). As an elitist and an aristocrat, like Xenophon, he faced a nearly intractable ideological challenge because of the oligarchs; as a moral philosopher, he faced an even greater challenge from the quarter of Callicles, Thrasymachus, and their ilk. Even if the oligarchs had shown in practice that idealizing greed produced uncontroversially immoral results, the theorists' attacks on justice were still left largely unanswered. As immensely complex and multifaceted as the *Republic* is, it would be wrong to impoverish it by reading it as a historical "document" or sign of the times. Nevertheless, our understanding of its specific content and focus can be enriched if we interpret it as responding both to the recent experience of the oligarchic revolutions and to the long discourse on greed and injustice that I have traced.[2]

If Plato hoped in part to rehabilitate aristocratic ideology, one diffi-

[1] Plato *Epistle* 7 (324d4–8). For arguments on the authenticity of the letter, see Morrow 1962, 3–16; Brunt 1993b, 313–25.

[2] Among several recent attempts to read Plato in his historical context, see Wood and Wood 1978, Lycos 1987 (esp. 7–18), Rose 1992, Ober 1998, and Schofield 2000. A striking example of this approach from an earlier period is Gouldner 1965. Annas (1999), examining ancient traditions of interpreting Plato, argues that it is anachronistic and inappropriate to view Plato (1) as a political philosopher and (2) as a thinker deeply engaged with his contemporary culture. That the ancient tradition reacted to Plato primarily as an ethical thinker is not incompatible with Plato's engagement with the ethics and politics of his time; it may be an interesting feature of the ancient tradition of moral commentary, particularly Platonic commentary, that the inspiration of one of its founding texts was in part the "real" world of politics and society.

culty was that the Athenian oligarchs themselves had also advanced the claims of aristocratic ideology in their respective coup attempts. They had asserted that their management of the polis would embody principles of effective public leadership. Their proposal was highly traditional.[3] As the genuine nobility (*kalokagathoi*), they claimed, they alone had sufficient moral and intellectual training to govern Athens fairly and according to rigorous canons of (aristocratic) intelligence and taste. Hence Plato had to show that his Guardians—and his Guardians alone—could live up to the aristocracy's vaunted social and moral ideals. Along the way, he wanted to explain what went wrong in the revolutionary decade. Why, that is, did real-life aristocrats such as Critias, who had once held out such promise of virtue and reform, fail to fulfill their own self-proclaimed ideals? Are such ideals simply impossible to achieve in the world of practical politics?

Moreover, and perhaps more importantly, the oligarchs of 404 played out the ideals of greed expressed by Callicles, Thrasymachus, Eteocles, and the interlocutors of the Anonymus Iamblichi. Their assaults on justice, along with their promotion of excessive desires to get more, were still alive at least insofar as no one had yet produced an argument to the effect that fair-mindedness and self-restraint were better for a human agent than successfully pursued greed and injustice. Unlike the Anonymus Iamblichi, however, Plato tried to refute such ideas on their own terms by showing that they imply a fundamentally misguided conception of the human good, which harms both the greedy agent and the wider political order. In other words, Plato attempted to show that greed does not reward even those who successfully achieve their immoralist ends.

The *Republic* begins and ends by concentrating on the individual's virtue and happiness. Plato's revisionist account of justice in the individual is his response to the late fifth-century immoralists, and it should come as no surprise that his novel vision of justice has much to do, so to speak, with limiting excessive appetites to get more.[4] The dialogue is set during the late fifth-century heyday of the immoralists. Socrates' conversation with Cephalus, which opens the dialogue, focuses on the bodily appetites and the role of wealth in creating happiness. After describing his contemporaries' regret over the lost pleasures of youth—sex, drinking, and feasting—Cephalus declares that he has found old age something of a relief, because, "When the appetites [*epithumiai*] lose their intensity and relax, . . . then we escape from many mad masters" (329c7–d1). Cephalus's em-

[3] The best discussion of the aristocratic tradition is that of Donlan 1980; cf. Rose 1992.

[4] With Annas (1981, 11–13) and Vlastos (1995, 70–78), I take Plato's *dikaiosunē* to mean the same as our term "justice," and not "righteousness" in some broader sense; Vlastos (1995, 75) rightly points out that Plato contrasts it with *pleonexia* (359c5–6). Hence, Plato, like Aristotle, opposes specifically distributive justice to *pleonexia*.

phasis on the bodily desires invites Socrates to ask whether it is his wealth, rather than his character, that allows him to enjoy his old age. His transition between bodily appetite and the means to satisfy it is smooth but predictable; we saw the same progression in Xenophon's *Memorabilia* and in Plato's presentation of Callicles. "What do you think is the greatest good you have received from being very wealthy [*tou pollēn ousian kektēsthai*]," Socrates wants to know (330d2–3). According to Cephalus, wealth keeps us from having to cheat other people, and it helps us pay our debts to gods and fellow human beings (331b1–4). His comment on paying debts enables Socrates to propose that their topic is really justice (331c1–5). The progression of argument leading up to the central question of justice—from appetites to money to justice—is one we have encountered frequently in the discourse on greed.

Contemporaries would be poignantly aware that this Cephalus was the father of Lysias, whose brother was killed by the Thirty Tyrants, and who lost a great deal of family wealth during the revolution. The historical circumstances immediately invite a question about whether wealth actually is a basic good in human life—or does the contemporary understanding of "good" need to be utterly revised? Without overtly criticizing Cephalus, Socrates follows the lead of Solon and Herodotus, whose critiques of greed had centered on the attempt to undermine the conceptions of happiness, and even the self-conceptions, of those they criticized. Within this tradition, Plato's striking move is to insist that such a critique *must* be centered on the role of justice in creating human happiness, or, conversely, on the role of injustice in destroying it. Never before had there been such a vigorous attempt to unite the inner health of the individual with the virtuous behavior of the individual in regard to others.[5]

After several brief exchanges, it quickly becomes apparent that no traditional conception of justice, such as those offered by Cephalus and his son Polemarchus, can survive Socrates' cross-examination. Absent the guidance and security provided by traditional morality, Thrasymachus's skepticism is one easy response; again the chronological progression of the dialogue is replaying a cultural progression experienced in late fifth-century Athens. Plato's representation of Thrasymachus's views, along with the expansion of his position by Glaucon and Adeimantus, focuses attention on greed and injustice as the central moral problems he wants to address.[6] His emphasis on the term *pleonexia* (greed) and related forms of that word, specifically in relation to Thrasymachus and the tyrannical

[5] At a much earlier date, Solon pushed in the direction of arguing that justice was central to individual well-being, but, as we will see, Plato takes this idea much further.

[6] Lycos (1987) argues that the dialogue is a "philosophical intervention in the socio-political climate of Plato's time" (viii); Algra (1996) draws attention to *pleonexia* as a key term in Plato's presentation of Thrasymachus.

individual in book 9, has led one critic to suggest, "We appear to be dealing with key-words."[7] If so, then we are undoubtedly dealing with the key terminology of the culture at large rather than simply the dialogue. More broadly, we are dealing with the key ideas, expressed by *pleonexia* and a variety of related terms, of the history, ideology, and ethical and political thought of Athens in its archaic and classical periods.

Without reprising Thrasymachus's arguments, suffice it to say that his ideal is the extravagantly successful tyrant: "When someone, in addition to taking their possessions, kidnaps and enslaves the citizens as well [*pros tois tōn politōn chrēmasin kai autous andrapodisamenos doulōsētai*], instead of these shameful names he is called happy and fortunate, not only by the citizens themselves, but also by all others who learn that he has done the whole of injustice [*tēn holēn adikian ēdikēkota*]" (344b5–c2). Like the Thirty Tyrants, Thrasymachus bridges the gap between possession and control of others by idealizing the all-powerful tyrant's capacity to enslave his fellow citizens. By claiming that the massively successful immoralist wins glory, Thrasymachus also tries to subvert the standard moralist's opposition between honor and greed. In his own formulation of the "immoralist" position, Glaucon similarly argues that "injustice pays" and that material profits and pleasures are more abundantly available to those willing to commit injustice. Indeed, he argues, the pursuit of material prosperity is altogether natural (359c5), even if it involves violating the just claims of others. According to Socrates, finally, the entire tradition of poetry and prose also praises the happiness of the unjust and represents heroes and sons of gods as greedy (392a13–b4; cf. 390d7–391a1, 391c1–6, 408c1–4). This is certainly a revisionist literary history. But Plato is forcefully, and rightly, asking why, despite cultural indications to the contrary, and despite the obvious material gains of the unjust, justice is good for the individual himself, apart from any external rewards it may bring.

Socrates can explain this only by completely redefining the nature of the goods that contribute to a flourishing human life.[8] Throughout the dialogue, he holds up the life of greed as a false ideal. He later says, for example, that the well-governed city can be established only if the "truly rich" (*hoi tōi onti plousioi*), namely philosophers, rule: "not those who are rich in gold but in that which the happy individual [*ton eudaimona*] must have, namely, a good and rational (*agathēs te kai emphronos*) life" (521a2–4). This is a truly revolutionary project. An early indication of the proj-

[7] Algra 1996, 51. *Pleonexia* (along with the related words *pleonektein* and *pleon echein*) occurs at 343d5–6, 344a1, 349b3, 349b8, 349c1, 349c4, 349c6, 349c8, 349c12, 349e12, 349e12–13, 350a2, 350b1, 350b8, 350b14, 350c1, 359c5, 362b7 (twice), 365d6, 574a8–9, 586b1.

[8] Cf. Adkins 1960, 250–56, 282–84.

ect's revisionist ambitions is Thrasymachus's frustration and incomprehension—injustice *does* pay, at least if one hopes, by whatever means, to acquire as many material goods as possible. "And how am I to persuade you?" he said. "If you aren't persuaded by what I said just now, then what more can I do? Am I to take my argument and put it into your very soul?" (345b4–6).

Thrasymachus is right. There may simply be no way to convince the hard-core immoralist by grounding one's arguments in premises he already accepts.[9] And as for the premises that Thrasymachus already accepts, it is easy to see where they come from. The competitive striving to get more had always been positively evaluated within Greek culture at large.[10] The views expressed by Plato's leading immoralists represented only an amplification of competitive values that were themselves deeply maintained even within Athenian democratic culture.[11] If Solon had once said, "I desire to have wealth, but I am unwilling to possess it unjustly" (fr. 13), then Athenian culture as a whole tended to override his moral scruples. In this context, Plato took on the task of saying why wealth was unimportant and justice of the greatest importance both for social and individual health. Thus, his project is indebted to, but represents a departure from, earlier attempts to curb individual excess through moral and religious argument. For Hesiod, Solon, and Herodotus, greedy aggressors could not ultimately fulfill their immoral aims because of the divine guarantee that justice would eventually prevail in human relations.[12] In the wake of sophistic critiques of conventional morality, however, new philosophical arguments were needed to ground morality in a non-religious framework.

In book 2, seeing that Socrates' arguments need to be informed by a

[9] Cf. Williams 1985, 22–74. The only way to change Thrasymachus's view is to reeducate him altogether through turning his soul in the proper direction, as Plato understood: "Education takes for granted that sight is there but that it isn't turned the right way or looking where it ought to look, and it tries to redirect it appropriately" (518d5–7). Socrates' argument is really for the sake of Glaucon and Adeimantus, interlocutors already convinced of the so-called moral point of view. As Schofield (1999, 71) points out, books 2–4 illustrate that the views on justice offered by each party in book 1 depend on views about a wide range of other topics.

[10] Weber 1967, 21–22; Adkins 1960; this issue is also considered briefly in the introduction.

[11] Adkins (1960, 232–40) helpfully formulates some of these issues in relation to the competitive ethics of Greek culture generally, but I think Plato's project makes more sense in relation to the specific notion of greed that I have traced; this seems substantiated by his focus on *dikaiosunē* as distributive justice, that is, the opposite of *pleonexia* (greed). Adkins (1960, 283–93) is much too severe in his criticisms of Plato's success in rationally justifying the importance of justice for leading a flourishing human life.

[12] As we saw in chapter 3, Solon's moral vision is more complicated than this, but by comparison with Plato he is firmly in the religious camp of Hesiod and Herodotus.

variety of other propositions about the human condition, Plato widens his lens through the soul-state analogy. Individual justice must be understood in the much broader framework of society as a whole. Formally, his argument's agenda is still to solve a question about the ethics of the individual, but the real content of the dialogue advances a dialectic conception of the relationship between individual and society.[13] He aims to secure both the psychic health of the individual and the well-being of the polis through organizing greed and injustice out of individual and social life altogether. His key insight is that rehabilitating justice requires the reformation of both individual and society. This dual concern parallels his dual ambition of refuting the immoralists and recuperating aristocratic ideology.

The transition to a broader focus on the city provides the first hints of Plato's rejection of the real-life Athenian oligarchs and his attempt to put the aristocratic ideal on a new footing. Socrates' "first city" (369b5–372d3), the simple and non-luxurious polis that precedes his formation of the Callipolis, appears to be a strange non-starter until we view it as an effort to emphasize the anti-pleonectic virtues of his Callipolis.[14] The inhabitants of the minimalist city have few and only necessary desires; as if giving them a treat, Socrates imagines that he ought at least to allow them a few luxuries, such as salt, figs, and peas (372c4–d1).[15] Presumably, it is in this "primitive" city if anywhere that just men could be found, because most of the typical temptations to behave unjustly, such as the possibility of luxury, are simply not present.[16]

Hearing Socrates' minimalist proposals about the first city, Glaucon immediately protests that Socrates has constructed a community of pigs, which fails to enjoy the amenities of civilized society (372d4–e1). This is a key moment in the argument. Looking back to Callicles in the *Gorgias*, Socrates *should* now argue that Glaucon's desires for unnecessary goods are harmful to himself and to society at large. Instead, he agrees to allow in many of the well-known luxuries, such as fine furniture, gold, and ivory. Why would Plato take this apparent detour into a luxurious city,

[13] Schofield 1999, 69–71; Annas 1981, 146–51.

[14] Annas 1981, 78–79: "The first city adds nothing, except a context in which the Principle of Specialization is introduced in a plausible way"; cf. Reeve (1988, 170–78), who argues that "the First Polis is that part of the Kallipolis in which money-lovers, and only money-lovers, are made as happy as it is possible for them to be" (176). On this city, see also Schofield 1999; Ober 1998, 220–22.

[15] On the desires of the inhabitants of the "First City," see Reeve 1988, 176–78.

[16] Interestingly, Plato seems to echo the thinking of Phaleas of Chalcedon in assuming that the inhabitants of a minimalist society will conceive few desires. But we might rightly, with Aristotle, wonder why that should be true: as Aristotle himself points out, human beings often appear insatiable, and, once given an inch, they take an ell. On Phaleas, see Aristotle *Politics* 1266a39–1267b21, with Balot forthcoming b.

especially since the luxurious city will ultimately have to be purged of its "fevers" before the true Callipolis can come into being (399e5–6)? I would suggest that Glaucon, Plato's brother and the son of Ariston, is meant to be expressing the characteristic desires of a well-meaning, albeit conventional, aristocrat.[17] Glaucon's protest acts as a marker within the text, which emphasizes the overgrown desire for more that has characterized the Athenian elite throughout its history and especially in the revolutionary decade. By specifically pointing up the characteristic tendencies of the Athenian elite to want more, Plato paves the way for a dramatic contrast between his own Guardians and the actual Athenian aristocracy.

The consequences of Glaucon's overgrown appetites become apparent immediately. To Socrates, the new city is "a city with a fever" (372e8), he says—and "by examining it, perhaps we might see how justice and injustice arise in cities" (372e4–6). Again we find the progression from materialistic appetites to a consideration of justice. The introduction of luxury brings about the stimulation of even further harmful appetites that lead the feverish city to aggressive imperialism and to the need to defend itself against neighboring imperialists. Like the feverish city, other cities have all likewise "given themselves over to the unlimited acquisition of money [*epi chrēmatōn ktēsin apeiron*] and have overstepped the limit of their necessities" (373d9–10). These consequences of luxury require the introduction of Plato's Guardians to defend the city, along with an elaborate education that will keep them from harming their fellow citizens. Thus, to Plato, greed to get more is the origin of war, civic strife, and personal immorality (373e4–7). Much of the next section of the dialogue will be taken up with purging the luxurious city of the uncontrollable desires that infect it (399e5–6). Major changes have resulted from Glaucon's seemingly harmless request for proper aristocratic furniture.

Once the community possesses luxuries, it needs Guardians to defend it, but these Guardians must know when, how, whom, and ultimately why to defend. According to Socrates, this knowledge will require both an appropriate education and appropriate material circumstances in which the Guardians' faculties can be developed (416b9–d1). It is in Plato's stipulations about the Guardians that I want to look for his effort to deal with the moral and political implications of the revolutionary period. To deal with the environment of their upbringing first, Plato stipulates that his Guardians must be propertyless (417a1–6), because, as Socrates explains, "If they acquire private property in land, houses, or

[17] At 372d7–e1, Plato emphasizes Glaucon's conventionality: when asked how the fictional inhabitants of the city should be fed, Glaucon replies, "In the conventional way [*haper nomizetai*]. If they aren't to suffer hardship, they should recline on proper couches, dine at a table, and have the delicacies and desserts that people have nowadays."

money, they will become . . . harsh tyrants instead of the allies [*summachōn*] of their fellow citizens, with whom they will live on terms of mutual hatred and suspicion" (417a6–b1). Once the powerful Guardians get their first taste of material pleasures, that is, they will abuse their power in order to gratify their base material acquisitiveness. Plato's underlying anxiety about the elite abuse of power for the sake of greed resonates at a variety of levels with the recent Athenian experience of the Thirty Tyrants. Socrates wants to create an unbridgeable separation of power and the temptation to desire more.[18] Socrates believes that if the Guardians acquire material possessions, then they will act like harsh masters and live in fear, driving themselves and the city to ruin (417a5–b2).

To make these points absolutely clear, Plato has Adeimantus object that other rulers must be happier than Socrates' Guardians, since they are allowed all the characteristic trappings of power—large estates, finely furnished palaces, and gold and silver (419a1–10).[19] At least within competitive aristocratic circles, these are all the things commonly thought to make a person happy. And, Socrates adds, "They'll have nothing to give their mistresses or to spend elsewhere in whatever way they wish, as people do who are considered happy [*eudaimones*]" (420a4–6). Socrates responds to all this with his well-known dictum that he is trying to make the city happy as a whole, rather than attending to the interests of a particular class within it (420b5–8). But this certainly isn't enough for the likes of Thrasymachus. Why should he give priority to the city's needs over his own—as if he were the living embodiment of Pericles' self-sacrificial Athenian soldiers?[20]

Before looking at Plato's answer to this question, we must see that his construction of the ideal society implicitly involves a critique of contemporary Athenian aristocrats and Athenian society as a whole. He scru-

[18] His way of doing so, it must be stressed, constitutes a blunt rejection of "proportional" or "geometric" equality, which he (along with many others, including Isocrates and Aristotle) accepts elsewhere (e.g., Plato *Laws* 757c1–7, Isocrates *Nicocles* 15; cf. Vlastos 1973, 164–203; Harvey 1965, 1966). As Vlastos (1995, 88) puts it, "Plato repeatedly mandates not bigger and juicier Plums for the bigger contributors [the Guardians], but smaller and drier ones, hygienic prunes instead of hedonic plums." As Vlastos (1995, 88) rightly points out, however, the Guardians will be "billionaires of honor" in the Callipolis—thus again reformulating the honor-greed dichotomy that I have traced throughout this book.

[19] Rose (1992, 356) relates Adeimantus's outburst rather to the deep Athenian context provided by Solon. I would argue that Plato is much more heavily influenced by the recent experience of the revolutions than by the deep Solonian context—to the extent that the two can readily be separated in the history of ideologies. Vlastos (1995, 85–89) understands Plato's stipulations as a matter of "political hygiene" that indicates his impartiality, that is, his equal regard for rights, regardless of any personal connections he himself may have felt with the new aristocracy.

[20] On the patriotism Socrates expects of his Guardians, see 502e2–503a1; on Pericles' ideology of the collective good, see chapter 5.

pulously organizes material temptations out of his Guardians' lives. Their characters must be appropriately nurtured in a carefully controlled environment that encourages self-restraint. But if ordinary Athenian aristocrats, such as Glaucon and Adeimantus, as well as oligarchs like Critias and Charmides, conceive excessive and potentially harmful appetites, then where did their excess acquisitiveness originate? Here Plato blames Athenian culture itself. The people themselves, here the Athenian demos, are responsible for improperly educating the citizens of their polis through their habits of praise and blame. Plato is especially concerned about the corruption of talented young men: "What kind of private education can withstand it and not be swept away by that kind of praise or blame and be carried by the flood wherever it goes, so that he will have the same opinions about what is beautiful or ugly as the crowd does, behaving like the crowd and becoming one of them?" (492c4–8). The people, in short, are the fathers of tyrants like Critias (568e4–5, 569a8–b2). Unruly members of the demos are tyrant makers (*turannopoioi*, 572e5): they implant in the souls of their premier individuals a vast, insatiable desire to get more, which Socrates calls *erōs* (572e4–573a2).[21] Thus, those with the most vigorous natures become capable of the worst injustices, and the most extravagant acquisitiveness, when nurtured by the excessively appetitive demos (491e1–6). Because the Athenian oligarchs lived in a corrupt moral climate, they could not receive a wholesome education. Instead, the democracy led them astray by wrongly educating them to regard its own beliefs about desire as healthy and just.

Plato's critique takes on an even sharper focus in connection with the Athenian history and ideology of greed. Imperialistic Athens provided a bad education not just in its inculcation of shadowy misperceptions about the nature of justice, truth, and political behavior. Rather, more specifically, the revolutionaries adopted the views of Thucydides' Athenians as their own—that might makes right, that power justifies the satisfaction of crude appetites, and that greed is the ultimate basis of the human good. These are the specific, pragmatic lessons that a powerful individual within Athens could learn, by analogy, from his experience of the pleonectic Athenian Empire within the Panhellenic community. Although original in its philosophical deployment, Plato's soul-state analogy had a deep context in the individual-polis relationship analyzed especially by Thucydides and experienced by all Athenians during the fifth century. On Plato's account, it turns out to be democracy itself, invested as it is in greed, injustice, and imperialism, that accounts at least in part for the deep perversions of the Thirty Tyrants. Greed is a lesson, now

[21] Here the relationship to Thucydides' account of the Sicilian expedition becomes clear: on Thucydides' portrayal of Alcibiades, and his use of the language of *erōs*, see chapter 5.

applicable to domestic politics, which the Athenians have taught themselves in the long experience of acquiring and governing their empire. Proof of this, for Socrates and his interlocutors, is that the traditional educators in Athens, the poets, such as the outstandingly wise Euripides (568a8–9), "call tyranny godlike [*isotheon*] and praise it in many other ways" (568b3–4). That's not to mention the corruption of desire occasioned by the likes of Pericles (cf. *Gorgias* 516–19). Plato's cultural critique, then, helps him explain why particular individuals, such as Critias and Charmides, would have exhibited such abusive, acquisitive tendencies once they seized power in 404. Individual and society moved in tandem.

Seen in this light, Glaucon's excessive desires for more resonate not only with Athens's recent domestic experience but also with its tradition of empire. Later in the dialogue, in a passage that recalls the present exchange, Socrates explains that wealth and poverty in a city both lead to revolution (422a1–3), while Callipolis's greatest source of military strength will be its unity. Other cities are readily conquerable because, in fact, they consist of two cities, the rich and the poor—and even these groups can be further subdivided. Thus, "if you treat them as many and offer to give to the one city the money, power, and indeed the very inhabitants of the other, you will always find many allies and few enemies" (423a3–5). Even though Socrates' focus is on defending Callipolis, his analysis of the closely symbiotic relationship between domestic harmony and successful external aggression—or, conversely, between civic strife and polis weakness—resonates deeply with Herodotus's and Thucydides' presentations of Athenian imperialism.[22] If circumstances were different, Socrates might have been writing a prescription for successful imperialism. But imperialism must be, for Callipolis, the road not taken.[23]

Here, however, we are brought back directly to the first book and to the question we postponed. Why shouldn't those with power, whether individuals within a city or unified cities within a larger geographical area, want to get as many of the things normally considered good, such as material possessions, as possible? Why should anyone want to be a Guardian in the first place, at least if he starts with the materialistic premises of most of the earlier interlocutors, such as Cephalus and Thrasymachus? Why should a city refrain from dominating its neighbors

[22] For the combination of domestic harmony and external greed in the earlier tradition, see chapters 3, 4, and 5.

[23] When he allowed in Glaucon's overgrown desires, as we saw, Socrates recognized the need for an army both to defend his own territory and to annex parts of the neighbors' territory (373d7–10). Presumably, once the city has been "purged" of its harmful desires (399e5–6; cf. 420–421), and the Guardians educated, the Callipolis will stop pursuing imperialism.

in order to satisfy the greed of its inhabitants? In part Plato tries to respond to these questions with reference to the individual's proper notion of happiness. His response illustrates his engagement with the discourse on greed: "If a guardian seeks happiness in such a way that he's no longer a guardian and isn't satisfied with a life that's moderate, stable, and—as we say—best, but a thoughtless, adolescent idea of happiness [*eudaimonias*] seizes him and drives him to use his power to take everything in the city for himself, he will understand that Hesiod was truly wise when he said that somehow the 'half is greater than the whole'" (466b5–c3).

Plato has taken us full circle to offer a response to those like Callicles, who, a fallen Guardian with an impoverished notion of happiness, desired power as an instrumental good that would help him satisfy his materialistic appetites. The key for Plato is education. In his conception, the educational process assumes that intellectual vision already exists within each soul, and it takes as its task the attempt to focus the mind's eye in appropriate directions (518d3–7). The structure of society teaches vigorous natures to have only the right sorts of desires. Equally, the more specialized training of the Guardians will produce a proper structure within their souls—that structure commonly referred to as "psychic health" or "psychic harmony." In this condition reason rules the spirited and appetitive parts of the soul. In other words, in this condition each of the three parts of the soul, to quote Plato's famous formulation, will be "doing its own work" (441d12–e2). That order in the soul, according to Plato, makes the person just.

Needless to say, there are numerous problems with the conception of justice as psychic health—primarily that it seems to have nothing to do with the agent's relationship with other people. And justice, to return to book 1, is ordinarily seen as a social virtue, a virtue one exhibits in relation to others. Plato *declares* that a person with a just and healthy soul would keep his hands off others' property and have nothing to do with temple robberies, thefts, and so on (442e4–443a4). He is able to *demonstrate* this only later in the argument, through developing an elaborate metaphysics. In his analogies of Sun, Line, and Cave, Plato constructs a teleological system of knowledge and truth according to which the eternal Forms, and especially the Form of the Good, are the ultimate objects of desire and human understanding. For Plato, justice arises only when the individual understands the Form of the Good itself and exemplifies his knowledge in the way he lives his life. That, to put it simply, is how Plato tries to bridge the gap between psychic health and ordinary justice.

What is important here is that, through his metaphysics, Socrates redefines the nature of what it is good to possess—now, according to him, not worldly power and wealth, but knowledge of the eternal forms. His vision of justice draws on, and attempts to reverse, the common opinions about what contributes to a good human life. More specifically, it draws on the two critiques of greed that we have traced throughout this book. The first of these suggests that excessive acquisitiveness drives individuals to act unfairly or unjustly within society; the second, that greed harms the individual himself. Plato unites the two critiques and reverses them in his conception of justice. For him justice is the state of soul that guarantees the individual's well-being and also his appropriate behavior within society.

To move again from the individual to the social level, Plato argues that it is knowledge of the Forms that creates virtue in the Guardians and that therefore justifies the Guardians' rule of the state (484b9–485b3). Hence, Plato is elaborating the kind of education necessary for his strict separation of power and desire; in other words, he is attempting to show not only why ordinary Athenian civic education went wrong, but also how to do it right. And his answer has much to do with allowing certain members privileged access to "goods"—now not the ordinary "goods" of material wealth but the essential goods embodied in the Forms. The metaphysical system enables Plato to restrict political authority to a narrow group. In his ideal state, philosophical education, which is the only way to gain political authority, is made available only to those who are capable of grasping it in its fullest significance. For Plato, such a restriction is based on nature: it is inherent in the nature of certain individuals to be suitable for philosophy and thus for membership in the ruling class, while others are naturally suitable only for banausic occupations (434a9–b7, 474b5–c3).[24] Such, in short, is how Plato situates his own literary effort within the traditional aristocratic ideology of nature, inherited excellence, and elite preeminence within the political community.[25]

At the broadest level of intellectual history, Plato's metaphysical project created a bifurcation of reality into that which is genuinely real, the intelligible world, and the mundane realm of ordinary objects, the sensible world. His bifurcation was an attempt to justify preexisting and hitherto unexplained bifurcations in social practice—commonplace Greek distinctions between Greek and barbarian, reason and appetite, and so

[24] A similar idea is captured by Plato's "myth of metals," which stresses the inborn capacity of the Rulers, who have gold in their souls, to rule (415a1–c7). A certain degree of upward and downward mobility is still possible, though unlikely; cf. Wood and Wood 1978, 144. There is a tension in Plato's advocacy of inherited excellence and his apparently meritocratic system of providing education for those most capable. Plato seems to be arguing that there will usually be a close correlation between one's genetic inheritance and one's intellectual capacity—for example, "golden" parents will usually have "golden" children, so that any apparently meritocratic features of his system are subsumed within the discourse on inherited excellence.

[25] Cf. Rose 1992, 331–69.

on. For him, aristocratic history had been a failure of aristocratic ideals—the ideals of pursuing honor and the higher goals of rational achievement—in favor of the gross, appetitive, and materialistic side of our humanity, the side, as Aristotle says, we share with the beasts (*EN* 1118a1–3, 1118a23–25). Gregory Vlastos believed that "Plato's bifurcation of reality produces a bifurcation of humanity," but the historical reality supports a reversal of that view.[26] The traditional bifurcations and distinctions, such as that constructed between Greek and barbarian, were felt to need justification, and Plato's explanation, if it can be called that, was a global, cosmological projection of beliefs that were already inherent in social practice, especially the belief in the primacy of reason as distinctive of our humanity. In such a context, it is fitting that greed, and especially those who recommended unbridled greed as the highest ideal of humanity, should be Plato's primary targets, because they promoted precisely the opposite ideals from those he found most honorable. Moreover, they had convinced many Athenians, even Athens as a whole, of their materialistic—even brutish—views, and they had been radically successful in pursuing their own ideals in practical politics. Plato's philosophical conception of justice arises in part from a deep engagement with the history of practical politics, and his hierarchical metaphysics reformulates the traditional hierarchy between honor and base material desires that we have found throughout the archaic and classical periods. But now he had found something even better than honor, the aims and satisfactions of reason.

Hence Plato's hierarchy between the Forms and the sensible world could be reenvisioned in the hierarchy he creates in his description of the imperfect individuals and constitutions in books 8 and 9. Balancing individual and state as equally important subjects of investigation, Plato charts in these books the progressive degeneration of desire[27]—from the *erōs* that strains after truth, to the aspiration to win honor in the timocratic man, to, finally, the emergence of the appetitive part, the multiform beast (588c7–10), as the victor in the souls of the oligarchic, democratic, and tyrannical men. Once the ideal state is transformed by a mathematical mistake (546a1–547a5), the rulers begin to exhibit characteristics not only of silver and gold souls, but also of iron and bronze, which draw them ineluctably toward profit seeking and self-aggrandizement (547b2–c4). The struggle between acquisitive and virtuous desires leads to a dra-

[26] Vlastos 1995, 94.

[27] To put it more precisely, these books concern the disorder created in society and the soul by the inability to maintain the primacy of reason's desire for the good, and thus by the inability of reason to continue ruling soul and society. On the "imperfect" states and souls, see Kraut 1973, 211–13, 216–22; 1997, 210–12; Irwin 1995, 281–97; Cooper 1999b, 127n13, 132n18.

matic compromise: the reintroduction of private property and the enslavement of the productive classes (547b2–c4), the first steps in disintegration (547c5).

Acquisitive desires and the instrumental use of power play a key role at each stage of political disintegration. Despite his general devotion to the honor-loving part of his soul, for example, the timarchic man will conceive a fierce passion for money, which leads to the socially destructive accumulation of wealth in few hands (548a5–7, 550d9–12). The timarchic man, pulled in every direction by the three parts of the soul, finally comes to rest in the middle, valuing the desires of his spirited part most of all. But he still "shares in the money-loving nature [*tēs tou philochrēmatou phuseōs*]" (549b2) and is inevitably drawn downward by it, until the appetitive part takes over. The key is that "virtue and wealth are so opposed that if they were set on scales, they'd always incline in opposite directions" (550e6–8). It is not for nothing that justice is opposed to greed throughout this dialogue and throughout the entire discourse I have traced.

The oligarch, by contrast with the timocrat, has abandoned honor as a value in itself and honors nothing other than wealth and the wealthy (553d1–7). Living in a society that overvalues wealth to the exclusion of everything else, he places his appetitive desires on a throne in his soul, rabidly acquiring as much as he can, through whatever means present themselves (553b7–c7).[28] The oligarchic city destroys itself through its own desire: greedy oligarchs impoverish their fellow citizens in order to win further wealth. Once a large and powerful enough class of poor people has been built up, however, the poor rise up and kill or exile the rich, instituting freedom and equality for all citizens (557a2–5). In a democracy, the leaders "rob the rich, keep as much of the proceeds as they can for themselves, and distribute the rest to the people" (565a6–8).[29] Attacked by a conspiracy of the demos and its leaders, the rich citizens (called "drone-fodder," 564e13) are compelled to defend themselves and ultimately to become unwilling oligarchs (565b2–c4). It is a pattern we saw in late fifth-century Athens, now transformed to make the oligarchs more presentable. Finally, the tyrant, raised to greatness by the people against the rich, turns on the demos itself, subjecting his fatherland to slavery in a crude attempt to gratify his greed. To Socrates, the tyrant lives the worst and unhappiest life both because he is most unjust to his

[28] On the different types of appetitive desires pursued by the oligarchic, democratic, and tyrannical individuals, see Reeve 1988, 44–49; Cooper 1999b, 127n13.

[29] In Plato's image of democracy, we should note again the "conspiracy theory" in which the demos and its leaders unite in an attack on the rich. We should also note, in what follows, Plato's use of food imagery to describe the greed of the democrats.

fellow men and because his lack of self-control enslaves him permanently to his base desires (579d9–e6).

Plato's analysis of political disintegration should be read in conjunction with his presentation of Thrasymachus and with the provisions he makes in constructing his ideal state. Plato specifically rejects Thrasymachus's vision of acquisitive politics in favor of a politics that accords ultimate authority to the most fair-minded and self-restrained of rulers. His picture of the disintegrating constitutions is the reverse of his ideal state. As he created a state that pointedly rejected greed both institutionally and individually, so too did he show in books 8 and 9 why that particular exclusion was necessary. Drawing on his knowledge of Athenian politics, especially the recent oligarchic revolutions, Plato directed his efforts toward eliminating greed, with all its destructive consequences, from his own political vision. When he turned to real politics, however, he found that political activity was almost inevitably governed by greed at its deepest levels. This pessimistic view is one that Plato had good reason to maintain in the post-revolutionary context. He found its antidote only by constructing a *logos* in the sky.

Bibliography

Texts and Translations

Bowersock, G. W., ed. and trans. 1968. *Pseudo-Xenophon: Constitution of the Athenians*. In *Xenophon. Scripta Minora*, edited and translated by E. C. Marchant. Cambridge, Mass.: Harvard University Press.

de Sélincourt, Aubrey, trans. 1971. *Livy. The Early History of Rome*. Harmondsworth: Penguin Books.

———, trans. 1996. *Herodotus. The Histories*. Revised by John Marincola. Harmondsworth: Penguin Books.

Dodds, E. R., ed. 1959. *Plato. Gorgias*. Edited with introduction and commentary. Oxford: Clarendon Press.

Edwards, M., ed. and trans. 1995. *Greek Orators*. Vol. 4: *Andocides*. Warminster: Aris & Phillips.

Frisch, Hartvig, ed. and trans. 1942. *The Constitution of the Athenians: A Philological-Historical Analysis of Pseudo-Xenofon's* [sic] *treatise "De Re Publica Atheniensium."* Copenhagen: Gyldendalske boghandel, Nordisk forlag.

Gagarin, M., and D. MacDowell, trans. 1998. *Antiphon and Andocides*. Austin: University of Texas Press.

Gagarin, M., and Paul Woodruff, eds. and trans. 1995. *Early Greek Political Thought from Homer to the Sophists*. Cambridge: Cambridge University Press.

Gernet, L., and M. Bizos, eds. and trans. 1955. *Lysias. Discours*. Paris: Société d'Édition "Les Belles Lettres."

Grube, G.M.A., trans. 1992. *Plato. Republic*. 2d ed. Revised by C.D.C. Reeve. Indianapolis: Hackett Publishing.

Hamilton, Walter, trans. 1971. *Plato. Gorgias*. Harmondsworth: Penguin Books.

Handford, S. A., trans. 1963. *Sallust. The Jugurthine War: The Conspiracy of Catiline*. Harmondsworth: Penguin Books.

Irwin, Terence, trans. 1999. *Aristotle. Nicomachean Ethics*. 2d ed. Indianapolis: Hackett Publishing.

Jowett, B., trans. 1885. *Aristotle. Politics*. Oxford: Clarendon Press.

Kovacs, David, ed. and trans. 1998. *Euripides*. Vol. 3. Cambridge, Mass.: Harvard University Press.

Lattimore, Richmond, trans. 1961. *The Iliad of Homer*. Chicago: University of Chicago Press.

———, trans. 1967. *The Odyssey of Homer*. New York: Harper Perennial.

Lee, Desmond, trans. 1987. *Plato. The Republic*. 2d ed. Harmondsworth: Penguin Books.

Lord, Carnes, trans. 1984. *Aristotle. The Politics*. Chicago: University of Chicago Press.

Mastronarde, D. J., ed. 1994. *Euripides. Phoenissae*. With introduction and commentary. Cambridge: Cambridge University Press.

Reesor, Margaret E., trans. 1972. "Anonymus Iamblichi." In *The Older Sophists*,

edited by Rosamond Kent Sprague, 271–78. Columbia: University of South Carolina Press.
Rhodes, P. J., trans. 1984. *Aristotle. The Athenian Constitution.* With introduction and notes. Harmondsworth: Penguin Books.
Ross, W. D., trans. 1980. *Aristotle. The Nicomachean Ethics.* With an introduction. Revised by J. L. Ackrill and J. O. Urmson. Oxford: Oxford University Press.
Saunders, Trevor J., trans. 1995. *Aristotle. Politics. Books I and II.* With commentary. Oxford: Clarendon Press.
Thalheim, T., ed. 1913. *Lysias. Orationes.* Leipzig: B. G. Teubner.
Todd, S. C., trans. 2000. *Lysias.* Austin: University of Texas Press.
Warner, Rex, trans. 1979. *Xenophon. A History of My Times.* With an introduction and notes by George Cawkwell. Harmondsworth: Penguin Books.
———, trans. 1986. *Thucydides. History of the Peloponnesian War.* Harmondsworth: Penguin Books.
West, M. L., ed. 1978. *Hesiod. Works and Days.* With prolegomena and commentary. Oxford: Clarendon Press.
———, ed. 1992. *Iambi et Elegi Graeci.* 2 vols. 2d ed. Oxford: Clarendon Press.
Woodruff, Paul. 1993. *Thucydides on Justice, Power, and Human Nature.* Indianapolis: Hackett Publishing.
Wyckoff, Elizabeth, trans. 1959. *Euripides. The Phoenician Women.* In *Euripides V: Three Tragedies,* edited by David Grene and Richmond Lattimore. Chicago: University of Chicago Press.

Secondary Sources

Adkins, A.W.H. 1960. *Merit and Responsibility.* Oxford: Clarendon Press.
———. 1971. "Homeric Values and Homeric Society." *Journal of Hellenic Studies* 91: 1–14.
———. 1972. *Moral Values and Political Behavior in Ancient Greece.* New York: Norton.
———. 1991. "The Connection between Aristotle's *Ethics* and *Politics.*" In *A Companion to Aristotle's "Politics,"* edited by David Keyt and Fred D. Miller, Jr., 75–93. Oxford: Blackwell.
———. 1994. Review of *Aidōs: The Psychology and Ethics of Honour and Shame in Ancient Greek Literature,* by Douglas Cairns. In *Ethics* 105.1: 181–83.
———. 1995. Review of *Hybris: A Study of the Values of Honour and Shame in Ancient Greece,* by N.R.E. Fisher; *Shame and Necessity,* by Bernard Williams; *Aidōs: The Psychology and Ethics of Honour and Shame in Ancient Greek Literature,* by Douglas L. Cairns. *Classical Journal* 90.4: 451–55.
Algra, Keimpe. 1996. "Observations on Plato's Thrasymachus: The Case for Pleonexia." In *Polyhistor: Studies in the History and Historiography of Ancient Philosophy. Presented to Jaap Mansfeld on His Sixtieth Birthday,* edited by Keimpe Algra, Pieter Willem van der Horst, David T. Ruina, and Jaap Mansfeld, 41–59. Leiden: Brill.
Allen, Archibald W. 1949. "Solon's Prayer to the Muses." *American Journal of Philology* 70: 50–65.

Allen, Danielle S. 2000. *The World of Prometheus: The Politics of Punishing in Democratic Athens*. Princeton: Princeton University Press.

Allison, J. 1989. *Power and Preparedness in Thucydides*. Baltimore: Johns Hopkins University Press.

Ambler, Wayne H. 1984. "Aristotle on Acquisition." *Canadian Journal of Political Science* 27.3: 486–502.

Anderson, Benedict. 1992. *Imagined Communities: Reflections on the Origins and Spread of Nationalism*. 2d ed. London: Verso.

Andrewes, A. 1960. "The Melian Dialogue and Pericles' Last Speech." *Proceedings of the Cambridge Philological Society* 186: 1–10.

———. 1982. "The Growth of the Athenian State." In *Cambridge Ancient History*, 3.3, edited by John Boardman and N.G.L. Hammond, 360–91. 2d ed. Cambridge: Cambridge University Press.

Anhalt, Emily Katz. 1993. *Solon the Singer: Politics and Poetics*. Lanham, Md.: Rowman and Littlefield.

Annas, J. 1981. *An Introduction to Plato's Republic*. Oxford: Oxford University Press.

———. 1999. *Platonic Ethics, Old and New*. Ithaca, N.Y.: Cornell University Press.

Appadurai, A. 1986. *The Social Life of Things*. Cambridge, Mass.: Harvard University Press.

Avery, Harry C. 1982. "One Antiphon or Two?" *Hermes* 110.2: 145–58.

Badian, E. 1993. "Thucydides and the Outbreak of the Peloponnesian War: A Historian's Brief." In *From Platea to Potidaea: Studies in History and the Historiography of the Pentacontaetia*, 125–62. Baltimore: Johns Hopkins University Press.

Baker, Keith. 1990. *Inventing the French Revolution: Essays on French Political Culture in the Eighteenth Century*. Cambridge: Cambridge University Press.

Balot, Ryan. Forthcoming a. Review of *The Swineherd and the Bow: Representations of Class in the "Odyssey,"* by William G. Thalmann. *Classical Philology*.

———. Forthcoming b. "Aristotle's Critique of Phaleas: Justice, Equality, and Pleonexia." *Hermes*.

Barker, E. 1918. *Greek Political Theory: Plato and His Predecessors*. London: Methuen.

———. 1959. *The Political Thought of Plato and Aristotle*. New York: Dover.

Barnes, Jonathan. 1982. *Aristotle*. New York: Oxford University Press.

Baron, H. 1988. *In Search of Florentine Civic Humanism*. Vol. 1. Princeton: Princeton University Press.

Barth, H. 1965. "Das Verhalten des Themistokles gegenüber dem Gelde." *Klio* 43–45: 30–37.

Betant, E.-A. 1843. *Lexicon Thucydideum*. 2 vols. Geneva. Reprint, Hildesheim: Georg Olms Verlag, 1961.

Bischoff, Heinrich. 1962. "Der Warner bei Herodot." In *Herodot: Eine Auswahl aus der neueren Forschung*, edited by Walter Marg, 302–19. Munich: C. H. Beck.

Bloomfield, Morton W. 1952. *The Seven Deadly Sins: An Introduction to the History of a Religious Concept, with Special Reference to Medieval English Literature*. East Lansing: Michigan State College Press.

Bolotin, David. 1986. "Thucydides." In *History of Political Philosophy*, edited by Leo Strauss and Joseph Cropsey, 7–31. 3d ed. Chicago: University of Chicago Press.

Booth, William James. 1981. "Politics and the Household: A Commentary on Aristotle's *Politics* Book One." *History of Political Thought* 2.2: 203–26.

Bowersock, G. W. 1966. "Pseudo-Xenophon." *Harvard Studies in Classical Philology* 71: 33–55.

Bowie, A. M. 1997. "Tragic Filters for History: Euripides' *Supplices* and Sophocles' *Philoctetes*." In *Greek Tragedy and the Historian*, edited by C.B.R. Pelling, 39–62. New York: Oxford University Press.

Bowie, Ewen L. 1986. "Early Greek Elegy, Symposium, and Public Festival." *Journal of Hellenic Studies* 106: 13–35.

Bradeen, Donald W. 1960. "The Popularity of the Athenian Empire." *Historia* 9: 257–69.

Brunt, P. A. 1993a. "The Hellenic League against Persia." In *Studies in Greek History and Thought*, 47–74. Oxford: Clarendon Press.

———. 1993b. "Plato's Academy and Politics." In *Studies in Greek History and Thought*, 282–331. Oxford: Clarendon Press.

Burckhardt, Jacob. 1898–1902. *Griechische Kulturgeschichte*. 4 vols. Berlin: W. Spemann.

Burian, P. 1985. "*Logos* and *Pathos*: The Politics of the *Suppliant Women*." In *Directions in Euripidean Criticism*, edited by P. Burian, 129–55. Durham, N.C.: Duke University Press.

Cairns, Douglas. 1993. *Aidōs: The Psychology and Ethics of Honour and Shame in Ancient Greek Literature*. Oxford: Clarendon Press.

———. 1996. "*Hybris*, Dishonour, and Thinking Big." *Journal of Hellenic Studies* 116: 1–32.

Calhoun, G. M. 1913. *Athenian Clubs in Politics and Litigation*. Bulletin of the University of Texas 262, Humanistic Series 14. Austin: University of Texas Press.

Carey, Christopher. 1994. "Comic Ridicule and Democracy." In *Ritual, Finance, Politics: Athenian Democratic Accounts Presented to David Lewis*, edited by Robin Osborne and Simon Hornblower, 69–93. Oxford: Clarendon Press.

Carter, L. B. 1986. *The Quiet Athenian*. Oxford: Clarendon Press.

Cartledge, Paul. 1996. "Comparatively Equal." In *Dēmokratia*, edited by Josiah Ober and Charles Hedrick, 175–85. Princeton: Princeton University Press.

———. 1997. "'Deep Plays': Theatre as Process in Greek Civic Life." In *The Cambridge Companion to Greek Tragedy*, edited by P. E. Easterling, 3–35. Cambridge: Cambridge University Press.

Castoriadis, Cornelius. 1978. "From Marx to Aristotle, from Aristotle to Us." *Social Research* 45.4: 667–738.

Chartier, Roger. 1990. *The Cultural Origins of the French Revolution*. Paris: Seuil.

Chiasson, C.C. 1986. "The Herodotean Solon." *Greek, Roman, and Byzantine Studies* 27: 249–62.

Cobb-Stevens, V. 1985. "Opposites, Reversals, and Ambiguities: The Unsettled World of Theognis." In *Theognis of Megara*, edited by Thomas J. Figueira and Gregory Nagy, 159–75. Baltimore: Johns Hopkins University Press.

Cobb-Stevens, V., Thomas J. Figueira, and Gregory Nagy. 1985. Introduction. In *Theognis of Megara*, edited by Thomas J. Figueira and Gregory Nagy, 1–8. Baltimore: Johns Hopkins University Press.
Cochrane, C. N. 1929. *Thucydides and the Science of History*. London: Oxford University Press.
Cogan, M. 1981. *The Human Thing: The Speeches and Principles of Thucydides' History*. Chicago: University of Chicago Press.
Cohen, David. 1992. *Law, Sexuality, and Society: The Enforcement of Morals in Classical Athens*. Cambridge: Cambridge University Press.
———. 1995. *Law, Violence, and Community in Classical Athens*. Cambridge: Cambridge University Press.
Cole, A. T., Jr. 1961. "The Anonymus Iamblichi and His Place in Greek Political Theory." *Harvard Studies in Classical Philology* 65: 127–63.
Cole, Thomas. 1991. *The Origins of Rhetoric in Ancient Greece*. Baltimore: Johns Hopkins University Press.
Connor, W. R. 1962. *Theopompus and Fifth-Century Athens*. Princeton: Princeton University Press.
———. 1971. *The New Politicians of Fifth-Century Athens*. Princeton: Princeton University Press.
———. 1984. *Thucydides*. Princeton: Princeton University Press.
Cooper, John M. 1985. "Aristotle on the Goods of Fortune." *Philosophical Review* 94: 173–96.
———. 1996. "Justice and Rights in Aristotle's *Politics*." *Review of Metaphysics* 49: 859–72.
———. 1999a. *Reason and Emotion: Essays on Ancient Moral Psychology and Ethical Theory*. Princeton: Princeton University Press.
———. 1999b. "Plato's Theory of Human Motivation." In *Reason and Emotion*, by John M. Cooper, 118–37. Princeton: Princeton University Press.
———. 1999c. "The Psychology of Justice in Plato." In *Reason and Emotion*, by John M. Cooper, 138–49. Princeton: Princeton University Press.
———. 1999d. "Socrates and Plato in Plato's *Gorgias*." In *Reason and Emotion*, by John M. Cooper, 29–75. Princeton: Princeton University Press.
Cornford, F. M. 1907. *Thucydides Mythistoricus*. London: Edward Arnold.
Crane, Gregory. 1998. *Thucydides and the Ancient Simplicity: The Limits of Political Realism*. Berkeley: University of California Press.
Cropsey, Joseph. 1977. *Political Philosophy and the Issues of Politics*. Chicago: University of Chicago Press.
Curzer, Howard J. 1995. "Aristotle's Account of the Virtue of Justice." *Apeiron* 28.3: 207–38.
Davidson, James. 1997. *Courtesans and Fishcakes: The Consuming Passions of Classical Athens*. New York: St. Martin's Press.
Davies, J. K. 1971. *Athenian Propertied Families*. Oxford: Oxford University Press.
———. 1975. Review of *The New Politicians of Fifth-Century Athens*, by W. R. Connor. *Gnomon* 47: 374–78.
Davies, Malcolm. 1989. "Sisyphus and the Invention of Religion ('Critias' *TrGF* 1 (43) F19 = B 25 DK)." *Bulletin of the Institute of Classical Studies* 36: 16–32.

Davis, Michael. 1986. "Aristotle's Reflections on Revolution." *Graduate Faculty Philosophy Journal* 11.2: 49–63.

———. 1996. *The Politics of Philosophy: A Commentary on Aristotle's "Politics."* Lanham, Md.: Rowman and Littlefield.

Delebecque, E. 1951. *Euripide et la Guerre du Péloponnèse*. Études et Commentaires X. Paris: C. Klincksieck.

de Polignac, François. 1995. *Cults, Territory, and the Origins of the Greek City-State*. Translated by Janet Lloyd. Chicago: University of Chicago Press.

de Romilly, J. 1963. *Thucydides and Athenian Imperialism*. Translated by Philip Thody. New York: Barnes and Noble.

———. 1967. "*Phoenician Women* of Euripides: Topicality in Greek Tragedy." *Bucknell Review* 15.3: 108–32.

———. 1971. "La vengeance comme explication historique dans l'oeuvre d'Hérodote." *Revue des Études Grecques* 84: 314–37.

———. 1992. *The Great Sophists in Periclean Athens*. Translated by Janet Lloyd. Oxford: Clarendon Press.

Derow, Peter. 1994. "Historical Explanation: Polybius and His Predecessors." In *Greek Historiography*, edited by Simon Hornblower, 73–90. Oxford: Clarendon Press.

de Ste. Croix, G.E.M. 1954. "The Character of the Athenian Empire." *Historia* 3: 1–41.

———. 1956. "The Constitution of the Five Thousand." *Historia* 5: 1–23.

———. 1972. *The Origins of the Peloponnesian War*. London: Duckworth.

———. 1977. "Herodotus." *Greece and Rome* 24.2: 130–48.

de Souza, Philip. 1995. "Greek Piracy." In *The Greek World*, edited by Anton Powell, 179–98. London: Routledge.

Detienne, Marcel. 1996. *The Masters of Truth in Ancient Greece*. Translated by Janet Lloyd. New York: Zone Books.

Develin, R. 1984. "Solon's First Laws." *Liverpool Classical Monthly* 9.10: 155–56.

Dickie, M. W. 1984. "Hēsychia and Hybris in Pindar." In *Greek Poetry and Philosophy: Studies in Honour of Leonard Woodbury*, edited by Douglas Gerber, 83–109. Chico, Calif.: Scholars Press.

Dillery, J. 1995. *Xenophon and the History of His Times*. London: Routledge.

Dodds, E. R. 1963. *The Greeks and the Irrational*. Berkeley: University of California Press.

Donlan, Walter. 1970. "Changes and Shifts in the Meaning of *Demos* in the Literature of the Archaic Period." *La Parola del Passato* 135: 381–95.

———. 1979. "The Structure of Authority in the *Iliad*." *Arethusa* 12: 51–70.

———. 1980. *The Aristocratic Ideal in Ancient Greece: Attitudes of Superiority from Homer to the End of the Fifth Century B.C.* Lawrence, Kans.: Coronado Press.

Dover, K. J. 1968. *Lysias and the Corpus Lysiacum*. Berkeley: University of California Press.

———. 1972. *Aristophanic Comedy*. Berkeley: University of California Press.

———. 1974. *Greek Popular Morality in the Time of Plato and Aristotle*. Oxford: Oxford University Press.

Doyle, R. E. 1970. "*Olbos, Koros, Hybris,* and *Atē* from Hesiod to Aeschylus." *Traditio* 26: 293–303.

Earl, D. C. 1961. *The Political Thought of Sallust*. Cambridge: Cambridge University Press.

Easterling, P. E., ed. 1997. *The Cambridge Companion to Greek Tragedy*. Cambridge: Cambridge University Press.

Edelmann, H. 1975. "Demokratie bei Herodot und Thukydides." *Klio* 57: 313–27.

Eder, Walter. 1986. "The Political Significance of the Codification of the Law in Archaic Societies: An Unconventional Hypothesis." In *Social Struggles in Archaic Rome: New Perspectives on the Conflict of the Orders*, edited by K. A. Raaflaub, 262–300. Berkeley: University of California Press.

Edmunds, Lowell. 1973. "Thucydides' Ethics as Reflected in the Description of *Stasis*." *Harvard Studies in Classical Philology* 79: 73–92.

———. 1975. *Chance and Intelligence in Thucydides*. Cambridge, Mass.: Harvard University Press.

———. 1987a. "The Aristophanic Cleon's 'Disturbance' of Athens." *American Journal of Philology* 108.2: 233–63.

———. 1987b. *Cleon, "Knights," and Aristophanes' Politics*. Lanham, Md.: University Press of America.

Ehrenberg, V. 1954. *Sophocles and Pericles*. Oxford: Oxford University Press.

———. 1973. *From Solon to Socrates*. 2d ed. London: Methuen.

Engberg-Pedersen, Troels. 1988. *Aristotle's Theory of Moral Insight*. Oxford: Oxford University Press.

Euben, J. Peter. 1990. *The Tragedy of Political Theory: The Road Not Taken*. Princeton: Princeton University Press.

Evans, J.A.S. 1963. "Histiaeus and Aristagoras: Notes on the Ionian Revolt." *American Journal of Philology* 84: 113–28.

———. 1991. *Herodotus, Explorer of the Past: Three Essays*. Princeton: Princeton University Press.

Everson, Stephen. 1998. "The Incoherence of Thrasymachus." *Oxford Studies in Ancient Philosophy* 16: 99–131.

Farrar, Cynthia. 1988. *The Origins of Democratic Thinking: The Invention of Politics in Classical Athens*. Cambridge: Cambridge University Press.

Feldherr, Andrew. 1998. *Spectacle and Society in Livy's History*. Berkeley: University of California Press.

Finley, John. 1942. *Thucydides*. Cambridge, Mass.: Harvard University Press.

Finley, M. I. 1962. "Athenian Demagogues." *Past and Present* 21: 3–24.

———. 1971. "The Ancestral Constitution." Inaugural Lecture, Cambridge University. London: Cambridge University Press.

———. 1977. "Aristotle and Economic Analysis." In *Articles on Aristotle 2: Ethics and Politics*, edited by Jonathan Barnes, Malcolm Schofield, and Richard Sorabji, 140–58. London: Gerald Duckworth.

———. 1978a. "The Fifth-Century Athenian Empire: A Balance-Sheet." In *Imperialism in the Ancient World*, edited by P.D.A. Garnsey and C. R. Whittaker, 103–26. Cambridge: Cambridge University Press.

———. 1978b. *The World of Odysseus*. 2d ed. New York: Viking Press.

———. 1983. *Politics in the Ancient World*. Cambridge: Cambridge University Press.

Fisher, N.R.E. 1992. *Hybris: A Study of the Values of Honour and Shame in Ancient Greece*. Warminster: Aris and Phillips.

Flory, Stewart. 1987. *The Archaic Smile of Herodotus*. Detroit: Wayne State University Press.

Forde, Steven. 1986. "Thucydides on the Causes of Athenian Imperialism." *American Political Science Review* 80: 433–48.

———. 1989. *The Ambition to Rule: Alcibiades and the Politics of Imperialism in Thucydides*. Ithaca, N.Y.: Cornell University Press.

Fornara, Charles W. 1971. *Herodotus: An Interpretive Essay*. Oxford: Clarendon Press.

Forrest, W. G. 1966. *The Emergence of Greek Democracy: 800–400 BC*. New York: McGraw-Hill.

———. 1975. "An Athenian Generation Gap." *Yale Classical Studies* 24: 37–52.

———. 1984. "Herodotus and Athens." *Phoenix* 38: 1–11.

Forsdyke, Sara. 1997. "Exile in Athenian Political Development and Historical Imagination." Ph.D. dissertation, Princeton University.

Foucault, Michel. 1979. *Discipline and Punish: The Birth of the Prison*. Translated by Alan Sheridan. New York: Vintage Books.

———. 1984. "Polemics, Politics, and Problematizations: An Interview with Michel Foucault." In *The Foucault Reader*, edited by Paul Rabinow, 381–90. New York: Pantheon Books.

Foxhall, Lin. 1997. "A View from the Top: Evaluating the Solonian Property Classes." In *The Development of the Polis in Archaic Greece*, edited by Lynette G. Mitchell and P. J. Rhodes, 113–36. London: Routledge.

Frankfurt, Harry. 1999. "On Caring." In *Necessity, Volition and Love*, 155–80. Cambridge: Cambridge University Press.

Freeman, K. 1926. *The Work and Life of Solon*. London: Humphrey Milford.

Frost, F. J. 1984. "The Athenian Military before Cleisthenes." *Historia* 33: 283–94.

Fuks, Alexander. 1953. *The Ancestral Constitution: Four Studies in Athenian Party Politics at the End of the Fifth Century B.C.* London: Routledge and Paul.

Furley, W. D. 1989. "Andokides IV ('Against Alkibiades'): Fact or Fiction?" *Hermes* 117: 138–56.

Galpin, Timothy J. 1983–84. "The Democratic Roots of Athenian Imperialism in the Fifth Century B.C." *Classical Journal* 79: 100–109.

Garlan, Yvon. 1988. *Slavery in Ancient Greece*. Translated by Janet Lloyd. Ithaca, N.Y.: Cornell University Press.

Garnsey, Peter. 1997. *Ideas of Slavery from Aristotle to Augustine*. New York: Cambridge University Press.

Georges, Pericles. 1994. *Barbarian Asia and the Greek Experience: From the Archaic Period to the Age of Xenophon*. Baltimore: Johns Hopkins University Press.

Goldhill, S. 1990. "The Great Dionysia and Civic Ideology." In *Nothing to Do with Dionysos? Athenian Drama in Its Social Context*, edited by J. J. Winkler and F. Zeitlin, 97–129. Princeton: Princeton University Press.

———. 1997. "The Audience of Athenian Tragedy." In *Cambridge Companion to Greek Tragedy*, edited by P. E. Easterling, 54–68. Cambridge: Cambridge University Press.

Gomme, A. W. 1938. "Aristophanes and Politics." *Classical Review* 52: 97–109.

———. 1962. "The Old Oligarch." In *More Essays in Greek History and Literature* 38–69. Oxford: Oxford University Press.

Gould, John. 1989. *Herodotus*. London: Weidenfeld and Nicolson.

Gouldner, Alvin. 1965. *Enter Plato: Classical Greece and the Origins of Social Theory*. New York: Basic Books.

Graham, D. 1986. *Aristotle's Two Systems*. Oxford: Clarendon Press.

Graver, Margaret. 1995. "Dog-Helen and Homeric Insult." *Classical Antiquity* 14.1: 41–61.

Gray, Vivienne. 1997. "Reading the Rise of Pisistratus: Herodotus 1.56–68." *Histos*, on-line journal <www.dur.ac.uk/Classics/histos/>.

———. 1998. *The Framing of Socrates: The Literary Interpretation of Xenophon's "Memorabilia." Hermes* Einzelschriften. Stuttgart: Franz Steiner Verlag.

Greenblatt, Stephen Jay. 1980. *Renaissance Self-Fashioning: From More to Shakespeare*. Chicago: University of Chicago Press.

Grene, David. 1965. *Greek Political Theory*. Chicago: University of Chicago Press. Originally published as *Man in His Pride*. 1950.

Griffith, M. 1995. "Brilliant Dynasts: Power and Politics in the *Oresteia*." *Classical Antiquity* 14: 62–129.

Griffiths, A. Phillips. 1967. "Ultimate Moral Principles: Their Justification." In *The Encyclopedia of Philosophy*, edited by Paul Edwards, 8:177–82. New York: Macmillan and Free Press.

Gutglueck, J. 1988. "From *Pleonexia* to *Polypragmosunē*: A Conflation of Possession and Action in Plato's *Republic*." *American Journal of Philology* 109: 20–39.

Hall, Edith. 1989. *Inventing the Barbarian. Greek Self-Definition through Tragedy*. Oxford: Clarendon Press.

Halperin, David. 1990. *One Hundred Years of Homosexuality and Other Essays on Greek Love*. New York: Routledge.

Halverson, John. 1986. "The Succession Issue in the *Odyssey*." *Greece and Rome* 33: 119–28.

Hammer, D. 1997. "'Who Shall Readily Obey?': Authority and Politics in the *Iliad*." *Phoenix* 51.1: 1–24.

———. 1998. "The Politics of the *Iliad*." *Classical Journal* 94.1: 1–30.

Hansen, M. H. 1989. "Solonian Democracy in Fourth-Century Athens." *Classica et Mediaevalia* 40: 71–99.

———. 1991. *The Athenian Democracy in the Age of Demosthenes: Structure, Principles, and Ideology*. Oxford: Blackwell.

Hanson, V. D. 1995. *The Other Greeks: The Family Farm and the Agrarian Roots of Western Civilization*. New York: Free Press.

———. 1996. "Hoplites into Democrats: The Changing Ideology of Athenian Infantry." In *Dēmokratia*, edited by Josiah Ober and Charles Hedrick, 289–312. Princeton: Princeton University Press.

Hardie, W.F.R. 1968. *Aristotle's Ethical Theory*. Oxford: Clarendon Press.

Harris, Edward. 1997. "A New Solution to the Riddle of the *Seisachtheia*." In *The Development of the Polis in Archaic Greece*, edited by Lynette G. Mitchell and P. J. Rhodes, 103–12. London: Routledge.

Harry, Avery. 1982. "One Antiphon or Two?" *Hermes* 110.2: 145–58.

Hartog, François. 1988. *The Mirror of Herodotus: The Representation of the Other in the Writing of History*. Translated by Janet Lloyd. Berkeley: University of California Press.

Harvey, F. 1965, 1966. "Two Kinds of Equality." *Classica et Mediaevalia* 26: 101–46; 27: 96–100 (corrigenda).

———. 1966. "The Political Sympathies of Herodotus." *Historia* 15: 254–55.

Havelock, Eric A. 1957. *The Liberal Temper in Greek Politics*. London: Camelot.

Heath, Malcolm. 1987. *Political Comedy in Aristophanes*. Göttingen: Vandenhoeck and Ruprecht.

Helm, James J. 1993. "*Koros*: From Satisfaction to Greed." *Classical World* 87.1: 5–11.

Henderson, J. J. 1990. "The *Dēmos* and the Comic Competition." In *Nothing to Do with Dionysos? Athenian Drama in Its Social Context*, edited by J. J. Winkler and F. Zeitlin, 271–313. Princeton: Princeton University Press.

———. 1993. "Comic Hero vs. Political Elite." In *Tragedy, Comedy, and the Polis: Papers from the Greek Drama Conference: Nottingham 18–20, July 1990*, edited by A. H. Sommerstein, S. Halliwell, J. Henderson, and B. Zimmerman, 307–19. Bari: Levante Editori.

Herman, Gabriel. 1987. *Ritualised Friendship and the Greek City*. Cambridge: Cambridge University Press.

Hignett, C. A. 1952. *A History of the Athenian Constitution to the End of the Fifth Century BC*. Oxford: Clarendon Press.

Hirschman, A. 1977. *The Passions and the Interests: Political Arguments for Capitalism before Its Triumph*. Princeton: Princeton University Press.

Holmes, Stephen T. 1979. "Aristippus In and Out of Athens." *American Political Science Review* 73: 113–28.

Hopper, R. J. 1966. "The Solonian 'Crisis.'" In *Ancient Society and Institutions: Studies presented to Victor Ehrenberg on His 75th Birthday*, edited by E. Badian, 139–46. Oxford: Blackwell.

Hornblower, Simon. 1987. *Thucydides*. Baltimore: Johns Hopkins University Press.

———. 1991. *A Commentary on Thucydides*. Vol. 1. Oxford: Clarendon Press.

———, ed. 1994. *Greek Historiography*. Oxford: Clarendon Press.

Houby-Nielsen, Sanne. 1992. "Interaction between Chieftains and Citizens?" *Acta Hyperborea* 4: 343–74.

———. 1995. "'Burial Language' in Archaic and Classical Kerameikos." *Proceedings of the Danish Institute at Athens* 1: 129–91.

How, W. W., and J. Wells. 1912. *A Commentary on Herodotus*. 2 vols. Oxford: Oxford University Press.

Howe, T. B. 1958. "Linear B and Hesiod's Breadwinners." *Transactions of the American Philological Association* 89: 44–65.

Huart, P. 1968. *Le vocabulaire de l'analyse psychologique dans l'oeuvre de Thucydide*. Paris: Klincksieck.

Hunt, Lynn. 1989. "Introduction: History, Culture, and Text." In *The New Cultural History*, edited by Lynn Hunt, 1–22. Berkeley: University of California Press.

Immerwahr, Henry. 1956. "Aspects of Historical Causation in Herodotus." *Transactions of the American Philological Association* 87: 241–80.

———. 1966. *Form and Thought in Herodotus*. APA Philological Monographs 23. Cleveland: Case Western Reserve University Press.

———. 1973. "Pathology of Power and the Speeches of Thucydides." In *The Speeches in Thucydides*, edited by P. A. Stadter, 16–31. Chapel Hill: University of North Carolina Press.

Irwin, Terence H. 1988. *Aristotle's First Principles*. Oxford: Clarendon Press.

———. 1989. *A History of Western Philosophy*. Vol. 1: *Classical Thought*. Oxford: Oxford University Press.

———. 1991. "Aristotle's Defense of Private Property." In *A Companion to Aristotle's "Politics,"* edited by David Keyt and Fred D. Miller, Jr., 200–225. Oxford: Blackwell.

———. 1995. *Plato's Ethics*. New York: Oxford University Press.

Jacoby, F. 1913. "Herodotus." *RE* Supplement 2:226–42. Stuttgart: J. B. Metzler.

Jaeger, Werner. 1943–45. *Paideia: The Ideals of Greek Culture*. 3 vols. Translated by Gilbert Highet. Oxford: Oxford University Press.

———. 1948. *Aristotle: Fundamentals of the History of His Development*. Translated by Richard Robinson. 2d ed. Oxford: Clarendon Press.

Johnson, Curtis N. 1990. *Aristotle's Theory of the State*. London: Macmillan.

Johnson, Laurie M. 1993. *Thucydides, Hobbes, and the Interpretation of Realism*. DeKalb: Northern Illinois University Press.

Johnston, A. W., and R. E. Jones. 1978. "The 'SOS' Amphorae." *Annual of the British School at Athens* 73: 103–41.

Johnstone, S. 1994. "Virtuous Toil, Vicious Work: Xenophon on Aristocratic Style." *CP* 89: 219–40.

Kagan, Donald. 1965. *The Great Dialogue: History of Greek Political Thought from Homer to Polybius*. New York: Free Press.

Kahn, Charles H. 1983. "Drama and Dialectic in Plato's *Gorgias*." *Oxford Studies in Ancient Philosophy* 1: 75–121.

Kallet-Marx, Lisa. 1993. *Money, Expense, and Naval Power in Thucydides' History 1–5.24*. Berkeley: University of California Press.

Kateb, G. 1964. "Thucydides' History: A Manual of Statecraft." *Political Science Quarterly* 79.4: 481–503.

———. 1998. "Socratic Integrity." In *Integrity and Conscience*, edited by I. Shapiro and R. Adams, 77–112. New York: New York University Press.

Keaney, John J. 1992. *The Composition of Aristotle's* Athēnaiōn Politeia*: Observation and Explanation*. New York: Oxford University Press.

Kerferd, G. B. 1981. *The Sophistic Movement*. Cambridge: Cambridge University Press.

Keynes, John Maynard. 1973. *The Collected Writings of John Maynard Keynes*, Vol. 7: *The General Theory of Employment, Interest, and Money*. London: Macmillan.

Keyt, David. 1988. "Injustice and Pleonexia in Aristotle: A Reply to Charles Young." *Southern Journal of Philosophy* 27, suppl.: 251–57.

———. 1991a. "Aristotle's Theory of Distributive Justice." In *A Companion to Aristotle's "Politics,"* edited by David Keyt and Fred D. Miller, Jr., 238–78. Oxford: Blackwell.

———. 1991b. "Three Basic Theorems in Aristotle's *Politics*." In *A Companion to Aristotle's "Politics,"* edited by David Keyt and Fred D. Miller, Jr., 118–41. Oxford: Blackwell.

King, Benjamin. 1997. "Wisdom and Happiness in Herodotus' 'Histories.'" Ph.D. dissertation, Princeton University.

Konstan, D. 1985. "The Politics of Aristophanes' *Wasps*." *Transactions of the American Philological Association* 115: 27–46.

———. 1987. "Persians, Greeks, and Empire." *Arethusa* 20.1–2: 59–74.

Kramer, Lloyd. 1989. "Literature, Criticism, and Historical Imagination: The Literary Challenge of Hayden White and Dominick LaCapra." In *The New Cultural History*, edited by Lynn Hunt, 97–128. Berkeley: University of California Press.

Kraut, Richard. 1973. "Reason and Justice in Plato's *Republic*." In *Exegesis and Argument: Studies in Greek Philosophy Presented to Gregory Vlastos*, edited by E. N. Lee, A.P.D. Mourelatos, and R. M. Rorty, 207–24. *Phronesis*, suppl. vol. 1. Assen, The Netherlands: Koninklijke Van Gorcum.

———. 1997. "The Defense of Justice in Plato's *Republic*." In *Plato's Republic*, edited by Richard Kraut, 197–221. Lanham, Md.: Rowman and Littlefield.

Krentz, P. 1982. *The Thirty at Athens*. Ithaca, N.Y.: Cornell University Press.

Kurke, Leslie. 1992. "The Politics of *Habrosunē* in Archaic Greece." *Classical Antiquity* 11.1: 91–120.

———. 1995. "Herodotus and the Language of Metals." *Helios* 22.1: 36–64.

———. 1999. *Coins, Bodies, Games, and Gold*. Princeton: Princeton University Press.

LaCapra, Dominick. 1983. *Re-thinking Intellectual History: Texts, Contexts, Language*. Ithaca, N.Y.: Cornell University Press.

———. 1985. *History and Criticism*. Ithaca, N.Y.: Cornell University Press.

Lamberton, Robert. 1988. *Hesiod*. New Haven: Yale University Press.

Lang, Mabel. 1967. "Revolution of the 400: Chronology and Constitutions." *American Journal of Philology* 88: 176–87.

———. 1984. *Herodotean Narrative and Discourse*. Martin Classical Lectures, 28. Cambridge, Mass.: Harvard University Press.

Lateiner, Donald. 1977. "No Laughing Matter: A Literary Tactic in Herodotus." *TAPA* 107: 173–82.

———. 1982. "A Note on the Perils of Prosperity in Herodotus." *Rheinisches Museum* 125: 97–101.

———. 1985. "Limit, Propriety, and Transgression in the *Histories* of Herodotus." In *The Greek Historians: Papers Presented to A. E. Raubitschek*, 87–100. Saratoga, Calif.: ANMA Libri; Department of Classics, Stanford University.

———. 1987. "Nonverbal Communication in the *Histories* of Herodotus." *Arethusa* 20.1–2: 83–119.

———. 1989. *The Historical Method of Herodotus*. Toronto: University of Toronto Press.

Levine, Daniel B. 1985. "Symposium and the Polis." In *Theognis of Megara*, edited by Thomas J. Figueira and Gregory Nagy, 176–96. Baltimore: Johns Hopkins University Press.

Lewis, T. J. 1978. "Acquisition and Anxiety: Aristotle's Case against the Market." *Canadian Journal of Economics* 11: 69–90.

Linforth, I. 1919. *Solon the Athenian*. Berkeley: University of California Press.

Lintott, A. 1982. *Violence, Civil Strife, and Revolution in the Classical City*. London: Croom Helm.

Little, Lester K. 1971. "Pride Goes before Avarice: Social Change and the Vices in Latin Christendom." *American Historical Review* 76.1: 16–49.

———. 1978. *Religious Poverty and the Profit Economy in Medieval Europe*. Ithaca, N.Y.: Cornell University Press.

Lloyd, G.E.R. 1968. "The Role of Medical and Biological Analogies in Aristotle's Ethics." *Phronesis* 13: 68–83.

Lloyd-Jones, Hugh. 1971. *The Justice of Zeus*. Berkeley: University of California Press.

Loening, Thomas C. 1987. *The Reconciliation Agreement of 403/402 BC in Athens*. Stuttgart: Franz Steiner.

Long, A. A. 1970. "Morals and Values in Homer." *Journal of Hellenic Studies* 90: 121–39.

Loraux, Nicole. 1984. "Solon au milieu de la lice." In *Aux origines de l'Hellénisme: la Crète et la Grèce: Hommage à Henri van Effenterre*, 199–214. Paris: Centre Gustave Glotz.

———. 1986. *The Invention of Athens: The Funeral Oration in the Classical City*. Translated by Alan Sheridan. Cambridge, Mass.: Harvard University Press.

Luce, T. J. 1977. *Livy: The Composition of His History*. Princeton: Princeton University Press.

———. 1997. *The Greek Historians*. London: Routledge.

Lycos, Kimon. 1987. *Plato on Justice and Power: Reading Book I of Plato's "Republic."* Albany: State University of New York Press.

Macan, R. W. 1908. *Herodotus. The Seventh, Eighth, and Ninth Books*. 2 vols. London: Macmillan.

MacDowell, D. M. 1976. "*Hybris* in Athens." *Greece and Rome* 23: 14–31.

MacIntyre, Alisdair. 1984. *After Virtue: A Study in Moral Theory*. 2d ed. Notre Dame, Ind.: University of Notre Dame Press.

———. 1988. *Whose Justice? Which Rationality?* Notre Dame, Ind.: University of Notre Dame Press.

MacLeod, Colin. 1983. *Collected Essays*. Oxford: Clarendon Press.

Manville, P. B. 1990. *The Origins of Citizenship in Ancient Athens*. Princeton: Princeton University Press.

Martin, Richard. 1992. "Hesiod's Metanastic Poetics." *Ramus* 21: 11–33.

———. 1993. "The Seven Sages as Performers of Wisdom." In *Cultural Poetics in Archaic Greece: Cult, Performance, Politics*, edited by Carol Dougherty and Leslie Kurke, 108–28. Cambridge: Cambridge University Press.

Mattingly, Harold B. 1996. "Epigraphically the Twenties Are Too Late." In *The Athenian Empire Restored: Epigraphic and Historical Studies*, 281–314. Ann Arbor: University of Michigan Press.

Mazzarino, S. 1947. *Fra Oriente e Occidente: ricerche di storia greca arcaica*. Florence: Nuova Italia.

McGlew, James F. 1993. *Tyranny and Political Culture in Ancient Greece*. Ithaca, N.Y.: Cornell University Press.

Meier, Christian. 1990. *The Greek Discovery of Politics*. Translated by David McLintock. Cambridge, Mass.: Harvard University Press.

———. 1993. *The Political Art of Greek Tragedy*. Translated by Andrew Webber. Baltimore: Johns Hopkins University Press.

Meiggs, R. 1972. *The Athenian Empire*. Oxford: Clarendon Press.

Meikle, Scott. 1979. "Aristotle and the Political Economy of the Polis." *Journal of Hellenic Studies* 99: 57–73.

———. 1991. "Aristotle and Exchange Value." In *A Companion to Aristotle's "Politics,"* edited by David Keyt and Fred D. Miller, Jr., 156–81. Oxford: Blackwell.

———. 1995. *Aristotle's Economic Thought*. Oxford: Clarendon Press.

Merkelbach, R., and H. C. Youtie. 1968. "Ein Michigan-Papyrus über Theramenes." *Zeitschrift für Papyrologie und Epigraphik* 2: 161–69.

Michelini, A. 1978. "*Hybris* and Plants." *Harvard Studies in Classical Philology* 82: 35–44.

Miles, Gary B. 1995. *Livy: Reconstructing Early Rome*. Ithaca, N.Y.: Cornell University Press.

Miller, Fred D., Jr. 1995. *Nature, Justice, and Rights in Aristotle's "Politics."* Oxford: Clarendon Press.

Miller, Margaret C. 1997. *Athens and Persia in the Fifth Century BC: A Study in Cultural Receptivity*. Cambridge: Cambridge University Press.

Millett, Paul. 1984. "Hesiod and His World." *Proceedings of the Cambridge Philological Society* n.s. 30: 84–115.

Minogue, Kenneth. 1988. "Method in Intellectual History." In *Meaning and Context: Quentin Skinner and His Critics*, edited by James Tully, 176–93. Cambridge: Polity Press.

Missiou, Anna. 1992. *The Subversive Oratory of Andokides: Politics, Ideology, and Decision-Making in Democratic Athens*. Cambridge: Cambridge University Press.

Mitchell, B. 1975. "Herodotus and Samos." *Journal of Hellenic Studies* 95: 75–91.

Mitchell, Bonner. 1986. *The Majesty of the State: Triumphal Progresses of Foreign Sovereigns in Renaissance Italy c. 1494–1600*. Florence: L. S. Olschki Editore.

Mitchell, Lynette. 1997. "New Wine in Old Wineskins: Solon, *Arete* and the *Agathos*." In *The Development of the Polis in Archaic Greece*, edited by Lynette G. Mitchell and P. J. Rhodes, 137–47. London: Routledge.

Moles, John L. 1996. "Herodotus Warns the Athenians." *Papers of the Leeds International Latin Seminar* 9: 259–84.

Monoson, S. Sara. 1994. "Citizen as *Erastes*: Erotic Imagery and the Idea of Reciprocity in the Periclean Funeral Oration." *Political Theory* 22.2: 253–76.

Moretti, L. 1957. *Olympionikai, i vincitori negli antichi agoni olimpici*. Rome.

Morris, Ian. 1986. "The Use and Abuse of Homer." *Classical Antiquity* 5: 81–138.

———. 1987. *Burial and Ancient Society: The Rise of the Greek City-State*. Cambridge: Cambridge University Press.

———. 1994. "The Athenian Economy Twenty Years after *The Ancient Economy*." *Classical Philology* 89.4: 351–66.

———. 1996. "The Strong Principle of Equality and the Archaic Origins of

Greek Democracy." In *Dēmokratia*, edited by Josiah Ober and Charles Hedrick, 19–48. Princeton: Princeton University Press.
———. 1998. "Archaeology and Archaic Greek History." In *Archaic Greece*, edited by N. Fisher and Hans van Wees, 1–91. London: Duckworth.
———. 2000. *Archaeology as Cultural History: Words and Things in Iron Age Greece*. Oxford: Blackwell.
Morris, Sarah. 1984. *The Black and White Style*. New Haven: Yale University Press.
Morrison, Donald M. 1997. "Aristotle on the Common Good." Unpublished manuscript.
Morrison, J. S. 1942. "Meno of Pharsalus, Polycrates, and Ismenias." *Classical Quarterly* 36.1–2: 56–78.
Morrow, Glenn. 1962. *Plato's Epistles*. Translation with critical essays and notes. Indianapolis: Bobbs-Merrill.
Mossé, C. 1979. "Comment s'élabore un mythe politique: Solon 'père fondateur' de la démocratie athénienne." *Annales ESC* 34: 425–37.
Motto, A. L., and J. R. Clark. 1969. "*Ise Dais*: The Honor of Achilles." *Arethusa* 2: 109–25.
Mulgan, Richard. 1977. *Aristotle's Political Theory*. Oxford: Oxford University Press.
———. 1991. "Aristotle's Analysis of Oligarchy and Democracy." In *A Companion to Aristotle's "Politics,"* edited by David Keyt and Fred D. Miller, Jr., 307–22. Oxford: Blackwell.
Müller, F. 1958. "Die blonde Bestie und Thukydides." *Harvard Studies in Classical Philology* 63: 171–78.
Murphy, T. M. 1992. "Lysias 25 and the Intractable Democratic Abuses." *American Journal of Philology* 113.4: 543–58.
Murray, Oswyn. 1966. "*Ho Archaios Dasmos*." *Historia* 15: 142–56.
———. 1980. *Early Greece*. Cambridge, Mass.: Harvard University Press.
———. 1988. "The Ionian Revolt." In *Cambridge Ancient History*, vol. 4, edited by John Boardman, N.G.L. Hammond, D. M. Lewis, and Martin Ostwald, 461–90. 2nd ed. Cambridge: Cambridge University Press.
———. 1990. "Sympotic History." In *Sympotica: A Symposium on the* Symposion, edited by Oswyn Murray, 3–13. Oxford: Oxford University Press.
———. 1993. *Early Greece*. 2nd ed. Cambridge, Mass.: Harvard University Press.
Nagel, Thomas. 1991. *Equality and Partiality*. New York: Oxford University Press.
Nagler, M. 1974. *Spontaneity and Tradition: A Study in the Oral Art of Homer*. Berkeley: University of California Press.
Nagy, Gregory. 1979. *The Best of the Achaeans*. Baltimore: Johns Hopkins University Press.
———. 1985. "Theognis and Megara: A Poet's Vision of His City." In *Theognis of Megara*, edited by Thomas J. Figueira and Gregory Nagy, 22–81. Baltimore: Johns Hopkins University Press.
———. 1990a. *Greek Mythology and Poetics*. Ithaca, N.Y.: Cornell University Press.
———. 1990b. *Pindar's Homer*. Baltimore: Johns Hopkins University Press.

———. 1996. *Poetry as Performance*. Cambridge: Cambridge University Press.

Newman, W. L. 1887–1902. *The Politics of Aristotle*. 4 vols. Oxford: Clarendon Press.

Nichols, Mary P. 1983. "The Good Life, Slavery, and Acquisition: Aristotle's Introduction to Politics." *Interpretation: A Journal of Political Philosophy* 2.2: 171–83.

———. 1992. *Citizens and Statesmen: A Study of Aristotle's "Politics."* Lanham, Md.: Rowman and Littlefield.

Nicholson, P. P. 1974. "Unravelling Thrasymachus' Arguments in the *Republic*." *Phronesis* 19: 210–32.

Nightingale, Andrea Wilson. 1995. *Genres in Dialogue: Plato and the Construct of Philosophy*. Cambridge: Cambridge University Press.

North, Helen. 1966. *Sophrosyne: Self-Knowledge and Self-Restraint in Greek Literature*. Ithaca, N.Y.: Cornell University Press.

Nozick, R. 1981. *Philosophical Explanations*. Cambridge, Mass.: Harvard University Press.

Ober, Josiah. 1985. "Thucydides, Pericles, and the Strategy of Defense." In *The Craft of the Ancient Historian: Essays in Honor of Chester G. Starr*, edited by J. W. Eadie and J. Ober, 171–88. Lanham, Md.: University Press of America.

———. 1989. *Mass and Elite in Democratic Athens: Rhetoric, Ideology, and the Power of the People*. Princeton: Princeton University Press.

———. 1993. "Thucydides' Criticism of Democratic Knowledge." In *Nomodeiktes: Greek Studies in Honor of Martin Ostwald*, edited by R. M. Rosen and J. Farrell, 81–98. Ann Arbor: University of Michigan Press.

———. 1994. "Civic Ideology and Counterhegemonic Discourse: Thucydides on the Sicilian Debate." In *Athenian Identity and Civic Ideology*, edited by A. Boegehold and A. Scafuro, 102–26. Baltimore: Johns Hopkins University Press.

———. 1996a. "How to Criticize Democracy in Late Fifth- and Fourth-Century Athens." In *The Athenian Revolution*, 140–60. Princeton: Princeton University Press.

———. 1996b. *The Athenian Revolution*. Princeton: Princeton University Press.

———. 1998. *Political Dissent in Democratic Athens: Intellectual Critics of Popular Rule*. Princeton: Princeton University Press.

O'Connor, David. 1988. "Aristotelian Justice as a Personal Virtue." In *Midwest Studies in Philosophy*, vol. 13, *Ethical Theory: Character and Virtue*, edited by Peter A. French, Theodore E. Uehling, Jr., and Howard K. Wettstein, 417–27. Notre Dame, Ind.: University of Notre Dame Press.

———. 1991. "The Aetiology of Justice." In *Essays on the Foundations of Aristotelian Political Science*, edited by Carnes Lord and David K. O'Connor, 136–64. Berkeley: University of California Press.

Olson, S. Douglas. 1996. "Politics and Poetry in Aristophanes' *Wasps*." *Transactions of the American Philological Association* 126: 129–50.

Orwin, Clifford. 1986. "Justifying Empire: The Speech of the Athenians at Sparta and the Problem of Justice in Thucydides." *Journal of Politics* 48: 72–85.

———. 1994. *The Humanity of Thucydides*. Princeton: Princeton University Press.

Osborne, R. G. 1985. "Law in Action in Classical Athens." *Journal of Hellenic Studies* 105: 40–58.

———. 1989. "A Crisis in Archaeological History? The Seventh Century B.C. in Attica." *Annual of the British School at Athens* 84: 297–322.

———. 1996. *Greece in the Making: 1200–479 BC*. London: Routledge.

Ostwald, M. 1969. *Nomos and the Beginnings of the Athenian Democracy*. Oxford: Oxford University Press.

———. 1972. "*Isokratia* as a Political Concept (Herodotus 5.92a.1)." *Islamic Philosophy and the Classical Tradition. Essays Presented by His Friends and Pupils to Richard Walzer on His seventieth birthday*, edited by S. M. Stern, Albert Hourani, and Vivian Brown, 277–91. Oxford: Oxford University Press.

———. 1986. *From Popular Sovereignty to the Sovereignty of Law*. Berkeley: University of California Press.

———. 1991. "Herodotus and Athens." *Illinois Classical Studies* 16.1–2: 137–48.

———. 1996. "Shares and Rights: 'Citizenship' Greek Style and American Style." In *Dēmokratia*, edited by Josiah Ober and Charles Hedrick, 49–61. Princeton: Princeton University Press.

Owen, G. 1979. "Logic and Metaphysics in Some Earlier Works of Aristotle." In *Articles on Aristotle 3: Metaphysics*, edited by Jonathan Barnes, Malcolm Schofield, and Richard Sorabji, 13–32. London: Duckworth.

———. 1986. *Logic, Structure, and Dialectic: Collected Papers in Greek Philosophy*. London: Duckworth.

Parker, Robert. 1996. *Athenian Religion: A History*. Oxford: Clarendon Press.

Parry, Jonathan, and Maurice Bloch. 1989. "Introduction: Money and the Morality of Exchange." In *Money and the Morality of Exchange*, 1–32. Cambridge: Cambridge University Press.

Patzig, Günther, ed. 1990. *Aristoteles' "Politik": Akten des XI. Symposium Aristotelicum, 1987*. Göttingen: Vandenbroeck and Ruprecht.

Pearson, L. 1962. *Popular Ethics in Ancient Greece*. Stanford: Stanford University Press.

Pelling, C.B.R. 1997a. "East is East and West is West: Or Are They?: National Stereotypes in Herodotus." *Histos*, on-line journal <www.dur.ac.uk/Classics/histos/>.

———, ed. 1997b. *Greek Tragedy and the Historian*. New York: Oxford University Press.

Pendrick, Gerard. 1987. "Once Again Antiphon the Sophist and Antiphon of Rhamnus." *Hermes* 115.1: 47–60.

Pohlenz, M. 1937. *Herodot, der erste Geschichtsschreiber des Abendlandes*. Leipzig: Teubner.

Polansky, Ronald. 1991. "Aristotle on Political Change." In *A Companion to Aristotle's "Politics,"* edited by David Keyt and Fred D. Miller, Jr., 323–45. Oxford: Blackwell.

Polanyi, Karl. 1968. "Aristotle Discovers the Economy." In *Primitive, Archaic, and Modern Economies: Essays of Karl Polanyi*, edited by George Dalton, 78–115. Boston: Beacon.

Pope, M. 1988. "Thucydides and Democracy." *Historia* 37: 276–96.

Powell, Anton. 1988. *Athens and Sparta: Constructing Greek Political and Social History from 478 BC*. London: Routledge.

Powell, J. E. 1938. *A Lexicon to Herodotus*. Cambridge: Cambridge University Press.

Qviller, Bjørn. 1981. "The Dynamics of the Homeric Society." *Symbolae Osloenses* 56: 109–55.

Raaflaub, K. A. 1980. "Des freien Bürgers Recht der freien Rede." *In Studien zur antiken Socialgeschichte: Festschrift F. Vittinghoff*, edited by Werner Eck, Hartmut Galsterer, and Hartmut Wolff, 7–57. Cologne: Böhlau.

———. 1987. "Herodotus, Political Thought, and the Meaning of History." *Arethusa* 20: 221–48.

———. 1988. "Homer and the Beginning of Political Thought in Greece." *Proceedings of the Boston Area Colloquium Series in Ancient Philosophy* 4: 1–25.

———. 1989. "Contemporary Perceptions of Democracy in Fifth-Century Athens." *Classica et Mediaevalia* 40: 33–70.

———. 1994. "Democracy, Power, and Imperialism in Fifth-Century Athens." In *Athenian Political Thought and the Reconstruction of American Democracy*, edited by J. Peter Euben, John R. Wallach, and Josiah Ober, 103–46. Ithaca, N.Y.: Cornell University Press.

———. 1996. "Equalities and Inequalities in Athenian Democracy." In *Dēmokratia*, edited by Josiah Ober and Charles Hedrick, 139–74. Princeton: Princeton University Press.

———. 1997. "Homeric Society." In *A New Companion to Homer*, edited by I. Morris and B. Powell, 624–48. Leiden: Brill.

———. 1998. "A Historian's Headache: How to Read 'Homeric Society'?" In *Archaic Greece*, edited by N. Fisher and Hans van Wees, 169–93. London: Duckworth.

Raubitschek, A. E. 1973. "The Speech of the Athenians at Sparta." In *Speeches in Thucydides*, edited by P. A. Stadter, 32–48. Chapel Hill: University of North Carolina Press.

Rawlings, Hunter R., III. 1981. *The Structure of Thucydides' History*. Princeton: Princeton University Press.

Rawls, J. 1971. *A Theory of Justice*. Cambridge, Mass.: Harvard University Press.

———. 1993. "Distributive Justice." In *Justice*, edited by Alan Ryan, 73–94. Oxford: Oxford University Press.

Rawson, E. 1970. "Family and Fatherland in Euripides' *Phoenissae*." *Greek, Roman, and Byzantine Studies* 11: 111–27.

Reckford, Kenneth J. 1987. *Aristophanes' Old-and-New Comedy*. Chapel Hill: University of North Carolina Press.

Redfield, James. 1985. "Herodotus the Tourist." *Classical Philology* 80: 97–118.

Reeve, C.D.C. 1988. *Philosopher-Kings: The Argument of Plato's "Republic."* Princeton: Princeton University Press.

Rhodes, P. J. 1972. "The Five Thousand in the Athenian Revolutions of 411." *Journal of Hellenic Studies* 92: 115–27.

———. 1981. *A Commentary on the Aristotelian "Athēnaiōn Politeia."* Oxford: Clarendon Press.

Robertson, A. F. 2001. *Greed: Gut Feelings, Growth, and History*. Cambridge: Polity Press.

Roberts, Jennifer T. 1994. *Athens on Trial: The Antidemocratic Tradition in Western Thought*. Princeton: Princeton University Press.

Robinson, R. 1953. *Plato's Earlier Dialectic*. 2d ed. Oxford: Clarendon Press.

———. [1962] 1995. *Aristotle's Politics, Books III and IV*. Translated with commentary by Richard Robinson. Oxford: Oxford University Press.

Rose, Peter W. 1988. "Thersites and the Plural Voices of Homer." *Arethusa* 21: 5–25.

———. 1992. *Sons of the Gods, Children of Earth: Ideology and Literary Form in Ancient Greece*. Ithaca, N.Y.: Cornell University Press.

———. 1997. "Ideology in the *Iliad*: Polis, *Basileus*, *Theoi*." *Arethusa* 30.2: 151–99.

Rosenbloom, David. 1992. "The Tragedy of Power: Myth, Memory, and Hegemony in the Theater of Aischylos." Ph.D. dissertation, Princeton University.

Rosenmeyer, T. 1982. "History or Poetry? The Example of Herodotus." *Clio* 11: 239–59.

Ross, W. D. [1923] 1995. *Aristotle*. 6th ed. London: Routledge.

Rowe, Christopher. 1991. "Aims and Methods in Aristotle's *Politics*." In *A Companion to Aristotle's "Politics,"* edited by David Keyt and Fred D. Miller, Jr., 57–74. Oxford: Blackwell.

Ruschenbusch, E. 1966. *Solonos Nomoi*. Wiesbaden: F. Steiner.

Ryffel, Heinrich. 1956. *Metabolē Politeiōn: Der Wandel der Staatsverfassungen*. Bern: Paul Haupt.

Sacks, David Harris. 1998. "The Greed of Judas: Avarice, Monopoly, and the Moral Economy in England, ca. 1350–ca. 1600." *Journal of Medieval and Early Modern Studies* 28.2: 267–311.

Saxonhouse, Arlene W. 1996. *Athenian Democracy: Modern Mythmakers and Ancient Theorists*. Notre Dame, Ind.: University of Notre Dame Press.

Schmitt-Pantel, Pauline. 1990. "Sacrificial Meal and *Symposion*: Two Models of Civic Institutions in the Archaic City?" In *Sympotica: A Symposium on the* Symposion, edited by Oswyn Murray, 14–33. Oxford: Clarendon Press.

Schofield, Malcolm. 1990. "Ideology and Philosophy in Aristotle's Theory of Slavery." In *Aristoteles' "Politik": Akten des XI. Symposium Aristotelicum*, edited by G. Patzig, 1–27. Göttingen: Vandenbroeck and Ruprecht.

———. 1999. *Saving the City: Philosopher-Kings and Other Classical Paradigms*. New York: Routledge.

———. 2000. "Approaching the *Republic*." In *The Cambridge History of Greek and Roman Political Thought*, edited by Christopher Rowe and Malcolm Schofield, 190–232. Cambridge: Cambridge University Press.

Schumpeter, Joseph A. 1954. *History of Economic Analysis*. Edited by Elizabeth Boody Schumpeter. New York: Oxford University Press.

Seaford, Richard. 1994. *Reciprocity and Ritual: Homer and Tragedy in the Developing City-State*. Oxford: Clarendon Press.

Sealey, R. 1976. *A History of the Greek City-States, 700–338 BC*. Berkeley: University of California Press.

Shames, L. 1989. *The Hunger for More: Searching for Values in an Age of Greed*. New York: Times Books.

Shapiro, Susan O. 1996. "Herodotus and Solon." *Classical Antiquity* 15.2: 348–64.

Shaw, Brent D. 1991. "The Paradoxes of People Power." *Helios* 18: 194–214.

Shimron, Binyamin. 1989. *Politics and Belief in Herodotus*. *Historia* Einzelschriften, 58. Stuttgart: F. Steiner Verlag.

Shklar, Judith N. 1990. *The Faces of Injustice*. New Haven: Yale University Press.

Shorey, Paul. 1893. "On the Implicit Ethics and Psychology of Thucydides." *Transactions of the American Philological Association* 24: 66–88.

Shulsky, Abram N. 1991. "The 'Infrastructure' of Aristotle's *Politics*: Aristotle on Economics and Politics." In *Essays on the Foundations of Aristotelian Political Science*, edited by Carnes Lord and David K. O'Connor, 74–111. Berkeley: University of California Press.

Sinclair, R. K. 1988. *Democracy and Participation in Athens*. Cambridge: Cambridge University Press.

Sinclair, T. A. 1967. *A History of Greek Political Thought*. 2d ed. London: Routledge and Kegan Paul.

Sinos, Rebecca H. 1993. "Divine Selection: Epiphany and Politics in Archaic Greece." In *Cultural Poetics in Archaic Greece: Cult, Performance, Politics*, edited by Carol Dougherty and Leslie Kurke, 73–91. New York: Cambridge University Press.

Skinner, Quentin. 1988a. "Some Problems in the Analysis of Political Thought and Action." In *Meaning and Context: Quentin Skinner and His Critics*, edited by James Tully, 97–118. Cambridge: Polity Press.

———. 1988b. "Language and Social Change." In *Meaning and Context: Quentin Skinner and His Critics*, edited by James Tully, 119–32. Cambridge: Polity Press.

Slatkin, Laura. 1996. "The Poetics of Measurement in Hesiod's *Works and Days*." Paper presented at the AIA-APA convention, New York.

Smith, Nicholas D. 1991. "Aristotle's Theory of Natural Slavery." In *A Companion to Aristotle's "Politics,"* edited by David Keyt and Fred D. Miller, Jr., 142–55. Oxford: Blackwell.

Snell, Bruno. 1953. *The Discovery of the Mind*. Translated by T. G. Rosenmeyer. Cambridge, Mass.: Harvard University Press.

Snell, F. J. 1979. *Lysias. Epitaphios*. New York: Arno Press.

Snodgrass, Anthony. 1980. *Archaic Greece: The Age of Experiment*. London: J. M. Dent & Sons.

Solmsen, F. 1974. "Two Crucial Decisions in Herodotus." *Mededelingen der koninklijke Nederlandse Akademie*, AFD Letterkunde (Amsterdam) 37: 139–70.

Sommerstein, A. H. 1977. "Aristophanes and the Events of 411." *Journal of Hellenic Studies* 97: 112–26.

———. 1997. "The Theatre Audience, the Demos, and the *Suppliants* of Aeschylus." In *Greek Tragedy and the Historian*, edited by C.B.R. Pelling, 63–80. New York: Oxford University Press.

Sommerstein, A., S. Halliwell, J. Henderson, and B. Zimmerman, eds. 1993. *Tragedy, Comedy, and the Polis: Papers from the Greek Drama Conference: Nottingham, 18–20 July 1990*. Bari: Levante editori.

Sparshott, F. E. 1966. "Socrates and Thrasymachus." *Monist* 50: 421–59.

———. 1994. *Taking Life Seriously: A Study of the Argument of the "Nicomachean Ethics."* Toronto: University of Toronto Press.

Springborg, Patricia. 1984. "Aristotle and the Problem of Needs." *History of Political Thought* 5: 393–424.
Stadter, P. A., ed. 1973. *The speeches in Thucydides*. Chapel Hill: University of North Carolina Press.
———. 1989. *A Commentary on Plutarch's "Pericles."* Chapel Hill: University of North Carolina Press.
———. 1992. "Herodotus and the Athenian ARCHE." *Annali della Scuola Normale Superiore di Pisa* 22: 781–809.
Stahl, H.-P. 1973. "Speeches and Course of Events in Books Six and Seven of Thucydides." In *Speeches in Thucydides*, edited by P. A. Stadter, 60–77. Chapel Hill: University of North Carolina Press.
———. 1975. "Learning through Suffering? Croesus' Conversations in the History of Herodotus." *Yale Classical Studies* 24: 1–36.
Starr, Chester. 1977. *The Economic and Social Growth of Early Greece, 800–500 B.C.* New York: Oxford University Press.
———. 1982. "Economic and Social Conditions in the Greek World." In *Cambridge Ancient History*, 3.3, edited by John Boardman and N.G.L. Hammond, 417–441. 2d ed. Cambridge: Cambridge University Press.
———. 1988. "Athens and Its Empire." *Classical Journal* 83: 114–23.
Strasburger, H. 1962. "Herodot und das Perikleische Athen." In *Herodot: Eine Auswahl aus der neueren Forschung*, edited by Walter Marg, 574–608. 2d ed. Munich: C. H. Beck.
Strauss, B. 1986. *Athens after the Peloponnesian War: Class, Faction, and Policy, 403–386*. Ithaca, N.Y.: Cornell University Press.
———. 1991. "On Aristotle's Critique of Athenian Democracy." In *Essays on the Foundations of Aristotelian Political Science*, edited by Carnes Lord and David K. O'Connor, 212–33. Berkeley: University of California Press.
Strauss, Leo. 1964. *The City and Man*. Chicago: University of Chicago Press.
Stroud, Ronald S. 1968. *Drakon's Law on Homicide*. Berkeley: University of California Press.
Swanson, Judith A. 1992. *The Public and the Private in Aristotle's Political Philosophy*. Ithaca, N.Y.: Cornell University Press.
Szegedy-Maszak, Andrew. 1978. "Legends of the Greek Lawgivers." *Greek, Roman, and Byzantine Studies* 19.3: 199–209.
———. 1993. "Thucydides' Solonian Reflections." In *Cultural Poetics in Archaic Greece: Cult, Performance, Politics*, edited by Carol Dougherty and Leslie Kurke, 201–14. New York: Cambridge University Press.
Tandy, David W. 1997. *Warriors into Traders*. Berkeley: University of California Press.
Taplin, Oliver. 1992. *Homeric Soundings: The Shaping of the "Iliad."* Oxford: Clarendon Press.
Thalmann, William G. 1988. "Thersites: Comedy, Scapegoats, and Heroic Ideology in the *Iliad*." *Transactions of the American Philological Association* 118: 1–28.
———. 1998. *The Swineherd and the Bow: Representations of Class in the "Odyssey."* Ithaca, N.Y.: Cornell University Press.
Thomas, R. 1989. *Oral Tradition and Written Record in Classical Athens*. Cambridge: Cambridge University Press.

———. 1994. "Law and Lawgiver in the Athenian Democracy." *In Ritual, Finance, Politics: Athenian Democratic Accounts Presented to David Lewis*, edited by Robin Osborne and Simon Hornblower, 119–34. Oxford: Clarendon Press.

Thompson, Norma. 1996. *Herodotus and the Origins of the Political Community: Arion's Leap*. New Haven: Yale University Press.

Tompkins, Daniel P. 1972. "Stylistic Characterization in Thucydides: Nicias and Alcibiades." *Yale Classical Studies* 22: 181–214.

Tuplin, C. J. 1985. "Imperial Tyranny: Some Reflections on a Classical Greek Political Metaphor." In *Crux: Essays in Greek History Presented to G.E.M. de Ste. Croix on His 75th Birthday*, edited by P. A. Cartledge and F. D. Harvey, 348–75. London: Duckworth.

———. 1993. *The Failings of Empire: A Reading of Xenophon "Hellenica" 2.3.11–7.5.27. Historia* Einzelschriften 76. Stuttgart: Franz Steiner Verlag.

Urmson, J. O. 1980. "Aristotle's Doctrine of the Mean." In *Essays on Aristotle's Ethics*, edited by A. O. Rorty, 157–70. Berkeley: University of California Press.

van Wees, Hans. 1992. *Status Warriors: War, Violence, and Society in Homer and History*. Amsterdam: J. C. Gieben.

Vernant, Jean-Pierre. 1982. *The Origins of Greek Thought*. Ithaca, N.Y.: Cornell University Press.

———. 1990. *Myth and Society in Ancient Greece*. New York: Zone Books.

Vlastos, Gregory. 1946. "Solonian Justice." *Classical Philology* 41: 65–83.

———. 1953. "*Isonomia*." *American Journal of Philology* 74: 337–66.

———. 1964. "*Isonomia Politikē*." In *Isonomia: Studien zur Gleichheitsvorstellung im Griechischen Denken*, edited by J. Mau and E. G. Schmidt, 1–35. Berlin: Akademie Verlag. Reprinted in *Platonic Studies*, 164–203.

———. 1973. *Platonic Studies*. Princeton: Princeton University Press.

———. 1995. "The Theory of Social Justice in the *Polis* in Plato's *Republic*." In *Studies in Greek Philosophy*, vol. 2, edited by Daniel W. Graham, 69–103. Princeton: Princeton University Press.

Von Reden, Sitta. 1995. *Exchange in Ancient Greece*. London: Duckworth.

———. 1997. "Money, Law and Exchange: Coinage in the Greek Polis." *Journal of Hellenic Studies* 117: 154–76.

Wallace, R. W. 1983. "The Date of Solon's Reforms." *American Journal of Ancient History* 8: 81–95.

———. 1989. *The Areopagos Council, to 307 BC*. Baltimore: Johns Hopkins University Press.

———. 1997. "Solonian Democracy." In *Democracy 2500? Questions and Challenges*, edited by Ian Morris and Kurt Raaflaub, 11–29. Dubuque: Kendall/Hunt.

Waldron, Jeremy. 1992. "The Irrelevance of Moral Objectivity." In *Natural Law Theory*, edited by Robert P. George, 158–87. Oxford: Clarendon Press.

Walzer, Michael. 1983. *Spheres of Justice*. New York: Basic Books.

———. 1988. "Introduction: The Practice of Social Criticism." In *The Company of Critics*, 3–28. New York: Basic Books.

Waters, K. H. 1985. *Herodotus the Historian: His Problems, Methods and Originality*. Norman: University of Oklahoma Press.

Wellman, R. R. 1976. "Socratic Method in Xenophon." *Journal of the History of Ideas* 37: 307–18.

Weber, H. O. 1967. "Die Bedeutung und Bewertung der Pleonexie von Homer bis Isokrates." Inaugural dissertation, Bonn.

Weil, Raymond. 1977. "Aristotle's View of History." In *Articles on Aristotle 2: Ethics and Politics*, edited by Jonathan Barnes, Malcolm Schofield, and Richard Sorabji, 202–17. London: Duckworth.

Wenzel, E. 1968. "Zur Echtheitsfrage von Thukydides 3, 84." *Wiener Studien* 81: 18–27.

West, M. L. 1974. *Studies in Greek Elegy and Iambus*. Berlin: de Gruyter.

West, Stephanie. 1988. "Commentary on Books 1–4." In *A Commentary on Homer's "Odyssey,"* eds. Alfred Heubeck, Stephanie West, and J. B. Hainsworth. Vol. 1. Oxford: Clarendon Press.

Wheeler, M. 1977. "Aristotle's Analysis of the Nature of Political Struggle." In *Articles on Aristotle 2: Ethics and Politics*, edited by Jonathan Barnes, Malcolm Schofield, and Richard Sorabji, 159–69. London: Duckworth.

White, James Boyd. 1984. *When Words Lose Their Meaning: Constitutions and Reconstitutions of Language, Character, and Community*. Chicago: University of Chicago Press.

Whitehead, David. 1982–83. "Sparta and the Thirty Tyrants." *Ancient Society* 13–14: 105–130.

———. 1983. "Competitive Outlay and Community Profit: *Philotimia* in Democratic Athens." *Classica et Mediaevalia* 34: 55–74.

———. 1993. "Cardinal Virtues: The Language of Public Approbation in Democratic Athens." *Classica et Mediaevalia* 44: 37–75.

Whitley, James. 1994. "Protoattic Pottery: A Contextual Approach." In *Classical Greece: Ancient Histories and Modern Ideologies*, edited by Ian Morris, 51–70. Cambridge: Cambridge University Press.

Whitman, C. H. 1958. *Homer and the Heroic Tradition*. Cambridge, Mass.: Harvard University Press.

Wickersham, John. 1994. *Hegemony and Greek Historians*. London: Rowman and Littlefield.

Will, Frederic. 1958. "Solon's Consciousness of Himself." *Transactions of the American Philological Association* 89: 301–11.

Williams, Bernard. 1980. "Justice as a Virtue." In *Essays on Aristotle's Ethics*, edited by A. O. Rorty, 189–99. Berkeley: University of California Press.

———. 1985. *Ethics and the Limits of Philosophy*. Cambridge, Mass.: Harvard University Press.

———. 1993. *Shame and Necessity*. Sather Classical Lectures, vol. 57. Berkeley: University of California Press.

Winkler, J. J., and F. Zeitlin, eds. 1990. *Nothing to Do with Dionysos? Athenian Drama in Its Social Context*. Princeton: Princeton University Press.

Wood, E. M., and Neal Wood. 1978. *Class Ideology and Ancient Political Theory: Socrates, Plato, and Aristotle in Social Context*. Oxford: Blackwell.

Woodman, A. J. 1988. *Rhetoric in Classical Historiography*. Portland: Areopagitica Press.

Yack, Bernard. 1993. *The Problems of a Political Animal: Community, Justice, and Conflict in Aristotelian Political Thought*. Berkeley: University of California Press.

Young, Charles M. 1988. "Aristotle on Justice." *Southern Journal of Philosophy* 27 (suppl.): 233–49.

Yunis, Harvey. 1991. "How Do the People Decide? Thucydides on Periclean Rhetoric and Civic Instruction." *American Journal of Philology* 112: 179–200.

———. 1996. *Taming Democracy*. Ithaca, N.Y.: Cornell University Press.

Zeitlin, F. 1990. "Thebes: Theater of Self and Society in Athenian Drama." In *Nothing to Do with Dionysos? Athenian Drama in Its Social Context*, edited by J. J. Winkler and F. Zeitlin, 130–67. Princeton: Princeton University Press.

Zelizer, Viviana. 1994. *The Social Meaning of Money*. New York: Basic Books.

Index Locorum

General Index

GPSR Authorized Representative: Easy Access System Europe - Mustamäe tee 50, 10621 Tallinn, Estonia, gpsr.requests@easproject.com

www.ingramcontent.com/pod-product-compliance
Ingram Content Group UK Ltd.
Pitfield, Milton Keynes, MK11 3LW, UK
UKHW020703130326
468955UK00003B/2452
9780691048550